D1566829

Books

Augustinian Heritage Institute, Inc.

www.augustinianheritage.org

THE WORKS OF SAINT AUGUSTINE
A Translation for the 21st Century

Part I – Books
Volume 19:
The Manichean Debate

THE WORKS OF SAINT AUGUSTINE
A Translation for the 21st Century

The Manichean Debate

The Catholic Way of Life and the Manichean Way of Life
(*De moribus ecclesiae Catholicae et De moribus Manichaeonum*)
The Two Souls (*De duabus animabus*)
A Debate with Fortunatus, a Manichean
(*Contra Fortunatum Manichaeum Disputatio*)
Answer to Adimantus, a Disciple of Mani
(*Contra Adimantum, Manichaei i discipulum*)
Answer to the Letter of Mani known as the Foundation
(*Contra epistulam Manichaei quam vocant Fundamenti*)
Answer to Felix, a Manichean (*Contra Felicem Manichaeum*)
The Nature of the Good (*De natura boni*)
Answer to Secundinus, a Manichean
(*Contra Secundinum Manichaeum*)

I/19

introductions and notes
by
Roland Teske, S.J.

editor
Boniface Ramsey

New City Press
Hyde Park, New York

Published in the United States by New City Press
202 Cardinal Rd., Hyde Park, New York 12538
©2006 Augustinian Heritage Institute

Library of Congress Cataloging-in-Publication Data:

Augustine, Saint, Bishop of Hippo.
    The works of Saint Augustine.
    "Augustinian Heritage Institute"
    Includes bibliographical references and indexes.
    Contents: — pt. 3, v .15. Expositions of the Psalms, 1-32
—pt. 3, v. 1. Sermons on the Old Testament, 1-19.
— pt. 3, v. 2. Sermons on the Old Testament, 20-50 — [et al.] — pt. 3,
v. 10 Sermons on various subjects, 341-400.
    1.   Theology — Early church, ca. 30-600.   I. Hill,
Edmund.   II. Rotelle, John E.   III. Augustinian
Heritage Institute.   IV. Title.
BR65.A5E53   1990   270.2   89-28878
ISBN 1-56548-055-4 (series)
ISBN-10: 1-56548-247-6 (pt. 1, v. 19)
ISBN 13: 978-1-56548-247-0 (pt. 1, v. 19)

Printed in the United States of America

Table of Contents

Answer to Adimantus, a Disciple of Mani

Answer to the Letter of Mani known as *The Foundation*

Answer to Felix, a Manichean

The Nature of the Good

Answer to Secundinus, a Manichean

General Introduction

The present volume contains eight works of Augustine of Hippo written against the Manicheans, namely, *The Catholic Way of Life and the Manichean Way of Life* (*De moribus ecclesiae Catholicae et de moribus Manichaeorum*), *The Two Souls* (*De duabus animabus*), *A Debate with Fortunatus, a Manichean* (*Contra Fortunatum Manichaeum disputatio*), *Answer to Adimantus, a Disciple of Mani* (*Contra Adimantum Manichaei discipulum*), *Answer to the Letter of Mani Known as The Foundation* (*Contra epistulam Manichaei quam vocant Fundamenti*), *Answer to Felix, a Manichean* (*Contra Felicem Manichaeum*), *The Nature of the Good* (*De natura boni*), and *Answer to Secundinus, a Manichean* (*Contra Secundinum Manichaeum*). Augustine's *Answer to Faustus, a Manichean* (*Contra Faustum Manichaeum*), a huge work containing thirty-three books, will follow in the next volume of this section of the current series.

There are, of course, other works of Augustine that were explicitly written against the Manicheans. *The Advantage of Believing* (*De utilitate credendi*) was written while Augustine was still a priest for his friend Honoratus, who was caught up in the Manichean error. *The True Religion* (*De vera religione*) was similarly written for his friend and patron, Romanianus, whom Augustine had led into Manicheanism and wanted to bring back to Catholicism. Likewise, *On Genesis: A Refutation of the Manicheans* (*De Genesi contra Manichaeos*), which was composed soon after Augustine's return to Africa, is obviously directed against the Manichean interpretation of Genesis. Many other earlier works, especially the dialogues and even the *Confessions*, are to a large extent aimed at the Manicheans.

There are several good introductions to Manichean doctrine. The articles on Mani and Manicheanism and on the individual works in *Augustine through the Ages: An Encyclopedia* provide an excellent starting point for further study.[1] A great deal of our knowledge of Manicheanism is derived from the writings of Augustine who, though not always unbiased, is still one of the best and most reliable sources available to us.[2]

Mani, the founder of the Manichean religion, was born in 216 in Persia. His family belonged to a Jewish Christian sect from which Mani may have become

---

1. Edited by Allan D. Fitzgerald (Grand Rapids: Eerdmanns, 1999). The articles on Manicheanism and the anti-Manichean works in this volume were done by J. Kevin Coyle.
2. Augustine was often attempting to convert Manicheans from their heresy to the Catholic Church, and he could not succeed in such an attempt if he described the tenets of Mani and of the Manichean religion incorrectly.

familiar with the Christian faith and various Gnostic ideas. He received several revelations which convinced him that the revelations attained by the founders of previous religions — such as Buddha, Zoroaster, and Jesus — were incomplete and that he, Mani, was destined to bring them to completion. Though Mani enjoyed the favor of Shapur, the king of Persia, he fell into disfavor under his successor, Bahram I, who had him executed in 277.

Manicheanism was a missionary religion that spread rapidly, reaching much of the Roman empire by the time of Augustine and later spreading eastward as far as China, Siberia, and Manchuria. Manicheanism's basic tenet was that there were two and only two substances or natures, the nature of good and the nature of evil. It taught that there were three times or eras: the beginning, the middle, and the end. In the beginning the two substances were separate and unmingled with each other. In the middle times, in which we are now living, good and evil are mingled with each other so that throughout the whole world particles of the good nature or of the nation of light are held captive in the evil nature or in the nation of darkness. The struggle within each human being between good and evil is explained by Manicheanism as part of the cosmic struggle between the good nature and the evil nature. Mani taught that the human soul was literally a part of God or of the nature of light, while the human body was part of the evil nature or nature of darkness. The Manicheans appealed to Saint Paul's words in Romans 7 about our not doing what we will and doing what we do not will as evidence of the conflict between the two natures. In the end times the two natures will once again be separate, at least to a large degree, and this separation will be attained through the knowledge and asceticism practiced by the Manichean Elect.

Mani's explanation of how the two natures, which were separate in the beginning, came to be mingled in the present middle times and of how the two natures can be once again separated in the end times is a key point of Manichean doctrine. Mani taught that the nation of darkness threatened to ruin and destroy the kingdom of light and that, to prevent this devastation of his realms, God sent forth against the nation of darkness a powerful deity, which was taken captive by the nation of darkness, in which to a large extent it is still held captive. Augustine repeatedly attacks the Manichean account of the mingling of the two natures on the grounds that it presupposes that the nature of God can be changed, violated, and corrupted. For, if the nation of darkness could do no harm to God or his realms, which are parts of him, God had no reason to do battle with the nation of darkness. But if the nature of darkness could do harm to God, as the Manichean myth teaches, then one is left with the blasphemy that God was subject to change, violation, and corruption, even before he was mingled with the nature of evil.

Equally important to Mani's teaching was the knowledge of how the two natures can once again attain separation. Manichean ethics was summed up in the so-called three seals. The seal of the mouth emphasized abstinence from forbidden foods, such as meat and wine. The seal of the hands stressed the avoidance of killing, for God is present in all living things. And the seal of the breast chiefly concerned abstinence from sexual intercourse, since conception of a child meant the imprisonment of a part of God in the flesh of the child. Manichean asceticism differed for the two classes of Manicheans. The Elect, or first rank of Manicheans, were held to a stricter set of rules, while the Hearers, or second rank, were allowed more freedom. For example, the Elect were not allowed to marry, but the Hearers were, though they were urged to avoid conception. Neither were the Elect permitted to pick fruit or harvest other crops since, by doing so, they would cause death to the fruits or vegetables, though the Hearers were permitted to pick fruits and harvest other crops in order to eat them themselves and to present them to their Elect for their food. In the middle times the nature of the good or of light is everywhere mingled with the nature of evil or of darkness, but more of the good or of light is found in light or bright foods. The Manicheans held that, by eating such foods, their Elect were able to release particles of God from their captivity in the realm of darkness when they belched forth those particles. Augustine ridicules at great length the Manichean moral and ascetical practices and mocks them so successfully that we now find it difficult to believe that a man of his intelligence remained a Manichean Hearer for at least nine years of his life.

One of the basic reasons for Augustine's having been a Manichean for so long was his inability to conceive of an incorporeal or spiritual substance until he discovered the books of the Platonists in Milan, where he heard the preaching of Bishop Ambrose who, Augustine noted, did not think of anything bodily when he spoke of God or of the soul. The Manicheans shared with the Stoics the philosophical assumption prevalent throughout the Latin West that everything that exists is a body. Given such a corporealist metaphysics, Augustine inevitably pictured God either in human form, as he believed the Catholics did, or in the form of a great shining mass, as the Manicheans did. Furthermore, he either had to deny that evil existed or to hold that evil was a body. Rather than deny the existence of evil, Augustine thought of it as a body — and a body that limited the otherwise infinite nature of the good, like a wedge driven into the good. Once he had attained the Neoplatonic insight that the real and the corporeal are not coextensive, Augustine was not only able to conceive of God and the soul as non-bodily but could also understand evil as real, not as a bodily substance but as a privation of being and goodness.

Manicheanism was a religion with a scripture. Mani had himself allegedly written seven works, none of which survive in their complete form. In Augustine's works passages from Mani's *Letter of the Foundation* and *Treasury* survive, though the extant fragments are unfortunately not nearly as extensive as one would like. The Manicheans rejected the Old Testament and its God. While they accepted the New Testament, they rejected parts of it that were in conflict with Manichean doctrine. For example, they rejected the genealogies of Jesus because they rejected the incarnation of Christ and boasted that they followed a spiritual savior. The Manichean Bishop Faustus proclaimed that the genealogies were not the gospel and that the good news began with the preaching of Jesus. The Manicheans also rejected the Acts of the Apostles because it contained an account of the coming of the Holy Spirit. For, in their view, the Holy Spirit came in the person of Mani, who brought the fullness of the truth that Jesus had promised. The Manicheans rejected as well many other passages from the New Testament that cited with approval passages from the Old.

The Manichean Jesus was neither incarnate nor born of the Virgin, but he was embodied in all living things and suffered not on the tree of the cross but on every tree whose fruits were plucked. The Manicheans found their eucharist in all bright fruits and foods. They did not celebrate the passion of Christ since they did not hold that he really suffered and died, but they did celebrate Mani's death with their feast of the Bema, which tended to replace the paschal triduum. The Manicheans had a hierarchical church with bishops and laity, though these divisions did not correspond perfectly to the Elect and the Hearers. They certainly thought of themselves as Christians, even as full Christians, and called the Catholics semi-Christians because of their clinging to the Old Testament. During his years as a Manichean Hearer Augustine would have considered himself a Christian — and a more intelligent Christian than the Catholics, whose naive beliefs and what he saw as a blind faith had driven him into the arms of the Manicheans, who promised him the truth without the yoke of superstition and belief.

Texts and Translations

I have translated the Latin text found in the CSEL edition by J. Zycha, Vienna, 1891, though I have also on occasion followed the text in PL or in the BA edition by R. Jolivet and M. Jourdon (Paris 1961), which has excellent notes to the texts of six works. For *The Nature of the Good* I also consulted the Latin text in A. A. Moon's edition as well as the text and notes in the BA edition by B. Roland-Gosselin. The BA edition also contains the text of *The Catholic Way of Life and the Manichean Way of Life.*

Three of the works in this volume have never been previously translated into English: *Answer to Adimantus, a Disciple of Mani, Answer to Felix, a Manichean,* and *Answer to Secundinus, a Manichean.* Three others, *Two Souls, A Debate with Fortunatus, a Manichean,* and *Answer to the Letter of Mani Known as The Foundation* have been translated in the Library of Nicene and Post-Nicene Fathers (1887; reprinted 1956). *The Catholic Way of Life and the Manichean Way of Life* was most recently translated into English by Donald and

Idella Gallagher in The Fathers of the Church 56 (1966). *The Nature of the Good* was most recently translated into English by J. H. S. Burleigh in *Augustine: Earlier Writings* (Philadelphia 1953) and by A. A. Moon in *The De Natura Boni of Saint Augustine: A Translation with an Introduction and Commentary* (Washington, D.C. 1955). *The Catholic Way of Life and the Manichean Way of Life* and *The Nature of the Good* were translated into French by B. Roland-Gosselin in the BA 1 (Paris 1949), and all the rest were translated into French by R. Jolivet and M. Jourdan in another volume of BA 17 (Paris 1961). All the works have been translated into Italian by L. Alici and A Pieretti in *Polemica con i manichei*, Nuova Biblioteca Agostiniana 13 (Rome 1997). They have all been translated into Spanish in Obras de San Agustín: *The Nature of the Good* by M. Lanseros in volume 3 (Madrid 1951), *The Catholic Way of Life and the Manichean Way of Life* by T. Prieto in volume 4 (Madrid 1948), and the rest by P. de Luis in volume 30 (Madrid 1986). *The Two Souls* has been translated into German by C. Perl (Paderborn 1966), and *The Catholic Way of Life and the Manichean Way of Life* has been translated into German by P. Keseling (Regensburg 1948).

The Catholic Way of Life
and the Manichean Way of Life

(De moribus ecclesiae Catholicae et De moribus Manichaeorum)

Introduction

Augustine began *The Catholic Way of Life and the Manichean Way of Life* in 387, when he was still in Rome, while waiting for the chance to return to Africa after his baptism in Milan at the hands of Bishop Ambrose. He tells us in the *Revisions* that he could no longer endure the pretenses of sexual continence by which the Manicheans were leading astray ignorant Catholics and that, for that reason, he began the first of his works that directly attacked the Manichean religion, in which he himself had been a Hearer, that is, a member of second rank below the Elect, for over nine years. Of the work's two books, the first is a philosophical and scriptural defense of the superiority of the Catholic way of life over that of the Manicheans, while the second aims to expose the deficiencies and contradictions in the Manichean way of life.

Structure and Content of the Work

The first book, *The Catholic Way of Life*, has three introductory paragraphs followed by two principal parts. The first part argues that human happiness consists in the possession of the highest good of a human being, namely, God, and that we come to the possession of God by loving him, while the second principal part spells out the life of the cardinal virtues and their relation to the love of God and neighbor as they are lived in the Catholic Church. The book ends with an exhortation to the Manicheans to embrace the way of life of the Catholic Church.

Augustine begins by stating that he has countered the Manichean attacks on the Old Testament in other unnamed books, presumably in his *On Genesis: A Refutation of the Manicheans*.[1] He points out that one should seek an explanation of the scriptures from people who profess to teach them rather than from those who attack them (paragraph 1). But the Manicheans attempt to ensnare the unwary not only by criticizing the scriptures but also by parading before them their image of a life of chastity and continence. Hence, in this book Augustine's aim is to present the Catholic teaching on the moral life based on the New Testament, which the Manicheans accept, though he will also show how the ideals of the Christian way of life are found in the Old Testament as well (paragraph 2). Despite the priority of authority over reason, Augustine will in the present work

---

1. Though Augustine began *The Catholic Way of Life* before *On Genesis: A Refutation of the Manicheans*, he finished it after he completed his first commentary on Genesis.

accede to the demands of the Manicheans and start by using reason (paragraph 3).

Augustine then begins the first principal part, which focuses upon human happiness and the love of God, by stating that all human beings want to live happily, that no one can be happy who does not have what he loves, and that no one can be happy if what he loves and has is harmful or can be taken from him against his will. Hence, he concludes that the happy life consists in the love and possession of the highest good of a human being (paragraph 4). This highest good is, Augustine argues, a good greater than a human being and the sort of good than which a greater is not possible and which one need have no fear of losing (paragraph 5). Regardless of whether a human being is both body and soul or only body or only soul, the highest good of a human being is not the highest good of the body but that of both body and soul or that of the soul alone (paragraph 6). We must, then, discover whether there is anything superior to the soul that makes the soul to be the best it can be, for this will rightly be called the highest good of a human being (paragraph 7). In asking about the manner of life according to which we should live in order to attain happiness, we need to investigate only what it is that makes the soul best (paragraph 8). No one doubts that it is virtue that makes the soul best, and virtue is either merely a habit or quality of the soul or something else that exists apart from the soul, which the soul pursues in order to become virtuous and wise (paragraph 9). This something else can only be a wise human being or God, but, if it is a wise human being, it can be taken away from us against our will. Hence, it must be God (paragraph 10).

Human reason is weak when it tries to rise up to see God, but divine authority comes to our rescue in accord with God's providential plan through miraculous events and the written word (paragraph 11). God has in his providence provided a path for us by the calling of the patriarchs, by the law of Moses, by the predictions of the prophets, by the incarnation of the Son of God, by the testimony of the apostles, by the blood of the martyrs, and by the conversion of the nations. Hence, from here on Augustine proceeds from the word of God (paragraph 12). In the gospel the Lord commands that we love God with our whole heart, soul, and mind, and the apostle Paul assures us that nothing can separate us from the love of God. Therefore we know whom we ought to love and how much we ought to love him (paragraph 13). Augustine shows that the authority of the Old Testament is in full accord with the words of the gospel and of the apostle, though the Manicheans try to claim that the citations from the Old Testament found in the New Testament are interpolations (paragraph 14). Augustine challenges the Manicheans either to deny that the words which Paul cites are actually found in the Old Testament or to claim that those words are not in agreement with the statements of the apostle (paragraph 15). The Manicheans argue that we should love God, but not the God of the Old Testament, whom they find objectionable for many reasons. Augustine warns them that they should rather listen to the pious and learned men in the Catholic Church who interpret the Old Testament quite differently from them (paragraph 16). He tells the Manicheans that, though there are little ones in the Catholic Church who remain at the level of simple faith and think of God as having a human form, there are others who are adults in the faith and who understand that God is not confined in space and is not bodily at all (paragraph 17). The pursuit of God, the highest good, is the desire for happiness, and the attainment of God is happiness itself. Hence, we ought to love God above all else (paragraph 18). Augustine spells out in detail Saint Paul's claim that nothing can separate us from the love of God (paragraph 19) and emphasizes the wisdom of the apostle's having said that no creature other than the soul can separate us from the love of God. For in that way the apostle reminds us that the soul is a creature, though the Manicheans had maintained that the soul was literally a part of God (paragraph 20). The soul is subject to change, wandering off from God and returning to him, but God is absolutely immutable (paragraph 21). Paul says that the love of God is found in Christ Jesus our Lord, and Augustine shows that Paul also tells us that this Christ is the power and wisdom of God, who says of himself that he is the truth and that no one comes to the Father except through him (paragraph 22). Love conforms us to God and cuts us off from this world, but this love is poured out in our hearts by the Holy Spirit, who also is God, not a creature (paragraph 23). Hence, our love of God is a love for the Trinity of the Father, the Son, and the Holy Spirit (paragraph 24).

In the second principal part of this first book Augustine turns to virtue and the Church. Though he is tempted simply to identify virtue with the love of God, he is aware of the four cardinal virtues, each of which he defines as a form of love (paragraph 25). Then he shows how the Old Testament contains testimonies to the love of God similar to those that he has been using from the New (paragraphs 26 to 29). Hence, Augustine insists that there is one God of both the New and the Old Testaments and that the two Testaments are in harmony with each other, though many things are expressed in a lowly manner for the less talented and many other things are expressed in symbols to challenge the more studious (paragraph 30). In the present work Augustine is not trying to get the Manicheans to understand the scriptures but only trying to get them to *want* to understand them, and it is the love of God that will bring this about (paragraph 31). He quotes at length from the Book of Wisdom and urges the Manicheans to bring themselves into the Catholic Church with great speed, sincere love, and solid faith, for it is within the Church that they will understand the scriptures (paragraph 32). Augustine admits that, when he was a Manichean, he too had scorned the teaching of the Catholic faith that leads to the highest peak of wisdom and truth (paragraph 33), and he pleads with the Manicheans to see the harmony of the Old and the New Testaments, which teach the Catholic way of life and the end to which everything is to be directed (paragraph 34).

Returning to the four virtues, Augustine shows how we can derive from each of them a rule of life. For example, temperance promises us a certain integrity and incorruptibility of the love that unites us to God. It holds in check and quiets those desires that turn us away from the happy life (paragraph 35). Paul declared that covetousness was the root of all evils, and Augustine illustrates how his words are in harmony with the Old Testament (paragraph 36). The New Testament warns us against the love of sensible things and admonishes us to seek those that are eternal. Hence, Augustine argues that the Manicheans, who worship the sun and the moon, cannot be Christians (paragraph 37). The New Testament also warns us against the desire for popular acclaim, against curiosity about this world, and against pride, if we are to preserve our souls as chaste for God (paragraph 38). So too, the New Testament commands us not to love this world, and Augustine cites the words of Ecclesiastes on the vanity of the things of this world in order to show how the Old Testament agrees with the New (paragraph 39). As the love of God is called temperate when the soul does not love the things of this world, so it manifests fortitude, another of the four virtues, in facing their loss. There is, then, no need to say much about fortitude. Augustine notes, however, that in this life the body is a human being's greatest chain, which afflicts and troubles the soul because of our habit of loving the body (paragraph 40). We still face a great struggle with pain, and the intense love that some have for earthly things ought to teach us how we should endure all things out of love for God (paragraph 41). Again Augustine shows how the Old Testament is in harmony with the New by appealing to the courageous sufferings of Job, to the mother of the Maccabees, and to a cluster of verses from the Psalms (paragraphs 42 to 43). As for the remaining two virtues, justice teaches us to worship God with the service we owe him, and prudence teaches us to discern what we should seek and what we should avoid. Augustine again illustrates these points from the two Testaments (paragraphs 44 to 45).

God, then, is the highest good of a human being, and to seek that highest good is to live well, and to live well is nothing but to love God with one's whole heart, soul, and mind. Temperance preserves this love whole and entire, fortitude keeps it from being crushed by difficulties, justice prevents it from serving anything else, and prudence is vigilant lest it be deceived by error. Why, then, Augustine asks, do the Manicheans reject the scriptures that they do not understand (paragraph 46)? Eternal life is to be the reward of our love of God, and eternal life is the knowledge of God, the truth. Augustine notes the error on the part of the Manicheans, who suppose that they teach the knowledge of God in order that people *may* become perfect, though such knowledge is rather the reward of those who *have* become perfect. He also notes the Catholic Church's wisdom in beginning with authority rather than with reason (paragraph 47).

It is impossible to love God and to fail to love oneself, and the love of one human being for another is the surest step toward the love of God (paragraph

48). The second commandment, namely, to love one's neighbor as oneself, means that we should love ourselves and our neighbor. But we love ourselves in a more salutary way if we love God more than ourselves, and we should love our neighbor by bringing him to the love of God (paragraph 49). We sin against our neighbor in two ways: either by harming him or by not helping him when we can. The acts of love for our neighbors are the cradle of our love of God (paragraph 50). Either these two loves rise up together, or perhaps the love of God begins in us first, and the love of neighbor is the first to reach perfection. In any case Augustine wisely notes that, in order to love our neighbor, good will is not enough. Rather, we need much thought and prudence (paragraph 51). Since a human being as seen by another human being is a rational soul using a mortal and earthly body, our love for our neighbor does good both to his soul and to his body. For the body love provides medicine, that is, anything that protects or restores its well-being, and for the soul it provides discipline (paragraph 52). Those who dutifully and humbly provide such medicine for the body are called merciful, even if the wise do not feel misery with their neighbor (paragraph 53). Augustine warns against the mistake of shunning mercy as a failing and notes that, as mercy demands that we repel troubles from our neighbor, so innocence forbids us to inflict them (paragraph 54). Discipline for the soul includes instructing others to help people by being merciful, but God's providence has also provided a discipline or medicine for the soul without which we could have no hope of salvation (paragraph 55). This discipline or medicine of the soul is divided into deterrence and instruction. Deterrence is brought about by instilling fear, but instruction is brought about by instilling love. Though fear is dominant in the Old Testament, while love is dominant in the New, both fear and love are found in each of them (paragraph 56). The Manicheans agree that we should love God and our neighbor, but they deny that these loves are contained in the Old Testament. Augustine, however, points out that the Old Testament commandments to love God and neighbor were cited by the Lord in the gospel (paragraph 57). He expresses his frustration at the continued evasiveness on the part of the Manicheans (paragraph 58), and he argues that, if love of God and love of neighbor are good—something that no one can deny—then it cannot be right to blame what depends upon those two commandments, namely, the whole of the law and the prophets (paragraph 59). If the Manicheans deny that Christ said this, they say something that the pagans have not dared to say and something that ultimately destroys the credibility of all books, both religious and secular (paragraph 60). Augustine points out that, if the Manicheans want to argue that certain passages found in the New Testament are interpolations, they need to produce more accurate and older manuscripts that are free from such corruption (paragraph 61)

Augustine concludes that it is evident that the Manicheans who criticize the Christian scriptures cannot be Christians. For Christians were given as their rule of life the twofold commandment of the love of God and neighbor. Augustine then begins to apostrophize the Catholic Church, speaking of her as the mother of Christians, who teaches us to worship God chastely and not to worship any creature (paragraph 62). She instructs all her children in ways that are suited to them and unites in society and brotherhood persons of every people and nation, teaching them to love everyone and to do injury to no one (paragraph 63). When this human love nourishes and strengthens the soul that clings to the breasts of the Church, God begins to reveal himself and to kindle within that soul the fire of love for him, which burns away all the vices and makes the soul pure and holy (paragraph 64). Augustine points to the lives of those Christians who have withdrawn from human society to live lives of perfect continence and chastity (paragraph 65). He does not want to praise too much the contemplative lives of the Eastern hermits, who are thought by some to have gone too far (paragraph 66). But if the lives of the desert hermits are too extreme, the Manicheans should certainly see the goodness of the lives of those men who have abandoned the world for the common life of monasteries (paragraph 67). Augustine also points to the holy and chaste lives of women religious in the Church (paragraph 68). So too, he appeals to the holy lives of bishops, priests, deacons, and other ministers of the sacraments (paragraph 69), and to houses of men and women religious dwelling in the midst of cities (paragraph 70). These men and women fast and abstain from various foods not because they regard any food as unclean but in order to subdue their passions (paragraph 71). Many Catholics do not eat meat or drink wine, but unlike the Manicheans they do not think that they would be defiled if they did (paragraph 71). Those who are able to do so abstain from meat and from wine, either to avoid scandalizing their weaker brothers or as an expression of their own freedom, but always out of love (paragraph 73).

Augustine challenges the Manicheans to compare their fasts, their chastity, their attire, their meals, their modesty, their commandments, and their love with the same practices of these Catholic Christians (paragraph 74). He admits that there are some in the Catholic Church who fail to live the lives they profess to live, but he challenges the Manicheans to find even one of their Elect who keeps the Manichean commandments (paragraph 75). He calls upon the Manicheans to stop speaking ill of the Catholic Church because of the misconduct of some of its members. For they will either be corrected or they will remain on the threshing floor, like chaff among the wheat, until the judgment (paragraph 76). Augustine asks the Manicheans to focus not upon sinners in the Church but upon the countless good people in every walk of life (paragraph 77). He especially challenges the Manichean prohibitions against procreation and the ownership of property, since Paul permits these (paragraph 78). Though Paul wanted all Christians to live a celibate life as he himself did, Augustine insists that marital chastity comes close to that ideal (paragraph 79). He asks the Manicheans to cease from their attempts to recruit ignorant Catholics into their sect by criticizing Catholic sinners and claims that such recruits will soon discover more failings among the Manicheans after joining them. But proof of this charge, Augustine explains, will be found in the second book (paragraph 80).

This second book, *The Manichean Way of Life*, can be divided into three parts. The first part points out the Manichean errors regarding the principles of morality. The second part highlights their errors about particular moral precepts, which were classified under three seals. The third part treats of the corruption of the actual lives lived by the Manicheans. Augustine wishes that we could bring to this investigation of the highest good so clear a gaze of the mind that we could see this highest good, but unfortunately our minds have been wounded and dulled by trivial ideas and sins. The highest good is God, who is immutable being and whose contrary is utter nothingness (paragraph 1). The Manicheans often ask those whom they are trying to win over to their heresy where evil comes from. Augustine insists that we must first ask what evil is. Moreover, the Manicheans say that for each kind of thing what is contrary to its nature is evil, but they also say that the evil is itself a nature and a substance. They ought to see that evil is simply a falling away from being (paragraph 2). When Catholics profess that God is the creator of all natures and substances, those with understanding realize that God cannot be the author of evil. As the cause of the being of all things, he cannot also be the cause of their falling away from being. The Manichean nation of evil, that is, the eternal evil substance opposed to God, cannot be the greatest evil and cannot be a substance (paragraph 3). Though some Manicheans cannot understand these ideas and though others are filled with bad will, Augustine still hopes that this work of his will lead some of them to abandon their error and keep others from being deceived by the Manicheans' words (paragraph 4).

Augustine then returns to the question about what evil is. If the Manicheans say that evil is that which does harm, which is not incorrect, they should see that their evil nation cannot be harmed if it has nothing good. Moreover, since God, who is the highest good, is incorruptible and inviolable, he cannot be harmed either. Hence, there is nothing that evil can harm (paragraph 5). Catholic doctrine, on the other hand, maintains that God is the highest good, who is good by his own nature, but that other good things, namely, creatures, are good by participating in and having goodness. These creatures can be harmed by evil. Evil, however, is not an essence but a privation (paragraph 6). Again Augustine asks what evil is. The Manicheans perhaps answer that it is corruption. Augustine agrees that this is evil in general, yet corruption is not found in itself but in some substance that it corrupts. If the Manichean nation of darkness lacked every good, it could not be corrupted (paragraph 7). Catholic doctrine, on the other hand, holds that God, the uncreated substance and the highest good, is incorruptible, but that created substances can be corrupted, while corruption itself, which is the greatest evil, cannot be corrupted and is not a substance.

Created substances can become better or worse. In becoming worse they lose their order to some extent in tending toward non-being (paragraph 8). God puts in order creatures that fall away from their order. Thus rational souls fall away from God by their free choice, and they are set in order by God's judgment so that they are unhappy in accord with their merits (paragraph 9). In summary, whatever is, insofar as it is, comes from God, but, insofar as it falls away from being, it does not come from God. Divine providence, however, sets it in order in such a way as is fitting for the universe (paragraph 10). Perhaps the Manicheans will make the childish claim that fire or poison or a wild animal or whatever they dislike is evil. Certainly a scorpion is evil, that is, harmful to certain other things, because of its unsuitability for them, but such unsuitability is not a substance. It is, rather, inimical to a substance (paragraph 11). Some things are suitable for one kind of being and unsuitable for another (paragraph 12). Augustine points out to the Manicheans that, if any substance is evil because it does harm, then the very light that they worship cannot be defended from this charge since its rays cause blindness (paragraph 13). Hence, he asks the Manicheans to stop saying that evil is an immense land, a mind wandering in that land, the five caves of the elements, and so on, for these elements of their myth cannot exist as the Manicheans describe them (paragraph 14). Furthermore, there are in the Manichean kingdom of evil many great goods (paragraph 15). If unsuitability is an evil and suitability a good, what is more suitable for the animals of the evil kingdom than the elements in which they live (paragraph 16)? Moreover, how could the nation of darkness gaze upon and desire the kingdom of light, while our eyes are so weak that we see nothing at all in the dark (paragraph 17)? Likewise, if corruption is said to be evil, the animals in the kingdom of evil were less subject to corruption than the animals of the present world (paragraph 18).

Having shown the great errors of the Manicheans about good and evil in general, Augustine turns to their doctrine of the three seals — of the lips, of the hands, and of the breast. The Manicheans say that they observe these seals so that they may be chaste and innocent with their lips, hands, and breast. Augustine points out the inconsistency and inadequacy of their attempt to classify the avoidance of sins under these three seals (paragraph 19).

The Manicheans say that to refrain from blasphemy pertains to the seal of the lips. No one blasphemes, however, worse than the Manicheans. For God, as everyone knows, is incorruptible, immutable, and inviolable (paragraph 20), but when the Manicheans begin to tell their myths, they argue that God is corruptible, mutable, and violable (paragraph 21). The human soul is corrupted. Because it is now foolish, it has changed since it was wise. It has been violated since it has lost its perfection. It is now weak and in need. Inasmuch as the Manicheans claim that the soul is a part of God, they make God subject to all these. Or, if they do not admit these facts about the soul, then the soul does not need the· teaching of the apostle or the healing and deliverance of Christ (paragraph 22).

Even if a part of God is not God, the Manicheans cannot escape from these blasphemies (paragraph 23). Augustine points to various truths of mathematics, which even the nation of darkness cannot violate, and asks how that kingdom could violate God, who is the highest good (paragraph 24). He recalls an objection that bothered him even when he was a Hearer among the Manicheans, namely, what the nation of darkness would do if God refused to fight with it. For, if the nation of darkness were not going to harm him, why were we sent into these present woes and treated so cruelly? But if the nation of darkness were going to harm him, God's nature was not incorruptible as it ought to have been (paragraph 25). Augustine mentions that at Carthage he recently heard someone claim that God himself could not be violated but that his kingdom had certain borders that could be invaded by the enemy nation. He points out that, if this were the case, there would be three natures: one inviolable, a second violable, and a third violating (paragraph 26).

If the seal of the lips means abstinence from meat and wine, Augustine asks what the end is on account of which the Manicheans practice such abstinence, for it is the end that makes such actions praiseworthy or blameworthy (paragraph 27). The wicked Catiline endured cold, thirst, and hunger, just as the apostles did, but the ends for which the apostles did so were very different from the ends of Catiline (paragraph 28). Augustine points out that a Manichean can feast more lavishly without meat or wine than a Catholic who eats simple fare with a bit of meat and some wine (paragraph 29). He mocks the Manichean gourmet who keeps the seal by avoiding meat and wine while indulging in all sorts of delicacies (paragraph 30). Catholics abstain from meat and wine either to control their passions or to avoid giving scandal (paragraph 31). Augustine cites the whole of Romans 14 to put the apostle's words about abstinence from meat and wine in their context (paragraph 32). He also cites two long passages from the First Letter to the Corinthians in which Paul discusses abstinence from meat sacrificed to idols (paragraphs 33 and 34). Hence, Augustine concludes that the apostle gives three reasons for abstinence from meat and wine: to suppress the delight found in such food and drink, to avoid scandal to the weak on account of meat or drink offered as sacrifices or libations, and to show love by avoiding giving offense to the weak. But, contrary to the teaching of Paul, the Manicheans believe meat and wine are unclean and, for that reason, defile someone who consumes them (paragraph 35). The reason for the Manichean abstinence from meat and wine is their belief that the members of God have been mingled in every part of the world and that his members are daily purified through the consumption and digestion by the Elect of grains and fruit (paragraph 36). But, according to Manichean belief, though the divine nature escapes through the digestive processes of the Elect, flesh, which is the product of sexual intercourse, is most foul and defiles the soul of anyone who eats meat (paragraph 37). Hence, Augustine sets out to refute these false and absurd ideas (paragraph 38).

He asks, first of all, why the Manicheans say that a part of God is present in grains, plants, flowers, and fruit. He mocks their claim that God's presence is evident from their bright color, pleasant smell, and sweet taste and points to the absurdities that follow from the idea that God is to be found by the nose and tongue (paragraph 39). If, for example, scent is to be a guide to God's presence, he should certainly be more present in roast pork than in beans (paragraph 40). A combination of goodness of color, taste, and smell fares no better than each of these alone (paragraph 41). Augustine continues to badger the Manicheans by indicating the difficulties that they need to face, given their position (paragraph 42). They have no criterion for testing the presence of God in bodies or for their claim that the substance of the good escapes from bodies over time (paragraph 43). Augustine mentions the inconsistency of the Manichean denunciation of wine as the bile of the princes of darkness, while they continue to eat grapes (paragraph 44), and the absurdity of their claim that the nature of the good flees from the bodies of living things when they die, since dry branches of trees burn more brightly than those still full of sap (paragraph 45). Likewise, he offers examples of things that are improved by motion, though the Manicheans claim that motion allows the divine nature to escape (paragraph 46). He concludes that the Manicheans have no grounds for their claim that the good abandons fruits and vegetables if they are picked and stored away (paragraph 47). If they claim that God is present in foods that are a source of strength, they ought to notice that athletes eat meat (paragraph 48). He shows that the Manicheans have no basis for their claim that meat is unclean (paragraph 49), and he argues that, if the Elect release the divine substance from the foods they eat, they also ought to eat meat (paragraph 50). The Manicheans have fallen into incredible absurdities because of their myths and would do much better to hold that a person becomes unclean because of his evil desires (paragraph 51). They hold that it is wrong for anyone else to eat the food that the Hearers offer to the Elect in order to release the members of God contained in it (paragraph 52), and for this reason they refuse to give bread to a hungry beggar (paragraph 53).

Turning to the seal of the hands, Augustine first says that, when he sent the demons into a herd of pigs and cursed the fig tree, Christ showed by his actions that the Manicheans' abstention from killing animals or from felling trees was pure superstition (paragraph 54). Augustine asks the Manicheans, who make great promises to provide reasons and truth, what harm it does to a tree if one completely uproots it, since the rational soul in a tree, after all, cannot make any progress in wisdom (paragraph 55). If the Manicheans, on the other hand, claim that trees hear our voices and perceive our thoughts, Augustine wonders why they do not also preach to trees. (paragraph 56). He notes the inconsistency on the part of the Elect who refuse to pick apples or pull up plants but who command that their Hearers do this for them (paragraph 57). According to the

Manichean teaching, a member of the Elect will not pick a piece of fruit to save the life of a starving person (paragraph 58).

Augustine asks the Manicheans what it is that they think is wrong with killing an animal, since even a Hearer is forbidden to do such a thing (paragraph 59). Mani had claimed that it was justifiable for Hearers to pick fruits and vegetables for the Elect because the Elect purified the members of God contained in such food. Why, Augustine asks, would a Manichean butcher not be justified in selling meat in order to buy food for the Elect (paragraph 60)? He says that the Manicheans cannot consistently defend their prohibition against killing all living things (paragraph 61). He asks them about a Manichean Hearer who is also a farmer and has to kill locusts, rats, or mice and to pull out thorns and weeds in order to protect his crops. Either he goes against Mani's command or he cannot cultivate his fields (paragraph 62). The Elect themselves do not refrain from killing lice, fleas, and bedbugs (paragraph 63). If the Manicheans permit the killing of a flea because of its smallness, it is easy to move from fleas to larger bugs and from there to still larger living beings (paragraph 64).

By their seal of the breast the Manicheans forbid not intercourse but marriage, for their Hearers are not forbidden to have wives but are forbidden to beget children, which is the sole justification of intercourse (paragraph 65). The Manicheans try to prevent a soul from being entangled in the flesh as a result of intercourse. But they eat grain, beans, lentils, and other seeds, and Augustine hints at what the Elect might do in private with the seed of animals (paragraph 66). If the Manicheans observed the precepts contained under their three seals, they would be foolish and stupid, but since they praise and teach them without practicing them, they are deceitful and insidious (paragraph 67).

Augustine admits that he was a Manichean Hearer for nine years, but he says that he never came to know any of the Elect who lived out the precepts of the three seals. He reports various ways in which he witnessed sinful behavior on the part of the Elect (paragraph 68) and suggests that they only escaped punishment because the Manichean assemblies were illegal (paragraph 69). He mentions an incident in which a Manichean woman was violated in one of the assemblies (paragraph 70) and recounts a vicious quarrel between two of the Elect (paragraph 71). He recalls another member of the Elect who made a virgin pregnant and justified himself on the ground that even Adam, according to Mani's teaching, became holier after he sinned (paragraph 72). The Manichean version of Adam's fall can, Augustine argues, easily be turned to justifying anyone's giving in to lust (paragraph 73). He describes how a Manichean Hearer established a house in which the Elect were supposed to live out the life of the three seals. The experiment was a complete failure (paragraph 74). If, finally, the Manicheans protest that Augustine should not attack those who fail to live up to the Manichean code, he asks why they attack the Catholics, for there are many Catholics who live good lives, but very few Manicheans who do (paragraph 75).

Revisions I, 6 (7)

Two Books on the Catholic Way of Life and the Manichean Way of Life

1. When I was in Rome after having been baptized, I was unable to endure in silence how the Manicheans boasted about their false and deceitful continence or abstinence in order to mislead the uneducated. Because of this continence they prefer themselves to true Christians, to whom they should not be compared. Hence, I wrote two books, one on the way of life of the Catholic Church, the other on the Manichean way of life.

2. In the one which is about the Catholic way of life, where I gave the testimony that reads: *On your account we are afflicted the whole day; we have been treated like sheep*, the defectiveness of our manuscript misled me, less mindful (as I was) of the scriptures in which I was not yet adept. For other copies of the same translation do not have *On your account we are afflicted* but *On your account we are afflicted with death* (Ps 42:22),[1] which others express in a single word, *We are being put to death* (*mortificamur*). The Greek books indicate that this is more correct, and from that language the translation into Latin was made in accord with the seventy translators of the old divine scriptures. Arguing accord with these words, however, that is, *On your account we are afflicted*, I said many things which I do not reject as false in these matters. But I did not prove the compatibility of the old and the new scriptures, which I wanted to prove at least from these words. I have, however, stated the source of the error that crept up on me, and I sufficiently proved the same compatibility from other testimonies.

3. Likewise, shortly thereafter I cited a testimony from the Book of Wisdom according to our manuscript in which it said: *Wisdom teaches sobriety, justice, and power* (Wis 8:7).[2] And in terms of those words I discussed ideas that were certainly true, but ones discovered on the basis of a faulty text. After all, what is truer than that wisdom teaches the truth of contemplation, which I thought was signified by the term *sobriety*, and the goodness of action, which I wanted to be understood by those other two, that is, by *justice* and *power*, though the more accurate manuscripts of the same translation have: *For it teaches sobriety and wisdom and justice and power*? For by those terms the Latin translator mentioned the four virtues that are frequently found on the lips of the philosophers, calling temperance *sobriety*, giving to prudence the name *wisdom*,

---

1. *The Catholic Way of Life* I, 9, 14–15.
2. *Ibid.* I, 16, 27.

expressing fortitude by the term *power* and translating only justice by its own name. But much later in the Greek manuscripts we found these four virtues in the same Book of Wisdom called by their own names, as the Greeks refer to them.

4. Likewise, I read in many manuscripts what I cited from the Book of Solomon, *Vanity of the vain, said Ecclesiastes*,[3] but the Greek does not have this. Instead it has *Vanity of vanities*, which I saw afterward, and I found that the Latin manuscripts are more correct that have *vanities*, not *the vain*. Whatever I said as a result of this defectiveness, nonetheless, is seen to be true from the facts themselves.

5. But when I said that we should love him whom we want to know,[4] that is, God, with full love, it would have been better to say "sincere" rather than "full," lest it be thought that the love of God will not be greater when we see him face to face. In that way, then, it would be understood in the sense that the love than which there cannot be any greater was said to be full. As long as we walk by faith, there will certainly still be a fuller love to come, and in fact the absolutely fullest love.

6. Likewise, what I said about those who help the needy, namely, that they are called merciful, even if they are so wise that they are no longer upset by any mental anguish,[5] should not be understood as if I stated definitively that in this life the wise were such. I did not say "since they are" but "even if they are."

7. In another passage I said,[6] "Now, when this human love has nourished and strengthened the soul that clings to your breasts and has become suited to pursuing God, when his majesty begins to reveal itself to the extent that is sufficient for a human being dwelling upon this earth, so great an ardor of love is kindled and such a great conflagration of love of God arises that, once all the vices have been burned away and a person has been made pure and holy, it is seen with sufficient clarity in what sense God said: *I am a consuming fire*" (Ex 20:5; Dt 4:24). The Pelagians could suppose that I said that this perfection comes about in this mortal life. But they should not think that. To be sure, the ardor of love, having become suited to following God and so great that it consumes all sins, can begin and grow in this life, but it cannot as a result bring to perfection what is begun so that there remains no sin in a human being, although that great reality is brought to perfection by the same ardor of love where and when it can be brought to perfection. Thus, just as the bath of rebirth cleanses one from the guilt of all the sins that human birth inherited and wickedness contracted, so that perfection will cleanse one from all stain of the sins without which human weakness cannot live in this world. In the same way we must

3. *Ibid.* I, 21, 39.
4. *Ibid.* I, 25, 47.
5. *Ibid.* I, 27, 53.
6. *Ibid.* I, 30, 64.

understand the words of the apostle: *Christ loved the Church and handed himself over for her, cleansing her in the bath of water and the word in order to present to himself a glorious Church, having neither stain nor wrinkle nor anything of the sort* (Eph 5:25.27). This is the bath of water and the word by which the Church is purified, but since the whole Church says, as long as it is here, *Forgive us our debts* (Mt 6:12), it is of course here not without stain or wrinkle or anything of the sort. Still, from that which it receives here, it is brought to that glory and perfection that does not exist here.

8. In the other book, whose title is *The Manichean Way of Life*, I said, "The goodness of God orders all the things that are falling away in such fashion that they may be where they can be most appropriately until by their well-ordered movements they return to that from which they fell away."[7] This should not be taken in the sense that all things return to that from which they fell away, as Origen thought, but only all the things that do return. For those who will be punished by eternal fire will not return to God from whom they fell away, although all things that fall away will be set in order so that they are where they can exist most suitably. After all, those who do not return to God are set in order most suitably in punishment.

In another passage I said, "Almost no one has any doubt that beetles come to be from dung rolled into a ball and buried by them,"[8] though many doubt whether this is true and many have not even heard this.

This book begins: "In other books I think that we have sufficiently discussed."

---

7. *The Manichean Way of Life* II, 7, 9.
8. *Ibid.* II, 17, 63.

Book One

1, 1. In other books I think that we have sufficiently discussed how we can meet the onslaughts of the Manicheans, by which they ignorantly and wickedly attack the law, which is called the Old Testament, and express their minds with empty boasting amid the applause of the ignorant.[9] I can also briefly mention this here. After all, who with a mind that is even moderately sound would not understand that one should ask for an explanation of the scriptures from those who profess to be the teachers of them? For it is possible — in fact it always happens — that many ideas seem absurd to the unlearned which, when they are explained by teachers, seem the more highly praiseworthy the more they had seemed worthy of being more abjectly scorned. And these ideas are accepted, once they are explained, with all the more pleasure to the extent that, when unexplained, they were more difficult to explain. This is almost exactly what happens with the holy books of the Old Testament, if only the person who is offended by them seeks out a pious teacher of them rather than an impious attacker of them and is first imbued with the desire of a student rather than the rashness of a critic. And if in the desire to learn these things he should perhaps come upon some bishops or priests or any sort of prelates or ministers of the Catholic Church who either occasionally avoid explaining the mysteries to just anyone or take no care to learn more profound matters, inasmuch as they are content with simple faith, he should not give up hope that there is knowledge of the truth where not all from whom it is sought can teach it and not all who seek it are worthy of learning it. One must, therefore, use diligence and piety — the first in order that we may find men with knowledge, the second in order that we may deserve to learn.

2. But there are in particular two snares of the Manicheans by which the unwary are led astray so that they want to have them as their teachers — one when they criticize the scriptures, which they either understand incorrectly or want others to understand incorrectly, the other when they parade about the image of a chaste life and of a remarkable continence. Hence, this book will contain our view in conformity with Catholic teaching concerning life and morality. In it you will perhaps understand how easy it is to pretend to have virtue and how difficult it is actually to have it. I shall, of course, observe such moderation, if I can, that I do not attack their diseases, which I know very well, as severely as they attack what they do not know. For I want them to be healed, if possible, rather than battered. I shall use the testimonies from the scriptures that

---

9. See *Revisions* I, 6 (7), 10.

they have to believe, that is, those from the New Testament, and yet I shall not cite any of the testimonies that they are accustomed to say are interpolations when they are cornered and in great difficulties. Rather, I shall cite those that they are forced to approve and to praise. Nor shall I leave any statement taken as a testimony from the teaching of the apostle without comparing it to a similar statement from the Old Testament so that, if they are willing to wake up and set aside their stubborn dreams and to desire the light of the Christian faith, they may notice how the life that they exhibit is not the Christian life and how the scripture that they tear to shreds is the scripture of Christ.

2, 3. Where, then, shall I begin? From authority or from reason? The natural order is, of course, such that authority precedes reason when we learn something. For a reason can seem weak if, once it has been given, it afterwards appeals to authority to be shored up. But the minds of human beings obscured by their familiarity with the darkness, by which they are veiled in the night of sins and vices, cannot direct a suitable gaze toward the clarity and purity of reason. Hence, it has been most salutarily arranged that authority, shaded as it were by the branches of humanity, leads the wavering eye into the light of the truth. But since we are dealing with people who think, say, and do everything out of order and above all say nothing else but that a reason must be given first, I shall go along with them and undertake what I admit is a defective manner of arguing. For I find delight in imitating, as much as I can, the gentleness of my Lord Jesus Christ, who clothed himself even with the evil of the death of which he wanted to strip us.

4. Let us, then, investigate by reason how a human being ought to live. We certainly all want to live happily,[10] and there is no one in the human race who would not agree with this idea before it is spoken aloud. But, from my perspective, a person cannot be said to be happy who does not have what he loves, whatever it might be. Nor can he be said to be happy who has what he loves if it is harmful. Nor can he be said to be happy who does not love what he has, even if it is the highest good. For someone who desires what he cannot obtain is tormented, and someone who has obtained what he ought not to have desired is deceived, and someone who does not desire what he ought to desire is sick. But a mind meets with none of these without unhappiness, and unhappiness and happiness have not learned how to dwell in the same person at the same time. None of these persons, then, is happy. A fourth possibility remains, as I see it , where the happy life can be found: when that which is the highest good of a human being is both loved and possessed. After all, what else is it that we call enjoyment but to have present what you love? No one is happy who does not enjoy that which is the highest good of a human being, nor is anyone who enjoys

---

10. See Cicero, *Hortensius;* Augustine, *The Trinity* XIII, 1, 7.

it unhappy. Our highest good, then, must be available to us if we contemplate living happily.

3, 5. It follows that we should investigate what the highest good of a human being is, which is something that certainly cannot be less good than a human being. For whoever pursues something less good than himself becomes less good himself. But every human being ought to pursue that which is the highest good. The highest good, then, is not something less good than a human being. Is it, therefore, perhaps the same sort of good as a human being is? That would of course be the case if there were nothing better than a human being for a human being to enjoy. But if we find something that is both more excellent than a human being and can be available to a human being who loves it, who would have any doubt that, in order to be happy, a human being should strive for that which is clearly more excellent than the one who strives for it? For, if to be happy is to arrive at the sort of good than which a greater is not possible, that is, at what we call the highest good, how can someone be included in that definition who has not yet arrived at his highest good? Or how is it the highest good if there is something better at which we can arrive? If, then, this is the highest good, it ought to be the sort of thing that one does not lose against one's will. Certainly no one can be confident about the sort of good that he thinks can be taken away from him, even if he wants to hold onto it and cling to it. But how can anyone who is not confident about the good he is enjoying be happy amid such a great fear of losing it?

4, 6. Let us, then, investigate what is better than a human being.[11] It is, of course, difficult to discover this without first considering and examining what a human being is. Nor do I think that a definition of a human being should now be demanded of me. Almost everyone agrees, or at least it is accepted by me and the people with whom I am now dealing (and that is quite enough), that we are composed of soul and body. Hence, what I think we must investigate at this point is whether a human being is both of the things that I mentioned or only a body or only a soul. After all, soul and body are two things, and neither of them would be called a human being if the other were not present. For a body would not be a human being if there were no soul, nor, on the other hand, would a soul be a human being if it did not animate a body. And yet, it is still possible that one of these should be considered and called a human being. What, then, do we call a human being? A soul and a body, like a pair of horses or like a centaur? Or a body alone, which is for the use of the soul that rules it, just as we do not call a lamp the flame along with the vessel, but the vessel alone, though we call it a lamp on account of the flame? Or do we say that a human being is nothing but a soul, but say it on account of the body it rules, just as by a horseman we do not

---

11. See *The City of God* XIX, 3 where Augustine uses Varro's work, *Philosophy*, to develop the topic found in this and the following paragraph.

mean a man and a horse together but only a man, though we call him a horseman because he is able to control a horse? It is difficult to settle this controversy, or if it is easy for reason, it takes long to discuss it, but there is no need to take up this labor and to undergo this delay. For, whether both of them or only the body or only the soul should bear the designation "human being," the highest good of a human being is not what the highest good of the body is, but the highest good of a human being is the highest good of the body and soul together or of the soul alone.

5, 7. But if we ask what the highest good of the body is, a certain argument forces us to admit that it is that which makes the body to be in the best condition. But none of all those things that give life to the body is better and more excellent than the soul. The highest good of the body, then, is not its pleasure, not freedom from pain, not strength, not beauty, not speed, nor anything else that is counted among the goods of the body, but it is certainly the soul. For by its presence it gives to the body both those goods that were mentioned and — what surpasses them all — life. Hence, I do not think that the soul is the highest good of a human being, whether we say that a human being is the body and the soul or the soul alone. For, as reason found that the highest good of the body is that which is better than the body and gives it vigor and life, so, whether the body and the soul or the soul alone by itself is the human being, we must discover whether anything surpasses the soul itself which, when the soul pursues it, makes the soul the best it can be in its own kind. If we can find this, it will certainly be what should be — with all doubts removed — rightly and deservedly called the highest good of a human being.

8. But if the body is a human being, I cannot deny that the soul itself is the highest good of a human being. At least, however, when we are dealing with morality, when we are asking what manner of life we should follow in order to be able to attain happiness, we do not deliver commands to the body, nor do we investigate the discipline of the body. Finally, the part of us that inquires and learns is going to perform good actions, and these are characteristics of the soul. Our question, then, does not have to do with the body when we are striving to attain virtue. But if it follows, as it does, that, when a body is ruled by a soul that possesses virtue, it is ruled in a far better and more honorable way and is best off by the mere fact that the soul that is governed by just law is best, then what makes the soul best will be the highest good of a human being, even if we call the body a human being. But if, in obedience to me, a charioteer feeds and controls in a most suitable manner the horses of which he has charge, and if he enjoys my generosity to the extent that he is more obedient to me, can anyone deny that it is due to me that not only the charioteer but also the horses are in the best condition? And so, whether the body alone or the soul alone or both of them are a human being, I think that I need especially to investigate only what makes the soul best. For, once that has been attained, a human being cannot but be either in

the best condition or certainly in a much better condition than if this one thing were lacking.

6, 9. No one, however, doubts that virtue makes the soul best. But one can correctly ask whether this virtue can also exist by itself or only in the soul. There again arises a very deep question that requires a very long discussion, but I shall perhaps do well to use this shortcut. I hope that God will provide his help in order that we may teach not merely clearly but also briefly concerning these important topics as much as our feebleness permits. For, whichever of these is the case, that is, whether virtue can also exist by itself without the soul or can only be present in the soul, the soul undoubtedly pursues something in order that it may attain virtue. That will be either the soul itself or virtue or some third thing. But if it pursues itself in order that it may attain virtue, it pursues something foolish. For the soul is foolish before it has attained virtue. But our highest desire when we are in pursuit of something is that we may attain what we are pursuing. Either, then, the soul will not desire to attain what it is pursuing — than which nothing more absurd or disordered can be said — or, when it pursues itself in its folly, it attains the same folly that it is avoiding. But if the soul pursues virtue with the desire to attain it, how does it pursue something that does not exist? Or how does it desire to attain what it has? Either, then, virtue exists apart from the soul or — if we do not want to call virtue anything but the habit and quality, as it were, of the wise soul, which can only exist in the soul — the soul must pursue something else in order that virtue can begin to be in it, since it cannot, to the extent that my reason grasps it, attain wisdom either by pursuing nothing or by pursuing folly.

10. This other thing, then, by the pursuit of which the soul comes to possess virtue and wisdom, is either a wise human being or God. As I said above, it ought to be the sort of thing that we cannot lose against our will. But who would think that we should doubt that a wise human being, if we thought it enough to pursue him, could be taken away from us not merely when we are unwilling but even when we fight back? God, therefore, remains. If we pursue him, we live well; if we attain him, we live not merely well but also happily. If there are those who deny that he exists, why should I consider the words by which to persuade them when I do not know whether I should be conversing with them at all? But if it seems that I should, a far different starting point, a far different line of argument, and a far different approach must be taken than we have taken at present. Now, therefore, I am dealing with those who do not deny that God exists — and not only that, but they also admit that he has care of human affairs. After all, I do not think that anyone has any claim to being religious who does not think that divine providence has care at least of our souls.

7, 11. But how do we pursue him whom we do not see, or how do we see? After all, we are not only human beings but also human beings without wisdom. For, though he is seen not with the eyes but with the mind, what mind can ever be found suitable so that, though it is covered with the cloud of folly, it can drink in that light or even try to do so? We must, therefore, have recourse to the directives of those who probably were wise. Reason could be brought to this point. For it was dealing with human affairs more with a security stemming from habit than with a certainty coming from the truth. But when it comes to divine realities, it turns away; it cannot see; it gropes, is set afire, gasps with love, is struck by the light of the truth, and turns back, not by choice but out of fatigue, to its own familiar darkness. How one should at this point fear, how one should tremble lest the soul develop a greater weakness from that in which it seeks rest in its weariness! Hence, when we desire to take refuge in the darkness, that shadiness of authority comes to meet us and charms us through the providential plan of ineffable wisdom both by miraculous events and by the words of the holy books, as if by gentler signs and by shadows of the truth.

12. What more could have been done on behalf of our salvation? What can be said to be more beneficent, what can be said to be more generous than divine providence? It did not completely abandon man, who had fallen away from its laws and who rightly and deservedly begets mortal offspring because of his desire for mortal things. For in marvelous and incomprehensible ways, through certain most hidden sequences of things which it has created and which obey it, that most just power exercises both severity in punishing and clemency in setting free. We shall never be able to understand how beautiful, how great, how worthy of God, how — finally— true is that which we seek unless we begin from things that are human and close by. If we keep the faith of the true religion and the commandments, we shall not abandon the path that God has constructed for us by the calling of the patriarchs, by the bonds of the law, by the predictions of the prophets, by the mystery of the man whom God assumed, by the testimony of the apostles, by the blood of the martyrs, and by the conversion of the nations. Hence, from now on let no one ask me my opinion, but let us rather listen to the oracles and subject our frail arguments to the words of God.

8, 13. Let us see how the Lord himself commanded in the gospel and how the apostle Paul also commanded that we should live. For the Manicheans do not dare to condemn these scriptures. Let us, then, hear what the goal is of good persons that you, Christ, set for us. There is no doubt that it will be the goal to which you command that we make our way with the highest love. He says, *You shall love the Lord your God* (Mt 22:37). Tell me also, I ask you, what the manner of this love is, for I fear that I may be inflamed with desire and love for my Lord more or less than I ought. He says, *With your whole heart.* That is not enough. *With your whole soul.* Not even that is enough. *With your whole mind* (Mt 22:37). What more do you want? I would perhaps want more if I saw what more there could be. What does Paul say to this? He says, *We know that for those who love God all things move toward the good* (Rom 8:28). Let him also state the manner of this love. He says, *Who, then, will separate us from the love of*

*Christ? Will tribulation? Or difficulty? Or persecution? Or hunger? Or naked-
ness? Or danger? Or the sword?* (Rom 8:35) We have heard what we ought to
love and how much we ought to love. Toward that goal we must by all means
make our way; to it we must direct all our plans. God is for us the sum of all
goods. God is for us the highest good. We must not remain with less than that nor
seek anything beyond that. For the first is dangerous, and the second is non-existent.

9, 14. Come now, let us investigate or rather pay attention to — for it is before
our eyes and quite easy to see — whether the authority of the Old Testament is
also in accord with these statements drawn from the gospel and the apostle.
What shall I say about the first statement, since it is evident to all that it was taken
from the law that was given through Moses?[12] For it is written there: *You shall
love the Lord your God with your whole heart, with your whole soul, and with
your whole mind* (Dt 6:5). But the apostle himself added a passage from the Old
Testament that I might compare to his words so that I need search no longer. For,
after he said that we are separated from the love of Christ by no tribulation, by no
difficulty, by no persecution, by no demands of bodily need, by no danger, by no
sword, he immediately added, *As scripture says: For we are afflicted on your
account all day long; we have been reckoned as sheep for the slaughter* (Rom
8:36; Ps 44:22).[13] The Manicheans usually say that these words were inserted by
persons who corrupted the scriptures. Since they have nothing at all to say in
opposition, the wretches are forced to make this response. But who would fail to
understand that the last cry of those who have been refuted could have been
nothing else?

15. Still I ask them whether they deny that this statement is found in the Old
Testament or whether they say that it is not in accord with the statement of the
apostle. I shall prove the first point from those books. I shall, however, either
call back to peace human beings who are hesitating over the second point and
fleeing along the edges of cliffs, if they are willing to reflect a little and consider
what is said, or I shall pursue them with the intelligence of others who judge
impartially. After all, what could sound more compatible than these two ideas?
For tribulation, difficulty, persecution, hunger, nakedness, and danger gravely
afflict a human being in this life.[14] All these words are included in that one testimony of the old law where it said, *On your account we are afflicted* (Ps 44:22a).
There was left the sword, which does not make this life painful but takes away
the life it finds. To this, then, there corresponds: *We were counted as sheep for
the slaughter* (Ps 44:22b). But love itself cannot be signified more explicitly
than where it said, *On your account.* Pretend, then, that this testimony was not

---

12. See Jn 1:17.
13. See *Revisions* I, 6 (7), 2.
14. See Rom 8:35.

found in the apostle Paul but was produced by me. Is there anything else for you to prove, you heretic, but that this was not written in the old law or that it does not agree with the apostle? You do not dare to say either of these. For you are trapped when the volume is read in which it obviously was written, and people understand that nothing could be more perfectly in agreement with the apostle. Why, then, do you suppose that you accomplish anything when you dare to pretend that the scriptures have been corrupted? Finally, what are you going to reply to someone who says to you, "I understand the scripture in that sense, I accept it in that sense, I believe it in that sense, and I read those books for no other reason than because everything in them is in harmony with the Christian faith." If you dare and are thinking of speaking against me, say this instead: "We should not believe that the apostles and martyrs are said to have been afflicted with great sufferings on account of Christ and that they were counted as sheep for the slaughter by their persecutors." If you do not dare to say this, why do you utter lies about a book in which I find what you admit that I ought to believe?

10, 16. Or do you say that you grant that we should love God, but not the God who is worshiped by the people who accept the authority of the Old Testament? You say, therefore, that we should not worship the God who *made heaven and earth* (Gn 1:1). For he is proclaimed in every part of those volumes. But you yourselves admit that this whole world, which is signified by the words *heaven and earth*, has God — and the good God — as its author and maker. We must, of course, make a distinction in speaking with you when God is mentioned. After all, you maintain that there are two gods, a good God and an evil God. But if you say that you worship and think that one should worship the God by whom the world was made,[15] but not the one whom the authority of the Old Testament commends, you act impudently. For you try — and utterly in vain — to interpret in a bad sense an idea and a statement quite foreign to you, which we accept in a good sense and with profit. Your stupid and wicked arguments cannot be compared in any way, after all, to the words of pious and most learned men who explain those scriptures in the Catholic Church to people who are willing and worthy. We certainly interpret the law and the prophets far, far differently than you suppose. Give up your error. We do not worship a God who is repentant, jealous, needy, or cruel; we do not worship a God who seeks pleasure from the blood of human beings or animals, nor a God who takes pleasure in sins and crimes, nor a God who limits his ownership of the earth to a certain small piece of it. For you are accustomed to inveigh violently and at length against these silly ideas and other similar ones. Hence, your attack does not touch us. Rather, you tear into certain opinions of old wives or even of children[16] with language that is more inept the more violent it is. If anyone is moved by it and crosses over

---

15. See Jn 1:10.
16. See 1 Tm 4:7.

to you, he does not condemn the teaching of our Church but shows that he is ignorant of it.

17. Hence, if you have any humanity in your heart, if you care about yourselves, seek rather with diligence and piety the sense in which those things are said. Seek, you poor wretches. For we very strongly and at great length denounce such a faith as would believe something unsuitable about God. For, when some people understand those passages that were mentioned in their literal sense, we correct their simplicity and mock their stubbornness. And Catholic discipline forbids those who pass beyond the childhood of the mind and advance toward the gray hairs of wisdom,[17] not by reason of years but by reason of their desire and understanding, to believe many other things that you cannot understand. For it teaches how foolish it is to believe that God is contained in some place, even in an endless space through any stretches whatsoever of expanse. And it is regarded as a sacrilege to think that he or some part of him moves and passes from place to place. And if anyone thinks that something of his substance and nature can in any way suffer change or transformation, he will be condemned for an astonishing madness and impiety. In that way it turns out that there are found among us certain children who think of God in a human form and believe that he is that way. Nothing is more base than that opinion. But there are also found many elders who see by the mind that his majesty, which is not only above the human body but also above that same mind, remains inviolable and immutable. We have already said that these ages are not to be distinguished by time but by virtue and wisdom. Among you, however, no one is found who limits the substance of God by the shape of the human body, but, by the same token, no one is found who is free from the stain of human error. And so, those whom the breasts of the Catholic Church sustain like wailing infants, if they do not fall prey to heretics, are fed, each in accord with his capacity and strength, and are guided, one in this way, another in that. And they come first to complete manhood,[18] then to maturity and the gray hairs of wisdom,[19] in order that, to the extent that they desire, they may live — and live most happily.

11, 18. The pursuit of God, therefore, is the desire for happiness, but the attainment of God is happiness itself. We pursue him by loving, while we attain him not when we become exactly what he is but when we become very close to him, touching him in a marvelous and intelligible way, and are enlightened and seized by his truth and holiness. For he is the light, but we are allowed to be enlightened by that same light.[20] *The greatest and first commandment*, then, which leads to eternal life, *is: You shall love the Lord your God with your whole heart and your whole soul and your whole mind* (Mt 22:38.37). After all, *for*

---

17. See Wis 4:8; Sir 6:18.
18. See Eph 4:13.
19. See Wis 4:8; Sir 6:18.
20. See Jn 1:9.

those who love God all things move toward the good. For this reason the same Paul says a little later, *I am certain that neither death nor life, neither an angel nor a power, neither present things nor those to come, neither height nor depth nor any other creature will be able to separate us from the love of God, which is found in Christ Jesus our Lord* (Rom 8:38-39). *For those,* then, *who love God all things move toward the good,* and no one doubts that we should not merely love the highest good, which is also called the best, but that we should love it so that we love nothing more. And that is signified and expressed in the words, *with your whole heart and your whole soul and your whole mind.* Once all these points are established and most firmly believed, who, I ask, has any doubt that for us nothing else but God is the highest good and that we ought to hasten to attain him in preference to all other things? Likewise, if nothing separates us from his love,[21] what can be not only better but also more certain than this good?

19. But let us briefly turn our attention to each point. No one separates us from the love of God by the threat of death. After all, that by which we love God can only die if it does not love God. For it is death not to love God, and that is nothing else than to prefer anything to him in our love and pursuit. No one separates us from the love of God by promising life. For no one separates us from a fountain by promising water. An angel does not separate us from the love of God. For, when we cling to God, an angel is not stronger than our mind. A power does not separate us from the love of God.[22] For, if in this case we mean by a power that which has some authority in this world, a mind that clings to God is absolutely superior to the whole world. But, if we mean power in the sense of virtue, that is, a perfectly correct disposition of our mind, when it is present in someone else, it fosters our union with God, but if it is present in us, it unites us with him. Present troubles do not separate us from the love of God. For we find them lighter to the extent that we cling more tightly to him from whom they try to separate us. The promise of things to come does not separate us from the love of God. For God promises with more certainty whatever good is to come, and nothing is better than God himself, who is of course present to those who firmly cling to him. *Neither height nor depth* separate us from the love of God. For, if these words perhaps signify the height or the depth of knowledge, I shall not be curious for fear that I may be separated from God. And no one's teaching separates me from him as if in order to keep me from error, for only someone separated from him is in error. But if height and depth signify the higher and lower parts of this world, who would promise me heaven in order to separate me from the maker of heaven? Or what lower world would terrify me so that I would abandon God? For I would not come to know the lower world if I never aban-

---

21. See Rom 8:39.
22. The Latin *virtus* can mean a power or a virtue. Augustine explains how in neither sense can such a *virtus* separate one from God.

doned him. Finally, what place would tear me away from the love of him who would not be whole everywhere if he were contained by any place?

12, 20. No other creature, he says, separates me from the love of God.[23] Oh, a man of the deepest mysteries! He was not content to say, "no creature," but he says, *not any other creature*, reminding us that that by which we love God and cling to God, that is, the soul and mind, is a creature. The other creature, then, is the body. And if the soul is an intelligible reality, that is, one that becomes known only by being understood, the other creature is everything sensible, that is, everything that offers some knowledge, as it were, of itself through the eyes or ears or smell or taste or touch and that is necessarily inferior to what is grasped by the intelligence alone. God too can be known by worthy souls only through the intelligence, though he is nonetheless more excellent than the mind by which he is understood, for he is, of course, its creator and author. Hence, there was reason to fear that the human mind might think that it is of the same nature as he is who created it because it is counted among invisible and intelligible things. And in that way it might by pride fall away from him to whom it should be united by love. For the mind becomes like God, insofar as it is granted this, when it subjects itself to him to be enlightened and illumined. And if it becomes very close to him through that subjection by which it becomes like him, the audacity by which it wants to be more like him must become far removed from it. This is the audacity by which it refuses to obey the laws of God when it wants to be in its own power, as God is.[24]

21. The soul, then, is filled with folly and unhappiness the farther it wanders off from God to things lower than itself not by place but by love and desire. It returns to God, therefore, by the love by which it desires not to make itself equal to God but to make itself subject to him. The more earnestly and zealously it does this, the happier and loftier it will be, and it will be most free when God alone is its lord. Hence, it should know that it is a creature. For it should believe that its creator, as he truly is,[25] always remains in the inviolable and immutable nature of truth and wisdom, but it should admit that folly and falsehood can overtake it, at least because of the errors from which it desires to be set free. But, again, it should beware that it is not separated by love for another creature, that is, for this sensible world, from the love of God himself, by which it is made holy in order that it may remain most blessed. Since we ourselves are a creature, no other creature, therefore, separates us *from the love of God, which is found in Christ Jesus our Lord.*

13, 22. Let the same Paul tell us who this Christ Jesus our Lord is. He says, *To those who have been called we preach Christ, the power of God and the wisdom*

---

23. See Rom 8:39.
24. See Gn 3:5.
25. See 1 Jn 3:2.

of God (1 Cor 1:23-24). Why does he say this? Does not Christ himself say, *I am the truth* (Jn 14:6)? If we, therefore, ask what it is to live well, that is, to strive for happiness by one's life, that will of course be to love power, to love wisdom, to love truth, and to love *with your whole heart and your whole soul and your whole mind* the power that is inviolable and unconquered, the wisdom to which no folly draws near, and the truth that cannot change and be otherwise than it always is. Through him we see the Father, for he said, *No one comes to the Father except through me* (Jn 14:6). To him we cling through becoming holy. For, having been made holy, we are ablaze with a love that is whole and entire, a love that alone prevents our being turned away from God and makes us conformed to him rather than to this world.[26] *For he predestined us*, as the same apostle says, *to become conformed to the image of his Son* (Rom 8:29).

23. Love, then, will see to it that we are conformed to God and, having been conformed and configured by him and cut off from this world,[27] that we are not confused with the things that ought to be subject to us. But this is done by the Holy Spirit. For the apostle says, *Hope does not produce confusion, since the love of God has been poured out in our hearts by the Holy Spirit who has been given to us* (Rom 5:5). In no way, however, could we be restored to wholeness by the Holy Spirit if he himself did not always remain whole and immutable. He could not do this, of course, unless he were of the nature and substance of God, which alone always has immutability and, so to speak, unchangeability. *For creation*, not I but the same Paul cries out, *is subject to vanity* (Rom 8:20). And what is subject to vanity cannot separate us from vanity and unite us to the truth. The Holy Spirit does this for us. He is not a creature, therefore, because everything that exists is either God or a creature.

14, 24. Hence, we ought to love God, a certain triple oneness, Father, Son, and Holy Spirit, and I shall say that God is nothing other than being itself. For God is truly and sovereignly, *from whom are all things, through whom are all things, and in whom are all things* (Rom 11:36a). These are Paul's words. What does he add next? *To him be glory* (Rom 11:36b). He adds this with absolute truth. For he does not say "to them," since God is one.[28] What does *to him be glory* mean but that the knowledge of him may be the best and the highest and the most widespread? For the better and the more extensively he is known, the more he is desired and the more ardently he is loved. When this happens, the human race does nothing but advance with a sure and constant step toward the best and happiest life. Since our question concerns morals and life, I do not think that we need to seek further what the highest good of a human being is to which all things must be directed. It has become evident, after all, that it is nothing but

---

26. See Rom 12:2.
27. See Phil 3:10; Col 2:11.
28. See Dt 4:35; Mk 12:32; Rom 3:30; Rom 11:36.

God himself — both from reason, to the extent that we were capable, and from that divine authority which surpasses our reason. For what else will be the greatest good for a human being but he to whom it is most blessed to cling.[29] But that is God alone, to whom we can certainly only cling by longing, desire, and love.

15, 25. But if virtue brings us to the happy life, I would say that virtue is absolutely nothing but the highest love of God. For virtue is said to be fourfold, insofar as I understand it, because of a certain varied disposition of love. And so I do not hesitate to define those four virtues — I wish that their power were in the minds of all as their names are on their lips — as follows: Temperance is love offering itself in its integrity to the beloved. Fortitude is love easily tolerating all things on account of the beloved. Justice is love serving the beloved alone and as a result ruling righteously. And prudence is love that wisely separates those things by which it is helped from those by which it is impeded. But we said that this love is not a love of just anything but of God, that is, of the highest good, the highest wisdom, and the highest harmony. Hence, it is also permissible to define them as follows: Temperance is love preserving itself whole and entire for God. Fortitude is love readily enduring all things for God. Justice is love that serves only God and, for this reason, correctly governs other things that are subject to a human being. And prudence is love distinguishing correctly those things by which it is helped toward God from these things by which it can be impeded.

16, 26. I shall explain in a few words what sort of life one may lead with respect to each of these virtues after I have compared (as I promised) testimonies from the New Testament, which I have been using for a long time, to similar testimonies from the Old Testament. After all, does Paul alone say that we ought to be subject to God so that there is nothing in between that separates us?[30] Does not the prophet signify this most aptly and briefly when he says, *But it is good for me to cling to God* (Ps 73:28)? Is not what Paul said at such great length about love here contained in the one word the prophet uses, *cling*? So too, do not the words he added, *it is good*, correspond to the words that were used by Paul, *For those who love God all things move toward the good*, so that by one short sentence with its two parts the prophet reveals the forcefulness and benefit of love?

27. Paul said that the Son of God is the power and wisdom of God,[31] and power is understood to have to do with action, while wisdom is understood to have to do with teaching. For this reason these two are signified in the gospel. It says there, *All things were made through him* (Jn 1:3). For this has to do with action and power. Then, with regard to teaching and the knowledge of the truth,

---

29. See Ps 73:28.
30. See 1 Cor 15:27; Phil 3:21.
31. See 1 Cor 1:24.

it says, *And the life was the light of human beings* (Jn 1:4). Could anything fit better with these testimonies from the New Testament than the words of the Old Testament about wisdom: *But it reaches from end to end mightily and arranges all things pleasingly* (Wis 8:1)? For "to reach mightily" rather signifies power, while "to arrange pleasingly" signifies in a sense art and reason. But if this seems obscure, look at what follows. It says, *And the Lord of all loved her, for she teaches God's discipline and chooses his works* (Wis 8:3-4). Here nothing seems as yet to have been said about action. For to choose works is not the same as to do them. Hence, these have to do with discipline. The activity of power is needed in order that the idea which we want to demonstrate may be complete. Read, therefore, what follows next. It says, *If wealth that is desired in this life is honorable, what is more honorable than the wisdom that produces all things?* (Wis 8:5) Can anything be said that is clearer, more obvious, or even more useful? If you think it is not enough, listen to another verse that makes the same point: *For wisdom teaches sobriety and justice and power* (Wis 8:7).[32] Sobriety seems to me to pertain to the knowledge of the truth, that is, to teaching, but justice and power to activity and action. I do not know what I should compare to these two, that is, to the effectiveness of action and the sobriety of contemplation, which the power of God and the wisdom of God,[33] that is, the Son of God, gives to those who love him. For the prophet himself immediately says how highly these should be valued. He expressed it in this way: *For wisdom teaches sobriety and justice and power, than which there is nothing more useful in life for human beings* (Wis 8:7).

28. Someone may perhaps think that this was not said about the Son of God. What else, then, do these words show: *Sharing his tent with God, he reveals his noble origin* (Wis 8:3)? Does *noble origin* usually signify anything else than one's parents? Does not *sharing his tent* cry out and assert his equality with the Father? Secondly, since Paul says that the Son of God is *the wisdom of God* and since the Lord himself says, *No one knows the Father but the only-begotten Son* (Mt 11:27; Jn 1:18), what could the prophet have said that is more in harmony with this than his words: *And with you is wisdom who knows your works, who was present when you made the world and knew what would be pleasing in your eyes* (Wis 9:9)? But as for Christ's being the truth,[34] the same thing that is revealed when he is called the splendor of the Father,[35] is there anything surrounding the sun but the splendor that the sun itself begets? What, then, from the Old Testament could more evidently and clearly correspond to this idea than the words: *Your truth surrounding you* (Ps 89:9)? Finally, wisdom himself says in the gospel, *No one comes to the Father except through me* (Jn 14:6). The

---

32. See *Revisions* I, 6 (7), 3.
33. See 1 Cor 1:24.
34. See Jn 14:6.
35. See Heb 1:3.

prophet says, *Who, then, knows your mind unless you give wisdom?* (Wis 9:17) And a little later he says, *Men have learned what pleases you and have been healed through wisdom* (Wis 9:18-19).

29. Paul says, *The love of God has been poured out in our hearts through the Holy Spirit who has been given to us* (Rom 5:5). The prophet says, *For the Holy Spirit of discipline will banish deceit* (Wis 1:5). For, where there is deceit, there is no love.[36] Paul says that we are becoming conformed to the image of the Son of God.[37] The prophet says, *The light of your countenance, O Lord, has been impressed upon us* (Ps 4:7). Paul shows that the Holy Spirit is God and for that reason not a creature. The prophet says, *And you will send the Holy Spirit from the greatest heights* (Wis 9:17). For God alone is the most high, than whom there is nothing higher. Paul shows that this Trinity is one God when he says, *To him be glory.* In the Old Testament it says, *Hear, O Israel: the Lord your God is one God* (Dt 6:4).

17, 30. What more do you want? Why do you rage in ignorance and impiety? Why do you upset uneducated souls with your harmful views? There is one God of the two Testaments. For, just as those testimonies that we quoted from the two Testaments are in harmony with one another, so the others are as well, if you are willing to pay attention to them carefully and with an unbiased mind. But many things are said in a rather lowly manner and in a way better suited to minds that creep along the ground in order that they may rise through what is human to what is divine, and many things are also said in a symbolic manner in order that a studious mind may have more useful exercise in the questions it asks and may have richer delight in the answers it finds. And so you misuse the marvelous providential plan of the Holy Spirit to deceive and ensnare your hearers. It would take a long time to discuss why divine providence allows you to do this and how truthfully the apostle said, *It is necessary that there be many heresies in order that the tried and true among you may become known* (1 Cor 11:19),[38] and, as has to be said to you, it is beyond your ability to understand these things. After all, I am not lacking knowledge of you. For you bring minds that are too dense and sick, because of the deadly food of bodily images, to pronounce judgment on the things of God, which are much more lofty than you think.

31. Hence, we should not at present work with you in order that you may now understand these ideas, for that is not possible, but in order that you may desire to understand them at some point. For the simple and pure love of God, which is especially seen in one's way of life, brings this about, and we have already said many things about this love. Once it has been breathed into us by the Holy

---

36. See 1 Cor 13:4-5.
37. See Rom 8:29.
38. Here and in *True Religion* 8, 44 Augustine's text adds "many" (*multas*).

Spirit,[39] it leads us to the Son, that is, to the wisdom of God,[40] through whom the Father himself comes to be known. For, if wisdom or truth is not desired by the full strength of the mind, it cannot in any way be found. But if it is sought, as it should be, it cannot withdraw itself and hide itself from its lovers. This is the reason for those words that you too often have on your lips: *Ask and you shall receive; seek and you shall find; knock and it shall be opened for you* (Mt 7:7; Lk 11:9). *Nothing is hidden that will not be revealed* (Mt 10:26; Lk 12:2). Love asks; love seeks; love knocks; love reveals; love, finally, remains in what has been revealed. The Old Testament does not deter us from this love of wisdom and from diligence in seeking it, as you constantly say with your lies; rather, it most vigorously urges us on to this.

32. Listen, therefore, at long last, and notice, please, without stubbornness what the prophet says. He says, *Wisdom is bright and never fades; she is easily seen by those who love her and found by those who seek her. She anticipates those who desire her and reveals herself to them. He who keeps watch for her will not labor, for he will find her sitting at his door. For to think of her is perfect knowledge, and he who keeps watch on account of her will quickly be free of worries. For she goes about seeking those who are worthy of her, joyfully reveals herself to them in the streets, and helps them with all her foresight. For the truest beginning of her is the desire for discipline. A concern for discipline, therefore, is love, and love is the observance of the laws. But the observance of the laws is an assurance of incorruptibility, and incorruptibility makes one close to God. The desire for wisdom, therefore, leads to the kingdom.* (Wis 6:12-20) Will you still bark against this? Expressed in this way, even if they are not yet understood, do these words not signify to anyone that they contain something lofty and ineffable? Oh, how I wish that you could understand what was said! You would quickly cast off all the nonsense of your myths and all the utterly vain images of bodies, and you would bring yourselves whole and entire with great speed, sincere love, and the firmest faith to the most holy bosom of the Catholic Church.

18, 33. In accord with my modest ability I could have discussed each point and singled out and demonstrated those that I grasped and those at whose excellence and depth words generally fail, but as long as you bark in opposition, I ought not to do that. After all, it was not said in vain: *Do not give what is holy to the dogs* (Mt 7:6). Do not become angry. I too barked in opposition and was a dog when people rightfully dealt with me not with the food of doctrine but with the rods of refutation. But if you had the love we are now discussing or even if you will ever have it as much as the greatness of the truth to be known demands, God will be there to show you that the Manicheans do not have the Christian

---

39. See Rom 5:5.
40. See 1 Cor 1:24.

faith that leads to the highest peak of wisdom and truth, the enjoyment of which is nothing other than to live most happily, and that this faith is found nowhere but within the Catholic discipline. For what else do we see that the apostle longs for when he says, *On this account I bend my knees before the Father of our Lord Jesus Christ, from whom all fatherhood in the heavens and on earth takes its name, that he may grant you courage according to the riches of his glory, that you may be strengthened by the Spirit in your inner self, that Christ may dwell in your hearts through faith, in order that, rooted and grounded in love, you may be able to grasp with all the saints what is the height and the length and the breadth and the depth, that you may also know the love of Christ, which surpasses knowledge, in order that you may be filled with the complete fullness of God* (Eph 3:14-19)? Can anything more clear be said?

34. I beg you, pay a little attention; see the harmony of the two Testaments that sufficiently discloses and teaches the manner of our way of life and the end to which all things are to be directed. The gospels stir up the love of God when they say: Ask, seek, and knock.[41] Paul stirs up love when he says, *In order that, rooted and grounded in love, you may be able to grasp.* The prophet also stirs up love when he says that wisdom can be easily known by those who love it, seek it, desire it, keep watch for it, think of it, and are concerned about it.[42] The salvation of the soul and the path to happiness are revealed by the harmony of the two books of scripture, and you prefer to bark at them rather than to obey them. I shall say what I think in a few words: Listen to the learned men of the Catholic Church with great peace of mind and with that desire with which I listened to you. There will be no need of the nine years during which you mocked me.[43] In a far, far shorter time you will see the difference between truth and vanity.

19, 35. But it is time to return to those four virtues and to draw and derive from each of them a rule of life. And so let us look first at temperance, which promises us a certain integrity and incorruptibility of the love by which we are united to God.[44] For its function lies in checking and quieting the desires by which we long for those things that turn us away from the laws of God and from the fruit of his goodness, that is, to put it briefly, from the happy life. For there is found the throne[45] of the truth, and when we enjoy the contemplation of it and cling closely to it, we shall undoubtedly be happy. But those who fall away from it are entangled in great errors and sorrows. For, as the apostle says, *the root of all evils is covetousness, and some who have followed after it have suffered shipwreck in the faith and have plunged themselves into many sorrows* (1 Tm 6:10). For those who understand well, this sin of the soul is signified quite clearly in the Old

---

41. See Mt 7:7; Lk 11:9.
42. See Wis 6:13-21.
43. See *Confessions* IV, 1, 1 and, in this work, II, 19, 68.
44. See Wis 6:19-20.
45. I have followed the reading *sedes* found in PL rather than *fides* found in CSEL.

Testament by the transgression of the man who was in paradise. *In Adam, indeed, we all die*, as the same apostle says, *and in Christ we shall all rise* (1 Cor 15:22). Oh, the depth of the mysteries![46] But I will hold myself back. For I have not now undertaken to teach you what is correct but to disabuse you of what is wrong if I can, that is, if God favors our aim in your regard.

36. Paul, then, says that the root of all evils is covetousness, and the old law indicates that the first man fell because of it.[47] Paul warns that we should strip off the old man and put on the new.[48] But he wants us to understand that the Adam who sinned is the old man, while the man whom the Son of God assumed in a mystery in order to set us free is the new man. For he says in another passage, *The first man from the earth is earthly, but the second man from heaven is heavenly. As the earthly man was, so are the earthly people. As the heavenly man, so are the heavenly people. Just as we have borne the image of the earthly man, let us also bear the image of the heavenly man.* (1 Cor 15:47-49) That is, strip off the old man and put on the new man.[49] The whole function, then, of temperance is to strip off the old man and to put on the new man and to be made new in God,[50] that is, to hold in contempt all the allurements of the body and popular acclaim and to bestow one's whole love on things that are invisible and divine. From this there follow these words, which are remarkably expressed: *Even if our outer self is being corrupted, our inner self is being renewed from day to day* (2 Cor 4:16). Listen also to the prophet as he sings, *Create a clean heart in me, O God, and renew a righteous spirit in my innermost self* (Ps 51:12). What can be said against this harmony except by those who bark in their blindness?

20, 37. But the allurements of the body are found in all the things that the bodily senses attain, which some people also call "sensible things." Among them this common light especially stands out because none among these senses of ours, which the soul uses through the body, is preferable to the eyes. And for this reason in the holy scriptures all sensible things are referred to by the expression "visible things." And so in the New Testament we are warned against a love for them in this way: *Let us not have our eyes on the things that are visible but on those that are not visible. For the things that are visible are temporal, but those that are not visible are eternal.* (2 Cor 4:18) From this one can understand that they are not Christians who think that the sun and the moon should not only be loved but should also be worshiped. After all, what do we see if we do not see the sun and the moon? But we are forbidden to turn to the things that are visible. These things, then, are not to be loved by one who thinks of offering to God that uncorrupted love. But there will be another place where I shall inquire more thoroughly into this. For at present I have

---

46. See Rom 11:33; 1 Cor 15:51.
47. See Gn 2:16-17.
48. See Col 3:9-10.
49. See Col 3:9-10.
50. See Eph 4:23-24.

begun to speak not about faith but about the way of life by which we may merit to know what we believe. God alone, therefore, should be loved, but this whole world, that is, all sensible things, should be held in contempt. We must, however, use them for the needs of this life.

21, 38. But in the New Testament popular acclaim is cast aside and held in contempt in this way: *If I wanted to please human beings,* it says, *I would not be Christ's servant* (Gal 1:10). There is also something else that the soul grasps concerning bodies through certain acts of the imagination, and it calls it the knowledge of things. For this reason we are also forbidden to be curious, something that is a great function of temperance. From this there comes that warning: *Take care that no one leads you astray by philosophy* (Col 2:8a). And if we consider the word *philosophy,* it signifies something important that we should seek with our whole soul, for philosophy is the love and pursuit of wisdom. Hence, the apostle adds with great caution, for fear that he might seem to deter us from the love of wisdom, *and the elements of this world* (Col 2:8b). For there are some who, having abandoned the virtues and not knowing what God is nor how great the majesty of his nature is, which always remains the same, think that they do something important if they investigate with great curiosity and intensity this entire mass of body that we call the world. From this there also arises such great pride that they suppose that they dwell in heaven, about which they often debate. Let the soul, therefore, hold itself back from the desire for such vain thoughts if it wants to preserve itself chaste for God. For it is very often deceived by such a love that either it thinks that there is nothing but body or — even if, moved by some authority, it admits that there is something incorporeal — it can nonetheless only think of it by means of bodily images and can only believe it to be something of the sort that the deceitful senses of the body impress upon it. The commandment that we should avoid images also applies to this.[51]

39. To this authority of the New Testament, therefore, by which we are commanded to love nothing belonging to this world,[52] that command especially pertains which says, *Do not be conformed to this world* (Rom 12:2). For it is necessary to show at the same time that one becomes conformed to that which one loves. If, then, I look for something from the Old Testament that I might compare to this authority, of course I find many things. But the one book of Solomon called Ecclesiastes goes to great lengths to bring all these things into the highest contempt. For it begins as follows: *Vanity of the vain, said Ecclesiastes, vanity of the vain, and all things are vanity. What riches does a man have from all his labor that he endures under the sun?* (Eccl 1:2-3)[53] If we pay attention to all these words, if we weigh them, if we examine them, we find many

---

51. See 1 Jn 5:21.
52. See 1 Jn 2:15.
53. See *Revisions* I, 6 (7), 4.

ideas that are quite necessary for those who desire to flee this world and to take refuge in God. But that would take a long time, and my tongue rushes on to other ideas. Nonetheless, after having established that one principle, the author moves on to all the others, showing that they are vain who are deceived by such things. But he calls vanity that by which they are deceived, not because God did not create these things but because human beings, by means of their sins, want to make themselves subject to the things that would have been subject to them by God's law if they had acted correctly. After all, what else is it to be mocked and deceived by false goods than to think that you should admire and desire things inferior to you? A man who is temperate in such mortal and passing things, then, has a rule of life supported by both Testaments so that he loves none of those things and thinks that none of them should be desired for themselves, but he employs them to the extent that it suffices for the necessities of this life and its duties with the moderation of someone who *uses* them, not with the disposition of someone who *loves* them. I have stated these ideas concerning temperance briefly, given the importance of the matter, but still perhaps more amply than was necessary, given the task I have undertaken.

22, 40. But concerning fortitude not many things need be said. For that love of which we are speaking, which ought to be ablaze for God with complete holiness, is called temperate when it does not desire these things and is called strong when it gives them up. But among all the things that we possess in this life the body is for a human being the heaviest chain, in accord with the completely just laws of God, on account of the ancient sin. Nothing is discussed with greater familiarity, nothing is more obscure to understand. This chain, then, afflicts the soul with a fear of labor and pain, that the body may be stricken and troubled, and with a fear of death, that it may be taken away and destroyed. The soul, after all, loves the body by force of habit, not understanding that, if it uses the body well and intelligently, the resurrected and restored body will, by the help and law of God, be made subject to the soul's rule without any difficulty. But when it turns the whole body to God with this love, the soul will not only hold death in contempt as a result of this knowledge but will even desire it.

41. But there remains a great struggle with pain. Yet nothing is so hard and so unbending that it is not conquered by the fire of love. When the soul turns to God with love, it will fly freely and admirably above all torture with the most beautiful and perfect wings, by which chaste love strives toward God's embrace, unless God will allow lovers of gold, lovers of praise, and lovers of women to be stronger than his own lovers, though that former love is more appropriately called not love but covetousness or lust. In it, nonetheless, one can see how great is the surge of the soul that tends on its twisted course through any great difficulties toward those things that it loves, and it is an argument for us as to how we must endure all things so that we might not abandon God, if those people endure such great difficulties in order to abandon him.

23, 42. Why, then, should I gather here authorities from the New Testament where it has been said, *Tribulation produces patience, but patience produces testing, and testing produces hope* (Rom 5:3-4) — and has not merely been said but has also been proved and confirmed by the examples of those who said it? Rather, from the Old Testament, against which the Manicheans madly rage, I shall take an example of patience. Nor shall I recall that remarkable man who amid great torments of the body and a terrible wasting away of his members not only endured human woes but even discussed divine things.[54] In his individual words it is seen clearly enough, if someone pays attention with an unbiased mind, how much value we should place on the things that human beings want to possess as masters of them. But they themselves are possessed by them through covetousness, and they become slaves to mortal things when they ignorantly desire to be their masters. For that man lost all his riches and, having suddenly become very poor, he kept his mind so unshaken and fixed upon God that he showed quite well that his riches were not more important than he but that he was more important than they, while God was more important than he. If human beings of our time were able to have such an attitude, the New Testament would not so strongly forbid us to possess riches in order that we might become perfect.[55] After all, it is much more admirable not to cling to riches, though you possess them, than not to possess them at all.

43. But since we are not now dealing with enduring the pain and torments of the body, I shall leave aside that man who, though great, though unconquered, was nonetheless a man. For those scriptures present to me a woman of awesome fortitude and they compel me now to move to her.[56] She surrendered her whole body along with her seven sons to the tyrant and torturer rather than utter one sacrilegious word. After she strengthened by her encouragement her sons, in whose members she herself was tortured, she still had to suffer in her own person what she had commanded them to endure. What, I ask, could be added to such suffering? Yet why is it surprising if the love of God, having penetrated to the very marrow of her bones, resisted the tyrant and her torturer and her pain and her body and her sex and her feelings? Had she not heard: *Precious in the sight of the Lord is the death of his holy ones* (Ps 116:15)? Had she not heard: *A patient man is better than a very strong one* (Prv 16:32)? Had she not heard: *Accept everything that happens to you; endure it in pain and have patience in your humiliation. For gold and silver are tested in fire* (Sir 2:4-5)? Had she not heard: *The furnace tests vessels of clay, and the trial of tribulation tests righteous men* (Sir 27:6)? Of course she had learned these divine commandments and many others concerning fortitude that the one Holy Spirit had written in

---

54. Augustine refers to Job.
55. See Mt 19:21.
56. See 2 Mc 7.

those books of the Old Testament, which were the only ones in existence at that point, just as he had in these books of the New Testament.

24, 44. What shall I say about justice in relation to God? Though the Lord says, *You cannot serve two masters* (Mt 6:24; Lk 16:13), and the apostle rebukes those who serve *a creature rather than the creator* (Rom 1:25), was it not first said in the Old Testament, *You shall adore the Lord your God and serve him alone* (Dt 6:13; 10:20)? But what need is there to say more on this since all the scriptures are full of such ideas? Justice, then, will give this rule of life to this lover whom we are discussing, namely, that he should most gladly serve the God he loves, that is, the highest good, the highest wisdom, the highest peace. And with regard to all other things he should rule those that have been made subject to him and undertake to subject others to himself. This norm for living, as we have taught, is confirmed by the authority of both Testaments.

45. Nor do we need to spend much time discussing prudence, to which there pertains the discernment of what we should seek and what we should avoid. If it is lacking, none of those things about which we have already spoken can be done. But to it there belongs watchfulness and most diligent vigilance so that we are not deceived by an evil idea that gradually sneaks up on us. On this account the Lord often cries out, *Be on guard* (Mt 24:42; 25:13; 26:38.41; Mk 13:33.35.37; Lk 21:36), and he says, *Walk so that the darkness does not overtake you* (Jn 12:35). So, too, the apostle says, *Do you not know that a little yeast leavens the whole lump?* (1 Cor 5:6; Gal 5:9) But can anything clearer be brought forth from the Old Testament against this sleepiness of the mind, because of which we do not perceive destruction as it creeps up as if by inches, than the words of the prophet: *One who scorns little things falls little by little* (Sir 19:1)? If it were useful for us, who are in a hurry, to discuss this statement at great length, and if the task we have undertaken now demanded it of us, we would perhaps point out how deep are the mysteries that these most ignorant and sacrilegious persons mock, and as a result they do not fall little by little but fall headfirst in a great plunge.

25, 46. Why should I argue more about ways of life? For, if God is the highest good of a human being, something that you cannot deny, it certainly follows that to seek the highest good is to live well and that to live well is nothing other than to love God with one's whole heart, one's whole soul, and one's whole mind.[57] God brings it about that this love is preserved whole and entire, which is a mark of temperance; that it is crushed by no difficulties, which is a mark of fortitude; that it serves no one else, which is a mark of justice; and that it is watchful in discernment, so that falsity or deceit does not overtake it little by little, which is a mark of prudence. This is the one perfection of a human being, and by it alone one comes to enjoy the purity of the truth. This perfection sings out to us from

57. See Dt 6:5; Mt 22:37.

both Testaments; we are urged to this perfection by each of them. Why do you still hurl slanders at the scriptures that you do not understand? With what great ignorance you tear apart those books! The only persons who criticize them are the ones who do not understand them, and the only persons who do not understand them are the ones who criticize them. For no one who is an enemy of them is permitted to know them, and one can only be a lover of them once they are known.

47. Let all of us who have set our mind on attaining eternal life, then, love God with our whole heart, our whole soul, and our whole mind.[58] For eternal life is the whole reward, and we rejoice over the promise of it. The reward cannot come before it is earned and cannot be given to a human being before he is worthy of it. After all, what would be more unjust than this, and what is more just than God? We ought, therefore, not to demand the reward before we have merited to receive it. Here perhaps one not inappropriately asks what eternal life is. But let us instead listen to him who gives it. He says, *This is eternal life, that they may know you, the true God, and Jesus Christ whom you sent* (Jn 17:3). Eternal life, then, is the knowledge of the truth. Hence, notice how perverse and mixed up they are who think that they teach the knowledge of God in order that we may be perfect, though that knowledge is the reward of those who are perfect. What, then, are we to do? What, I ask, but first desire with full love him whom we want to know?[59] From this there arises the principle that we worked to establish from the beginning, namely, that the Catholic Church does nothing more conducive to salvation than to have authority come before reason.

26, 48. But let us look at other points. For it seems that we have said nothing about human beings themselves, that is, about those who do the loving. But someone who thinks this is not thinking clearly enough. For it is impossible that someone who loves God should fail to love himself; on the contrary, only a person who loves God knows how to love himself. After all, he loves himself sufficiently who takes care to act so that he may enjoy the highest and true good, and if that is nothing other than God, as what has already been said has taught us, who can doubt that a person who is a lover of God loves himself? What else? Ought there not to be a bond of love among human beings themselves? Indeed, there ought to be to the point that we believe that there can be no more certain step toward the love of God than the love of one human being for another.

49. Having been asked about the commandments leading to life,[60] then, the Lord himself gives us the second commandment. For he was not content with one commandment, since he knew that God is one thing and a human being another and that there is as great a difference between them as between the

---

58. See Dt 6:5; Mt 22:37.
59. See *Revisions* I, 6 (7), 5.
60. See Mt 19:16.

creator and what was created in the likeness of the creator.[61] He therefore states the second commandment: *You shall love your neighbor as yourself* (Mt 19:19). You love yourself, however, in a salutary way if you love God more than yourself. You should do for your neighbor, then, what you do for yourself. That is, you should bring him to love God with a perfect love. For you do not love him as yourself if you do not bring him to that good toward which you yourself are striving. For that is the one good that does not become crowded when all strive for it along with you. From this commandment there arise the duties of human society, in which it is difficult not to go astray. But we must strive, first of all, to have good will, that is, to exercise no malice, no evil deceit against a human being.[62] After all, what is more a neighbor to a human being than another human being?

50. Listen as well to what Paul says. He says, *Love does no harm to one's neighbor* (Rom 13:10). I am using very short testimonies but, unless I am mistaken, ones that are suitable and sufficient for what I have undertaken. For who does not know how many words on the love of neighbor — and words of great weight — are spread throughout those books? But someone sins against a human being in two ways: in one way if he is harmed, in another way if he is not helped when he can be. And these ways of acting are the reasons why human beings are called evil, and someone who loves acts in neither of these ways. Hence this statement, I think, proves well enough what we want: *Love does no harm to one's neighbor.* And if we cannot attain the good unless we stop doing evil, the actions by which we love our neighbor are the cradle, so to speak, of the love of God. As a result, since *love does no harm to one's neighbor*, we rise from there to the words: *We know that for those who love God all things move toward the good* (Rom 8:28).

51. Somehow or other either these two loves rise up together to their fullness and perfection, or the love of God is the first to begin and the love of neighbor is the first to reach perfection. For the love of God perhaps pulls us more quickly to itself in the beginning, but we more easily bring lesser things to perfection. Whichever the case may be, we must above all maintain that no one should think that he will come to happiness and to the God he loves if he holds his neighbor in contempt.[63] And I wish that it were just as easy for someone well instructed and full of good will to help his neighbor or not to harm him as it is easy to love him. For good will is not enough for this; rather, there is need of much thought and prudence, which no one can have unless God, the source of all good things,[64] grants it. On this very difficult matter we have, in my opinion, tried to express a

---

61. See Gn 1:26; Jas 3:9.
62. See 1 Pt 2:1.
63. See 1 Jn 3:14-15.
64. See Jas 1:17.

few ideas in accord with the task we have undertaken, placing our whole hope in him who alone gives these gifts.

27, 52. A human being, then, as seen by another human being, is a rational soul using a mortal and earthly body. One who loves his neighbor, therefore, does good in part to the body but in part to the soul of a human being. With regard to the body this is called medicine; with regard to the soul it is called discipline. But I am now calling medicine whatever in any way either protects or restores the well-being of the body. To this, therefore, there pertain not only those things that are taught by the art of those called physicians in the proper sense but also food and drink, clothing and shelter and, finally, every defense and protection by which our body is preserved against external attacks and accidents. For hunger and thirst, cold and heat, and all the things that seriously afflict it from outside do not allow that well-being of ours, which we are now discussing, to continue.

53. Hence, those who dutifully and humbly provide all these means by which such evils and difficulties are warded off are called merciful, even if they are so wise that they are no longer upset by any mental anguish.[65] For who can fail to know that mercy received its name because it makes miserable the heart of a person who suffers along with another's woes? And who would not concede that a wise person ought to be free from all misery when he helps someone in need, when he offers food to someone hungry and drink to someone thirsty, when he clothes the naked, when he receives a traveler into his home, when he sets free someone oppressed and, finally, when he extends his humanity to the burial of the dead?[66] Even if he does this with a tranquil mind, driven by no goads of pain but guided by the duty of kindness, he should still be called merciful. For this term does him no harm since he is without any misery.

54. But when fools shun mercy as if it were a failing because they cannot be sufficiently roused by duty unless they are also stirred by feeling, they grow cold through the hardness of their inhumanity rather than become calm through the tranquility of reason. And so it is much wiser to say that God himself is merciful.[67] But how he may be said to be merciful remains for those to understand who have made themselves capable by religion and study. Otherwise, when we foolishly use the words of the learned, we may make the souls of the unlearned grow hard by shunning the practice of mercy before we make them meek by loving goodness. And as mercy commands us to repel these troubles from a human being, so innocence forbids us to inflict them.

28, 55. But discipline restores health to the mind, and, if that health is lacking, the health of the body is useless for driving off misery. This discipline is some-

---

65. *Misericordia* ("mercy" or "pity") is derived from *miser* ("miserable" or "wretched") and *cor* ("heart"). See *Revisions* I, 6 (7), 6.

66. See Tb 4:17-18; Is 58:6-7; Ez 18:7.16; 4 Ezr 2:20-23; Mt 25:35-36.

67. See Dt 4:31; 2 Ezr 9:17; Ps 86:15; Sir 2:13; Jon 4:2; Lk 6:36; Jas 5:11.

thing very difficult in every way. And, as we said in the case of the body, it is one thing to cure diseases and wounds, something that only a few can do well, but it is something else to quiet hunger and thirst and to perform the other actions by which one human being can commonly help another when the occasion arises. In the same way, in the case of the soul there are certain occasions that do not require at the moment those excellent and precious teachings, for example, when we exhort and teach people to give to the needy those things that we said should be provided for the body. For, when we do these things, we assist the body with help, and when we teach people to do them, we assist the mind with instruction. But there are other means by which all sorts of different diseases of the soul are healed by a certain great and in fact ineffable plan. Unless God sent this medicine, there would be no hope of salvation for those who advance so excessively in sin, although, if you search out more deeply the origin of things,[68] you find that even the body's medicine is available to human beings only from God, to whom we should attribute the existence and well-being of all things.

56. This discipline, nonetheless, which we are now discussing, which is the medicine of the soul, is divided, insofar as we can infer from these divine scriptures, into two areas: deterrence and instruction. Deterrence is produced by fear, but instruction by love — I mean the love of the one who is helped by being taught. For of these two the one who offers help has only love. In these two God himself, whose goodness and clemency brings it about that we are anything at all, gave us the rule of discipline in the two Testaments, the Old and the New. For, though both are found in each of them, fear is dominant in the Old Testament, while love is in the New. The apostles point to servitude in the Old and freedom in the New.[69] It would take a very long time to speak about the wonderful order and divine harmony of those Testaments, and many religious and learned men have done so. This topic calls for many books in order that it might be explained and taught as it deserves, insofar as a human being can. One *who loves his neighbor* (Rom 13:8), then, works insofar as he can so that he may be healthy in body and healthy in soul, but the care of his body ought to be directed to the health of his soul. With regard to the soul, therefore, he works by these steps in order that his neighbor may first fear and then love God. This is the best way of life by which we attain even the *knowledge of the truth itself* (Sir 24:32),[70] to which we are drawn by all our desire.

57. And on these two commandments, that is, that we should love God and our neighbor, the Manicheans and I are in agreement, but they deny that this is contained in the Old Testament. How much they are mistaken on this point is, I think, sufficiently evident from the passages that we quoted above from each of

---

68. See Virgil, *Aeneid* I, 372; VI, 371; *Georgics* IV, 285.
69. See Rom 8:15; Gal 4:21-31; 5:1; Heb 2:15.
70. See 1 Tm 2:4; Ti 1:1.

the two Testaments. I shall, nonetheless, say something brief — but the sort of thing that it would be incredible madness to deny. They deny that in the gospel the Lord himself most opportunely cited from the Old Testament these two commandments, which they are forced to praise. Do they not see that it was written there: *You shall love the Lord your God with your whole heart and with your whole soul and with your whole mind*, as well as that other commandment: *You shall love your neighbor as yourself* (Lev 19:18; Mt 22:39)? Or if they do not dare to deny that these commandments are found there, for they are compelled by the light of the truth, let them dare to deny that these commandments are conducive to salvation. Let them deny, if they can, that these commandments contain the best way of life, and let them say that we should not love God, that we should not love our neighbor, that for those who love God all things do not move toward that good,[71] and that love does no harm to one's neighbor.[72] For by these two commandments human life is ordered in the most salutary and the best way. But if they say this, they have nothing in common not only with Christians but even with human beings. If, however, they do not dare to say this and are forced to admit that they are God's commandments, why do they not stop tearing to pieces and blaming out of wicked impiety the books from which they are taken?

58. Are they going to say that it does not follow that everything is good where we were able to find these? For they are accustomed to say this. I do not readily see what I should reply to this evasion or how I should meet it. Should I examine the individual words of the Old Testament and prove to the stubborn and unlearned that there is in them a complete agreement with the gospel? But when will this come about? When shall I be up to it or will they allow it? What, then, shall I do? Shall I give up the cause and allow them to hide behind an opinion that, though wicked and false, is nonetheless difficult to dispel? I will not do that; God will be at my side, whose commandments they are, and he will not allow me to be helpless and abandoned in such great difficulties.

29, 59. Hence, pay attention, you Manicheans, if any of you are perhaps caught in that superstition, so that you may at last escape. Pay attention, I repeat, without any stubbornness or desire to fight back. Otherwise, it is most dangerous for you to pronounce judgment. After all, it is surely doubtful for no one, nor are you so turned away from the truth that you do not understand, that, if to love God and one's neighbor is good, which no one can deny, it cannot be right to censure whatever depends upon these two commandments. It is ridiculous, then, if you think that you should ask me what depends on these two commandments. Listen to Christ himself; listen, I repeat, to *Christ*; listen to *the*

---

71. See Rom 8:28.
72. See Rom 13:10.

wisdom of God (1 Cor 1:24). He says, *The whole law and all the prophets depend on these two commandments.*

60. With your most impudent stubbornness, what can you say about this passage? That Christ did not say this? These words of his are written in the gospel. Was what was written false? What can be found more impious than this sacrilege? What more impudent than this claim? What more audacious? What more criminal? The worshipers of idols, who hate even the name of Christ, have never dared to say this against those scriptures. For there will result the complete destruction of all the writings and the abolition of all the books that have been handed on to posterity if what has been supported by so great a religious faith of many peoples and confirmed by such a great consensus of human beings at different times is brought into doubt, so that it cannot obtain the credence and respect of even ordinary history. Finally, what will you be able to produce from any writings, where I would not be able to use this claim, if it is produced against my argument and aim.

61. But who could tolerate it if the Manicheans forbade us to believe books that are very well known and are found in the hands of all and if they commanded that we believe the books that they produce? If one ought to have doubts about some writings, about what ought one to have more doubts than about those which have not merited to be widely known but which could be a complete lie under someone else's name? If you force these writings on someone who is unwilling and coerce him into belief by reason of their authority, which you have exaggerated, shall I, then, like a poor wretch, have doubts about the writings that I consistently see have become very widely known and have been defended by the testimony of churches spread throughout the world and — what is more wretched — shall I have these doubts at your instigation? For, if you brought forth other copies of the scriptures, I ought to accept only those that are recommended by the agreement of the majority. But now, since you produce nothing to compare with them aside from that utterly empty and completely rash claim, do you think that the human race has become so perverse and so abandoned by the help of divine providence that it prefers to those writings not other writings that you have brought forth to refute them but your words alone? You must produce another manuscript containing the same writings — but an uncorrupted and more accurate manuscript in which only those passages are missing that you charge were inserted in this manuscript. For example, if you claim that the letter of Paul written to the Romans is corrupt, you should produce another uncorrupted letter — or rather another manuscript in which the same letter of the apostle is written without falsification and corruption. You say, "I will not do this for fear that I may be thought to have corrupted it." For this is what you are in the habit of saying, and you speak the truth. Even moderately intelligent persons will, of course, suspect nothing else if you do

this. See for yourself, then, what judgment you have pronounced on your own authority, and understand whether people ought to believe your words in opposition to those scriptures if it is a mark of great temerity to have faith in a manuscript for the sole reason that you produce it.

30, 62. But why should I say more on this? After all, who would not see that those who dare to say these things against the Christian scriptures, though they may not be what people suspect that they are, are nonetheless not Christians. For Christians were given this rule of life, namely, that we should love the Lord our God with our whole heart, our whole soul, and our whole mind,[73] and, secondly, our neighbor as ourselves.[74] *For on these two commandments depend the whole law and all the prophets.* O Catholic Church, O truest mother of Christians, you rightly teach not only that we should worship most purely and chastely God himself, whom to attain is the most happy life. You propose no creature for us to adore, which we might be commanded to serve, and you exclude everything that has been made, that is, subject to change, and that falls under time from that incorruptible and inviolable eternity, to which alone a human being should be subject and by adhering to which alone the human soul is not unhappy.[75] You do not confuse what eternity, what truth, and, finally, what peace itself distinguishes, nor do you separate what the one majesty joins together. But you also include love and charity toward one's neighbor, so that in you there is an abundance of every medicine for the various diseases with which souls are sick on account of their sins.

63. You train and teach children in a way suited to children, young people vigorously, and old people calmly, in accord with each one's age not of the body but of the mind. You make women subject in chaste and faithful obedience to their husbands not for the satisfaction of lust but for the procreation of children and for the establishment of family life.[76] You set husbands over their wives by the laws of sincere love, not in order to mock the weaker sex.[77] You subject children to their parents in a certain free servitude, and you set parents over their children in a loving lordship. You unite brothers and sisters to one another by a bond of religion that is stronger and closer than that of blood. You connect all the relationships of the family and bonds of affinity in mutual love, while preserving all the ties coming from nature and will. You teach slaves to cling to their masters not by the necessity of their condition but from delight in duty. Out of a consideration of God most high, their common master, you make masters gentle toward their slaves and more ready to take care of them than to coerce them. You unite — not merely in society but even in a kind of brotherhood —

---

73. See Mt 22:37; Dt 6:5.
74. See Mt 19:19; 22:39; Lv 19:18.
75. See Ps 73:28.
76. See Tb 6:22; 8:9.
77. See Gn 39:14; Jgs 19:25; 2 Kgs 4:28.

citizens with one another, nations with one another, and, of course, human beings with one another through the remembrance of their first parents. You teach rulers to look out for their people; you admonish people to be subject to their rulers. You carefully teach to whom we owe honor, to whom we owe love, to whom we owe reverence, to whom we owe fear, whom we should console, whom we should admonish, whom we should exhort, discipline, rebuke, and punish, for you show how we do not owe all things to all persons but owe love to all and injury to none.

64. Now, when this human love has nourished and strengthened the soul that clings to your breasts and has become suited to pursuing God, when his majesty begins to reveal itself to the extent that is sufficient for a human being dwelling upon this earth, so great an ardor of love is kindled and such a great conflagration of love of God arises that, once all the vices have been burned away and a person has been made pure and holy, it is seen with sufficient clarity in what sense God said, *I am a consuming fire* (Ex 20:5; Dt 4:24), and, *I came to cast fire upon the earth* (Lk 12:49).[78] These two statements of the one God recorded in the two Testaments reveal by their harmonious testimony how the soul is made holy so that at some point there may come about what the New Testament likewise borrowed from the Old: *Death has been swallowed up by victory. Where, O death, is your sting? Where, O death, is your strength?* (1 Cor 15:54)[79] If these heretics could understand this one passage, they would certainly, without pride and in complete peace, venerate the one God nowhere but within you and at your breast. It is right that in you the commandments of God are widely known and observed. It is right that in you it is correctly understood that it is more serious to sin with knowledge of the law than without knowledge of it, *for the sting of death is sin, but the power of sin is the law* (1 Cor 15:56), and that knowledge of a commandment that is held in contempt strikes a more serious blow at the law and destroys it. It is right that in you it is seen that actions under the law are worthless when passion ravages the soul and is restrained by fear of punishment, not overcome by love of virtue. It is right that for you so many are hospitable, so many merciful, so many dutiful, so many learned, so many chaste, so many holy, so many aflame with the love of God to the point that even solitude along with perfect continence and an incredible contempt for this world is their delight.

31, 65. What is it, I ask, that they see who cannot fail to love human beings and yet cannot see a human being? Certainly, whatever that is, it is more excellent than things that are merely human, for, by contemplating it, a human being can live without human beings. Now, you Manicheans, listen to the singular way of life and continence of perfect Christians who have judged that perfect chastity is not only to be praised but is also to be embraced, so that, if you have any sense of

78. See *Revisions* I, 6 (7), 7.
79. See Is 25:8; Hos 13:14.

shame, you will not venture to boast impudently before the minds of the uneducated of your abstinence, as if it were terribly difficult. Nor shall I speak of things that you do not know, but of those you conceal from us. After all, who does not know that the multitude of Christians living in perfect continence is spreading more and more each day throughout the whole world and especially in the East and in Egypt, a fact that you cannot fail to know?

66. I shall say nothing of the men whom I have just mentioned. Completely hidden from all human sight, content with bread alone, which is brought to them at set intervals of time, and with water, they dwell in the desert, enjoying conversation with God, to whom they have clung with pure minds, perfectly happy in the contemplation of his beauty, which can only be perceived by the intellect of the saints. I shall, I repeat, say nothing about these men, for some people think that they have abandoned human affairs more than they ought to have. Those people do not understand how much their mind at prayer and exemplary life benefits us, though we are not allowed to see their bodily persons. But it would, I think, take too long and be useless to debate this question. For, if someone does not spontaneously see that this lofty peak of holiness is worthy of admiration and honor, how can he be brought to see it by our words? These persons who boast vainly should only be informed that the temperance and continence of the most holy Christians of the Catholic faith has advanced so far that some persons think that they should be restrained and recalled, so to speak, to human limits. To such a point do these persons who find their conduct displeasing judge that their minds have risen above humankind!

67. But if this sort of life goes beyond what we can tolerate, who would not admire and praise those men who, having held in contempt and abandoned the allurements of this world, have joined together in a common life that is most holy and most chaste, and who pass their life together in prayer, in reading, in discussion, not swollen with pride, not restless out of stubbornness, not livid with envy? Rather, they modestly, reverently, and peacefully offer a life that is most harmonious and entirely directed toward God as a most pleasing sacrifice to him from whom they have merited the ability to live in that way. No one owns anything as his own;[80] no one is burdensome to anyone. They produce by their hands what can nourish the body but cannot hold the mind back from God.[81] But they offer their work to those whom they call deans, because they are set over ten men, in order that none of them may have the care of his own body, either in food or in clothing or in anything else required for his daily needs or as a result of a change in his health, as often happens.[82] But these deans arrange everything with great care and make available what that life demands by reason of the frailty of

---

80. See Acts 4:32.
81. See Eph 4:28; 1 Thes 4:11.
82. See Mt 6:25-34; Lk 12:22-31.

the body; they themselves, however, also give an account to one man, whom they call their father. But these fathers, who are not only most holy in their way of life but also excel in the knowledge of God and are superior in all regards, take care without any pride of those whom they call sons; they themselves exercise command with great authority, while the others obey with great willingness. They come together at the last hours of the day, each from his own dwelling, while they are still fasting, to listen to that father, and at least three thousand men gather around each father. For in even greater numbers they live under one father. They listen with incredible zeal and perfect silence, however, making known the dispositions of their own souls, insofar as the words of the speaker moves them, either with groans or with tears or even with a modest joy free from every outburst. Then the body is refreshed as much as is necessary for well-being and good health, with each restraining his concupiscence, for fear that it might rush forth even into those most ordinary foods that are at hand in small amounts. In that way they abstain not only from meat and from wine sufficiently to conquer their passions but also from the things that provoke the desire of the belly and the palate more sharply to the degree that they are considered by some to be purer, and under this pretext a shameful desire for exquisite foods is often foolishly and shamefully defended because that desire does not include meat.[83] Indeed, whatever is more than the monks need for nourishment — for there is a great abundance from the work of their hands and as a result of limiting their meals — is more carefully distributed to the needy than those who distribute it took care to acquire it. For they do not work in order that they themselves might have these things in abundance. Rather, so greatly do they strive not to have an abundance remain in their hands that they even send loaded ships to those places where the needy dwell. There is no need to say more about this very well-known fact.

68. This is also the life of women who serve God zealously and chastely. Separate in their dwellings and as far removed from men as is proper, they are united with them only in pious love and in the imitation of their virtue. No young monk has access to them, nor does any older monk, even though most grave and well-tested, except at the doorway for the sake of providing them with the necessities they require. They exercise and sustain their body by producing wool, and they give that very clothing to the brothers, while receiving from them in turn what they need as food. If I should want to praise this conduct, this way of life, this order, this institution, I cannot do so worthily, and I fear that I may give the impression of considering a mere description insufficient if I thought that I had to add to the simplicity of my account the lofty style of an encomium. Criticize

---

83. Augustine is referring to the Manichean practice of abstaining from meat but not from fine foods.

this, you Manicheans, if you can. Do not point out our weeds to blind persons who are incapable of discernment.[84]

32, 69. In any case the noblest ways of life in the Catholic Church are not so narrowly confined that I think that only the life of those whom I mentioned is praiseworthy. After all, how many bishops, excellent and very holy men, have I known, how many priests, how many deacons and ministers of every sort of the divine sacraments, whose virtue seems to me more admirable and worthy of greater praise the more difficult it is to preserve it amid many different kinds of human beings and in this more turbulent life. For they do not preside over persons who have been healed but over those in need of healing. The failings of the masses must be endured in order that they may be cured, and their disease must be tolerated before it subsides. It is very difficult in this case to maintain the best manner of life and a peaceful and tranquil mind. To put it briefly, these men work where one learns to live; the former where one lives.

33, 70. Still, I would not on that account hold in scorn the praiseworthy Christians who dwell in cities far removed from ordinary life. I saw at Milan a house of holy men, not few in number, over whom one priest, an excellent and most learned man, presided. I know that there are also many houses at Rome in which individuals who excel in gravity, prudence, and the knowledge of God preside over the others who dwell with them and live in Christian love, holiness, and freedom. They are not a burden to anyone, but, in the manner of the East and by the authority of the apostle Paul, they live by their own hands.[85] I learned that many practice fasts that are certainly incredible, not once daily taking refreshment for the body at nightfall, something that is most common everywhere, but very often going a continuous three days or more without food and drink. Nor did I find this only among the men but also among the women. Many widows and virgins likewise dwell together and seek their livelihood by working in wool and linen.[86] Individual women, very grave and well-tested, preside over them; they are not only trained and ready merely to form and order their conduct but also to instruct their minds.

71. No one among these is urged toward austerities that he or she cannot endure. Nothing that anyone refuses is imposed on him, nor do the others condemn someone who admits that he is unable to imitate them. For they recall how much all the scriptures praise love. They recall: *All things are clean to the clean* (Ti 1:15), and: *It is not what enters your mouth that makes you unclean, but what comes out of it* (Mt 15:11). And so all their effort is on guard not to reject certain kinds of food as if they were defiled but to overcome concupiscence and to maintain brotherly love. They recall: *Food is for the belly and the*

---

84. See Mt 13:24-30.
85. See 2 Thes 3:8-12.
86. See Terence, *Andria* 1, 75.

belly for food, but God will destroy them both (1 Cor 6:13), and elsewhere: *We shall not have more if we eat, nor shall we have less if we do not eat* (1 Cor 8:8). And there is above all this passage: *It is good, brothers, not to eat meat and not to drink wine and not to do anything else at which your brother takes offense* (Rom 14:21). For he shows here how all these things should be directed to the goal of love. *For one person believes in eating everything, but let one who is weak eat vegetables,* he says. *Let not the one who eats hold in contempt the one who does not eat. And let the one who does not eat not judge the one who eats, for God accepts him. Who are you to judge another's servant? He stands or falls in the eyes of his own lord. But he will stand, for God is able to make him stand.* (Rom 14:2-4) And a little later he says, *One who eats eats for the Lord and gives thanks to God, and one who does not eat refrains from eating for the Lord and gives thanks to God* (Rom 14:6). Likewise, in the following verses he says, *And so, each of us will give an account of himself. Let us, then, no longer judge one another. But judge rather that you should not set a stumbling block or obstacle in your brother's path. I know and trust in the Lord Jesus that there is nothing unclean in itself, but if someone thinks that it is unclean, it is unclean for him.* (Rom 14:12-14) Could he have shown better that the power to defile a person is not in the foods that we eat but in the mind and that, for this reason, those who are able to regard these things as of little importance and who know with certitude because of their deeper understanding that they are not defiled should, if they take some food without any shameful desire, still keep their eyes on love? See what follows: *For, if your brother is troubled on account of your food, you are no longer walking in accord with love* (Rom 14:15).

72. Read the rest, for it would take too long to include everything, and you will find that a commandment was given to the persons who could regard these things as of little importance, that is, to those who are stronger and more secure, that they should still practice temperance so that those who still need such temperance, given their weakness, would not be caused to stumble. Those about whom I was speaking know and practice this, for they are Christians, not heretics; they understand the scriptures in accord with the teaching of the apostles, not in accord with the proud and false title of apostle.[87] No one holds in contempt someone who eats; no one judges someone who eats; one who is weak eats vegetables. Many of the strong, nonetheless, do the same thing for the sake of the weak. Many do not have this reason for doing so, but they do so because they choose to live with more ordinary food and to lead a very tranquil life without sumptuous sustenance for the body. *For all things are permissible for me, but I will not be brought under the power of anything* (1 Cor 6:12). In that way many do not eat meat, yet they do not superstitiously think that meat is unclean. In that way the same persons who, when healthy, practice temperance will, when ill,

---

87. Mani had claimed for himself the title of apostle.

take meat without any fear if reasons of health demand it. Many do not drink wine, yet they do not suppose that they are defiled by it, for in a most human and moderate way they see to it that it is provided to particular individuals who are somewhat ill and indeed to all who cannot obtain bodily health without it. If some foolishly refuse to accept it, they admonish them in a brotherly manner for fear that, because of their vain superstition, they may become weaker more quickly than they become holier. They read to them the apostle as he commands his disciple that he should take a little wine on account of his various infirmi-ties.[88] In that way they zealously exercise piety, but they know, as the same apostle says, that bodily exercise pertains to the present short time.[89]

73. Those who can do so, therefore (and they are countless), abstain from meat and from wine for two reasons: either on account of the weakness of their brothers or on account of their own freedom. Above all, love is preserved. Their food is adapted to love; their speech is adapted to love; their attire is adapted to love; their countenance is adapted to love. They are united and grow into one love. An offense against this love is said to be a sin like an offense against God. If anything opposes it, they fight against it and cast it out. If anything injures it, they do not allow it to last one day.[90] They know that this love was praised by Christ and the apostles[91] to the point that, if this love alone is lacking, everything is empty, but if it is present, everything is full.[92]

34, 74. Face up to these people, you Manicheans, if you can. Look at them; name them, if you dare, without lies and without insults. Compare your fasts with their fasts, your chastity with their chastity, your attire with their attire, your meals with their meals, your modesty with their modesty, finally, your love with their love, and — what the situation especially demands — your command-ments with their commandments. Now you will see the difference between ostentation and sincerity, between the correct path and error, between trustwor-thiness and deception, between strength and bombast, between happiness and misery, between unity and division and, finally, what difference there is between the sirens of superstition and the harbor of religion.

75. Do not bring me those who make profession of the Christian name without either knowing or exhibiting the heart of their profession. Do not pursue the crowds of the ignorant who are either superstitious in the true religion or so given to their passions that they have forgotten what they promised to God. I know that there are many worshipers of tombs and of painted images. I know that there are many who, when they drink in excess over the dead, offering meals to corpses, bury themselves on top of those they have buried and attribute their

88. See 1 Tm 5:23.
89. See 1 Tm 4:7-8.
90. See Eph 4:26.
91. See 1 Cor 13:1-3.
92. See Rom 13:8; Gal 5:14; Col 3:14.

gluttony and drunkenness to religion. I know that there are many who have verbally renounced the world and want to be weighed down by all the burdens of this world and rejoice when they are so weighed down. Nor is it surprising that in so large a number of people you find those whose lives you may criticize in order to deceive the unwary and turn them away from Catholic salvation, though in your own small numbers you suffer great embarrassment when you are asked for even one from among those whom you call the Elect who keeps the commandments that you defend with your irrational superstition. But I have decided to show in another volume[93] how vain, how harmful, and how sacrilegious those commandments are and how they are not observed by a large part of your people and, in fact, hardly by any of you.

76. Now I warn you at long last to stop speaking ill of the Catholic Church by criticizing the conduct of persons whom she herself condemns and whom she strives daily to correct like bad children. But whoever of them are corrected by good will and the help of God recover by doing penance what they lost by sinning. Those who out of bad will persevere in their previous sins or even add more serious sins to their earlier ones, however, are allowed to exist in the field of the Lord and to grow with the good seed, but the time will come when the weeds will be separated out.[94] Or if on account of their Christian name they should now be considered to be among the chaff rather than among the thorns, he will also come to cleanse the threshing floor and separate the chaff from the wheat and with perfect justice assign to each part what is right in accord with the merit of each.

77. Meanwhile, why do you rage? Why are you blinded with partisan zeal? Why are you entangled in a long defense of so great an error? Look for the crops in the field and for the grain on the threshing floor; they will readily be seen and offer themselves to those who look for them. Why do you fix your eyes so much on the refuse? Why do you deter ignorant people from the richness of the lush garden by the roughness of the hedges? There is a certain entrance, though known to fewer people, by which one can enter, one which you either do not believe exists or do not want to find. There are in the Catholic Church countless believers who do not make use of this world; there are those who make use of it as though not making use of it, as the apostle says.[95] And this was already proved in those times when Christians were forced to the worship of idols. After all, how many wealthy men, how many heads of families in the country, how many businessmen, how many leaders of their cities, finally, how many senators and persons of both sexes, left all these vain and temporal things, by which they were not held back, though of course they used them! They underwent death for the

---

93. That is, in the second book of the present work.
94. See Mt 13:3-30.36-43.
95. See 1 Cor 7:31.

faith and religion that leads to salvation, and they proved to unbelievers that they owned all those things rather than that they were owned by them.

78. Why do you falsely state that believers, once renewed by baptism, ought not to procreate children and ought not to own fields, homes, or any money? Paul permits this. For it cannot be denied; after the enumeration of the sins of many who will not inherit the kingdom of God, [96] he wrote to believers: *And you were once such people, but you have been washed; you have been made holy; you have been made righteous in the name of the Lord Jesus Christ and in the Spirit of our God* (1 Cor 6:11). Certainly no one will dare to think that those who have been washed and made holy are any but believers and those who have renounced this world. But because he revealed to whom he was writing, let us see whether he permitted those things to them. For he continues as follows: *All things are permissible for me, but all things are not expedient. All things are permissible for me, but I will not be brought under the power of anything. Food is for the belly, and the belly for food, but God will destroy them both. The body, however, is not for fornication, but for the Lord, and the Lord is for the body. But God has raised up the Lord and will also raise us up by his power. Or do you not know that your bodies are members of Christ? Shall I, then, take the members of Christ and make them members of a prostitute? By no means! Do you not know that a man who clings to a prostitute becomes one body with her? For, scripture says, they will be two in one flesh. But one who clings to the Lord is one spirit with him. Shun fornication. Every other sin a man commits is outside his body, but one who commits fornication sins against his own body. Or do you not know that your members are the temple of the Holy Spirit, who dwells in you and whom you have from God, and that you are not your own? For you have been purchased at a great price. Glorify God and carry him in your body. But about those matters on which you wrote to me, it is good for a man not to touch a woman, but because of a lack of self-control each man should have his own wife and each woman her own husband. A husband should pay the debt to his wife, and a woman likewise to her husband. A woman does not have power over her own body, but her husband does. Likewise, a man does not have power over his own body, but his wife does. Do not deprive each other except perhaps by agreement for a time in order that you may be free for prayer, and then go back to it for fear that Satan may tempt you because of your lack of self-control. I say this, however, by way of concession, not by way of command. I want all to be as I am, but each has his own gift from God, one this gift, another that.* (1 Cor 6:12-7:7)

79. Does the apostle seem to you both to have sufficiently shown to the strong what is most perfect and to have permitted to the weaker what is close to that? He showed that not to touch a woman is most perfect when he said, *I want all to be as I am* (1 Cor 7:7). But marital chastity, by which a man avoids being defiled by

---

96. See 1 Cor 6:9-10.

fornication, is close to this perfection. Did he say that they were no longer believers because they made use of their spouses? He says, after all, that by this marital chastity not only is one spouse made holy by the other if one of them is a non-believer but also the children born of them. *For a non-believing husband*, he says, *is made holy in his believing wife, and a non-believing wife is made holy by her believing husband. Otherwise, your children would be unclean, but now they are holy.* (1 Cor 7:14) Why do you protest with stubbornness against such a great truth? Why do you try to obscure the light of the scriptures with empty shadows?

80. Do not say anymore that catechumens are permitted to make use of their spouses but that believers are not, and that catechumens are permitted to have money but that believers are not. For there are many who make use of them as if they were not making use of them.[97] And from that sacred bath the renewal of the new man is begun[98] in order that by making progress some may attain perfection more quickly, others more slowly. Still, many enter into a new life, if a person only pays attention not with hostility but with care. Indeed, the apostle speaks as follows: *Even if our outer man is being corrupted, our inner man is being renewed from day to day* (2 Cor 4:16). The apostle says that our inner man is being renewed from day to day in order that it may attain perfection, and you want to begin with perfection. I wish that you did want this, but instead you seek not the means to lift up the weak but the means to deceive the unwary. For you ought not to have spoken with such great audacity, not even if it were clear that you had attained perfection by those silly commandments of yours. But since your conscience knows that those people whom you bring into your sect will discover, when they begin to be more closely united with you, many failings that no one suspected were to be found in you when you were accusing others of them, what great impudence it is to look for perfection in weaker Catholics in order to turn the ignorant away from them and not in any way to display that perfection in yourself to those whom you have turned away. But for fear that we may now seem to be rash in pouring out any charges against you, let this be the end of this volume in order that we may at last come to an examination of your remarkable commandments and way of your life.

---

97. See 1 Cor 7:31.
98. See Ti 3:5.

Book Two

1, 1. I think that no one has any doubt that, when one asks about good and evil, this kind of question pertains to the doctrine of morality, with which we are dealing in this discussion. Hence, I would certainly want people to bring such a clear gaze of their mind to the investigation of these ideas that they could see that highest good, than which there is nothing better or higher and to which the pure and perfect rational soul is subject. For, when they understood and saw this highest good, they would at the same time see that it is what is most correctly said to exist in the highest manner and primordially. After all, that should be said to exist most of all, which is always in the same way, which is in every respect like itself, which can in no respect be corrupted and changed, which is not subject to time, and which cannot now be otherwise than it was before. For that is what is said to exist most truly. Now, under this expression there falls what is meant by the nature of that which remains in itself and exists immutably. We can call this nature nothing other than God, and, if you look for something contrary to it, there is absolutely nothing. For being does not have any contrary except non-being. There is, therefore, no nature contrary to God. But because we bring to the contemplation of these matters a gaze of the mind that is wounded and dulled by trivial ideas and by the wickedness of the will, let us try, to the extent we can, to come gradually and cautiously to some sort of knowledge of so great a reality, not in the way that those with sight are accustomed to search but in the way that those who are groping do.

2, 2. Often and almost always you Manicheans ask those whom you are trying to win over to your heresy where evil comes from. Suppose that I have now met you for the first time. Let me, please, obtain something from you, namely, that you set aside for a while the opinion by which you suppose that you know these things and try, as if you were uneducated people, to investigate this important issue with me. You ask me where evil comes from, but I in turn ask you what evil is. Who has the fairer question? Those who ask where it comes from, though they are ignorant of what it is, or someone who thinks that we should first ask what it is in order to avoid asking about the origin of something of which we are ignorant? For that is absurd. Quite correctly, you say, for who is so mentally blind that he does not see that for each kind of thing what is contrary to its nature is evil? But, if you grant this, your heresy is demolished, for no nature is something evil if what is contrary to nature is going to be evil. You, however, maintain that evil is a nature and a substance. Added to this there is also the fact that what is contrary to nature, whatever it is, is of course opposed to nature and strives to destroy it. It tends, therefore, to cause that which is not to be. For a nature is nothing else than that which is understood to be something in its own kind. And so, just as by a new term derived from being (*esse*) we now call "essence" what we usually also call "substance," so the ancients who did not have these terms used "nature" instead of "essence" and "substance." Evil itself, then, if you are willing to look beyond your obstinacy, is a falling away from being (*essentia*) and a tending toward non-being.

3. Hence, when in the Catholic Church it is said that God is the author of all natures and substances, it is at the same time understood by those who can understand this that God is not the author of evil. How, after all, can he who is the cause of the being of all the things that are also be the cause of their non-being, that is, of their falling away from being and tending toward non-being? The most correct reasoning cries out that this is evil in general. But how will that nation of evil of yours, which you want to be the greatest evil, be contrary to nature, that is, contrary to substance, since you say that it is a nature and a substance? For, if it acts against itself, it takes being from itself, and if it does this completely, it will ultimately come to the greatest evil. But it will not do this completely, because you want it not only to be but also to be everlasting. The greatest evil, therefore, cannot be what is called a substance.

4. But what am I to do? I know that there are many among you who cannot understand these ideas at all. I also know that there are some who, though they somehow see these points with their fine minds, still act stubbornly out of bad will, because of which they will also lose those fine minds. They seek what they might say against these ideas, which might easily convince the slow and feeble, rather than agree that these ideas are true. Yet I shall not regret having written something either in order that someone from among you may at last consider it with a fair judgment and leave your error or in order that talented persons who are subject to God and are still untainted by your influence may read it and be kept from being deceived by your words.

3, 5. Let us, then, investigate these points more carefully and, insofar as it is possible, more clearly. I ask you again what evil is. If you say that it is that which does harm, you will not be saying something false even here. But please pay attention; please be alert; please set aside partisanship and seek the truth — not for the sake of winning but for the sake of finding it. After all, whatever does harm deprives the thing that it harms of some good, for, if it does not take away any good, it certainly does no harm. What could be more obvious than this, I ask you? What could be more clear? What could be so plain to a person of average intelligence, provided he is not obstinate? But, granted this point, I think that you already see what follows. In that nation, of course, which you suppose is the greatest evil, it is not possible that anything be harmed where there is nothing good. But if, as you state, there are two natures, the kingdom of light and the kingdom of darkness, since you say that the kingdom of light is God, to whom you grant a simple nature so that there is in him nothing inferior to anything else, you must admit something that is certainly very much opposed to you. But you must admit it nonetheless, namely, that this nature, which you not only do not deny but even vigorously strive to prove, is the highest good, is immutable, impenetrable, incorruptible, and inviolable. For otherwise it will not be the highest good; the highest good is, after all, that than which nothing is better. But such a nature can in no way be harmed. If, however, to harm something is to deprive it of a good, as I showed, the kingdom of darkness cannot be harmed because there is nothing good in it. The kingdom of light cannot be harmed because it is inviolable. To what, then, will that which you call evil do harm?

4, 6. Hence, since you cannot free yourselves from this problem, see how the statement of Catholic doctrine is set free. It says that the good that is supremely good and good through itself, not by participation in another good but by its own nature and essence, is something other than the good that is good by participating in and having good. But the latter has its being good from the highest good, while the highest good nonetheless remains in itself and loses nothing. Catholic doctrine calls this good that we mentioned second a creature, and it can be harmed by a defect. Of that defect God is not the author because he is the author of existing and, so to speak, of being. In that way we are shown how evil is spoken of, for it is most truly spoken of not as an essence but as a privation. And we see a nature that can be harmed. For the nature from which a good is taken away when it is harmed is not the greatest evil. And the nature that can fall away from the good, because it is said to be good not by *being* good but by *having* good, is not the highest good. Nor is that thing good by its nature. For, since it is said to have been made, it has, to be sure, received its being good. In that way God is the highest good, and the things that he made are all good, though they are not as good as he who made them is. After all, who would be so insane as to demand that products be equal to their maker and creatures to their creator? What more do you want? Or do you want something even clearer?

5, 7. I ask for the third time, then, what evil is. You will perhaps answer: corruption. And who would deny that this is evil in general. For it is contrary to nature; it is that which does harm. But corruption is not found in itself but in some substance that it corrupts. For corruption itself is not a substance. The thing, then, that corruption corrupts is not something evil. For what is corrupted is deprived of integrity and purity. Something, therefore, that does not have any purity of which it might be deprived cannot be corrupted. But something that has some purity is, of course, good by reason of its participation in purity. Likewise, that which is corrupted is certainly perverted. But what is perverted is deprived of order. But order is something good. That which is corrupted, therefore, does not lack some good, for, when it is corrupted, it can only be stripped of what it does not lack. If that nation of darkness, as you say, lacked every good, it could not have been corrupted. For it did not have what corruption could take away from it, and, if corruption does not take anything away, it does not corrupt. Be so bold now as to say, if you can, that God and the kingdom of God could have been corrupted, if you do not find how the kingdom of the devil, as you describe it, could be corrupted.

6, 8. What, then, does the Catholic light say about this? What do you suppose but what the truth holds, that is, that a created substance can be corrupted, for that uncreated substance, which is the highest good, is incorruptible, and corruption itself, which is the greatest evil, cannot be corrupted, but that this latter is not a substance? But if you ask what it is, see to what it tries to bring the things that it corrupts. For of itself it affects the things that are corrupted. Through corruption, however, all things fall away from what they were, and they are forced not to remain; they are forced not to be. For to be means to remain. Therefore, that which is said to be in the highest and greatest way is said to be such by remaining in itself. For what is changed for the better is not changed because it remains, but because it was perverted to what is worse, that is, because it fell away from its essence. But he who is the author of the essence is not the author of this falling away from the essence. Some things, then, are changed for the better and, for this reason, they tend toward being and are not said to be perverted by this change but to turn back and to be converted. For perversion is contrary to order. But the things that tend toward being tend toward order, and, when they attain order, they attain being to the extent that a creature can attain it. Order, after all, brings what it orders to a certain fittingness. But to be is nothing else than to be one. And so anything is to the extent that it attains oneness. For the effect of oneness is the fittingness and harmony by which those things that are composite are insofar as they are. For simple things are by themselves because they are one. But those things that are not simple imitate oneness by the harmony of their parts, and they are to the extent that they attain it. Hence, the imposition of order forces them to be; a lack of order, then, forces them not to be. This is called perversion and corruption. Whatever, then, is corrupted tends toward non-being. Now it is up to you to consider that to which corruption forces something in order that you may be able to find the greatest evil. For it is that to which corruption tries to bring it.

7, 9. But the goodness of God does not permit the situation to go so far, and it orders all the things that are falling away in such fashion that they may be where they can be most appropriately until by their well-ordered movements they return to that from which they fell away.[1] And so, when rational souls fall away from the goodness of God to lower levels of creation, the goodness of God also sets those souls, in which free choice is most powerful, in order where it is fitting that such souls should be. They are made unhappy by God's judgment, therefore, when they are set in order in a way that corresponds to their merits. For this

---

1. See *Revisions* I, 6 (7), 8.

reason the verse that you are accustomed to attack most of all is very well expressed: *I make good things, and I create evil things* (Is 45:7). For "to create" means "to establish" and "to set in order." In several manuscripts, therefore, it says: *I make good things, and I establish evil things.* For one makes what does not exist at all. But "to establish" means to set in order what already was in some way so that it might be better and greater. For God establishes those things, that is, sets them in order, when he says, *I establish evil things* — things that are falling away, that is, that are tending to non-being, not those that have arrived at that toward which they are tending. For it has been said that divine providence permits nothing to come to the point that it does not exist at all.

10. These ideas could be treated more extensively and fully, but when we are dealing with you, this is enough. For we had to show you the door, over which you despair and over which you cause the ignorant to despair. For nothing brings you inside but a good will that divine mercy has rendered peaceful, as the gospel sings: *Glory on high to God, and on earth peace to men of good will* (Lk 2:14). It is enough, I say, that you see that there is no way out of the religious discussion of good and evil except this: Whatever is, insofar as it is, comes from God, but, insofar as it falls away from being, it does not come from God. Divine providence always sets it in order, nonetheless, as is fitting for the universe. If you do not yet see this, I do not know what more I should do now except go over in more detail the ideas that have been stated. For only piety and purity bring one to the more important ideas.

8, 11. After all, when I ask what evil is, what else are you going to reply but either that it is contrary to nature or that it does harm or that it is corruption or something of the sort? I have pointed out how you meet with shipwreck with these answers, unless perhaps you reply (as you usually do), like a child with children, that fire, poison, a wild animal, and other things of this sort are evil. For one of the leaders of this heresy, whom we listened to rather frequently and in a quite friendly context, said of a certain person who said that no substance is an evil, "I would like to put a scorpion in that man's hand and see whether he would not pull his hand away. If he did so, he would show, not by words but by the action itself, that evil is a substance, since he would not deny that a living being is a substance." He did not say this in the man's presence but when we were disturbed and reported to him what the man had said; then he replied, as I have said, like a child with children. For who is endowed with a somewhat better mind and has received some education and fails to see that in one case these things do harm on account of the unsuitability of the body's condition and in another case do no harm on account of its suitability but often even confer no small advantages? For, if that venom were something evil in itself, it would instead first destroy the scorpion. But if the venom were somehow completely removed from it, the scorpion would undoubtedly perish. For the scorpion's body, then, it is evil to lose what it is evil for our body to receive. Likewise, it is good for it to have what it is good for us to be without. Will one and the same thing, then, be both good and evil? In no way. Rather, it is evil because it is contrary to a nature. For this is an evil both for that animal and for us, namely, the very unsuitability, which is certainly not a substance and in fact is inimical to a substance. Where does evil come from, then? Pay attention to what the argument forces you to and you will learn — at least if a glimmer of the inner light is alive in you. For everything that destroys something forces it not to be. But God is the author of being, nor can that which forces that in which it is present not to be, be thought to be some being. That from which unsuitability does not come is said to be something, therefore, for nothing can be said to be that from which it comes.

12. By drinking in small amounts the poison that condemned persons drank in the precise amount that would induce their death, a certain wicked woman of Athens, as history discloses, brought it about that she could drink it without any or only a slight impairment to her health.[2] And so, when she was finally condemned, she took like the others the prescribed amount of poison, whose effect she had overcome by having gotten used to it, so that she was not killed like the others. Since this was taken to be a great miracle, she was sent into exile. What are we to think? If poison is something evil, did she cause it not to be something evil? What would be more absurd? But because unsuitability is something evil, she brought it about instead that that body became suited to her body through becoming gradually accustomed to it. For when could that woman have been able to bring it about by any cleverness that that unsuitability would not harm her? Why? Because that which is truly and generally evil always does harm to everything. Oil is good for our bodies, but it is very bad for the bodies of many living things that have six feet. Is not hellebore in one amount a food, in another a medicine, and in still another a poison? Who would not cry out that salt is a poison when ingested in too great a quantity? But who can count the many and great advantages to the body that come from it? When land animals drink sea water, it is harmful, but it is very beneficial and useful for the bodies of many others when they are bathed in it. Fish, however, find well-being and pleasure in both kinds of water. Bread nourishes a human being but kills a hawk. Does not excrement, which, if tasted or smelled, gravely offends and does injury, cool when touched in the summer and serve as a remedy for wounds caused by fire? What is more contemptible than dung? What is more lowly than ashes? But these bring such great benefits to fields that the Romans thought that they should

---

2. See Galen, *The Mixing and Powers of Simple Medicines (De simplicium medicamentorum temperamentis ac facultatibus)* 3, 18 in *Claudii Galeni Opera Omnia*, ed. C. G. Kühn, Vol. XI, 601 (Leipzig, 1821-1833; reprinted Hildesheim: Olms, 1964-1965), and Sextus Empiricus, *Outlines of Pyrrhonism (Hypotyposes)* I, 18.

offer divine honors to Stercutius, their inventor, from whom dung took its name.[3]

13. But why should I gather small examples, which are countless? Who would doubt that those four elements, which are readily available, are beneficial on account of their suitability but, when unsuitably used, are strongly opposed to nature? Earth and water kill us who live in the air, if they cover us over. But countless living beings creep through the sand and looser earth and live there, while fish die in this air. Fire destroys our bodies, but, when used suitably, it rescues us from the cold and wards off countless ills. This sun, to which you bend your knee, than which there is truly nothing more beautiful among visible things, enlivens the eyes of eagles but injures and dims our vision. Yet, through accustoming ourselves to it, we too are able to fix our gaze upon it without injury. You are not going to allow us, then, are you, to compare it with the poison that the Athenian woman rendered harmless by becoming accustomed to it? Consider at long last, then, and notice that, if any substance is an evil because it injures someone, the light that you worship cannot be defended from this accusation. See, rather, that this unsuitability, by which the ray of the sun causes eyes to go blind, though nothing is more pleasing to them than daylight, is evil in general.

9, 14. I have said these things in order that you might, if possible, stop saying that evil is a land immensely broad and long; that evil is a mind wandering through the land; that evil is the five caves of the elements, one full of darkness, another full of water, another full of the winds, another full of fire, and another full of smoke; that evil is the animals born in each of those elements, crawling ones in darkness, swimming ones in water, flying ones in the winds, four-legged ones in fire, two-legged ones in smoke. These beings, after all, could by no means exist as you describe them. For whatever is of such a kind is necessarily from the sovereign God insofar as it is, because of course it is good insofar as it is. For, if pain or weakness is an evil, there were animals there with such great bodily strength that you say that, after the world was fashioned from them, according to your sect, their aborted fetuses fell from heaven to earth and were unable to die. If blindness is an evil, they saw; if deafness, they heard. If to become mute or to be mute is an evil, their voices were so clear and distinct there that they decided to wage war against God, as you claim, when they were persuaded by one of them in an assembly. If sterility is an evil, there was present there a great fecundity for procreating children. If exile is an evil, they were in their own land and were inhabiting their own regions. If slavery is an evil, there were those who reigned there. If death is an evil, they were living, and they were

---

3. See *The City of God* XVIII, 15; Tertullian, *Ad nationes* II, 9, 20; Lactantius, *Divinae institutiones* I, 20, 36; Ep. 16 (21), 2.

living in such a way that you might proclaim that their mind could in fact never die, not even after God's victory.

15. Why, I ask you, do I find in the greatest evil such great goods contrary to the evils that I mentioned? Or, if these are not evils, will any substance insofar as it is a substance ultimately be an evil? If weakness is not an evil, will a weak body be an evil? If blindness is not an evil, will darkness be an evil? If deafness is not an evil, will a deaf person be an evil? If to be mute is not an evil, will a fish be an evil? If sterility is not an evil, how is a sterile human being an evil? If exile is not an evil, how is a human being in exile or someone sending a human being into exile an evil? If slavery is not an evil, how is a human being in slavery or forcing someone to be a slave an evil? If death is not an evil, how is a mortal human being or one inflicting death an evil? But if these are evils, how will bodily strength, sight, hearing, persuasive speech, fecundity, one's native soil, freedom, and life be evils — all of which you say existed in that kingdom of evil and which you dare to claim are the greatest evil?

16. Finally, if unsuitability is an evil, which is something that no one has ever denied, what is more suitable than each of those elements for its animals — darkness for crawling ones, water for swimming ones, the winds for flying ones, fire for more hungry ones, smoke for prouder ones? For you describe such great concord in the nation of discord and such great order in the seat of disorder. If that which does harm is evil, I omit the most powerful argument that was stated above, that no harm could be done where no good was present, but, if this argument is not clear, certainly that previous one stands out and is seen by all because, as I said, all agree that what does harm is evil. Smoke did not harm two-footed animals in that nation; it begat, nourished, and sustained them without harm as they were born, grew up, and ruled. But now, after the good was mixed in with the evil, smoke has been made more harmful; we who are two-legged cannot endure it, to be sure; it blinds, suffocates, and kills us. Has such a great savagery been added to the evil elements by their mixture with good? Is there such a great perversity under the kingship of God?

17. Why, at least do we see in the other things this suitability, which deceived your founder and led him to compose lies? Why, I ask, is darkness suited for serpents, water for fish, and wind for birds, whereas fire burns quadrupeds and smoke suffocates us? Why is it also that serpents see with great acuteness and exult in the presence of the sun and are found in greater abundance where the clearer air gathers clouds with greater difficulty and less often? What is more absurd than that animals which dwell in and love darkness are situated more suitably and fittingly where they can rejoice in the brightness of the light? But if you say that they rejoice more over the warmth than over the light, you should say that swift serpents are more suitably born in fire than the slow donkey, and yet who would deny that the asp is fond of this daylight since its eyes are compared to the eyes of an eagle? But I shall discuss the other animals later.

Please let us consider ourselves without stubbornness and strip our minds of vain and destructive myths. For who would endure the great perversity by which it is said that in the nation of darkness, with which no light was mixed, two-legged living beings have such a strong, such a vital and, finally, such an incredible power in the gaze of their eyes, that even in their darkness they saw the purest light of the kingdom of God, which you praise — for you want it to be visible even to such beings — and that they gaze upon it, contemplate it, delight in it, and desire it? But our eyes have been rendered so weak and so feeble by a mixture with the light, by a mixture with the highest good, and finally by a mixture with God, that we see nothing at all in the dark and can in no way endure looking at the sun but turn away from it and seek even what we saw?

18. The same things can also be said if corruption is an evil, something about which no one is honestly in doubt. For then smoke did not corrupt the kind of animals that it now corrupts. And, to avoid going through the individual kinds, which would be long and unnecessary, the animals that you imagine were present there were so much less subject to corruption that their aborted fetuses, which were not yet ready to be born, could, after having been cast down from heaven to earth, live, generate, and again form a conspiracy. Of course they had their pristine strength, because they had been conceived before the mingling of good and evil. For you say that the animals that were born from them after this mingling are those that we now see are very weak and readily yielding to corruption. Who could tolerate this error any longer except someone who either does not see these points or has become hardened in opposition to all the weight of reason out of some incredible force of habit and association with you?

10, 19. But because I have shown, I think, the great darkness and the great error in which you are involved regarding good and evil in general, let us now look at those three seals, which you claim with great praise and boasting are found in your conduct. What, then, are these seals? They are, of course, those of the lips, of the hands, and of the breast. What are they for? They exist, you say, so that a person may be chaste and innocent with his lips, his hands, and his breast. What if he should sin with his eyes, ears, or nose? What if he injures or even kills someone with his feet? How will we hold a man guilty who sinned with neither his lips nor his hands nor his breast? But, he says, when I mention the lips, I want you to understand all the senses that are found in the head. When I mention the hand, I want you to understand every action, and when I mention the breast, I want you to understand all sexual passion. Where, then, do you want blasphemies to belong? To the lips or to the hand? This is an action of the tongue. Hence, if you include every action in one kind, why do you join the action of the feet to the hands but hold separate the action of the tongue? Or, because the tongue signifies something by words, do you want to separate it from an action that is not done in order to signify something? Then the seal of the hands might be defined as refraining from an evil action that is not done for the sake of signifying something? But what are you going to do if someone sins by signifying something with his hands, as we do when we write or show by a gesture something that is understood? For you cannot attribute this to the lips and to the tongue, because it is done with the hands. After all, what is more absurd than that — though there are said to be three seals, of the lips, of the hands, and of the breast — certain sins associated with the hands are attributed to the lips? But if action in general is ascribed to the hands, what reason is there to add the action of the feet to this and not to add that of the tongue? Do you see how the desire for novelty, when accompanied by error, results in great difficulties? For you find no way to include the purification from all sins in this newfangled division that you teach.

11, 20. But divide them as you want; pass over whatever you want. Let us discuss the seals that you are accustomed to praise so much. For you say that it pertains to the seal of the lips to refrain from all blasphemy. But it is blasphemy when some bad things are said about good things. And so it is now commonly taken to be blasphemy only if one speaks evil words about God. For with regard to human beings there can be some doubt, but God is incontrovertibly good. If, then, reason shows that no one says worse things about God than you do, where will that famous seal of the lips be? After all, reason teaches — and surely not a hidden reason but one readily available and thrust before the understanding of all, a reason that is unconquered and even more than unconquered because no one is permitted not to know it — that God is incorruptible, immutable, and inviolable and that in him there can be no need, no weakness, no unhappiness. But all rational souls are of the same mind about these matters, to the point that even you agree when they are mentioned.

21. But when you begin to tell your myths, you are seized with an amazing blindness and argue that God is corruptible, changeable, violable, subject to need, susceptible to weakness, and not safe from unhappiness, and those seized by an amazing blindness you also convince of this. Nor is this enough. For you say not only that God is corruptible but that he has been corrupted, not only that he is changeable but that he has been changed, not only that he is violable but that he has been violated, not only that he can suffer need but that he is in need, not only that weakness can come over him but that weakness has come over him, and not only that he can be unhappy but that he is unhappy. Indeed, you say that the soul is God or a part of God. I do not see how what is said to be a part of God is not God. For a part of gold is gold, and a part of silver is silver, and a part of a stone is also stone. And, to move to these larger things, a part of the earth is earth, and a part of water is water, and a part of the air is air, and if you take some fire you will not deny that it is fire, and any part of the light cannot be anything else than light. Why, then, will a part of God not be God? Or is the form of God divided into members like that of a man and of the other animals? For a part of a man is not a man.

22. But I am coming down to each of these opinions, and I am considering each of them separately. For, if you want God to be like light, you cannot deny that a part of God is God. You do not deny that the soul has been corrupted since it is foolish, has changed since it was wise, has been violated since it does not have its proper perfection, is in need since it asks for help, is weak since it needs medicine, and is unhappy since it desires to be happy. Hence, when you say that the soul is a part of God, you pile all these defects upon God with your sacrilegious opinion. Or, if you do not admit these things about the soul, the apostle is also unnecessary to lead the soul to the truth because it is not foolish, nor is the soul renewed by the true religion because it has not been changed, nor is it made perfect by your seals because it is perfect, nor does God bring it help because it does not need it, nor is Christ its physician because the soul is healthy, nor is the happy life correctly promised to it. Why is it, then, that Jesus is called the deliverer, which he himself cries out in the gospel: *If the Son sets you free, then you will truly be free* (Jn 8:36)? And that the apostle Paul says, *You have been called into freedom* (Gal 5:13)? The soul, then, that has not attained this freedom is in slavery. According to you, therefore, if a part of God is God, God is corrupted by foolishness, has been changed by falling, has been violated by the loss of perfection, is in need of help, is weak from disease, overwhelmed by unhappiness, and disgraced by slavery.

23. But if a part of God is not God, God still cannot be uncorrupted if there is corruption in a part of him, nor unchanged if he is changed in some part, nor inviolate if he is not perfect in every part, nor free from need if he diligently works in order to restore to himself a part of himself, nor completely healthy if he is feeble in some part, nor perfectly happy if he has some part reduced to unhappiness, nor entirely free if some part of him suffers under slavery. You are forced to say all these things when you claim that the soul, which you see is overwhelmed by such calamities, is a part of God. Remove these and many such ideas from your sect if you can. Then finally say that your lips are free from blasphemy. Rather, abandon that sect. For, if you cease to believe and to say what Mani wrote, you will of course not be Manicheans.

24. God must be either understood or believed to be the absolutely highest good, than which nothing can be or be thought to be better if we plan to avoid blasphemies. The rule of numbers can in no way be violated or changed, nor does any nature bring it about by any violence that the number that follows after one does not coincide with its double. This can in no way be changed, and you say that God is changeable. This rule retains its inviolable integrity, and you do not want God to be at least its equal. Let any nation of darkness cause the third intelligible number, in which each one is so much a one that it lacks parts — let this nation of darkness cause this third number to be divided into two equal parts. Your mind certainly sees that this cannot be done by anyone's bad will. Could that, then, which could not violate the nature of a number, violate God? But if it

could not, what need, I ask you, was there that a part of him be mingled with evil and be shoved into such great unhappiness?

12, 25. For from this the objection arose, even when we were your eager Hearers, which overwhelmed us with great difficulties, nor did we find any way out when we asked what the nation of darkness was going to do to God if he were unwilling to fight with it, with so great a disaster for a part of himself. For, if the nation of darkness was not going to harm him when he was at peace, we protested that we who were sent into these woes were treated cruelly. But if it was going to harm him, we protested that his nature was not incorruptible as the nature of God ought to have been. On this question there was someone who said that God did not want to be without evil or did not take care that he was not harmed, but on account of his natural goodness he wanted to do good to the restless and disordered nature in order that it might be set in order. The books of Mani do not read that way; they very often indicate and very often state that God took care that he would not be invaded by enemies. But let us concede that Mani held these views, as that man said who did not find anything else to say. Is God defended from cruelty or weakness by this argument? After all, this goodness of his toward the opposing nation turned out to be a great disaster for his own people. In addition, if his nature could not be corrupted and changed, that plague would not change and corrupt us either, and the order that was supposed to be given to the alien nature could have been given without any disorder in us.

26. But that objection had not yet been stated which I recently heard at Carthage. For, when a certain man, whom I especially desire to be set free from that error, was being forced into the same difficulties by this question, he dared to say that the kingdom had certain of its borders that could be invaded by the opposing nation, for God himself could in no way be violated. But he said what even that author of your sect was not forced to say. For Mani perhaps saw that the consequent ruin for his sect was much easier through this view than through the other. And it is really true that, if anyone of average intelligence heard that in that nature one part was violable and another inviolable, he would readily understand that there were not two natures but three: one inviolable, a second violable, and a third that violates.

13, 27. Since these blasphemies, then, have come forth from your heart and daily dwell upon your lips,[4] stop at some point praising — in order to ensnare the ignorant — the seal of the lips as if it were something great. Or perhaps you think that the seal of the lips is something admirable and praiseworthy because you do not eat meat and drink wine. I ask you for what end you do this. For, if the end to which we direct what we do, that is, on account of which we do whatever we do, is not only blameless but also praiseworthy, then our actions are also worthy of some praise. But if the end that we have in sight and contemplate

---

4. See Mt 12:34; Lk 6:45.

when we are engaged in some activity is rightly and deservedly blamed, no one would doubt that that activity should be blamed and reprimanded.

28. History tells us that Catiline was able to endure cold, thirst, and hunger.[5] These qualities were common to that scurrilous and sacrilegious man and also to our apostles. How, then, is that parricide distinguished from the apostles except by the very different end that he was pursuing? For he endured those things in order to carry out his utterly unbridled and cruel desires. The apostles, on the other hand, endured them in order that they might suppress such desires and compel them to obey the reason that masters them. You yourselves are accustomed to say, when the multitude of Catholic virgins is praised in your hearing, "Even a mule is a virgin." You say this rashly out of an ignorance of Catholic teaching, but you still indicate that this continence is useless if it is not directed to some absolutely correct end by sure reasoning. Catholic Christians can also compare your abstinence from wine and meat to that of domesticated animals, of the many sparrows,[6] and finally even of countless kinds of worms. But for fear that I may fall into your rashness, I shall not be overly hasty and do that. Rather, I shall first examine the end for which you do this. For it is already agreed between us, I think, that we should look for nothing else in such conduct. If it is for the sake of frugality and for holding in check the desire that causes us delight and holds us captive in such foods and drink, I listen and approve. But that is not the case.

29. For I ask you: Suppose that there is someone (and this is possible), a man so sparing and frugal that, in governing the desire of the belly and the palette, he eats only once a day and, when he eats, there are set before this man vegetables with a little bacon, and the vegetables have been cooked and flavored with the same bacon. He eats as much as is enough for quieting his hunger and quenches his thirst with two or three well-diluted cups of wine, out of care for his health, and this is his daily fare. But suppose that another man, on the other hand, who touches no meat and no wine, gladly consumes at the ninth hour exquisite and imported cereals prepared in many different dishes and seasoned with much pepper. And, when he is about to consume such dishes at the beginning of the night, he drinks a beverage sweetened with honey, grape juice, and juices of squeezed fruits that imitate quite well the appearance of wine and even surpass it in sweetness. And he drinks not to the extent of his thirst but to the extent of his desire. He has that fare set before him every day and enjoys such foods and delicacies not out of any need but with great pleasure. Which of these two do you judge leads a life of more abstinence with regard to eating and drinking? I do not think that even you are so blind that you do not prefer that man with a little bacon and wine to this glutton.

---

5. See Sallust, *Bellum Catilinae* V, 3; Augustine, Letter 167, 7.
6. See Mt 10:31; Lk 12:7.

30. This is of course what the truth leads to, but your error sings quite a different tune. After all, if one of your Elect, someone praised for the three seals, should live on a daily basis like the second man whom we described, he could be criticized by perhaps one or two of your graver men, but he could not by any means be condemned as a violator of the seal. But if he has once had supper with that first man and greased his lips with a bit of ham, even if spoiled, and wet them with flat wine, he will be judged a violator of the seal and for this reason destined for hell in the opinion of your founder — to your surprise but nonetheless with your agreement. I beg you, leave your error; I beg you, heed reason; I beg you, at long last resist your habits. For what is more perverse than this depravity? What is crazier? What, moreover, can be said or thought that is more insane than that you do not find how a man with a full belly — who has devoured mushrooms, rice, truffles, pastries, grape juice, peppers, and curry, who with distended belly burps his condiments with a feeling of self-satisfaction and who daily requires such a menu — might seem to have fallen away from the three seals, that is, from the rule of holiness, while you think that another man — who seasons the most ordinary vegetables with smoked bacon, eats only as much of this as suffices to restore his body, drinks three glasses of wine for the sake of sustaining his health, and daily goes from that food to this drink — is destined for certain punishment?

14, 31. But the apostle says, to be sure, *It is good, brothers, not to eat meat and not to drink wine* (Rom 14:21). It is not, however, as if any of us would deny that this is good. Rather, he said this either with the end in mind that I mentioned above, in accord with which he says, *Do not make provision for the flesh with its concupiscences* (Rom 13:14), or with the ends that, again, the same Paul indicated, that is, either for the sake of restraining one's appetite, which is often carried off more insanely and immoderately in these matters, or in order to avoid giving offense to a brother or having the weak partake of food offered to idols. For at the time when the apostle wrote this, much meat that had been sacrificed to idols was sold in the butcher shops. And because libations of wine were also offered to the gods of the pagans, many of the weaker brothers, who used even these items that were sold, preferred to abstain completely from meat and wine rather than to fall unknowingly into what they considered communion with idols. But on account of these weaker brothers even those who were stronger and who judged, because of a greater faith, that they should place no value on these things (since they knew that nothing is unclean except as a result of a bad conscience and since they possessed the statement of the Lord, *It is not what enters your mouth that makes you unclean, but what comes out of it* [Mt 15:11]), ought nonetheless to have abstained from these things on account of the weaker brothers so that they would not take offense. Nor is this something inferred as a suspicion; rather, it is found clearly in the letters of the apostle. For you are accustomed to quote to us only: *It is good, brothers, not to eat meat and not to drink wine*, without adding what follows: *or anything over which your brother takes offense or is scandalized or is made weak* (Rom 14:21). After all, from this the end for which the apostle commanded these things is clear.

32. The preceding and the following passages, which would in fact take a long time to record, more clearly indicate this. But on account of those who are lazy about reading or studying the divine scriptures, we are forced to set forth this whole text. The apostle says, *Accept a person who is weak in faith, but not with arguments over opinions. For one person believes that he can eat all things, but let someone who is weak eat vegetables. He who eats should not hold in scorn one who does not eat, and he who does not eat should not condemn one who eats. For God accepts him. Who are you to judge another's servant? He stands or falls in the sight of his own master. But he shall stand. For God is able to make him stand. For one man distinguishes one day from another; another regards every day in the same way. Let each be convinced in his own mind. He who observes the day observes it for the Lord. He who eats eats for the Lord, for he gives thanks to God. And he who does not eat refrains from eating for the Lord, and he gives thanks to God. For none of us lives for himself, and none of us dies for himself. For if we live, we live for the Lord, and if we die, we die for the Lord. After all, whether we live or we die, we belong to the Lord. For Christ lived, died, and rose in order that he might be lord of both the living and the dead. But why do you judge your brother? Or why do you hold your brother in contempt? After all, we shall all stand before the judgment seat of God. For scripture says: As I live, says the Lord, every knee will bend before me, and every tongue will make confession to God. And so, each of us will give an account of himself to God. Let us, therefore, not judge one another any more, but rather judge that you should not set a stumbling block or hindrance before a brother. I know and am confident in the Lord Jesus that there is nothing unclean in itself except for someone who thinks something is unclean. For him it is unclean. For if your brother is saddened on account of your food, you are not now living in accord with love. Do not, because of your food, lose someone for whom Christ died. Let the good we have, therefore, not be subjected to blasphemy. The kingdom of God is not food and drink but righteousness, peace, and joy in the Holy Spirit. For one who serves Christ in this way is pleasing to God and receives the approval of men. Let us, therefore, pursue what leads to peace and to the edification of one another. Do not destroy God's work on account of food. All things are clean, to be sure, but it is bad for a person who eats and gives offense. It is good not to eat meat and not to drink wine or anything over which your brother takes offense or is scandalized or is made weak. You have faith within yourself; have faith also in God. Blessed is he who does not judge himself in what he approves. But he who has doubts is condemned if he eats, because he does not do so out of faith. But everything that does not come from faith is sin. We who are stronger, however, ought to support the weaknesses of those who*

are weak and ought not to please ourselves. Let each of us please our neighbor in order to build him up in goodness. For Christ did not please himself. (Rom 14:1-15:3)

33. Is it clear enough that the apostle commanded those who were stronger not to eat meat and not to drink wine because they were causing offense to the weak by not adapting to them and because they were causing the weak to think that those who with faith judged all things to be clean[7] were refusing to abstain from such foods and drink because it was part of their worship of idols? He also conveyed this to the Corinthians when he wrote to them: *But with regard to the meat of the sacrifices that are offered to idols, we know that there is no idol in the world and that there is no God but the one. For, even if there are those who are called gods either in heaven or on the earth, we nonetheless have one God, the Father, from whom all things are, and we are in him, and one Lord, Jesus Christ, through whom all things are, and we are through him. Knowledge, however, is not found in everyone. But some even now, because of their familiarity with idols, eat meat as if it were offered to an idol, and, since their conscience is weak, it is defiled. But food does not commend us to God. For, if we eat, we shall not be better off, and if we do not eat, we shall not be worse off. But see to it that your freedom does not become a stumbling block for the weak. If anyone sees someone with knowledge at table in the temple of an idol, will not his conscience, since it is weak, be encouraged to eat meat sacrificed to idols, and the weak brother, for whom Christ died, perish because of your knowledge? In that way, however, by sinning against your brothers and striking their weak conscience, you sin against Christ. Hence, if food scandalizes a brother, I will never eat meat for fear of scandalizing a brother.* (1 Cor 8:4-13)

34. In another passage he asks, *What, then, am I saying? That what has been sacrificed to idols is anything? That an idol is anything? But what the pagans sacrifice they sacrifice to demons and not to God. I do not want you to be associated with demons. You cannot drink of the cup of the Lord and of the cup of demons; you cannot partake of the table of the Lord and of the table of demons. Or are we provoking the Lord to jealousy? Are we stronger than he? All things are permitted me, but not all things are expedient. All things are permitted me, but not all things cause edification. Let no one seek his own interests but that of the other person. Eat anything that comes to the butcher shop without asking any question on account of your conscience. But if someone says, This has been sacrificed to idols, do not eat it for the sake of the one who indicates this to you and for the sake of conscience. I do not mean for the sake of your conscience but for the sake the other person's. After all, why should my freedom be subject to judgment by another's conscience? If I partake with thanksgiving, why am I blamed for that for which I give thanks? Whether you eat or drink or whatever*

---

7. See Lk 11:41; Rom 14:20; Ti 1:15.

you do, then, do it all for the glory of God. Do not give offense to the Jews or to the Greeks or to the Church of God, just as I too try to please all people in all things, not seeking what is beneficial for myself but what is beneficial for many in order that they may be saved. Be imitators of me, just as I am of Christ. (1 Cor 10:19-25.28-11:1)

35. It is clear, I think, with what end we should abstain from meat and wine. That end is threefold: in order to suppress the delight that is often found especially in these foods and that in such drinks often leads to drunkenness; in order to protect the weak, on account of the things that are sacrificed or poured out in libations; and, what is especially to be commended, out of love, lest the weakness of those frail people who abstain from these things should take offense. You say that certain foods are unclean, however, though the apostle says that all things are clean but are bad for someone *who eats and gives offense* (Rom 14:20). [8] And of course I believe that you are defiled by these banquets precisely because you think that they are unclean. For he says, *I believe and am confident in the Lord Jesus that nothing is unclean in itself except for someone who thinks something is unclean. For him it is unclean.* (Rom 14:14) Who, however, has any doubt that he called unclean what is impure and defiled? But it is foolish to discuss the scriptures with you since, by promising reasons, you mislead people and you say that those books that have great authority in religion have been corrupted by the insertion of falsified passages. Persuade me by reason, then, of how meat defiles those who eat it if they take it without giving offense, without any wavering conscience, and without any desire.

15, 36. It is worth the effort to know the whole reason behind this superstitious abstinence, which is given as follows. For, as is said, a member of God was mingled with the substance of evil in order to rein it in and hold it in check from its greatest fury — that, after all, is what you say — and that from the two natures mixed together, that is, of good and of evil, the world was constructed. But the divine part is daily being purified from every part of the world and taken back into its own kingdoms, but this part, being breathed forth through the earth and making its way toward heaven, enters into plants because their roots are fixed in the earth, and in that way it makes fertile and vivifies all the plants and all the trees. From these the animals take their nourishment, and, if they have intercourse, they bind that divine member in the flesh and envelop it in errors and sufferings, after it has been turned aside and held back from its certain journey. And so, if the foods that are prepared from grain and fruits come to the holy ones, that is, to the Manicheans, whatever is bright and divine in them is purified, that is, made perfect in every way, through their chastity, prayers, and psalms, in order that it may be returned to its own kingdoms without any trouble due to defilement. This is the reason why you are forbidden to give to a beggar who is

---

8. See Ti 1:15.

not a Manichean bread or anything made of grain or even water, which is inexpensive for everyone, for fear that the beggar might render foul by his sins and hold back from its return a member of God that is mingled with these things.

37. But you say that flesh is composed of such filth. For something of that divine part escapes, as you claim, when grains or fruit are plucked. It escapes when they are broken down by tearing or grinding or cooking or biting and chewing. It also escapes in all the movements of animals, when they leap or move about or labor or do anything at all. It also escapes in our very repose when that activity called digestion is carried out in the body by its inner heat. And so, as the divine nature escapes on so many occasions, a certain most foul element remains from which the flesh is formed through intercourse, while a soul of the good kind, because, though it is mostly good, it is not wholly good, flies off through the movements we mentioned. Hence, when the soul also abandons the flesh, the remaining foulness becomes very great, and for this reason the soul of those who eat meat is defiled.

16, 38. O what a cloak over falsity is provided by the obscure nature of things! Who is there who, when he hears these ideas, is not deceived by corporeal images, if he has not studied the causes of things and has not as yet been touched by even the slightest ray of the truth? For, by the very fact that these things are not apparent and are thought about through certain images of visible things and can be eloquently stated, they are thought to be true. Great crowds and herds of such human beings wander about, whom a religious fear rather than reason keeps safe from such deceptions. Hence, I shall try to refute these ideas, to the extent that God helps me, in order that it may be seen clearly enough how false and absurd they are not only in the judgment of the wise, by which they are rejected as soon as they are uttered, but also in the understanding of the common man.

39. I ask first why you teach that some part or other of God is present in grains, vegetables, plants, flowers, and fruits. "It is evident," they say, "from their bright color, from their pleasant smell, and from their sweet taste. And when such things are spoiled and do not have these qualities, they indicate that they are bereft of the same goodness." Are you not ashamed to think that God is found by the nose and palate? But I will leave this aside. For I shall speak to you in plain language, and, as is usually said, that is a bit much for you. If the presence of the good is seen in bodies from their color, a mind of any sort ought rather to understand that the excrement of animals, which is purged from their flesh, is bright with various colors, at times white, often gold, and others of the sort, which in fruits and flowers you accept as evidence of God's presence and inherence. What, then, is the reason why you claim that redness in a rose is proof of abundant goodness and condemn the same color in blood? Why in a spring flower do you cherish the same color as in cabbages but hold it in contempt in the disease of those with jaundice and also in the excrement of an infant? Why do

you think that the bright sheen of oil proclaims the amount of good mixed into it, and why do you prepare the gullet and belly to purify it but are afraid that your lips might touch fatty meat oozing drops of a similar sheen? Why do you think that a golden melon comes from the storehouses of God and not think this of the rancid fat of ham or the yoke of an egg? Why does whiteness in lettuce announce God to you, but the whiteness of milk does not? I am still talking about colors, after all, in which — to omit the others — you can compare no fields decked with flowers to the feather of a single peacock, which certainly came to be from intercourse and flesh.

40. For, if this good is also discovered by smell, perfumes with a wonderful scent are made from the flesh of some animals. Secondly, foods themselves, which are often cooked with somewhat better meats, smell much more pleasant than if they did not have meat. Finally, if you judge better what smells more pleasant, you ought to eat some mud more eagerly than drink water from a cistern, since the drier earth soaked with rain pleases the nose with a wonderful scent, and such mud smells better than if purer rainwater were caught. But if it is necessary that scent be a witness in order that we might know that something of God dwells in a body, that he dwells in dates and honey more than in pork, but in pork more than in beans and in figs more than in a liver fattened by figs, see, I grant this. But you too should grant that he dwells more in a liver fattened on figs than in a beet. What are you going to say about the fact that you are forced by this argument to admit that certain plants, all of which you of course want to be purer than meat, receive God from meat, if by their taste one recognizes that God is mingled in them? For even vegetables are tastier when cooked with meat, and we cannot taste the plants on which cattle feed, but we judge them more excellent in their color and most suitable in their taste after they have been converted into the liquid of milk.

41. Or do you think that where the three goods are present together, that is, good color and odor and taste, a larger part of the good is present? Do not, then, admire and praise flowers so greatly, which you cannot admit to the tribunal of the palate for judgment. Do not at least prefer purslane to meat, which meat surpasses in color and odor and taste when it is cooked. Roast suckling pig — for you force us to discuss good and evil with you not by means of writers and books but by means of cooks and bakers — a roast suckling pig, then, is glistening in color and attractive in odor and pleasing in taste. You have a perfect proof of the indwelling of the divine substance. The pig invites you by its threefold testimony and desires to be purified by your holiness. Attack it; why do you hesitate? What are you preparing to say to the contrary? An infant's excrement surpasses lentils in color alone; a grilled cutlet surpasses a mild and green fig in odor alone; goat meat surpasses in taste alone the grass on which a living goat feeds. We have also found meat whose cause is bolstered by all these three witnesses together. What more do you ask for? Or what are you going to say? Why should

pieces of meat make you unclean when you eat them and these astonishing arguments not make you unclean when you present them, especially when a beam of this sun, which you certainly prefer to all meats and grains, has neither an odor nor any taste but only stands out among other bodies by the excellence of its very bright color. It exhorts you mightily and forces you, even against your will, to prefer none among the other proofs of the presence of the intermingled good to the brightness of color.

42. You are reduced to such difficulties, then, that you say that a part of God dwells in blood and in the most disgusting but brightly colored droppings left by the flesh of animals in the streets rather than in the pale leaves of the olive tree. If you say — as you do say — that, when the leaves of the olive tree are burned, they emit a fire in which the presence of the light is seen, but when meat is burned, it does not do this, what will you reply regarding fat, which lights almost all the lamps of Italy? What will you reply concerning cow dung, which is surely filthier than beef, though, once it is dried, farmers use it in the hearth since nothing is handier than its fire and cleaner than its smoke? But if sheen and brightness reveal a greater presence of a part of God, why do you not purify it? Why do you not put your seal upon it? Why do you not set it free? But if God is especially present in flowers — to say nothing of blood and countless similar things in the flesh or from the flesh — you certainly cannot eat those flowers at your banquets, and, even if you ate meat, you certainly would not use in your foods the scales of fishes and certain worms and flies, all of which shine with their own light even in the dark.

43. What remains, then, but that you stop saying that you have adequate judges in your eyes, nose, and palate by which you can test the presence of a part of God in bodies? But, once these judges have been set aside, how will you show not only that a larger part of God is present in plants than in flesh but even that there is anything of God in plants? Does their beauty move you, not that which is found in the attractiveness of their color but that which is found in the harmony of their parts? I wish that this were the case! For when would you dare to compare gnarled trees to the bodies of animals in whose shape equal members correspond to each other? But if you find delight in the testimonies of the bodily senses, something that is necessary for those who cannot see the power of being with their mind, how do you prove that the substance of the good escapes from bodies over a period of time through a certain wear and tear except on the grounds that God leaves there, as you say, and moves from place to place? This is complete madness. Yet no signs or proofs have, as far as I can judge, led you to this view. After all, before many things plucked from trees or uprooted from the ground come to serve as our food, they are improved over an interval of time, for example, leeks and endives, lettuce, grapes, apples, figs, certain pears, and many other things, which have a better color, are eaten with greater benefit for the body, and are tastier in the mouth if they are not consumed as soon as they are

picked. Such a great advantage and sweetness should not be present in these things, according to your view, if they become emptier of the good the longer they are stored after being separated from the earth, as though from their mother. The meat of animals killed the day before is certainly tastier and healthier. But it ought not to be so if, as you claim, it had more of the good on the day when the animal was freshly killed than on the next day, when a greater flight of the divine substance had taken place.

44. But who would fail to know that wine becomes purer and better with age? Not with a finer bouquet for throwing the senses into confusion but with greater benefit for invigorating the body, provided that there is moderation, which ought to govern all things. For new wine usually introduces confusion into the senses more quickly, so that, if it remains in the vat for some time and ferments for a while, it affects the head of those who look down into it, causes them to fall in headfirst, and kills them unless they somehow receive help. For, as far as health goes, who would deny that bodies are bloated and dangerously distended by it? Are such disadvantages found in it because it has more good, while they are not present in old wine because a large part of the divine substance has departed? It is absurd for you to say this, especially since you prove the presence of a part of God by the eyes, nose, and palate when these senses are affected in a good manner. But what is so great a perversity as to think that wine is the bile of the princes of darkness and not to refrain from eating grapes? Will that bile be more present in the cup than in the cluster of grapes? But if, as the good departs, the evil remains more undiluted, so to speak, and that happens over a period of time, those same grapes should not become tastier, sweeter, and healthier after having been hung up and stored, nor should the wine itself, as we said previously, become clearer and brighter when the light departs and become healthier when the salutary substance leaves.

45. What shall I say about trees and branches, which over time dry up and which you cannot say become worse as a result? After all, they lose that which produces smoke, but they retain that from which a bright flame arises and testifies by that brightness, of which you are very fond, that the good is purer in drier branches than in greener ones. The result is that you either deny that the part of God is larger in the pure light than in the smoky light, and in that way you throw all your teachings into confusion, or you admit that it is possible that the nature of evil flees in greater quantity from branches that have been cut off or uprooted, if they are put aside for a longer time, than does the nature of the good. Once you have conceded this, we shall have your admission that greater evil can leave fruits and vegetables when they are picked and that in that way greater good can remain in meat. And let this indeed be enough as far as time is concerned.

46. For, if the divine nature finds a chance to escape in the motion, crushing, or rubbing of things, many similar things that become better because of movement are an argument against you. The barley liquor behaves like wine, which

becomes best as a result of movement. Certainly, and this is a point not to be passed over, this kind of drink makes someone drunk very quickly, and yet you have never said that barley liquor is the bile of the princes of darkness. Flour, when properly mixed with a little water, becomes slightly harder, so that it becomes better by being kneaded and — what is completely wrongheaded to say — becomes whiter when the light leaves. A candy maker works honey for a long time in order for it to come to that sheen and sweetness that is less harmful and more tasty. Explain how this happens through the departure of the good. But if you do not want to test the presence of God only by the delight of sight, smell, and taste, but also by that of hearing, it is flesh that provides strings for lyres and bones for pipes, and when these are dried, polished, and twisted, they become sonorous. In that way we are offered the sweetness of music, which you say came from the divine kingdoms, from the foul remains of dead flesh that have been dried over time, smoothed by rubbing, and stretched by twisting, the same sorts of mistreatment which you teach cause the divine substance also to flee from living things. And you also say that this happens as a result of their being cooked. Why, then, are boiled thistles not harmful to health? When they are cooked, are we to think that God or disease leaves them?

47. Why should I continue with other things, since it is neither easy nor necessary to mention them all? To whom, after all, does it not occur that many things are sweeter and healthier when cooked? They should not be if, as you suppose, they are stripped of the good by such actions. I think that you certainly do not find any way to prove by these senses of the body that meat is unclean and defiles the souls of persons who eat it, inasmuch as fruits and vegetables that have been picked are turned into meat through numerous transformations. This is especially the case since you think old wine that has turned to vinegar is purer than wine, and since we see that the beverage you drink[9] is nothing other than cooked wine. For it ought to be more unclean than wine if the members of God depart from bodily things as a result of motion and cooking. But if this is not the case, there is no reason why you should think that, when fruits and vegetables are picked, stored, handled, cooked, and digested, they are abandoned by the good as it leaves them and, for this reason, provide a very sordid material for the generation of bodies.

48. But if you are not guided by color, shape, smell, and taste in order that you may judge the presence of good in these things, what other evidence can you offer? Do you want to use as an argument a certain strength and resistance that seems to be taken away from these things when they are removed from the earth and handled? But if this is what motivates you — although one can quickly see that it is false on account of the increased strength of some things after they have

---

9. Augustine uses the term *caroenum*, which refers to a sweet wine that had been boiled down to a third of its original amount.

been removed from the earth, as I have already mentioned concerning wine, which becomes stronger with age — if, nonetheless, this strength is, as I said, what motivates you, you will find that a more ample part of God is found in no food more than in meats. For athletes, who most of all need that strength and vigor, do not eat vegetables and fruit but do eat meat.

49. Or is it because flesh is fed from trees, but trees are not fed with flesh, that you think that the bodies of trees are better than our bodies? You do not consider a fact right before your eyes, namely, that trees become healthier and more fertile and crops become richer when fed with manure, though you think that you say nothing worse when you bring accusations against the flesh than that it is a house of dung. The things that you regard as clean, then, are fed from things that, from among those that you regard as unclean, you declare to be much more unclean. But if you scorn the flesh because it comes into existence after inter-course, then the flesh of worms — which come into existence in such great numbers and magnitude in apples, trees, and even in the earth itself without any intercourse — should be a source of delight for you. But this is some sort of a pretense. For, if you were displeased by the flesh, which is formed by the union of a father and a mother, you would not say that those princes of darkness were born from the fruits of their trees, since you certainly shun those princes more than the meat that you refuse to taste.

50. You suppose that all the souls of animals come from the food that their parents eat, and you boast that you set free from those prisons the divine substance, which is contained in your foods. This is very much against you and drives you most insistently to eat meat. Why, after all, do you not take the meat first and eat it and in that way deliver the souls that those who eat meat are going to chain to a body? But, you say, they do not chain to the body any of the good part from meat but from the fruits and vegetables that they eat along with meat. What about the souls of lions, whose only food is meat? They drink, you say, and that soul, therefore, is drawn from the water and bound to the flesh. What will you say about countless birds? What can you say about eagles, which eat nothing but meat and do not need any drink? Certainly you give up here and do not find any answer. For, if the soul comes from food and if there are animals that give birth to young and drink nothing and eat only meat, the soul is present in the meat, and in accord with your practice you ought to go to its aid in order to purify it by eating the meat. Or perhaps you think that a pig that is fed on fruits and vegetables and drinks water has a soul of light but that an eagle, for which the sun is most natural, has a soul of darkness because it eats only meat.

51. O what difficulties! O what incredible absurdities! You would certainly not have fallen into them if you were free from your utterly vain myths and, regarding abstinence from foods, followed what the truth approves. That is, you would judge that you ought to reject delicious foods for the sake of holding concupiscence in check, not for the sake of avoiding something unclean, since

there is nothing unclean. For, if someone who does not pay much attention to the nature of things and to the power of the soul and the body concedes that the soul is defiled by food, you have much better reason to concede that the soul becomes unclean because of its desires. What reason — or rather madness — is there in expelling from the number of the Elect someone who perhaps eats meat for the sake of his health without any desire, but, if he passionately desires to eat peppered truffles, in perhaps only reprimanding him for a lack of moderation but not condemning him for violating the seal? In that way it turns out that a person cannot be one of your Elect who is shown to have eaten a part of a chicken not out of desire but for reasons of health, but that a person can be one of the Elect if he shows himself to have desired dill-flavored vegetables and other entrees without meat. You keep the one whom desire plunges into filth, therefore, but you do not keep the one whom food itself, as you suppose, defiles, although you admit that the defilement from concupiscence is far greater than that from food. You nonetheless embrace one who greedily tucks into most delicately seasoned fruits and vegetables and does not hold himself back, but you exclude one who, though he is ready to take food and ready to pass it up with indifference, takes any human food whatsoever without any desire and for the sake of suppressing hunger. There is your amazing way of life; there is your exemplary discipline; there is your remarkable temperance!

52. Now, how shameful and criminal it is that you think it wrong if anyone besides one of the Elect touches, in order to eat them, the foods that are offered you at your banquets for purification. For often so much food is provided that it cannot be easily consumed by a few. And because you consider it a sacrilege to give the leftovers to others and certainly to throw them out, you are forced into acts of great overindulgence, since you desire to purify, as it were, the whole amount that you were given. But once you are stretched to capacity and almost bursting, like cruel masters you force those youngsters who are under your discipline to devour the rest, with the result that the objection was raised against a certain man at Rome that, because of such superstition, he killed some poor children by forcing them to eat. I would not believe this if I did not know what a great crime you think it is either to give these foods to others who are not members of the Elect or even to have them thrown out. Hence, you are left with the need to eat that almost daily leads to a most shameful overeating but at times can even lead to murder.

53. Since this is so, you also forbid giving bread to a beggar. You nonetheless think that you should give him money out of mercy or rather out of hatred. What should I blame first here? Your cruelty or your madness? Suppose, after all, that this happens in a place where one cannot find food for sale? The man in need is going to die of hunger while you, a wise and kind man, show more mercy for a cucumber than for a human being. This is certainly— for what can I say more to the point and more clearly? — false mercy and true cruelty. Now let us look at

the madness. For what if the man buys bread for himself with the money you gave? Is not the part of your God that is going to suffer in the man who eats this bread from the merchant the same that was going to suffer if he had eaten it if you gave it? Because he was helped by your money to commit the crime, that sinful beggar, then, entangled in filth the part of God that wanted to fly off. And yet with all your wisdom you think that there is a difference if you do not surrender to a murderer the man whom he wants to kill but knowingly give him money by which he may buy someone to kill him. What can be added to this insanity? For in that way it turns out that either a man dies if he does not find food for sale or the food dies if he finds it. Of these the first is a real murder; the other is your sort of murder, which must be ascribed to you as if they were both real murders. For, as for the fact that you do not forbid your Hearers to eat meat but forbid them to kill animals, what could you do that is more foolish and more perverse? For, if that sort of food does not pollute them, eat it yourself as well. But if it pollutes them, what madness it is to think that it is a greater crime to release a pig's soul from its body than to defile a human soul with a pig's body!

17, 54. But now let us turn to consider and discuss the seal of the hands. First of all, Christ showed that your abstention from killing animals and from felling trees is utter superstition. For he taught us that we share no community of laws with animals and trees when he sent the demons into a herd of pigs[10] and withered with a curse the tree on which he found no fruit. [11] Those pigs and that tree had certainly committed no sin. For we are not so crazy as to think that a tree is willingly either fruitful or barren. Nor should you say at this point that our Lord wanted to signify certain other things by these actions. Who, after all, would fail to know this? But the Son of God certainly ought not to have given a sign by means of murder if, as you suppose, either to kill a tree or to kill animals is murder. For he also gave certain signs by means of human beings, with whom we are, of course, united in a community of laws, but he did so by healing them, not by killing them. [12] He would have also done this with animals and trees if he judged that we were united with them in a community, as you suppose.

55. Here I thought that I should appeal to authority, because one cannot hold a simple discussion with you about the soul of pigs or about the kind of life by which trees are said to live. But, in order to avoid being overwhelmed by the scriptures, you are protected by a kind of rule of your own, insofar as you say that they were falsified. You have, of course, never said that the passages that I mentioned concerning the tree and the herd of pigs were inserted by those who corrupted the scriptures. But you might realize how much they are opposed to you and want to say the same thing about them. Hence, I shall stick to my resolu-

---

10. See Mt 8:31-32; Mk 5:12-13; Lk 8:12-13.
11. See Mt 21:18-19; Mk 11:12-14.
12. See Mt 4:23; Mk 3:4.10; Lk 8:26-37.

tion. First of all I shall ask you, who make great promises of reason and truth, what harm it does to a tree — I do not mean if you pluck an apple or leaves from it (for, if someone does that, not unintentionally but knowingly, he will, according to you, undoubtedly be condemned as a violator of the seal), but if you completely uproot it. After all, that rational soul, which you suppose is present in trees, is released from its bonds when the tree is cut down — you yourselves say this — and from those bonds, in fact, in which it was held with great misery and to no benefit. For it is known that the founder of your sect used to threaten a human being with transformation into a tree as a great but not as the greatest punishment. And in a tree the soul cannot become wiser as it can in a human being. The reason for not killing a human being is most certain, namely, so that you do not kill either someone whose wisdom and virtue benefits others greatly or someone who could perhaps attain wisdom, if he were either admonished by someone externally or was enlightened by God with interior thoughts. But by the simplest reasoning and the most widely acknowledged authority the truth teaches that the soul of a human being leaves the body with greater benefit to the extent that it leaves the body with greater wisdom. Hence, someone who fells a tree sets free from that body a soul that is making no progress in wisdom. And so, you holy men, you, I say, ought most of all to cut down trees and to bring by your prayers and psalms their souls, which have been stripped of those bonds, to a better state. Or can this be done only with those souls that you receive in your belly, not with those that you help by your mind?

56. And yet, when you are asked why an apostle is not sent to trees as a teacher or why that apostle who is sent to human beings does not proclaim the truth to trees as well, very great difficulties, in my opinion, force you to admit that the souls of trees do not make progress toward wisdom as long as they are in trees. Here you are forced to answer that those souls cannot receive the commandments of God in those bodies. But you are pressed more violently from the other side since you claim that they hear our voices, understand our words, see our bodies and the motions of our bodies, and even perceive our thoughts. If these claims are true, why can they not learn from an apostle of light? Or why can they not learn even much more easily than we do, since they see even the inner reaches of the mind? For in that way that teacher, who scarcely teaches you by speaking, could, according to you, educate them by thinking, since they would see his thoughts in his mind before he expresses them in words. But if these claims are false, see at last the error in which you lie.

57. Now, as for the fact that you yourselves do not pick apples and pull up plants but command your Hearers to pick them, pull them up, and offer them to you, in order that you may benefit not only the people who bring them to you but also the things that are brought to you, who would in any way tolerate this, if he considers it well? For, first of all, it makes no difference whether you yourself commit the crime or want someone else to commit it for you. You say that you

do not want this. How, then, do you help the part of God that is found in lettuce and leeks if no one picks them and brings them to the saints to eat? Secondly, in passing through a field where the rights of friendship give you the authority to pick whatever you want, if you see a raven threatening a fig, what will you do? In accord with your opinion, do you not suppose that the fig itself speaks and pleads with you in a pitiful fashion that you yourself should pick it and bury it in your holy belly to be purified and resuscitated, rather than that the raven should devour it and mingle it with its dark body and from there send it on into other forms to be bound and tormented in them? What is more cruel than you if this is true? What is more silly if it is false? What is more contrary to your discipline if you violate the seal? What is more inimical than you to a member of God if you keep it?

58. But this stems from your false and absurd opinion. For a certain and obvious cruelty, which flows from the same error, is shown to be present in you. After all, suppose that someone with a body broken by disease, worn out from a journey, and half-dead from the plague, lies in the road, capable of doing nothing more than blurting out a few words. Giving him a pear would help to revive his body, and he begs you, as you pass by, to help him, and he pleads that you bring some fruit from a nearby tree — from which no human law, in fact no true law, prevents you from picking — to him who is soon going to die if you do not do so. You, a holy and Christian man, would rather pass by and abandon a person in such a condition, who is making such pleas, for fear that the tree might weep when the fruit is plucked and you might be doomed, as a violator of the seal, to the Manichean punishments. O what a way of life, and what a strange innocence!

59. But now I shall ask what bothers you about the killing of animals, and many points of this sort can be also raised on this subject. What wrong, after all, does one who kills a wolf do to the soul of a wolf? For that wolf is going to be a wolf as long as it lives and is not going to obey any preacher who tells it that it should hold back from the blood of sheep; and when the beast is killed, the rational soul, according to you, is set free from the bonds of the body. And you keep even your Hearers from this killing, for it seems greater than in the case of trees. Here I do not blame very much your senses, namely, your bodily ones. For we see and perceive from their cries that animals die in pain — something, of course, on which a human being places little value in the case of an irrational animal, that is, one without a rational soul, with which a human being is not united by any community of laws. But I am looking for those same senses of yours in observing trees, and I find you blind indeed. For, to omit the fact that in a tree the feeling of pain is not apparent from any movements, what is more evident than that a tree is in its best condition when it is thriving, covered with foliage, bright with flowers, and rich with fruit? But it generally gets this most of all from being trimmed. If it felt the knife, as you claim, it would waste away

when afflicted by many great wounds rather than revive and send forth new shoots from those places with such sure exuberance.

60. Yet why do you think it a greater wrong to kill animals than plants, since you think that plants have a purer soul than flesh does? Mani says that a certain exchange occurs, since a part of those things taken from the fields is given to the Elect and to the saints to be purified. These ideas were already torn to shreds above, and it was sufficiently proved, in my opinion, that there is no reason to say that there is a greater part of that good in fruit and vegetables than in flesh. But if someone earns his living by selling meat and uses all the income from that business to buy food for your Elect and offers to the saints more food than a farmer and a peasant do, will he not cry out that he is permitted to kill animals on the basis of the same exchange? There is, Mani says, another absolutely secret reason. For, in opposition to the ignorant, a clever man does not lack a refuge in the obscurity of nature. After all, he says, the heavenly princes who have been captured and bound in the kingdom of darkness have been placed by the creator of the world in those places, and each possesses on earth its own animals, that is, ones coming from his own kind and family. They hold guilty the killers of those animals, and they do not permit them to leave this world, and they wear down those they can by punishments and torments. Who among the ignorant would not fear this? And would not someone who can see nothing amid such great obscurity think that things are as they are said to be? But I shall not abandon my goal, if God will help me, in order that your obscure lies may be refuted by the perfectly plain truth.

61. For I ask whether the animals that live on the land and in the water come from that race of princes by way of generation and by the act of intercourse, since the origin of the beings that are born is traced back to those aborted fetuses. I ask once more whether, if this is so, it is permissible to kill bees and frogs and many other living beings that come to be without intercourse. You say that it is wrong. You do not keep your Hearers from the killing of living things, therefore, on account of their kinship with some princes or other. Or, if you say that there is some general kinship of all bodies, trees will also undoubtedly be linked to the same offense against the princes, though the Hearers are not commanded to spare them. We come back, then, to that feeble argument — that the injuries which the Hearers inflict on plants are expiated by the fruits which they bring to your church. For it was also said that in this way, if they are your Hearers, those who kill animals in a butcher shop, sell the meat, and bring you the income after they have bought fruits and vegetables, need not be concerned over that daily slaughter and that any sin involved in it is wiped out by your banquets.

62. You might say that, just in the case of fruits and vegetables, it is necessary to grant that such killing should merit pardon, but that, since this is not possible — the Elect, after all do not eat meat — the Hearers must abstain from the killing of animals. What, then, will you answer concerning thorns and weeds that

farmers kill by pulling them out when they weed the fields? For they cannot offer you any food from them. How will such devastation gain pardon, when no food for the saints is derived from it? Or do you perhaps, by eating some of those vegetables and fruits, also remove whatever sin is committed in order to grow vegetables and fruits? What if locusts or rats or mice ravage the fields, something that obviously happens often? Will the farmer, your Hearer, kill them with impunity because he sins precisely in order that fruit may grow? Here you are certainly caught in a corner. For you either grant your Hearers the killing of animals that your founder refused to grant them, or you forbid them the cultivation of fields that he did grant them. And yet you often venture to say that the moneylender is more innocent than the farmer. So much better friends are you of melons than of human beings! For, in order not to harm melons, you judge that it is better to slay a human being by usury. Is this the justice that one should seek and preach or rather a lie that one should curse and condemn? Is this a memorable act of mercy or rather a damnable act of cruelty?

63. Why is it that you yourselves do not refrain from the killing of living beings in the case of lice, fleas, and bedbugs? You consider it a great defense of this act when you say that these are the filth from our bodies. This is, first of all, clearly false concerning fleas and bedbugs. For who does not clearly see that these living things do not come from our body? Secondly, if you vehemently deplore intercourse, something that you certainly want us to think, why do you not think that those living beings that are born from our flesh without intercourse are cleaner? For, although they later have young by having intercourse, they are not first born from our body because we have intercourse. But if whatever is born from living bodies must be considered to be most foul, whatever is born from dead bodies must be considered most foul for even better reasons. With greater impunity, therefore, one kills a mouse, a snake, or a scorpion, which, we are accustomed to hear, especially from you, come to be from human corpses. But I omit points that are obscure and uncertain. Concerning bees the opinion is certainly quite widespread that they come to be from the dead bodies of cows.[13] They are, then, killed with impunity. But if this too is uncertain, hardly anyone has any doubt that beetles come to be from dung rolled into a ball by them and buried.[14] You certainly ought to consider these living beings, therefore, and others, which it would take a long time to run through, as more foul than your lice, and yet you think it is wrong to kill the former but silly to spare the latter, unless you perhaps consider these living things of no value because they are small. Of course, if it is true that one ought to consider a living being less valuable to the extent that it is smaller, one must necessarily prefer a camel to a human being.

---

13. See Varro, *On Farming* (*Rerum rusticarum de agricultura*) III, 6, 14.
14. See *Revisions* I, 6 (7), 9; Pliny the Elder, *Naturalis Historia* IX, 34, 98.

64. In addition to this there is that series of steps that often disturbed us when we were your Hearers. For there is no reason why a flea should be killed on account of the smallness of its body, while a fly, which comes to be from a bean, should not. And if that fly can be killed, why should this fly, which is a little bigger, not also be killed, since its offspring is smaller than that other fly. Now it follows that a bee is also killed without sin, since its offspring is not equal to this fly. And in that way we come to the offspring of a locust and to a locust and to the offspring of a mouse and to a mouse. And in order not to prolong this, do you not see that by these steps we come to an elephant, so that whoever thinks that the killing of a flea is not a sin on account of its small body cannot deny that he kills that huge beast without guilt? But now I think that I have said enough about such nonsense.

18, 65. There remains the seal of the breast, in which your chastity is quite unchaste. After all, you actually forbid not intercourse but marriage, as the apostle foretold long before,[15] though marriage is the one moral defense of that act. Here I have no doubt that you will cry out and stir up hatred by saying that you strongly recommend and praise perfect chastity yet do not forbid marriage, since your Hearers, who hold the second level of membership among you, are not forbidden to take and have wives. Since you say this loudly and with great indignation, I will quite calmly question you in this way. Are you not the people who think that the begetting of children, by which souls are bound in the flesh, is a more serious sin than intercourse? Are you not the people who are accustomed to admonish us to observe, as much as we can, the time at which a woman is ready for conception after her menstrual period and to abstain from intercourse at that time so that a soul does not become entangled in flesh? From this it follows that you think that taking a wife is not for the sake of procreating children but for the sake of satisfying lust. But marriage, as the very laws of marriage cry out, unite a man and a woman for the sake of procreating children. Whoever, then, says that to beget children is a more serious sin than to have intercourse certainly forbids marriage and makes the woman no longer a wife but a prostitute, who in return for certain compensation is given to the man to satisfy his lust. After all, if she is a wife, it is matrimony. But it is not matrimony when the effort is made that she not become a mother.[16] She is not, therefore, a wife. Hence, you forbid marriage, and you do not defend yourselves by any argument against this charge, which was foretold of you long ago by the Holy Spirit.

66. Now, since you make such a to-do lest a soul be entangled in the flesh through intercourse and vigorously maintain that a soul is set free from seeds

---

15. See 1 Tm 4:1-3.
16. In Latin the link between "matrimony" (*matrimonium*) and "mother" (*mater*) is more obvious than in English.

through the food of the holy, do you not confirm, you poor wretches, what people suspect of you? When people believe that you want to set the soul free when you eat grain, beans, lentils, and other seeds, why should they not believe this with regard to the seed of animals? For you say that the flesh of a dead animal is unclean because it does not have a soul, but you cannot say this of the seed of an animal, since you think that in it there is entangled the soul that will be seen in the offspring and in which you say that the soul of Mani himself was entangled. And because such seed cannot be brought to you by your Hearers to be purified, who would not suspect that you yourselves perform such a secret purification among yourselves and conceal it from them for fear that they might abandon you? If you do not do this, and I wish that were the case, you see the great suspicion to which your superstition is exposed and how you should not be angry at people who arrive at conclusions that they infer from your teaching, since you teach them that you set free souls from bodies and the senses by means of your food and drink. I do not want to delay over this any longer; you see how much room there is for attacking you. But because the matter is such that discussion shies away from it instead of pursuing it, and because my aim can be seen through the whole discussion in which I decided not to exaggerate anything but to deal, so to speak, with the bare facts and arguments, let us go on to another topic.

19, 67. For the character of your three seals is already sufficiently clear. This is your way of life; this is the end of your admirable commandments in which there is found nothing certain, nothing constant, nothing reasonable, nothing free from blame, but in which there is found everything doubtful—in fact without any doubt absolutely false—everything contradictory, everything absurd. Moreover, so many and such serious sins are detected in this way of life that, if anyone wanted to bring accusations against all of them, a person of any ability could devote at least an individual volume to each of them. If you observed these commandments and lived out your teaching, no one would be more inept, no one more foolish, no one more stupid than you, but since you praise and teach them without practicing them, who can be called or found more deceitful, more insidious, and more malicious than you?

68. I listened to you with great care and diligence for nine full years.[17] I was unable to come to know anyone among the Elect who in terms of these commandments was not either caught in sin or at least subject to suspicion. Many were found using wine and meat; many were found bathing in the baths. But these are things we heard of. Some were proven to have seduced other women, so that I simply cannot have any doubt about this. Granted, however, that this too is more rumor than truth, I myself — and not I alone but also the people who in part have already been set free from that superstition and who in

---

17. See I,18, 34; *Confessions* IV, 1,1.

part will still, as I hope, be set free from it — saw at a crossroads in Carthage, in a very well-known square, not one but more than three of the Elect, who were passing together behind some women or other, hustle them with such an immodest gesture that they outdid the impurity and impudence of all the scum of the earth. It was clear enough that this stemmed from a longstanding habit and that they lived in that way among themselves, since none of them was afraid of the presence of a companion, and in that way they demonstrated that all or almost all were involved in this evil. For they were not men from one house but men who certainly lived in different places; perhaps they had together come from the place where the meeting of all of them had been held. But we were seriously upset; we also complained seriously. Who, finally, did not think that this action should be punished — I do not mean by separation from the Church but at least by a severe rebuke in accord with the magnitude of the crime?

69. The only excuse for their going unpunished was that, at the time when their assemblies were forbidden by civil law,[18] there was fear that they might be harmed and would betray something. What happens, then, to their claim that they will have endless persecution in this world[19] and to their desire to be more highly esteemed for this reason? For they interpret in this sense the words that the world will hate them,[20] and they state that the truth should be sought among them for the reason that, in the promise of the Holy Spirit, the Paraclete, it was said that this world could not receive him.[21] This is not the place to discuss this question. But certainly, if you are going to have constant persecution right up to the end of the world, this corruption, the unpunished disease of such great shamefulness, will also be constant, as long as you are afraid to harm such men.

70. We also received this response when we reported to the leaders of the sect that a woman had complained to us. In an assembly where she was along with other women, where she felt confident because of the holiness of the Manicheans, after several of the Elect had entered and one of them had put out the light, she was seized in the dark in the embrace of one of them, though it was not certain who it was, and she would have been forcibly violated if she had not escaped by shouting. How great a habit must we think it was that led to this crime that is so well known to us? And this was done on the night when you celebrated the vigil of a feast. But really, even if there was no fear of betrayal, who could bring before the bishop for condemnation a man who had taken such precautions not to be recognized? As if all of them who had entered at the same time were not involved in the same crime! For the light was extinguished while they were all joking rudely.

---

18. See the edict of Diocletian of the year 297 and the law of Valentinian I of the year 372 in A. Adam, *Texte zum Manichäismus. Kleine Texte* 175 (Berlin 1954) 82-84.
19. See Jn 16:33.
20. See Jn 15:18-20.
21. See Jn 14:16-17.

71. But how widely were the doors opened to suspicions when we found them to be envious, greedy, connoisseurs of sumptuous banquets, frequently involved in quarrels, and most easily upset over little things! We certainly did not think that they could abstain from the things from which they profess to abstain if they found places to hide in darkness. There were two men of fairly good reputation, men of quick wit and leaders in those discussions of theirs, who were closer and friendlier to us than the others. One of them who was also more closely attached to us on account of his studies of the liberal arts is now said to be a priest in your sect. These men were very envious of each other, and one reproached the other, not with public accusations but with words and whispers in the ears of those he could reach, on the ground that the other man had violently attacked the wife of a certain Hearer. But that man, in defending himself in the meanwhile, accused of the same crime, in our presence, another member of the Elect who was living with the same Hearer as a most trusted friend. Since he had caught him with the woman when he suddenly entered the house, he said that his enemy and rival advised the woman and the adulterer to spread that slander against him in order that, if he revealed anything, it would not be believed. We were tormented and bore it very ill that, even if there was uncertainty about the woman who was seized, we saw a most bitter hatred in those two men who were the best we found in that sect, and it forced us to surmise other things.

72. Finally, we very often encountered in theaters, along with an old priest, members of the Elect who were, we thought, quite respectable in terms of their age and their way of life. I do not mention the youths whom we used to catch quarreling with actors and chariot drivers, and this fact is no small indication as to how they would be able to refrain from hidden desires, since they could not conquer the passion that exposes them to the eyes of their own Hearers and reveals them as blushing and fleeing. But would that awful action by that holy man, whose discussions we frequently attended in the quarter of the fig merchants, have been revealed if he had been able to make that consecrated virgin just his wife and not pregnant? Her swelling womb, however, did not allow the hidden and unbelievable sin to remain unknown. Though her mother, who was deeply grieved, revealed this to her young brother, he was nonetheless held back from a public accusation in the name of religion. And he saw to it — for no one could put up with this — that the man was expelled from that church, and, lest the action go completely unpunished, he planned, in the company of his friends, to beat the man with his fists and his feet. But when the man was seriously beaten, he cried out, so that he might be spared on the authority of Mani, that Adam, the first hero, had sinned and after his sin had become more holy.[22]

73. For such indeed is your opinion of Adam and Eve. It is a long tale, but I will touch upon the part of it that is sufficient for the present. You say that Adam

22. See Wis 9:19; 10:2.

was born of his parents, those aborted princes of darkness, in such a way that he had the greatest part of the light for his soul and a very small part of the opposing nation. Though he lived a holy life on account of the preponderant amount of good, that opposing part was nonetheless aroused in him so that he would turn to intercourse. In that way he fell and sinned, but he lived thereafter a holier life. Here I am not complaining about a sinner who, in the guise of a holy man and a member of the Elect, brought another family into great disgrace and infamy by his wicked crime. I am not raising that as an objection to you. Let this be ascribed to a man who was thoroughly wicked rather than to your habitual way of life. And so I do not accuse you but him of such a great crime. Nonetheless I do not know how anyone can bear and tolerate another point in all of you, namely, that, though you say that the soul is a part of God, you still claim that the small amount of evil which was mingled with it overcame its greater abundance and fecundity. After all, if anyone believed this and if lust attacked him, who would not have recourse to such a defense rather than to the bridling and suppression of his lust?

20, 74. What more shall I say about your way of life? I have stated what I discovered when I was in the city where these crimes were committed. But it would take a long time to explain everything that was done in Rome during my absence. I shall nonetheless say something briefly. For there an affair broke forth into the open in such a way that it could not remain hidden from those who were not there. And when I was later in Rome, I confirmed that I had heard the complete truth, though the man who was present there and who was on such friendly terms with me and was greatly trusted by me reported the matter to me, so that I absolutely could not doubt it. For a certain Hearer of yours, who took second place to none of the Elect in that memorable abstinence and who had received a liberal education and wanted and was accustomed to defend your sect at length, took it very badly that people often raised as objections to him in his discussions the utterly depraved morals of the Elect, who lived here and there as vagabonds in a very wicked manner. He desired, therefore, if it were possible, to gather into his home and to support by his resources all those who were prepared to live a life in accord with their commandments. For he was a man with no small contempt for money and a man of more than average wealth. But he complained that his great efforts were hindered by the corruption of the bishops by whose help he had to carry out his project. Meanwhile, there was a certain bishop of yours, a man who was clearly, as I myself experienced, an uneducated peasant, but somehow or other he seemed stricter in observing good morals because of that very toughness. This man seized upon him as someone whom he had long desired and at last had present; he explained to the man what he wanted. The bishop praised him and agreed. He chose to be the first to live in his house. After he did this, all of the Elect who could be found in Rome assembled there. When the rule of life from the letter of Mani was proposed, many found it intolerable and left. But out of shame, nonetheless, more than a few remained. They began to live as they had chosen and as so great an authority had prescribed, since the Hearer in the meanwhile was forcefully compelling everyone to perform every duty, although he compelled no one to do what he himself had not first undertaken. Meanwhile, very frequent quarrels broke out among the Elect, and they hurled charges at one another, which that Hearer heard with groans. And he tried to get them to reveal themselves in their disputes through a lack of caution, and they revealed terrible and wicked things. There we found out what sort of people they were who nonetheless thought that they among all the others should undertake the rigors of those commandments. Now what should one suspect or rather what should one judge concerning the others? What more shall I say? Compelled as they were, they at times murmured that they could not endure those commandments, and from there they turned to rebellion. The Hearer defended his position with a very brief dilemma: either they should observe all those commandments or they should regard as a complete fool the man who had given such commandments under such a condition that no one could carry them out. The utterly unbridled outcry of the many nonetheless overcame — nothing else could have happened — the opinion of the one man. After this the bishop himself gave in and ran off in great disgrace. For, contrary to the rule, his food was in fact brought to him, which he received in secret although it was frequently discovered, since he had a large amount of money available to him from his own carefully hidden purse.

75. If you say that these claims are false, you are resisting plain facts and ones commonly known. But I wish that you would say this. For, since these facts are so clear and very easily known to those who want to know them, we can understand to what extent those who deny that they are true are accustomed to speaking the truth. But you use other defenses that I do not attack. For you either say that there are some people who do observe your commandments and that they ought not to have accusations against the others poured out on them, or you say that one should not complain at all about the character of those who profess the teaching of your sect but about the character of the teaching they profess. I accept both of these, although you cannot point out either those faithful observers of the commandments or acquit your heresy of so many and such great absurdities and crimes. Still, I earnestly ask you why you attack Christians who bear the name "Catholic" with curses when you see some of them living a bad life? For concerning your own people you either impudently deny that there is any question or even more impudently do not deny that there is and want us to understand that in that small number of you there are hidden some persons or other who keep their commandments, while you do not want to admit this of the great multitude of Catholics.

The Two Souls

(De duabus animabus)

Introduction

The Two Souls (*De duabus animabus*) was written between 391 and 395 during the years when Augustine was a priest. The work is an argument against the Manichean theory of human nature, which, as Augustine understood it, held that there were two souls in each human being, one a part of the substance of God or of the kingdom of light and the other a part of the substance of evil or of the kingdom of darkness. Scholars question whether the Manicheans explicitly held a theory of two souls and claim that it would be more correct to say that they claimed that there were in each of us a soul, which was a part of the good substance or the kingdom of light, and a body, which was a part of the evil substance or the kingdom of darkness.[1] Augustine, on the other hand, could certainly defend his position on the grounds that the Manichean nation of darkness was populated with all sorts of living, sentient, and intelligent beings that performed the sort of activities that soulless bodies cannot perform.

Augustine's definitions of will and of sin in *The Two Souls* were later used against him by the Pelagians and especially by Julian of Eclanum, who in his long work, *To Florus*, used the two definitions to show that there could not be any sin in an infant who did not have free will and that the natural sin, which Augustine defended against the Pelagians, smacked of Manicheanism. In his *Unfinished Work in Answer to Julian*, especially in book five, Augustine replied to Julian's charges, but the rather lengthy comments in his *Revisions* also supply the necessary qualifications to what Augustine wrote in *The Two Souls*.

Augustine had led some of his best friends, such as Romanianus and Honoratus, into the Manichean heresy when he himself became a Hearer in that sect, in which he remained for over nine years. In *The Two Souls* Augustine explains to some of his lifelong friends how he would now refute the Manichean teaching on human nature by simple and clear definitions of the will and sin. He makes a touching plea to his long-standing friends who are still members of the Manichean sect to realize how untenable the Manichean view of human nature is, and in doing so he admits that two things kept him a Manichean for so long. One was the friendship of these men, who had the appearance of moral goodness, and the other was the delight that Augustine found in winning arguments with the less-well-educated Catholics.

---

1. See J. Kevin Coyle, "De duabus animabus," in *Augustine through the Ages: An Encyclopedia*, ed. by Allan D. Fitzgerald (Grand Rapids: Eerdmanns, 1999) 287-288.

Augustine begins *The Two Souls* by deploring the years during which he lingered in the Manichean sect, and he says that, if he had only realized that all life could have its source only in the one true God, he would have escaped from the snares of the Manicheans long before (paragraph 1). He continues in this remorseful vein and blames himself for not having realized the superiority of the intellect over the senses and of the objects of understanding over the objects of sensation. For, if he had done so, he would have seen that life, which we grasp by understanding and not by sensation, is superior to any objects that we perceive by the senses, including the sun and the moon, which the Manicheans regard as divine. So too, he would have seen that, if these lights come from the Father of Christ, as the Manicheans admit, any soul must also come from him (paragraph 2). Augustine accuses himself of having failed to see that the human soul with its intelligence was superior to those bodies that the Manicheans worship, and he wants to convince his friends from his Manichean days that they must admit that the light which they worship is less valuable than an evil soul, which they claim that we must flee from (paragraph 3). Even the soul of a tiny fly is capable of amazing activities which prove that it is superior to the bodily light which the Manicheans worship. For the soul of a fly is something intelligible that surpasses anything sensible (paragraph 4). Augustine faces a possible objection, namely, that injustice and intemperance, though vices, are grasped by the intellect, not by the senses, but that they are nonetheless not preferable to sensible things that we praise. He points out that not everything that we praise is preferable to everything that we blame but that each thing must be considered in its own class. Thus unjust and intemperate souls are still superior to the visible light, though such souls may be deserving of condemnation (paragraph 5). Augustine realizes, however, that the real question concerns not unjust and intemperate souls but injustice and intemperance, which as objects of understanding ought to be preferable to any sensible objects. Why are the vices, then, not ascribed to God as their author? Augustine undertakes a lengthy argument to show that, when light is decreased, we do not see the decrease but the lesser light. So too, virtue is like an intelligible light, and vice is the absence of virtue, and, just as a decrease in light is not properly something visible, so an absence of virtue or a vice is not properly something intelligible (paragraph 6). Augustine argues that, though intelligible souls are to be preferred to sensible bodies, the defects of souls, though known by the intellect, cannot be preferred to the defects of bodies, for defects are like mere negations. Yet he insists that it is worse to lack virtue than to suffer some bodily lack (paragraph 7). Hence, if the Manicheans maintain that any bright body comes from God, they ought also to admit that all life and hence all souls come from God, and they ought to prefer any soul, however vicious, to any body, however excellent (paragraph 8).

Augustine now insists that the Manicheans should admit that whatever exists comes from God. If they produce passages from the gospel, such as Christ's words to certain Jews, *You do not come from God* (Jn 8:47), he tells them that he will produce other passages that say just the opposite, such as Paul's words, *All things come from God* (1 Cor 11:12). He urges his Manichean friends to seek out with him a teacher who could resolve the apparent conflicts so that they might see that a person who is a living sinner comes from God insofar as he is living but does not come from God insofar as he is a sinner (paragraph 9). The Manicheans might perhaps ask where sins come from. Augustine chides them for trying to appear as if they know something by raising difficult questions and admits that he himself acted in that manner when he was with them. He asks them to admit that nothing can live without God if nothing can be bright without God, and he hopes that they might go on from there to know God, who is the highest good, though he concedes that it is a difficult task (paragraph 10). Augustine confesses that two factors kept him with the Manicheans. One was a sort of camaraderie with many of the Manicheans who maintained an appearance of moral goodness, while the other was that he enjoyed besting Christians with arguments that he got from the Manicheans, which led him to approve as true whatever they said (paragraph 11). Augustine admits that, when he was a Manichean, he could not distinguish sensible things from intelligible ones, but he wonders how he could have been so blind that he did not realize that sin could exist only in the will (paragraph 12). There is no need to worry about the distinction between intelligible and sensible things. It is enough for Augustine's purposes that a person admit that he is living and wills to live, which are points about which one cannot be mistaken (paragraph 13). Hence, Augustine defines will as "a movement of the soul, with nothing forcing it either not to lose something or to acquire something," and he wonders why, when he was a Manichean, he could not have grasped this obvious concept (paragraph 14). Before turning this definition against the Manicheans, Augustine adds a definition of sin, which he refers to as "the will to retain or to acquire what justice forbids and from which one is free to hold back." He admits that this concept too is obvious, and he asks himself how he could have supposed that there could be any sin without freedom of the will (paragraph 15). These two definitions destroy the whole heresy of the Manicheans in a few short but unbeatable arguments. For they hold that human beings have two souls. One of these souls is good and comes from God in such a way that it is a part of his substance. The other soul is evil and does not belong to God in any way. The Manicheans maintain that these two souls, which were once distinct, are now mingled with each other. Hence, Augustine asks whether the evil soul possessed a will before it was mingled with the good. If it did not, it was sinless, but if it was evil without a will, it was evil in the sense that it would corrupt what was good. In that case, however, the good soul, which is the highest good, could be corrupted. But if the evil soul had a will, it had the movement of the soul, with nothing forcing it either not to lose something or to acquire something. And this something was either good or at least thought to be good. Otherwise it could not be desired. How, then, could the greatest evil desire the good before it was in any way mingled with the good? If the greatest evil desired to do harm to the good, it had to do this for some good of its own. If the greatest evil knew the good, the greatest evil had an excellent mind. Hence, Augustine shows that there are great goods in the greatest evil (paragraph 16). He asks the Manicheans whether God condemns any souls. If he does not condemn any, then he does not judge souls on the basis of merit, and the world is governed not by providence but by chance. But no religion is going to deny God's providence. Hence, God either condemns some souls for their sins or there are no sins. But if there are no sins, there is no evil, and Manicheanism is done with. Hence, the Manicheans must agree that God condemns some souls, and these souls must be evil not by nature but by will. And so the souls which the Manicheans say are evil by nature do not exist (paragraph 17).

Turning to the good kind of soul, Augustine tells the Manicheans that it would be better if a soul recognized its proper rank and saw that, since it changed so often, it could not be the highest good, which is immutable. Souls cannot sin by reason of the fact that they are not what they cannot be. For this reason the evil souls, which the Manicheans say exist, cannot sin and do not exist at all. Hence, if there are sins, the Manicheans can ascribe them only to the good souls, which are the substance of God. Christ, they must admit, promised the forgiveness of sins. But if he forgives the sins of the evil souls, they can become good and inherit the kingdom of God. If he forgives the sins of the good souls, then those souls and only those souls sin (paragraph 18). As evidence for the existence of the two kinds of souls, the Manicheans had appealed to the fact that, in deliberating, our assent turns now to the good side and now to the evil side. Augustine asks why this is not rather a sign that a single soul can be carried by free will from one side to the other (paragraph 19). Even if we were to grant to the Manicheans that we are enticed to evil by some inferior kind of soul, it would not follow that such inferior souls are evil by nature or that the higher souls are the highest good. It is possible that the inferior souls became evil by their own will and that they can become good again (paragraph 20). Hence, deliberation offers us no evidence for the existence of the two kinds of souls. In any case no one can fail to know what Augustine stated about the will and about sin, and that is sufficient to prove that the heresy of the Manicheans is false (paragraph 21).

Augustine next turns to the question of repentance and asks to which kind of soul repentance belongs. It cannot belong to the kind of soul that cannot do evil or to the kind of soul that cannot do good. Repentance shows that the one who repents did evil but could have done good. The Manicheans must either deny the benefit of repenting, in which case they cease to be Christians, or stop teaching that there are two souls, one which does nothing evil and the other which does nothing good, in which case they cease to be Manicheans (paragraph 22). Augustine is just as sure that the Manicheans are in error as he is that he should repent of his sins. Anyone who admits the benefit of repenting cannot be a Manichean (paragraph 23). Finally, Augustine appeals to his dear Manichean friends and tells them that the ideas he proposes to them are more certain than those that he and they learned from the Manicheans. He ends with a prayer that God will not allow his long-standing friends who are still Manicheans to remain in disagreement with him over the worship of God (paragraph 24).

Revisions I, 15 (16)

The Two Souls in Answer to the Manicheans, One Book

1. After this book I wrote, while still a priest, *The Two Souls in Answer to the Manicheans*. They say that one of these souls is a part of God and that the other comes from the nation of darkness, which God has not created and which is coeternal with God, and they say in their madness that these two souls, the one good and the other evil, are present in one human being. They say that the latter, that is, the evil soul, is proper to the flesh and that the flesh belongs to the nation of darkness, but they say that the former, the good soul, comes from a part of God that has come here and has fought with the nation of darkness and mingled the two. They ascribe all the good in a human being to that good soul and all the evil to that evil soul. In this book I said, "There is no life whatever that, because it is life and insofar as it is life, does not belong to the highest source and principle of life."[1] I said this in the sense that a creature should be understood to belong to the creator, but not, however, in the sense that it should be thought to be a part of God.

2. Likewise I said, "Sin is found nowhere except in the will."[2] The Pelagians can suppose that this was said in their favor on account of the infants who they deny have a sin that is forgiven them in baptism because they do not yet have the use of the choice of the will. They suppose that the sin that we say they contract from Adam because of their origin, that is, insofar as they are held implicated in his guilt and for this reason subject to punishment, could not exist anywhere but in the will, that is, in the will by which the sin was committed when Adam transgressed the commandment of God.

One can also suppose that this statement is false, in which we said, "A sin is found nowhere except in the will," because the apostle said, *But if I do what I do not will, it is no longer I who do it but the sin that dwells in me* (Rom 7:20). For this will is so far from being in the will that he says, *I do what I do not will*. How, then, is sin found nowhere but in the will? But this sin about which the apostle spoke in this way is called sin precisely because it was caused by sin and is the punishment of sin, since he says this about concupiscence of the flesh, as he reveals in the following verses: *I know that the good does not dwell in me, that is, in my flesh. For I can will the good, but I cannot bring it to perfection.* (Rom 7:18) For the perfection of goodness means that the desire for sin to which one does not consent when one lives a good life does not exist in a human being. Yet

---

1. *The Two Souls* 1, 1.
2. *Ibid.* 9, 12.

one does not bring the good to perfection because there is still the concupiscence against which the will fights. The guilt of this concupiscence is forgiven in baptism, but the weakness remains, and, until it is healed, every believer who is making progress fights against it with very great earnestness. But the sin that exists nowhere but in the will should especially be understood as that upon which just condemnation follows. For this sin *entered the world through one man* (Rom 5:12), though the sin by which one consents to concupiscence of the flesh is also committed only by the will. On this account I also said in another place, "One sins only by the will."[3]

3. Likewise, I defined the will in another place where I said, "The will is a movement of the soul, with nothing forcing it either to lose something or to acquire something."[4] This was said in order to distinguish by this definition one who wills from one who does not will and to direct attention to those who, as the first, were the origin of evil for the human race when in paradise they sinned with nothing forcing them, that is, when they sinned by free will, because they knowingly went against the commandment and that tempter persuaded them to do this and did not force them. For someone who has sinned unknowingly can appropriately be said to have sinned against his will, although he still willingly did what he did unknowingly. In that way even his sin could not be without will. This will was, of course, defined in this way: it was "a movement of the soul, with nothing forcing it either not to lose something or to acquire something." A person has not been forced to do what he would not have done if he had not willed to. He did it because he willed to, therefore, even if he did not sin because he willed to, since he did not know that what he did was a sin. In that way even such a sin could not exist without the will—but the will to do the action, not the will to commit the sin, though the action was a sin. For this action that ought not to have been done was done. But whoever knowingly sins if he can without sin resist what is forcing him to sin and, nonetheless, does not do so certainly sins willingly. But if someone cannot resist desire with a good will and for this reason acts contrary to the commandments of righteousness, this is now sin in the sense that it is also the punishment of sin. Hence, it is completely true that sin cannot exist without the will.

4. Likewise, the definition of sin in which we said that "sin is the will to retain or to acquire what justice forbids and from which one is free to hold back"[5] is true because the sin that is only a sin was defined, not the sin that is also the punishment of sin. For, when a sin is such that it is also the punishment of sin, to what extent does the will still have power under the dominance of passion, unless perhaps, if it is pious, it asks for help? For it is free to the extent that it has

---

3. Ibid. 10,14.
4. Ibid.
5. Ibid. 11, 15; see also *Unfinished Work in Answer to Julian* I, 104.

been set free, and to that extent it is called will. Otherwise, the whole of it should properly be called passion rather than will, though it is not an addition from another nature, as the Manicheans foolishly think, but a defect in our nature from which our nature is healed only by the grace of the savior. And if someone says that this passion is nothing but will, but a defective will and one enslaved to sin, one should not be opposed to this, nor should there be a quarrel about words when there is agreement about facts. For in this way as well it is shown that there is no sin either in action or in origin without the will.

5. Again, I said, "I had begun to ask whether, before that evil kind of soul was mingled with the good, it had some will. For, if it did not, it was sinless and innocent and, for this reason, in no way evil."[6] Why, then, they ask, do you say that infants, whose will you do not regard as guilty, have any sin? The answer is that they are considered guilty not because of their personal will but because of their origin. For in terms of his origin what is every human being but Adam? But Adam surely had a will, and, when he sinned by that will, through him sin entered the world.[7]

6. Likewise, I said, "Souls can in no way be evil by nature."[8] If someone asks how we understand the words of the apostle, *We were also children of wrath, just like the others* (Eph 2:3), we reply that in these words of mine I wanted that nature to be understood that is properly called nature, that in which we were created without any defect. For on account of our origin this present nature is called nature, and its origin surely has a defect, which is contrary to nature.

And again, in my words, "It is the height of injustice and insanity to hold someone guilty of sin because he did not do what he could not do."[9] Why, then, they ask, are infants held guilty? The answer is that they are held guilty because of their origin from the one who did not do what he could do, that is, keep the commandment of God.

But I said, "Whatever those souls do, if they do it by nature and not by will, that is, if they lack the free movement of the soul both to do it and not to do it, and if, finally, they are given no ability to refrain from their action, we cannot maintain any sin on their part."[10] The question of infants does not raise a problem in that regard, since they are held guilty because of the origin of the one who sinned by his will when he did not lack "the free movement of the will to do it or not to do it." And he had the full ability to refrain from the evil action. The Manicheans do not say this about the nation of darkness which they introduced as part of their myth, and they contend that that nature was always evil and never was good.

---

6. *The Two Souls* 12, 16; see also *Unfinished Work in Answer to Julian* I, 104; *Expositions of the Psalms* 58, 18.
7. See Rom 5:12.
8. *The Two Souls* 12,17.
9. Ibid.
10. Ibid.

7. One can, however, also ask how I said: "Even if souls are assigned to bodily duties not because of sin but by nature—something that is for the present unclear—and even if, though they are inferior, they still touch us by some internal nearness, those souls should not be considered evil on the grounds that we are evil when we follow them and love bodies."[11] For I said this about the souls about which I had begun to speak previously, when I said, "And yet, even if we grant them that we are enticed to shameful acts by the other inferior kind of souls, they do not conclude from this either that these inferior souls are evil by nature or that those higher souls are the highest good."[12] For I continued the discussion concerning these souls up to the place where I said, "Even if souls are assigned to bodily duties not because of sin but by nature—something that is for the present unclear," and so on. One can, therefore, ask why I said, "something that is for the present unclear," since I certainly ought not to have had any doubt that such souls do not exist. But I said this because I know by experience that there are some people who say that the devil and his angels are good in their kind and in that nature in which God created them in their proper order, such as they are, but that it is bad for us if we are enticed and misled by them, while, if we avoid them and conquer them, it is honorable and glorious for us. And those who say this think that they use suitable testimonies from the scriptures to prove this, such as the passage in the Book of Job where the devil is described: *This is the beginning of the work of the Lord that he produced as a plaything for his angels* (Job 11:14), or the passage: *The dragon that you made as a plaything* (Ps 104:26). In order not to make the book longer than I wanted, I did not at that time want to consider and resolve this question, which needed to be taken up and dealt with not in opposition to the Manicheans who do not hold this but in opposition to the others who do hold this. For I saw that, even if this were granted, the Manicheans still ought to be and can now be refuted, when they introduce in their insane error a nature of evil that is coeternal with the good. For this reason I said, "something that is for the present unclear," not because I was in doubt about this but because the question between me and the people who had held these ideas was not yet resolved. Yet I did resolve this question in other and much later books of mine, *The Literal Meaning of Genesis*,[13] with as much clarity as I could.

8. In another passage I said, "We sin when we love bodily things because we are commanded by justice to love spiritual things and by nature we can, and, if we do love them, we are then the best and happiest in our kind."[14] Here someone can ask why I said that we can do this by nature and not by grace. But against the Manicheans the question turned on nature. And grace, of course, brings it about

---

11. Ibid. 13, 20.
12. Ibid.
13. *The Literal Meaning of Genesis* XI, 20-21.
14. *The Two Souls* 13,20.

that, once healed, nature can do through him who *came to seek and to save what was lost* (Lk 19:10; Mt 18:11) what it could not do when it was injured. Still, I then called to mind that grace and prayer for my friends who were still caught in that deadly error. I said, "Great God, almighty God, God of the highest goodness, whom it is right to believe and to understand to be inviolable and incorruptible, God three and one, whom the Catholic Church worships, I beg you as a supplicant, who has experienced your mercy toward me: Do not permit the men with whom I was in perfect agreement from boyhood on to disagree with me in our worship of you."[15] When I prayed in that way, I of course already held in faith not only that those who have been converted to God are helped by his grace to make progress and to attain perfection, where it can still be said that this grace is given them in accord with the merit of their conversion, but also that they may be converted to God, to this very grace of God, since I prayed for those who were completely turned away from him and that they might be converted to him.

This book begins as follows: "With the help of God's mercy."

---

15. Ibid. 15, 24.

The Two Souls

1, 1. With the help of God's mercy the snares of the Manicheans have been broken and abandoned, and I have been at last restored to the bosom of the Catholic Church. Now at least I want to consider and deplore that wretchedness of mine. For there were many things that I ought to have done so that the seeds of the true religion, which were implanted in me for my salvation from my childhood, would not so easily and in a few days have been dug up and driven from my mind by the error or deceit of false and deceitful human beings. For, first of all, if by myself, and with a mind turned to God in pious supplication, I had soberly and carefully considered the two kinds of souls to which they assign individual and proper natures, wanting one to be understood to be of the very substance of God, while God is not even accepted as the creator of the other, it would perhaps have been clear to me, had I done so, that there is no life of any sort that does not belong — by the very fact that it is life and insofar as it is life at all — to the highest source and principle of life. And we can confess that this is nothing other than the sovereign, one, and true God. Hence, the souls that the Manicheans call evil either lack life and are not souls, do not will or refuse anything, and do not desire anything or flee from anything, or, if they are living, so that they can be souls and do the sort of things that they imagine, they live only because of life. And if it were clear, as it is, that Christ said, *I am the life* (Jn 14:6), we would admit that there is no reason why all souls would not have been created and made by Christ, that is, by *the life*, since souls can only exist by living.

2, 2. At that time my thought was unable to endure and sustain the question about life itself and about participation in life. For this is certainly an important question and one requiring much calm discussion among those who are very learned. But I could perhaps have been able to see something that is perfectly evident to any person who considers the matter well without taking sides, namely, that everything that we are said to know and to be aware of is something grasped by either a sense of the body or by the intelligence. But who save someone ungracious or wicked would not grant me that the senses of the body are commonly counted as five — sight, hearing, smell, taste, and touch — and that intelligence far surpasses and is much more excellent than all these? Once this has been established and affirmed, it follows that all the things that are perceived by touch or sight or in a bodily manner by any other sense are as inferior to the things that we attain by understanding as we see that the senses are inferior to the intelligence. No life and, for this reason, no soul can be perceived by any sense of the body but only by the intellect, and the Manicheans themselves also say that the sun and the moon and every light that is seen by these mortal eyes are to be attributed to the true and good God. Hence, it is the height of madness to proclaim that what we see by means of the body belongs to God but to think that we should remove and separate from the same God, who is its author, what we grasp not merely by the soul but by the very summit of the soul, namely, by the mind and by the intelligence — I mean life of whatever sort it may be said to be, but life nonetheless. For, if I called upon God and asked myself what it is to live, and how removed it is from every sense of the body, and how absolutely incorporeal it is, would I be unable to reply? Or would the Manicheans not also admit that the souls that they detest not only live but live immortally? Would they not admit that what Christ said, *Let the dead bury their dead* (Mt 8:22), was said not about those who are not living at all but about sinners? For this alone is the death of an immortal soul. As Paul writes, *A widow who is living in pleasure is dead* (1 Tm 5:6). He said that at the same time she had died and was living. Hence, I should have paid attention not to the extent to which a sinful soul lives more shamefully but only to the fact that it lives. But if I could have perceived this only by the understanding, I think it would have come to my mind that any soul should be preferred to the light that we perceive through these eyes to the same extent that we prefer the intelligence to those very eyes.

2, 3. But the Manicheans affirm that that light also comes from the Father of Christ. Should I have doubted, then, that any given soul came from him? But not even a man as ignorant and young as I was would have had any doubt that not only the soul but also any body whatsoever came from him, if I had piously and carefully considered what form was or what it was to be formed, what beauty was and what it was to be endowed with beauty, and finally which of these was the cause of which.

3, 3. But I am saying nothing for the time being about the body. My complaint is about the soul, about its spontaneous and quick movement, its activity, life, and immortality. My complaint, finally, is that in my great misery I believed that something could have had all these in some other way than by the goodness of God, because I paid insufficient attention to how great they were. I think that I should groan and weep over this. I should have pondered these ideas within myself; I should have discussed them with myself; I should have referred them to others; I should have asked myself what the power of understanding was and how there was nothing in a human being that we could compare to its excellence. Once people had — if only they were human! — granted me this, I would have asked whether to see with these eyes was to understand. Once they had said that it was not, I would first have concluded that the intelligence of the mind was much to be preferred to the sensation of these eyes; then I would have added that we must necessarily judge to be better what we have perceived by means of something better. Who would not have granted this? Hence, I would have gone on to ask whether the soul that they call evil was perceived by these eyes or was understood by the mind. They would have admitted that it was understood by the mind. When all these points had been brought together and been agreed upon between us, I would have shown what we had established, namely, that the soul which they regarded as evil was better than this light which they venerated, since that soul was known by the mind's intellect, while this light was known by the body's sense. But here they would perhaps have hesitated and refused to follow the guidance of reason. So powerful is the force of longstanding opinions and of a false doctrine that has long been defended and believed! But I would have insisted more with them while they hesitated — but not harshly, nor childishly, nor obstinately. I would have repeated the points that they had granted and I would have shown how they should have granted these others. I would have urged them to consult together in common and to see at least which of them we needed to deny. Did they think that it was false that the intellect was to be preferred to the eyes of the flesh? Or did they think that it was false that what is known by the excellence of the mind was more excellent than what is known by a lowly sense of the body? Or did they refuse to admit that the souls that they believed to be of a foreign nature could be known only by understanding, that is, by the excellence of the mind? Or did they want to deny that the sun and the moon were known only by these eyes? But if they had seen that none of these could be denied without the greatest absurdity and impudence, I would have persuaded them that they must not doubt that this light, which they preached should be worshiped, was of less value than that soul, which they warned that we must flee from.

4, 4. And here, if they had perhaps been disturbed and had asked me whether I thought that even the soul of a fly was superior to this light, I would have replied that it was; and a fly would not have bothered me because of its smallness but would have supported me because it was alive. For we are seeking what enlivens those members which are so tiny, what leads so small a body back and forth in accord with its natural appetite, what rhythmically moves its feet when it runs, what governs and moves its wings when it flies. Whatever it is, for those who consider it well, it stands out as so great in something so small that it is preferable to any brightness that strikes the eyes.

5, 4. Certainly no one doubts that, whatever it is, it is something intelligible, which by the laws of God surpasses everything sensible and therefore even this light. After all, I ask, what do we perceive by thought if we do not perceive that it is one thing to understand by the mind and another to sense through the body, and that that former act differs from this latter by its incomparable sublimity, and that, for this reason, intelligible objects cannot fail to be preferred to sensible ones, since the intellect itself is so much preferred to the senses?

5, 5. From this I would also perhaps have come to know what clearly followed, namely, how it happened that, since injustice and intemperance and the other vices of the soul were not perceived by the senses but were grasped by the understanding, these vices, which we detest and judge should be condemned, were able, because they were intelligible, to surpass this light, though it was something praiseworthy in its own kind. For it occurs to a mind that properly subjects itself to God that, first, not everything that we praise should be preferred to everything that we blame. After all, it does not follow that, because I praise the purest lead, I value it for this reason more than gold with which I ought to find fault. Each thing must be considered in its own kind. I disapprove of a lawyer who is ignorant of many laws, but I still esteem him so much more than a highly experienced tailor that I do that even think that the comparison should be made. I praise the tailor because he is very well trained in his own art, but I rightly criticize the lawyer because he carries out his profession less well.

From this I ought to have discovered that this light is rightly praised because it is perfect in its proper kind. But, because it is included in the number of sensible things, which is the class that must yield to the class of intelligible things, it should be considered inferior to unjust and intemperate souls, because these souls are intelligible, though it is no injustice that we judge those souls most worthy of condemnation. For in those souls we look for their reconciliation with God, not for their being preferable to this brightness. Hence, if anyone had contended that this light came from God, I would not have opposed him, but I would have said that it was more necessary that souls, even vicious ones — not insofar as they are vicious but insofar as they are souls — confess that God is their creator.

6, 6. One of those people who was cautious and alert, and also more studious than stubborn, might have warned me that the question must be posed not about vicious souls but about the vices themselves. For, since the vices are not known by the senses of the body but still are known, they can only be taken to be intelligible objects. And if these surpass all sensible objects, why have we agreed that light should be ascribed to God as its author, though only someone sacrilegious would say that God is the author of vices? I would have replied to that person, if God had immediately and suddenly made the answer to this question clear to me, as often happens to good worshipers of God, or if I had had an answer prepared beforehand. And if I had neither merited nor been capable of either of these, I would have postponed what I had begun, and I would have admitted that what was set before us was difficult and arduous to discern. I would have returned to myself; I would have prostrated myself before God; I would have groaned deeply, asking that he would not allow me to be stuck in the middle ground to which I had advanced by unassailable arguments. Otherwise, I would have been forced by the unresolved question to subject and subordinate intelligible things to sensible ones or to say that he was the author of vices, though each of these was utterly false and impious. In no way could I think that God would have abandoned me when I was so disposed. He would instead have admonished me in those ineffable ways of his to consider again and again whether the vices of the soul over which I had been thrown into confusion should be counted among intelligible objects. In order to find this out, on account of the feebleness of my inner eye, which rightly befell me because of my sins, I would have devised a kind of stairway for myself in those sensible things in order to come to see those invisible ones. Though the knowledge of those sensible things is by no means more certain for us, our familiarity with them inspires more confidence. And so I would have immediately asked what properly pertained to the sense of the eyes. I would have found colors, among which this light would have held the chief place. After all, they are what no other sense attains. For, though the motions of bodies, their sizes, the places between them, and their shapes are perceived by the eyes, they are not perceived by them as their proper objects, since they can also be perceived by touch. From this I would have inferred that light surpasses the other bodily and sensible things as much as sight is more noble than the other senses. And so, having chosen from all the things that are perceived by the body this light, by which I would have tried to and in which I would necessarily have located that stairway for my investigation, I would have gone on to pay attention to what I should have done in this way, and I would have discussed these ideas with myself. If this sun, which is seen with such great brightness and is sufficient for the light of day, decreased little by little in our sight to the point of being like the moon, would we perceive anything else by the eyes than a light that is somewhat bright? For we would still be seeking light because we would not see the light that had been, and we would be drawing in light because we would see the light that was present. We would not see that decrease in light, therefore, but the light that remained from the decrease. But since we would not see that decrease, we would not sense it; for whatever we sense by sight cannot fail to be seen. Hence, if that decrease were not sensed by sight or by any other sense, it could not be counted among sensible things. After all, nothing that cannot be sensed is sensible.

Let us, therefore, apply this consideration to virtue. For we say with the greatest propriety that the soul is resplendent with the intelligible light of virtue. Now, a certain decrease in this light, which does not destroy the soul but darkens it, is called a vice. A vice of the soul, then, can by no means be correctly counted among intelligible things, just as a decrease in light is correctly removed from the number of sensible things. Nonetheless, that which remains of the soul, that is, the fact that it lives and is a soul, is something intelligible, just as that which is still bright in this visible light after a decrease of whatever amount is something sensible. And for this reason the soul, insofar as it is a soul and participates in life, without which it could in no way be a soul, is most correctly preferred to all sensible things. Hence, it is a mark of the greatest error to say that any soul does not come from God, from whom you boast that the sun and the moon come.

6, 7. But you might have wanted to call all those things sensible — not only those that we sense but also those that we still make out by means of the body, though not by sensing them. In this way we make out darkness with our eyes and silence with our ears. For we come to know darkness by not seeing and silence by not hearing. And again, you might want to call intelligible not only the things that we see when our mind is enlightened, such as wisdom itself, but also the things from which we turn away by the privation of this enlightenment, such as lack of wisdom, which we have appropriately called a darkness of the mind. If so, I would not have raised an argument over a word. I would instead have resolved the whole question by an easy distinction, and I would have immediately proved for those who were paying close attention that intelligible substances are preferred to sensible substances by the divine and inviolate law of the truth, but not the defects of those substances, although we might want to call the former defects intelligible and the latter ones sensible. Hence, those who admit that these visible lights and those intelligible souls are substances are in every way forced to grant and to attribute those loftier positions to souls, but the defects of each kind cannot be preferred to one another. For they only take something away and do not indicate any being, because they have exactly the same force as mere negations. For, when we say, "It is not gold," and "It is not virtue," though there is a big difference between gold and virtue, there is still no difference between the negations that we added to them. It is worse, however, that virtue does not exist than that gold does not exist. No sane person has any doubt about this. But who would fail to understand that this is the case not on account of the negations but on account of the things to which the negations are added? For, as preferable as gold is to virtue, so much more wretched is it to lack virtue than gold. Hence, since intelligible things surpass sensible things, we are right to tolerate a defect in intelligible things less easily than in sensible things, since we value more dearly or less dearly not those defects but the things that have the defect. From this we see that a defect of life, which is intelligible, is much more miserable than a defect of this sensible light for the very reason that life which is understood is much more valuable than the light which is seen.

6, 8. Since this is so, will anyone dare to refuse to grant that any souls, which of course are only souls because they are living, come from God, when he attributes to God the sun and the moon and whatever shines in the stars — whatever, finally, shines in this fire of ours and in this visible earthly light? For life surpasses this light by so much. And although that person speaks the truth who says, "Insofar as it is bright, it comes from God," shall I, then, O great God, be lying if I say, "Insofar as it lives, it is from God"? Please, let the blindness of the mind and the punishments of souls not increase to the point that human beings fail to understand these things! But, however great their error or stubbornness might have been, I believe that — relying on and armed with these arguments, after I had presented to them the issue that had been so carefully weighed and examined and after I had calmly conferred with them — I would have been afraid that I would not have thought any one of them to be a person of substance if he had tried to subordinate or even to compare the intellect or those things that are perceived by the intellect — though not through a defect — to a bodily sense and to the things that pertain in a similar way to the knowledge of the same sense. Once that had been established, when would he or anyone have dared to deny that souls, however evil they might have wanted them to be, were still included among the number of intelligible things because they were souls and that they were not understood through a defect? For they would not have been souls save insofar as they lived. After all, though they were understood to be vicious by reason of a defect, since they were vicious because of a lack of virtue, they were still not souls by reason of a defect, for they were souls because they were living. Nor is it possible that the presence of life is the cause of their failure, since anything fails to the extent that it is abandoned by life.

6, 9. Since it would have been perfectly evident, therefore, that no souls could be separated from the author from whom this light is not separated, I would not accept now whatever they might have brought forth, and I would instead have warned them to follow, along with me, those who proclaimed that everything that existed, whatever it was, because it was, and to the extent that it was, came from the one God.

7,9. They would have read out against me the words of the gospel: *You do not hear because you do not come from God; you come from your father, the devil* (Jn 8:47.44). I for my part would have read out against them: *All things were made through him, and without him nothing has been made* (Jn 1:3), and the words of the apostle: *There is one God from whom all things are, and one Lord Jesus Christ through whom all things are* (1 Cor 8:6); and, once more, the words of the same apostle: *From whom are all things, through whom are all things, in whom are all things, to him be glory* (Rom 11:36). And I would have urged these men—at least if I had found them to be men — that we should not have presumed that we had already ascertained something but that we should instead have sought teachers who would have demonstrated the peace and harmony between these statements, which seem to conflict with one another. For,[16] by one and the same authority of scripture, though in one place it says, *All things come from God* (1 Cor 11:12), elsewhere it says, *You do not come from God* (Jn 8:47). Since it would have been wicked to condemn the holy books rashly, who would not have seen that we had to find a learned teacher who knew the answer to this question? Of course, if he had been a man of good understanding and a spiritual person (as is said by God[17]), since he would necessarily have favored the true arguments concerning the intelligible and sensible natures that I had

16. I have followed the PL reading of *nam* instead of *non,* which is found in CSEL.
17. See 1 Cor 2:15.

examined and discussed as well as I could, he would in fact have explained them much better and in a way more suitable for teaching. We would have heard nothing else from him on this question but how it was not possible that any kind of souls do not come from God, although it was rightly said to sinners and unbelievers: *You do not come from God*. For we too could perhaps have easily seen, once we had implored the help of God, that to live was something other than to sin and that, although a life in sins was called death in comparison with a righteous life,[18] both could still be found in one human being, so that such a person would be both living and a sinner. But the fact that he is living comes from God, while the fact that he is a sinner does not come from God. In this distinction we use that side of the two which fits our intention, so that, when we want to convey the omnipotence of God the creator, we say even to sinners that they come from God. We say this, after all, to beings that are contained in some species; we say this to beings with souls; we say this to rational beings; finally—and this is especially relevant — we say this to living beings, since all these are of themselves gifts of God. But when our purpose is to blame bad people, we are right to say, *You do not come from God*. For we say this to those who turn away from the truth, to unbelievers, to criminals, to evil-doers, and — to use one word for them all — to sinners. Who, after all, doubts that none of these come from God? And so, why is it surprising that, in blaming the very fact that they were sinners and did not believe in him, Christ said, *You do not come from God*, though on the other side these statements are perfectly true: *All things were made through him* and *All things come from God*? For, if not to believe in Christ, to reject the coming of Christ, and not to receive Christ are certain signs of souls that do not belong to God, and if for this reason it was said, *You do not hear because you do not come from God* (Jn 8:47), how is that cry of the apostle true, when he said at the memorable beginning of the gospel, *He came unto his own, and his own did not receive him* (Jn 1:11)? How would they have been his own if they did not receive him? Or how would they not have been his own because they did not receive him, if not because human sinners belong to God insofar as they are human beings but belong to the devil insofar as they are sinners? The one, then, who says, *His own did not receive him*, takes the side of nature, but the other who said, *You do not come from God*, takes the side of the will. For the evangelist was praising the works of God; Christ was rebuking the sins of human beings.

8, 10. Here perhaps someone might say: Where do sins come from and where in general do evils come from? If they come from a human being, where does the human being come from? If from an angel, where does the angel come from? When one says that angels and human beings come from God, although one speaks correctly and truthfully, those who are uneducated and less capable of clearly seeing hidden matters think that evils and sins are linked to God as if by a

---

18. See 1Tm 5:6.

sort of chain. On this question the Manicheans think that they reign like kings, as if to ask a question were the same as to know something. Would that it were! No one would be found to have more knowledge than I. But somehow or other the person who poses a big question in an argument often takes on the guise of a great teacher, and generally he is less learned than the person he frightens on the issue about which he frightens him. And so these people think that they are better than the masses because they first ask questions about what they, along with the masses, do not know. But suppose that they had raised this as an objection for me when I was producing these arguments at the time when I was with them, not as I have now been for a long time, for I now regret how I acted. I would have said:

"Please, for the time being recognize with me something that is very easy: If nothing can be bright without God, much less can anything live without God. Otherwise, we would abide in such monstrous opinions that we would proclaim that some souls or other have life that is not from God. In that way it will perhaps turn out that we shall learn either together or sometime and in some order what neither you nor I know, namely, where evil comes from. What am I saying? After all, can a human being attain a knowledge of the greatest evil without a knowledge of the highest good? For we would not know darkness if we were always in darkness. But the knowledge of light does not permit its contrary to go unknown. The highest good, however, is that than which nothing can be higher. But God is good, and nothing is higher than God. God is, therefore, the highest good. Let us, therefore, know God, and in that way what we were seeking in the wrong order will not escape our knowledge. Do you think that the knowledge of God involves a middling effort or merit? What other reward is promised us than eternal life, which, after all, is the knowledge of God? For God, our teacher, said, *But this is eternal life, to know you, the only and true God, and Jesus Christ whom you have sent* (Jn 17:3). For, though the soul is immortal, its turning away from the knowledge of God is nonetheless rightly said to be its death, and, when it turns back to God, it merits to attain eternal life, so that eternal life is, as I said, that knowledge. But no one can turn back to God unless he turns away from this world. I see that this is arduous and most difficult for me. If it is easy for you, God himself will decide. I would want to believe that it is. But it troubles me that, though this world, from which we are commanded to turn away, is visible, and though the apostle said, *The things that are seen are temporal, but those that are not seen are eternal* (2 Cor 4:18), you ascribe more to the judgment of these eyes than to that of the mind. For your people teach and believe that no feather is bright that is not bright because of God but that there is a living soul that is not living because of God."

These and similar things I would also have said to them or would have pondered within myself. For perhaps even then, if I had beseeched God with all my heart and had been as intent as possible upon the scriptures, I could either have said such things or — what would have been enough for salvation — have thought them.

9, 11. But two things especially that easily ensnare that incautious age wore me down by their strange paths. One of these was a friendship of sorts that somehow crept up on me under a certain appearance of goodness, like some twisted chain wrapped many times around my neck. The other was that I almost always gained a certain harmful victory when I argued in discussions with Christians, who were unlearned but still striving to defend their faith in combat, as well as each of them could. My youthful ardor increased along with this frequent success and unwisely brought[19] me by its impetus into the great evil of stubbornness. Because I had taken up this kind of disputation after becoming their Hearer, I gladly attributed to the Manicheans whatever I could accomplish in it either by whatever talent I had or by other readings. In that way my passion for debating was daily renewed as a result of their words, and my love for them was daily renewed as a result of my success in debating. From this it came about that in certain strange ways I approved as true whatever they said, not because I knew that it was true but because I wanted it to be. Thus it happened that, although I followed those men slowly and cautiously, I nonetheless followed them for a long time, preferring shiny straw to a living soul.

9, 12. It is true. I could not at that time distinguish and differentiate sensible things from those that were intelligible, that is, carnal things from spiritual ones. It was due not to age nor to teaching nor to any habit nor, finally, to any merits. For it is a matter of no small joy or happiness. But was I so unable to grasp even the idea that nature itself places within the judgment of all human beings by the laws of the sovereign God?

10, 12. After all, suppose that some people, whom no madness had already torn away from the common sense of the human race, have brought to the exercise of judgment any desires they want, any lack of learning, or any slowness. I would like to find out what they would reply to me when I ask whether they think that someone asleep commits a sin if someone else has used his hand to write something sinful. Who would doubt that they would all deny that it was a sin, and that they would shout back because perhaps they would even be angry at my having thought that they deserved such questioning? Once I had calmed them down and restored them to peace as best I could, I would ask them not to become annoyed at me when I asked another question — one that would be within everyone's range of knowledge. Then I would ask this: If by the hand of someone who was not sleeping but awake, whose other members were bound and restrained, another stronger person did something evil in a similar way, would the bound man be held guilty of a sin because he knew it, although he did not will it at all?

---

19. I have followed the reading *vergebat* in one manuscript and the BA text rather than *urgebat* in the CSEL edition.

And at this point, amazed that I would ask such a question, they would all unhesitatingly reply that this person also had committed no sin whatsoever. Why? Because, if to do something evil someone uses another person who does not know it or is unable to resist, the latter person cannot in any way be rightly condemned.

And if I asked human nature itself in those persons why this was the case, I would easily arrive at what I wanted by asking questions in this way: What is that? If the person who was asleep had already known what the other person was going to do with his hand and deliberately put himself to sleep, having also drunk rather heavily so that he would not wake up, in order that he might deceive someone by an oath, would his sleep lend any support to his innocence?[20] What else would they declare him but guilty? Why? If he was also bound willingly in order that he might similarly deceive someone by his pretended defense, what good did those chains do him for keeping him free of sin? And yet he was really not able to resist because he was restricted by them, just as the man who was asleep did not at all know what happened then. Is there, then, any reason to doubt that both would be judged to have sinned? Once these points were granted, I would draw the conclusion that sin exists nowhere but in the will, since I would have also received help from the fact that justice holds people to be sinners because of an evil will alone, even though they were unable to carry out what they willed.

10, 13. Who could say that in considering these matters I was involved in obscure and abstruse ideas, where a suspicion of either deceit or ostentation often arises on account of the small number of those who understand them? Let us set aside the distinction between intelligible and sensible things for a little while. I do not want to meet with any animosity on the grounds that I go after slow minds with the goads of subtle arguments. Just allow me to know that I am living. Just allow me to know that I will to live. If the human race agrees with these points, our will and our life are already known to us. And when we profess to have this knowledge, there is no need to fear that someone might prove that we could be mistaken. For no one can be mistaken about this unless he either is not living or wills nothing. I do not think that I have introduced anything obscure, and I fear rather that someone may think me worthy of criticism because these points are too obvious. But let us consider where all of this is leading us.

10, 14. There is no sinning, then, apart from the will. But our will is very well known to us. After all, I would not know that I willed if I did not know what the will was. And so, the will is defined in this way: The will is a movement of the soul, with nothing forcing it either not to lose something or to acquire some-

---

20. Here one has to suppose that the sleeping man's hand is moved by another to write out an oath, which he can later deny.

thing. Why, therefore, could I not define it at that time? Was it difficult to see that unwilling is the contrary of willing, as we say that left is contrary to right, not as black is contrary to white? For the same thing cannot be both black and white at the same time, but someone placed in between two persons is left of the one and right of the other. At the same time, indeed, one person is both left and right, yet at the same time one cannot in any way be both of these in relation to a single human being. In the same way one mind can certainly be willing and unwilling at the same time. For, if you ask someone who does something unwillingly whether he willed to do it, he says that he did not will to do it. Likewise, if you ask him whether he willed not to do it, he will reply that he willed this. In that way you will find that he was unwilling to do something but willing not to do it — that is, one mind that at one time has both, but in relation to two distinct things. Why do I say this? Because, if we again ask why he does this unwillingly, he will say that he was forced. For everyone who does something unwillingly is forced, and everyone who is forced does it unwillingly, if he does it.

It remains that a person who is willing is free from being forced, even if someone thinks that he is being forced. And in this way, then, everyone who does something willingly is not forced, and everyone who is not forced either does it or does not do it willingly. Since in all human beings whom we could reasonably question, from boys to old men, from grade school to the chair of the sage, nature herself proclaims these truths, why did I then not see that I should have put in the definition of the will the phrase "with nothing forcing it," which I have put there now, thanks to the great caution that has accompanied my increased experience? But if this is obvious everywhere and available to all not through teaching but from nature, what obscurity remains unless perhaps anyone is unaware that we will to have something when we will to, and that our soul is moved to this, and that we either have it or do not have it, and that, if we have it, we will to retain it, but, if we do not have it, we will to acquire it? Hence, everyone who wills wills either not to lose something or to acquire something. For this reason, if all these points are clearer than daylight, as they are, and granted by the generosity of the truth not merely to my own knowledge but to that of the human race, why could I not even at that time have stated: Will is a movement of the soul, with nothing forcing it, either not to lose something or to acquire something?

11, 15. But someone will say: And how would this have helped you against the Manicheans? Wait a moment. Allow us first to define sin. For every mind reads it as something written within itself by God that sin cannot exist without the will. Sin, therefore, is the will to retain or to acquire what justice forbids and from which one is free to hold back. And yet, if it is not free, it is not a will. But I preferred to define it in rougher terms rather than in more precise ones. Did I have to examine obscure books even on this point in order to learn that no one deserves blame or punishment who either wills what justice does not forbid him to will or does not do what he cannot do? Are not these ideas sung by shepherds in the hills, by poets in the theaters, by the unlearned at street corners, by the learned in libraries, by teachers in schools, by priests in sanctuaries, and by the human race throughout the world? But if no one is worthy of blame or condemnation if he does not act contrary to the prohibition of justice or if he does not do what he cannot do, though every sin is to be either blamed or condemned, who has any doubt that there is sin when we will what is unjust and are free not to will it? And for this reason I could have declared that definition both true and very easy to understand not only now but also then: Sin is the will to retain or to acquire what justice forbids and from which one is free to hold back.

12, 16. Come now, let us see how these points might have helped us. First of all, they would have brought the whole case to an end, so that I would have desired nothing more. For, if anyone consults the depths of his own conscience and the laws of God, which are deeply embedded in nature, interiorly within his mind where they are clearer and more certain, and concedes that these two definitions of will and of sin are true, he can condemn without any hesitation the whole heresy of the Manicheans with a very few and very short but utterly invincible arguments. This can be seen as follows. They say that there are two kinds of souls. The one is good, which comes from God in such a way that it was not made from some matter or out of nothing but is said to proceed right out of his very substance as a certain part, but the other is evil, which they believe and teach that we should believe does not belong to God in any way whatsoever. And so they proclaim that the former is the highest good but that the latter is the greatest evil and that these two kinds were once distinct but are now mingled. I had not yet heard about the nature and cause of this mixture, but I was still able to ask whether, before that evil kind of soul was mingled with the good, it had some will. For, if it did not, it was sinless and innocent and, for this reason, in no way evil. If, however, it was evil because, though it was without a will, it would, like fire, violate and corrupt the good if it touched it, what a great outrage it is to believe that the nature of evil has such power to change any part of God and that the highest good is able to be corrupted and violated!

But if it had will, a movement of the soul was truly present in it, with nothing forcing it either not to lose something or to acquire something. But this something was either good or was thought to be good. For it could not otherwise be desired. But in the greatest evil before the mingling, which the Manicheans teach, there was never any good. And so, from where could it have got some knowledge or opinion about the good? Or did the evil souls want nothing that was within them and yet desire the true good that was outside them? But this will, by which the highest and true good is desired, is excellent and should be extolled with great praise. In the greatest evil, therefore, where does a movement of the soul most worthy of such great praise come from? Or did they desire it with the desire to do it harm? First of all, the argument comes to the same conclusion. For one who wants to do harm wants to deprive another of some good for the sake of some good of his own. There was in those souls, therefore, either some knowledge or some opinion about the good, which ought in no way to exist in the greatest evil.

Next, how did they know whether that good, which was located outside of them and which they desired to harm, existed at all? If they had understood that good, what would have been more excellent than such a mind? Or is there anything else toward which a good person would make every effort to apply himself intently if not toward understanding the highest and pure good? That pure evil, therefore, was then able to attain without the help of any good what is now granted to scarcely a few good and righteous persons. But if those souls had bodies and they saw it with their eyes, how many tongues, how many hearts, how many minds are enough for praising those eyes, which the minds of the righteous can scarcely equal! What great goods we find in the greatest evil! For, if it is evil to see God, God is not a good. But God is a good. And so it is good to see God, and I do not know what can be compared to this good. But how is it possible that it is evil to be able to see what it is good to see? Hence, whoever brought it about that the divine substance could be seen by them, whether by those eyes or by those minds, has accomplished a great good and one most worthy of ineffable praise. Yet if this was not accomplished, but this evil was by itself such and everlasting, it is difficult to find anything better than it.

12, 17. Finally, as those souls have none of the praiseworthy things that they are forced to have by the arguments of the Manicheans, I would have asked whether God condemns some souls or no souls. If he condemns no souls, there is no judgment on the basis of merits and no providence, and the world is governed — or rather not governed — by chance rather than by reason. Governance, after all, should not be attributed to chance. But if it is wrong for all those who are bound by the laws of any religion to believe this, what remains is either that some souls are condemned or that there are no sins. But if there are no sins, there is also no evil. If the Manicheans say this, they will slay their own heresy with one blow. They agree with me, then, that some souls are condemned by the law and judgment of God. But if these souls are good, what sort of justice is that? If they are evil, are they evil by nature or by will? But souls can in no way be evil by nature. On what basis do we teach this? On the basis of the previous definitions of the will and of sin. For to say both that souls are evil and that there is no sin is completely mad, but to say that they sin without a will is a great delusion. And it is the height of injustice and insanity to hold someone guilty of sin because he did not do what he could not do. Hence, whatever those souls do, if they do it by nature and not by will, that is, if they lack the free movement of the soul both to do it and not to do it, and if, finally, they are given no ability to refrain from their action, we cannot maintain any sin on their part. But all admit both that evil souls are justly condemned and that those that have not sinned are unjustly condemned. They admit, then, that those who sin are evil. But, as reason has taught us, the souls that the Manicheans speak of do not sin. Hence, that strange kind of evil souls, whatever it may be, which the Manicheans introduce, does not exist.

12, 18. Now let us look at that good kind that they again praise in such a way as to say that it is the substance of God. But how much better it is that each soul would know its own rank and merit and not give voice to such sacrilegious pride that, though the soul perceives that it changes often, it would believe that it is the substance of that highest good, which devout reason professes and teaches is immutable! For, you see, it is evident that souls do not sin by reason of the fact that they are not what they cannot be. Hence, it is already agreed that those souls, whatever they may be like, which the Manicheans have introduced, can in no way sin and for this reason do not exist at all. It remains, then, that, though they admit that there are sins, they find nothing to which to attribute them except to the good kind of souls and to the substance of God. But they are under very great pressure from Christian authority. After all, they have never denied that forgiveness of sins is granted when someone turns back to God. They have never said — as they have of many other things — that some falsifier has inserted this into the divine scriptures. Whose sins, then, are forgiven? If the sins of those alien evil souls are forgiven, they can also become good; they can inherit the kingdom of God with Christ. But because the Manicheans deny this and have no other kind of souls save those which they say come from the substance of God, it remains for them not only to admit that these souls sin too but also that only these souls sin. But I do not oppose this. Granted that only these very souls sin, nonetheless they do sin. But they are, after all, forced by that mingling with evil. If they are forced in such a way that there is no power to resist, they do not sin. If it is in their power to resist and they consent by their own will, why are we forced by the teaching of the Manicheans to find such great goods in the supreme evil and to find this evil in the highest good except because the evil that they introduce by their suspicion does not exist and the highest good that they pervert by their superstition does not exist either?

13, 19. But if I had taught or had at least learned that they were raving mad and in error about these kinds of souls, what reason could have remained why I should have thought that they should be listened to or consulted on any topic? Or would I have learned that the existence of the two kinds of souls is proven from the fact that, when we deliberate, our assent turns now to the good side and now to the bad? Why is this not rather a sign of one soul, which can be carried to one side and then to the other by free will? For, when it happens to me, I see that my one self considers both and chooses one of them. But generally the one is attractive and the other is right, and, placed between them, we waver back and forth. Nor is this surprising, for we are now constituted in such a way that we can be influenced by pleasure through the body and by goodness through the spirit.

Hence, why am I forced to admit two souls on this account? For it would be better and much easier for us to understand that there are two kinds of good things, though neither of them is alien to God their author, and that one soul is influenced by its two sides, the lower and the higher or — what can be correctly expressed in this way — the outer and the inner. These are the two kinds that we dealt with a little before under the names of sensible and intelligible things, which we more readily and usually call carnal and spiritual things. But it has become difficult for us to refrain from carnal things, though our truest bread is spiritual. For we now eat our bread with toil. After all, it was as a punishment for the sin of transgression that, from having been immortal, we became mortal. For this reason it happens that — when, as we strive for what is better, the familiarity that we have established with the flesh and our sins begin somehow to battle against us and to cause us difficulty — some fools suspect because of their utterly obtuse superstition that there is another kind of soul that does not come from God.

13, 20. And yet, even if we grant them that we are enticed to shameful acts by the other inferior kind of souls, they do not conclude from this either that these inferior souls are evil by nature or that those higher souls are the highest good. For it is possible that the former became evil, from having been good, by desiring with their own will what was not permitted, that is, by sinning, and that they can again become good, but that, as long as they remain in sin, they draw other souls to themselves by a certain hidden persuasion. And, finally, it is possible that they are not completely evil but carry out their own function at their own level, although a lower one, without any sin. But if those higher souls, to which the highest justice, which governs things, has given a far more excellent activity, choose to follow and imitate these inferior ones, they become evil by sinning, not because they imitate evil souls but because they imitate those inferior souls in an evil way. For these inferior souls are minding their own business, but those higher ones are seeking what belongs to others. Hence, the inferior souls remain at their own level, but the higher ones sink to lower levels, as is the case when humans imitate animals. A horse moves beautifully, walking on four feet. But if a human being imitates a horse on his hands and feet, who would think that he deserves even hay to eat? We are right, therefore, to disapprove of the imitator though we approve of what he imitates. We disapprove of him not because he was not successful, however, but because he wanted to do it at all. After all, in a horse we approve of that by which we are offended in a man when he imitates inferior beings, and we are offended at this in him to the extent that we prefer a man to a horse. Why? Among human beings themselves, in projecting the voice, would not a senator be insane if he did what it is good for a herald to do, even if the senator should do it more loudly and better? Look at the things in the sky. We praise the shining moon and are quite pleased by its course and cycles if we consider them well. If, nonetheless, the sun should want to imitate it — let us pretend, after all, that it could have such desires — who would not be very greatly and rightly displeased? From these examples you have the point that I want you to understand. Even if souls are assigned to bodily duties not because of sin but by nature — something that is for the present unclear — and even if, though they are inferior, they still touch us by some internal nearness, those souls should not be considered evil on the grounds that we are evil when we follow them and love bodies. For we sin when we love bodily things because we are commanded by justice to love spiritual things and by nature we can, and, if we do love them, we are then the best and the happiest in our kind.

13, 21. Hence, what sort of argument does deliberation pose when it is torn in two directions, now inclined to sin, now pulled toward acting rightly, such that we are forced to accept the two kinds of souls, of which the nature of one comes from God, while the nature of the other does not? For we can guess at so many other causes of our thought's wavering back and forth. But whoever is a good judge of things sees that these questions are obscure and are asked in vain by minds with squinting eyes. Hence, if the things that we stated about the will and about sin — which, I say, the highest justice permits no one with the use of reason not to know, which, if they are taken from us, we would have nothing left to learn virtue from, nothing by which we might rise from the death of the vices — if these things are considered over and over, they quite clearly and distinctly prove that the heresy of the Manicheans is false.

14, 22. What I shall now say about repentance is similar to this. For, as is agreed among everyone of sound mind — and the Manicheans themselves not only admit but also teach this — it is useful to repent for sin. Why, then, should I gather for this point the testimonies of the scriptures, which are scattered everywhere in them? This is also the cry of nature; no fool is left without knowledge of this matter. Unless this were deeply implanted in us, we would perish. Someone can say that he does not sin, but no barbarian would dare to say that he need not repent if he has sinned. Since this is so, I ask: Of those two kinds of souls, to which of them does repenting for sin belong? I know, of course, that it cannot belong to the kind that cannot do evil nor to the kind that cannot do good. Hence, to use their words, if the soul of darkness repents of a sin, that soul does not come from the substance of the greatest evil. If the soul of light repents, it does not come from the substance of the highest good. For that disposition of repenting, which is beneficial, bears witness that the one who repents did evil and could have done good. How, then, does nothing evil comes from me if I did something wrong? Or how do I rightly repent if I did not do something wrong? Listen to the other side: How does nothing good come from me, in whom there is a good will? Or how do I correctly repent if a good will is not found in me. Hence, let these people either deny the great benefit of repenting, so that they are repulsed not only by anyone bearing the Christian name but also by every reason, even an imaginary one, or let them cease to learn and to teach that there are those two kinds of souls, one from which nothing evil comes and the other from which nothing good comes. But, of course, if they do this they will already cease to be Manicheans. For this whole sect is based upon this two-headed or rather wrong-headed difference between souls.

14, 23. And for me it is quite enough to know that the Manicheans are in error in the same way as I know that one should repent of sin. And yet, if by the right of friendship I should challenge one of my friends who still thinks that he should listen to them, and if I should say to him, "Do you know that it is good to repent when one has sinned?" he will undoubtedly swear that he knows this. If, then, I bring you to know that the heresy of the Manicheans is false in the same way, will you desire anything more? Let him reply what more he can desire in this matter. It is fine up to this point. But when I begin to show him the compelling arguments that follow upon that proposition — bound to it, as they say, by adamantine chains — and when I bring the whole matter to the conclusion by which that sect is overthrown, he will perhaps deny that he knows the benefit of repenting, which no one learned or unlearned does not know, and he will instead contend that he knows that, when we doubt and deliberate, the two souls within us each add their proper support to the individual sides of the question. O the force of the habit of sin! O the punishment that accompanies sin! Back then you turned me away from a consideration of facts that were perfectly obvious, but you harmed me when I was not thinking. But now in my friends, who are likewise not thinking, you are wounding and tormenting me, who am now thinking.

15, 24. Pay attention to these ideas, my dear friends; I know your talents well. If you now grant me the mind and reason that any human being has, these ideas are much more certain than those that we either thought that we were learning in that error or, rather, were being forced to believe.

Great God, almighty God, God of the highest goodness, whom it is right to believe and to understand to be inviolable and incorruptible, God three and one, whom the Catholic Church worships, I beg you as a supplicant who has experienced your mercy toward me: Do not permit the men with whom I was in perfect agreement from boyhood on to disagree with me in our worship of you. I see that it is greatly expected now that I show how I would also at that time have defended the Catholic scriptures attacked by the Manicheans if, as I say, I had been cautious or how I would now show that they could be defended. But in other volumes God will help me with the goal that I have set for myself; for the present, however, the moderate length of this volume requires that we forego it.

A Debate with Fortunatus, a Manichean

(Contra Fortunatum Manichaeum Disputatio)

Introduction

On August 28 and 29, 392, while still a priest, Augustine debated the Manichean priest Fortunatus in the Basilica of Sossius in Hippo. In the present work we have the stenographic record of the lively discussion between the two, which was held over the course of two days before an interested crowd of people from Hippo. At the request of those in attendance the debate was to be based on rational arguments rather than scripture, largely because the Manicheans claimed that any passages from the New Testament that were opposed to their teaching were interpolations and also rejected the whole of the Old Testament. The topic was, furthermore, to be the Manichean and Catholic faith, not their ways of life.

The debate proceeded at a vigorous pace, with brief questions and replies, until the second day, when each of the men delivered lengthy statements of their faith. Fortunatus' statement of the Manichean creed offers an interesting perspective on his understanding of Manichean dualism, in accord with which there are two and only two substances, one good and one evil. Fortunatus repeatedly asks Augustine whether he does not admit that there is something besides God. For if there is nothing besides God, the good substance, and if there are evils, they are going to have to be in God. Much of the debate centers upon the incorruptibility of God, which the Manicheans wanted to maintain, though their myth about the sending by God the Father of souls to fight against the nation of darkness implies either that the evil substance could harm God or that God was cruel in sending souls, which are parts of himself, into the misery in which they are now found. Fortunatus was no match for the debating skills of Augustine, and he finally recognized that he had no answer to the questions Augustine had proposed. Though he withdrew to seek the counsel of his elders, he promised to return to Augustine for instruction if they could not answer the questions that Augustine had raised. We hear nothing more of him.

Augustine begins by stating what he now considers erroneous but had previously thought was true with regard to the Manichean faith. He singles out in particular the Manichean claim that God is in some respect able to be defiled, violated, and corrupted. For, though the Manicheans claim that God is incorruptible, their explanation of how our souls — which, according to them, are parts of the divine substance — have come to their present misery, from which they need deliverance, entails that God has suffered corruption. Fortunatus tries to turn the debate to the Manichean way of life, which he claims that Augustine knew well from his time with them as a Hearer (section 1). Augustine insists that the people have come to hear them debate about faith, not about morals, but Fortunatus claims that he wants to exonerate himself in the minds of those who have heard ugly rumors about the Manichean way of life (section 2). Augustine insists that, though he was a Hearer and was present at the Manichean prayers, he was not one of the Elect and never attended their eucharists. Hence, he does not know what the Elect did during them. He asks, therefore, that they return to the topic that was agreed upon. Fortunatus accordingly states briefly the faith he holds about God the Father, who sent the savior, his Word, into the world in order to bring souls back to the kingdom of God (section 3). Augustine asks what cause cast those souls down into death. Fortunatus challenges Augustine to deny what he has said if Augustine thinks that there is nothing besides God (section 4). Augustine repeats his question, and Fortunatus asks him whether there is anything besides God or whether all things exist in God (section 5). Augustine says that he knows that God cannot suffer any necessity and asks out of what necessity God sent souls here. Fortunatus rephrases Augustine's question so that it now asks why souls came here and need deliverance if there is nothing besides God (section 6). Augustine warns his opponent that they should not frustrate their distinguished audience by departing from the agreed-upon topic. He asks why, if God is inviolable, as they both agree, he sent souls here to suffer miseries if there was no reason to do this. Fortunatus replies by citing from the Letter to the Philippians the passage about Christ's assuming the form of a servant, and he claims that Christ's subjection to death and being raised up by the Father showed us how we were to think about our own souls (section 7). Augustine points out that the question concerns how we got here, not how we are delivered from death. Fortunatus replies that, as Christ entered into suffering and death by the will of the Father, so do we (section 8). Augustine says that everyone knows what Catholics believe concerning the incarnation, and he poses a dilemma that contradicts the Manichean myth: If the nation of darkness could harm God, he was not inviolable. If it could not, God was cruel in sending us here for no reason. Fortunatus asks whether the soul belongs to God or not (section 9). Augustine complains that Fortunatus is not answering the question, and Fortunatus asks his question again (section 10). Augustine claims that whether the soul came down from God is a big question but that, whether it did or not, the soul is not God. God is incorruptible, but the changes of the soul show that it is not of the substance of God. Fortunatus interprets Augustine as having denied that the soul comes from God, and he asks him whether the soul comes from God or not. He claims to have shown from Christ's coming and preaching that the soul comes from God (section 11). Augustine explains that he denied that the soul was of the substance of God but not that it was made by God. Fortunatus asks where God found the stuff out of which to make the soul if there was nothing besides God (section 12). Augustine replies that, because God is almighty, he did not need any matter out of which to make what he wanted to make but made everything out of nothing. Fortunatus then asks whether every-thing exists as the result of God's command (section 13).

Augustine agrees that everything God made exists as the result of his command. Fortunatus admits that everything God made is in harmony, but he points to the opposition between darkness and light, lies and truth, and death and life, as evidence that there is another substance besides God (section 14). Augustine explains that God made all things and arranged them well but that he did not make sin. Besides the evil of sin there is the evil of punishment for sin. For God gave to the rational soul free choice, and because of sin we experience its punishment. But God does not suffer evil. Fortunatus adds that God does not suffer but that he prevents evil (section 15). Augustine asks what God was going to suffer from. In reply Fortunatus explains that God wanted to prevent evil, and he cites a long passage from the Letter to the Ephesians on what Christ has done for us in redeeming us (section 16).

Augustine points out that the passage from the apostle Paul that Fortunatus cited favors the Catholic rather than the Manichean position, since it mentions our sins and our reconciliation with God. For the Manicheans cannot explain how sins come about or who can receive forgiveness of sins. They cannot explain how we were once children of wrath by nature, as Paul said. Fortunatus replies that the apostle said that we were children of wrath with respect to our body, not with respect to our soul (section 17). Augustine reminds Fortunatus that the apostle said that we were alienated from God by our way of life. Fortunatus, on the other hand, repeats his belief in the two substances, the good one and the evil one, and claims that Christ was sent for our deliverance, as the apostle taught (section 18).

Augustine points out that they had agreed to debate the belief in the two natures of good and evil by reasoned arguments, not by appealing to the scrip-tures. But since Fortunatus had cited the apostle Paul, Augustine cites the begin-ning of the Letter to the Romans, where Paul said that Christ was a descendant of David according to the flesh, which the Manicheans always deny. Against Christ's being a descendant of David according to the flesh, Fortunatus appeals to the passage where Paul stated, *Flesh and blood will not possess the kingdom of God* (1 Cor 15:50).

Here the audience created an uproar because they saw that Fortunatus was unwilling to accept the full text of the apostle. Then everyone in the crowd began to speak at the same time, and the first day of the debate came to an end.

The debate resumed on the following day, once again with a stenographer. Fortunatus says that God does not bring forth from himself anything evil and that what belongs to him remains inviolate, but that other things in this world, in contrast to the previous things, do not come from God. Hence, the Manicheans hold as a matter of faith that evils are alien to God (section 19). Augustine replies that the Catholic faith says that God has made no evil nature. Since both the

Catholics and the Manicheans hold that God is incorruptible, Augustine leaves it to the judgment of the faithful as to which of the two faiths is purer and more worthy of God: that which maintains that God is incorruptible or that which claims that some part of God is changed, violated, and corrupted. Furthermore, he insists that, if God had not given us free choice, there would be no justice in punishment nor any need for repentance. If we suffer evils, we should remember that, as God is good in creating all things, so he is just in punishing sins. But those sins could not exist unless we had free choice of the will. Augustine asks what evil the soul — which is supposed to be a part of God, according to the Manicheans — has done that it is punished by God, needs to repent, or merits forgiveness, since it had not sinned.

Fortunatus replies that he said that God was the creator only of the good but the avenger of evil, because evils do not come from him. If evils did come from him, he would either be found to be the author of everyone's sin because he gave human beings free choice, or he would have sinned in creating beings unworthy of himself in ignorance of what they would become. Fortunatus argues that, if there were no cause of our thinking about doing evil, we would not be forced to sin, but he claims that we are forced to sin by the evil substance. Mindful of its origin and of the evils in which it finds itself, the soul can establish the merit of its reconciliation before God with the help of the savior. If there were no enemy substance and the soul were alone in the body, it would be without sin (section 20).

Augustine insists that there is no sin without free will and that punishment and reward presuppose freedom. He states that his faith holds that almighty God made all things good but that the things he made cannot be equal to him. He maintains that the origin of evil is sin, and he cites the apostle Paul's words that covetousness is the root of all evils. He asks Fortunatus whether the Manichean evil nature is the totality of evil and whether evil can come only from it. For, if evil can come only from it, the soul does not commit sin and does not deserve punishment. Moreover, the soul need not repent and cannot receive forgiveness for what it did not do. Augustine points out the insanity of maintaining that the nation of darkness sins and the soul is granted forgiveness. He asks how Fortunatus can extricate himself from such problems.

Fortunatus says that the soul is forced to sin by the opposing nature, and he objects to the idea that covetousness is the root of all evils. He points out that there are other evils besides those in our bodies, of which he admits that covetousness may be the root. There are evils throughout the world, and these come from the evil source, which is the nature of evil. He appeals to Christ's words about the evil tree, which does not bear good fruit and which the Father did not plant, as proof that the Manichean belief in a nature of evil is correct. There is sin in a soul if it does not separate itself from the enemy race after it has heard the teachings of Christ and has received knowledge of the way things are so that it can be restored to the kingdom of God. Fortunatus also appeals to the apostle Paul's teaching on the wisdom of the flesh and the struggle between the spirit and the flesh in support of Manichean dualism (section 21).

Augustine replies that he accepts the testimonies of the scriptures, and he explains that Adam was created with free will in such a way that nothing would have resisted his will if he had willed to obey the commandments. But because Adam sinned, we who are his descendants have been reduced to our present necessity. Augustine illustrates his assertion by referring to the human experience of habits of sinful behavior and points out that, as long as the wisdom of the flesh is the wisdom of the flesh, it cannot be subject to the law of God, but that, when God enlightens our mind, the wisdom of the flesh is transformed into a good habit of the soul. He explains that the good tree and the bad tree, of which the Lord spoke, are not natures but wills, and he says that the Lord told us to make the tree good. So too, the apostle taught that every creature of God is good but that sin entered the world through one man, because of whose sin we are subject to the law of sin and death. Yet we are set from that law by grace. Finally, Augustine asks Fortunatus how sin is imputed to us who were sent into that nature not by our own will but by God.

Fortunatus replies that souls are sent here in the same way in which Christ sent his disciples like lambs into the midst of wolves, which represent the opposing nature of evil. He adds that God sends them forth in order to call them back to their proper substance, and he claims that souls were sent against the opposing nature before the creation of the world. Hence, evils do not exist merely in our bodies but everywhere in the world (section 22).

Augustine explains that the Lord sent his disciples like lambs into the midst of wolves because he was sending them like righteous men into the midst of sinners to preach the gospel. So too, the apostle spoke of our struggle with the principalities and powers because the devil and his angels also fell by sinning and because we are under their yoke as long as we are under the dominion of sin. Again Augustine asks Fortunatus whether or not God can be harmed, and Fortunatus answers that he cannot be (section 23). Augustine then asks why, according to Manichean belief, God sent us here. Fortunatus says that his faith holds that God cannot be harmed and that he sent us here, and he asks Augustine why our soul, which God now desires to set free, appeared here (section 24). Augustine again complains that Fortunatus has not answered his question, but he replies that our soul is now involved in misery because it sinned by its free will and was cast out of happiness and thrust into its present miseries. Once more he asks why God sent us here, though he could not be harmed. Fortunatus rephrases the question to ask why the soul came here (section 25). Augustine repeats his question. Fortunatus answers by appealing to the apostle Paul's question about whether the clay pot can object to the way the potter has made it. But he adds that, if God was under some necessity to send the soul here, he rightly had the will to set it free (section 26). Augustine jumps at Fortunatus' admission that God was under some necessity. Fortunatus tries to deny what he said (section 27). But Augustine insists that Fortunatus' last statement be read out from the records. After it has been read out, Augustine adds that, if God willed to send us here, though nothing could harm him, his will was cruel. Fortunatus tries to steer the debate to God's intention to adopt the soul as a sort of compensation for sending it into these miseries (section 28). Augustine points out that it was the apostle Paul who spoke about our adoption, but the topic of adoption is irrelevant to the debate. Fortunatus says that the soul went forth against the opposing nature that could not harm God (section 29). Augustine asks what need there was for the soul's going forth, and Fortunatus asks whether Augustine is certain that Christ came from God (section 30). Again Augustine protests at Fortunatus' refusal to answer his questions. Fortunatus says that he believes that Christ came here because of the will of God (section 31). Augustine again asks why almighty God, whom nothing could harm, sent the soul into these miseries. Fortunatus cites the words of Christ about laying down his soul and taking it up again as proof that the soul has gone forth by the will of God (section 32). Augustine asks why the soul has gone forth if nothing can harm God, and Fortunatus says that God sent the soul in order to impose a limit on the opposing nature and that, once the soul has imposed that limit, God will take it up again (section 33). Augustine insists that everyone knows that Christ said that he had the power to lay down his soul and take it up again because he was going to suffer and rise from the dead. He asks once more why God sent souls here, and Fortunatus repeats that it was in order to impose a limit on the opposing nature (section 34). Augustine asks whether God sent souls here to impose a limit on the opposing nature in order to make souls free from any limit. Fortunatus says that he did this in order to call souls back to himself (section 35). Augustine asks why — if God calls souls back from a lack of limit, from sin, error, and misery — the soul has to suffer these miseries until the end of the world. Fortunatus gives up (section 36). Augustine tells Fortunatus that the same question had stumped him when he was a Hearer and offers to explain the Catholic faith to those who are present, if Fortunatus admits that he has no response. Fortunatus chooses to take Augustine's questions to his elders and expresses his intention to return for further study of this question if he does not get satisfactory answers from them. To this Augustine says: "Thanks be to God" (section 37). And in that way the debate comes to an end.

Revisions I, 16 (15)

A Debate with Fortunatus, a Manichean, One Book

1. At the same time of my priesthood, I debated against a certain Fortunatus, a priest of the Manicheans who had lived a long time in Hippo and had led so many astray that he was delighted to live in Hippo on their account. This debate was taken down by stenographers as we spoke back and forth in the way in which judicial proceedings are recorded. For it gives the date and the consul. We took care to have this debate turned into a book for posterity. In it there is discussed where evil comes from. I said that it arose from man's free choice of the will, while Fortunatus tried to persuade people of a nature of evil coeternal with God. But on the following day he finally admitted that he found nothing to say against us. He of course did not become a Catholic, but nonetheless he left Hippo.

2. What I said in this book — "I say that the soul was made by God just like all the other things that were made by God, and that, among the things that almighty God made, the first place was given to the soul"[1] — was said in the sense that I wanted this to be understood in general regarding every rational creature, although in the holy scriptures it is either not possible at all or not easily possible to find that angels have souls, as we already said previously.[2] Likewise, I said in another place, "I say that there is no sin if we do not sin by our own will."[3] There I wanted that sin to be understood which is not also the punishment of sin. For in the same debate I said what needed to be said regarding that punishment.[4] Likewise I said, "So that afterwards the very same flesh that tormented us with punishments when we remained in sin might be made subject to us in the resurrection and might not afflict us with any opposition, so that we do not keep the law and commandments of God."[5] This should not be understood as if in that kingdom of God, where we shall have an incorruptible and immortal body, we shall have to derive the law and the commandments from the scriptures of God. Rather, there the eternal law of God will be observed most perfectly, and we shall have the two commandments about loving God and our neighbor[6] not in writing but in perfect and everlasting love.

---

1. *Answer to Fortunatus* I, 13.
2. *See Revisions* I, II, 4.
3. *Answer to Fortunatus* II, 21.
4. See ibid. I, 15; *Revisions* I, 15, 2.
5. *Answer to Fortunatus* II, 22.
6. See Lk 10:27; Mk 12:30; Mt 21:37-38.

This work begins as follows: "On the fifth day before the Kalends of September, under the consuls Arcadius Augustus in his second term and Rufinus, most illustrious men."

A Debate with Fortunatus, a Manichean

The First Day's Debate

On the fifth day before the Kalends of September,[7] under the consuls Arcadius Augustus in his second term and Rufinus, most illustrious men, a debate was held in the presence of the people against Fortunatus, a priest of the Manicheans, in the city of Hippo, in the Baths of Sossius.

1. Augustine said: "I now regard as an error what I earlier thought was the truth. I desire to hear from you, while you are present, whether I am right to think that."

Fortunatus said: "Begin to explain the error."

Augustine said: "First of all, I think it the worst error to believe that almighty God, in whom our one hope lies, can be violated, defiled, or corrupted in some respect. I know that your heresy affirms this, but not of course in the words that I just used. For, when you are asked, you admit that God is incorruptible, absolutely inviolable, and unable to be defiled, but when you begin to explain other points, you are forced to admit that he can be corrupted, penetrated, and defiled. For you say that some sort of nation of darkness rebelled against the kingdom of God. But when almighty God saw the great ruin and devastation that threatened his kingdoms unless he set something in the way of the enemy nation and resisted it, he sent forth this power, and this world was fashioned from this power's mingling with evil and the nation of darkness. For this reason good souls labor, are enslaved, fall into error, and are corrupted, so that they need a deliverer to purify them from error, to release them from this mingling, and to set them free from slavery. I think that it is wicked to believe that almighty God feared some enemy nation or suffered some necessity, so that he plunged us into suffering."

Fortunatus said: "Because I know that you were one of us, that is, that you had a role among the Manicheans, those are the principal points of our faith. But here we are discussing our way of life and the false charges by which we are being pummeled. Let the good people present, then, hear from you whether that with which we are being charged and pursued is true or false. For they will be able to know our way of life more correctly from your teaching and from your explanation and revelation, if you disclose it. Were you present at our prayers?"

---

7. That is, August 28, 392. In the CSEL edition Zycha conjectured: "On the sixth and fifth days before the Kalends of September," though the manuscripts have only the text I have translated.

2. Augustine said: "I was present. But the question about your faith is one thing; that about your way of life is another. I have proposed to debate your faith. But if those who are present prefer to hear about your way of life, I am not going to dodge that question either."

Fortunatus said: "Before your conscience, before which we are being defiled, I want first to exonerate myself by the testimony of a capable man, who in my view is capable, both now and in the future courtroom of Christ the just judge, of saying if he saw or found in us what people are saying about us."

3. Augustine said: "You are steering me toward something else, though I had proposed to discuss your faith. But only those who are your Elect can be fully informed about your way of life. You know, however, that I was not one of your Elect but a Hearer. And so, although I was present at your prayers, as you asked, only God and you can know whether you held some prayers separately among yourselves. Yet I saw nothing shameful take place at the prayers at which I was present. I only noticed as contrary to the faith (which I later learned and approved of) that you make your prayer facing the sun. Aside from this I discovered nothing new in your prayers. But whoever raises some question for you about your way of life raises it for your Elect. I cannot, however, know what you, the Elect, do among yourselves. For I have often heard from you that you receive the eucharist, but since the time when you receive it was kept hidden from me, how could I have known what you receive? And so, please keep the question about your way of life for discussion among your Elect, if it can be discussed. You gave me a faith that I reject today. That is precisely what I proposed; answer me about what I proposed."

Fortunatus said: "And this is our profession: God is incorruptible, bright, unable to be approached, unable to be held, unable to suffer; he dwells in an eternal light of his own. He brings forth from himself nothing corruptible, neither darkness nor demons nor Satan, and nothing can be found in his kingdom opposed to him. But he sent a savior like himself. The Word, born at the foundation of the world when he made the world, came among human beings after the world was made. He chose souls worthy of himself for his holy will, which were made holy by his heavenly commandments and were imbued with a faith in and a knowledge of heavenly things. Under his leadership the same souls will again return from here to the kingdom of God according to his holy promise. For he said, *I am the way, the truth, and the door* (Jn 14:6; 10:9), and, *No one can come to the Father except through me* (Jn 14:6). We believe these things because souls could not otherwise, that is, by some other means, return to the kingdom of God if they did not find him, who is the way, the truth, and the door. For he said, *He who has seen me has also seen my Father* (Jn 14:9), and, *He who believes in me will not taste death for eternity, but he will pass from death to life and will not come into judgment* (Jn 11:26; 5:24). We believe these things, and this is the aim of our faith: in accord with the strength of our mind to obey its commandments, following the one faith of this Trinity of the Father, the Son, and the Holy Spirit."

4. Augustine said: "You admit that these souls come from death to life through Christ. What cause cast them down to death?"

Fortunatus said: "Be so good now as to take up from here and contradict me if there is nothing besides God."

5. Augustine said: "Rather, you be so good as to reply to what you were asked. What cause handed these souls over to death?"

Fortunatus said: "Rather, you be so good as to say whether there is something besides God or whether all things are in God."

6. Augustine said: "I can answer what God wanted me to know, namely, that God can suffer no necessity and cannot be violated or corrupted in any respect. Since you also admit this, I ask under what necessity he sent here the souls that you say return through Christ."

Fortunatus said: "You have said that God has revealed to you that he is incorruptible, just as he has revealed this to me. We must seek an account of how and for what reason souls came into this world so that God now rightly sets them free from this world through his only-begotten Son, who is like him, if there is nothing besides him."

7. Augustine said: "We should not frustrate the very many people who are present and go from the question that was proposed to another one. We both admit, we grant to each other that God is incorruptible and inviolable and could not have suffered anything. It follows from this that your heresy is false. For it says that, when God saw that devastation and ruin was threatening his kingdoms, he sent a power to wage war with the nation of darkness, and that our souls labor here as a result of that mingling. My argument, therefore, is short and, I think, perfectly plain to anyone. If God could not suffer anything from the nation of darkness because he was inviolable; he sent us here for no purpose so that we might suffer these woes here. But if he could suffer something, he is not inviolable, and you deceive those to whom you say that God is inviolable. For your heresy denies this point when it explains the others."

Fortunatus said: "We hold what the blessed apostle Paul taught us. He said, *Have this mind in you that was also in Christ Jesus. Since he was established in the form of God, he did not think it robbery to be equal to God, but he emptied himself, taking the form of a servant, having come to be in the likeness of men, and, having been found in appearance like a man, he humbled himself and became subject even to death.* (Phil 2:5-8) We have this same mind about ourselves, then, as about Christ who, though he was established in the form of God, became subject even to death in order to show his likeness to our souls. And just as he showed the likeness of death in himself and that, having been raised up from among, he is in the Father and the Father is in him, so we think that it will also be the same way with our souls. For we shall be able to be set free from this death through him. Death is either foreign to God, or, if it belongs to God, his mercy ceases, as well as his title of deliverer and the works of the deliverer."

8. Augustine said: "I ask how we came into death, and you say how we are set free from death."

Fortunatus said: "The apostle said that we should think about our souls as Christ showed us. If Christ underwent suffering and death, we should as well. If he came down into suffering and death by the will of the Father, we should as well."

9. Augustine said: "Everyone knows that the Catholic faith holds that our Lord — that is, the power and the wisdom of God[8] and the Word through whom all things were made and without whom nothing has been made[9] — assumed a man for our deliverance. In the man whom he assumed, he showed us the things that you mention. But now, with regard to the substance of God himself and of his ineffable majesty, we are asking whether anything can or cannot harm it. For, if something can harm it, he is not inviolable. If nothing can harm it, what was the nation of darkness going to do to it? For you say that God waged war against the nation of darkness before the creation of the world, and you claim that in that war we, that is, our souls, which it is clear now need a deliverer, were mingled with every evil and entangled in death. Now I am returning to that very brief argument: If something can harm him, he is not inviolable; if it cannot, he sent us here out of cruelty in order that we might suffer these evils."

Fortunatus said: "Does the soul belong to God or not?"

10. Augustine said: "If it is fair that my questions are not answered and I am asked a question, I shall reply."

Fortunatus said: "Does the soul act by itself? This is what I ask you."

11. Augustine said: "I shall answer what you asked. Only remember that you refused to reply to my questions but that I replied to yours. If you ask whether the soul came down from God, that is certainly an important question, but whether it came down from God or not, I reply concerning the soul that it is not God. God is one thing, the soul another. God cannot be violated, corrupted, penetrated, or defiled. He cannot be corrupted in any respect, and he cannot be harmed in any respect. But we see that the soul is sinful, lives in distress, seeks the truth, and needs a deliverer. This changeableness on the part of the soul shows me that the soul is not God. For, if the soul is the substance of God, the substance of God is mistaken, the substance of God is corrupted, the substance of God is violated, the substance of God is deceived, and it is wicked to say this."

Fortunatus said: "And so you have denied that the soul is from God as long as it is enslaved to sins, vices, and worldly things, because it is impossible that

---

8. See 1 Cor 1:24.
9. See Jn 1:3.

either God or his substance should suffer this. For God is incorruptible, and his substance is immaculate and holy. But here you are being asked whether the soul is from God or not. We profess that it is and show this from the coming of the savior, from his holy preaching, and from his election, when he takes pity on souls; and the soul is said to have come in accord with his decision in order that he might set it free from death, lead it to eternal glory, and restore it to the Father. But what do you yourself say or hope for concerning the soul? Is it from God or not? And can the substance of God, from which you deny that the soul comes, be subject to no sufferings?"

12. Augustine said: "I said that the soul is not the substance of God in such a way as to deny that the soul is God, but it still comes from God as its author because it was made by God. He who made it is one thing; what he made is another. He who made it can absolutely not be corruptible, but what he made can in no way be equal to him who made it."

Fortunatus said: "I did not say that the soul was like God. But because you said that the soul was made and that there was nothing besides God, I ask where God found the substance of the soul."

13. Augustine said: "Just remember that I am replying to your questions but that you are not replying to mine. I say that the soul was made by God, just like all the other things that were made by God, and that, among the things that almighty God made, the first place was given to the soul. But if you ask out of what God made the soul, remember that I profess along with you that God is almighty. He is not almighty, however, if he seeks the help of some matter out of which to make what he wants. From this it follows that, according to our faith, God made out of nothing all the things that he made through his Word and wisdom. For we read as follows: *He commanded, and they were made; he gave the order, and they were established* (Ps 148:5)."

Fortunatus said: "Do all things exist as the result of God's command?"

14. Augustine said: "I believe that they do — but all the things that have been made."

Fortunatus said: "The things that have been made are in harmony with one another. But, from the fact that the things of which you speak are unsuited to one another, it is clear that there is not one substance, though it was as the result of the command of one substance that the same things came to produce the composition and appearance of this world. But from the facts themselves it is evident that darkness and light are not at all alike, that the truth and a lie are not at all alike, that death and life are not at all alike, that soul and body are not at all alike, nor are other things like these, which differ from one another by their names and appearances. And our Lord was right to say: *The tree that my heavenly Father has not planted will be uprooted* (Mt 15:13), because *it does not bear good fruit* (Mt 3:10), and there is also the tree that he has planted. Hence, it is very clear from the nature of things that there are two substances in this world, which differ in their appearances and names; one of these is that of the body, but the other is eternal, which we believe is the substance of the almighty Father."

15. Augustine said: "These contraries that bother you to the point that we should find them opposed to one another have come about on account of our sin, that is, on account of the sin of man. For God made all things good and arranged them well, but he did not make sin. And this is the only thing that we are at present calling evil: our voluntary sin. But there is another kind of evil, which is the punishment of sin. Since, then, there are two kinds of evil, sin and the punishment of sin, sin does not pertain to God, but the punishment of sin pertains to the one who punishes sin. For, as God is good because he created all things, so he is just in punishing sin. Since, then, all things are arranged in the best way, those that now seem to us opposed to one another come about because of the sin of the man who fell, who did not want to observe the law of God. For God gave free choice to the rational soul, which is present in a man. After all, in that way the soul could earn merit if we were good by will, not by necessity. Since, then, we were to be good not by necessity but by will, God had to give free choice to the soul. But he made all things subject to this soul without any opposition when it obeyed his laws, so that the other things that God created would obey it, if the soul had willed to obey God. If, however, the soul refused to obey God, the things that obeyed it would be transformed into its punishment. Hence, if all things have been correctly arranged by God, it is true both that they are good and that God does not suffer evil."

Fortunatus said: "He does not suffer but prevents evil."

16. Augustine said: "After all, from what was he going to suffer?"

Fortunatus said: "This is my point: He wanted to prevent evil, not thoughtlessly but by power and foreknowledge. But deny that evil exists apart from God, when he showed by his commandments that there are other things which come about apart from his will. A commandment is only introduced where there is also opposition. And the ability to live freely only exists as a result of the fall, according to the explanation of the apostle, who says, *And you were dead because of your transgressions and sins, in which you once walked according to the teaching of this world, according to the prince of the power of this air, the spirit who is now at work in the children of unbelief, among whom we all also once lived in the desires of our flesh, carrying out the desires of the counsels of our flesh. And we were naturally children of wrath, just as the others. But God, who is rich in all mercy, took pity on us. And though we were dead because of sins, he brought us to life in Christ, by whose grace you have been saved. And he has raised us up and placed us with him in the heavens with Christ Jesus in order to reveal in the coming ages the abundant riches of his grace in his goodness upon us in Christ Jesus. For you were saved by grace, and this does not come from you. For it is the gift of God, not because of works, in order that no one might boast. For we are his handiwork, created in Christ Jesus for the good works that God has prepared in order that we might walk in them. On account of this be mindful that you were once gentiles in the flesh, who were called the uncircumcised by those with the circumcision made by hand in the flesh. For at that time you were without Christ, separated from the life of Israel and strangers to the testaments, not having the hope of the promise and without God in this world. But now, in Christ Jesus, you who were once far away have been brought near in the blood of Christ. For he is our peace who made both one, tearing down the dividing wall of hostilities in his flesh, destroying the law of the commandments with its decrees in order to establish the two in himself as one new man, making peace in order to reconcile to God both of them in one body through the cross, slaying the hostilities in himself. And he came and brought the good news of peace for you who were far away and of peace for those who were near. For through him we both have access to the Father in the one Spirit."* (Eph 2:1-18)[10]

17. Augustine said: "Unless I am mistaken, this passage from the apostle that you chose to read aloud works very much in favor of my faith and against yours. First of all, it clearly reveals free choice, by which I said that the soul can sin, when the apostle mentions sins and when he says that our reconciliation with God comes about through Jesus Christ. For by sinning we had turned away from God, but by observing the commandments of Christ we are reconciled to God, so that we who were dead in our sins are brought to life when we keep his commandments and have peace with him in the one Spirit, from whom we were separated when we did not keep his commandments, just as we are taught in our faith concerning the man who was first created.

"Now, therefore, I ask you, according to the passage that you read, how we would have sins if the opposing nature forces us to do what we do. For someone who is forced by necessity to do something does not sin. But someone who sins sins by free choice. Why would we be commanded to do penance if it is not we who commit sin but the nation of darkness? I likewise ask who receives the forgiveness of sins: we or the nation of darkness? But if the nation of darkness receives the forgiveness of sins, it will also reign with God when it receives the forgiveness of sins. But if we receive the forgiveness of sins, it is obvious that we sinned by our will. After all, it is quite stupid to forgive someone who did nothing wrong. But he has done nothing wrong who did not do anything by his will. Suppose, therefore, that God promises the soul the forgiveness of sins and reconciliation if it stops sinning today and does penance for its sins. If the soul replied according to your belief, it would say, 'What sin have I committed? What have I merited? Why have you expelled me from your kingdoms in order to fight against some nation or other? I am downtrodden, mingled with that

---

10. The CSEL text omits from the above quotation from the middle of verse 7 to the middle of verse 16 on the basis of the manuscripts, which say, "And so on up to," though the early editions and PL include the whole text as I have here.

nation, corrupted, and worn out; I have lost my free choice. You know the necessity that has pressed me down. Why do you blame me for the wounds I received? Why do you force me to repentance, though you are the cause of my wounds, though you know that the nation of darkness has produced in me what I have suffered, despite the fact that you, who created me, could not be violated? And yet, wanting to look out for your kingdoms, which nothing could harm, you have cast me down to such miseries. Surely, if I am a part of you that has gone forth from deep within you, if I have come from your kingdom and from your lips, I ought to have suffered nothing in this kingdom of darkness. Rather, while I remain uncorrupt, that nation should be held in subjection if I was a part of the Lord. But now, since that nation could be subdued only by my corruption, how am I said to be a part of you? Or how do you remain inviolable? Or how are you not cruel, who wanted me to suffer in defense of your kingdoms, which could not be harmed in any way by that nation of darkness?' Reply to this, please, and be so good as to explain to me how the apostle Paul said, *We were naturally children of wrath* (Eph 2:3), since he says that we have been reconciled to God. If, then, they were naturally children of wrath, how do you say that the soul is naturally a child and a portion of God?"

Fortunatus said: "If the apostle had said that we were naturally children of wrath in terms of the soul, the apostle's lips would have alienated the soul from God. And by this reasoning you now show that the soul does not belong to God because the apostle says that we are naturally children of wrath. But if he had said this insofar as the same apostle was bound by the law since, as he himself testifies, he came from the family of Abraham,[11] it is clear that he said that we were children of wrath in terms of the body, just as others are as well.

"But he showed that the substance of the soul comes from God and that the soul could only be reconciled to God through our teacher, who is Christ Jesus. For, once the hostility was slain, the soul seemed to have emerged as unworthy of God. But we admit that the soul was sent, both taking its origin from almighty God and sent to do his will, just as we believe that Christ the savior also came from heaven to carry out the will of the Father. The will of the Father was to set free our souls from the same hostility, once the same hostility had been slain. If this hostility had not been opposed to God, the apostle would not even have mentioned it where there was unity, and he would not have mentioned slaying, nor would it have taken place where there was life."

18. Augustine said: "Remember that the apostle said that we were alienated from God by our way of life."

Fortunatus said: "I teach that there are two substances. In the substance of light God is considered, as we said previously, to be incorruptible, but there was the contrary nature of darkness. I confess that it is even today being conquered

---

11. See Rom 11:1.

by the power of God, and I teach that Christ was sent as a savior for the sake of my return, as the same apostle says."

19. Augustine said: "Our listeners have imposed upon us the task of discussing in rational arguments the belief in two natures. But since you have had recourse to the scriptures again, I descend to them, and I ask that nothing be passed over for fear that by using certain chapters we might cause obscurity for those who do not know the scriptures. Let us, therefore, consider from the beginning what the apostle has in his Letter to the Romans. For on the first page there is something that is strongly against you. For he says, *Paul, the servant of Christ Jesus, called to be an apostle, predestined for the gospel of God, which he had earlier promised through his prophets in the holy scriptures, concerning his Son who was born for him as a descendant of David according to the flesh, who was predestined to be the Son of God in power, according to the Spirit of holiness, by the resurrection from the dead of Jesus Christ our Lord* (Rom 1:1-4). We see that the apostle teaches us that our Lord was both predestined by the power of God before he assumed flesh and was born for him according to the flesh as a descendant of David. Since you always denied this latter point and still deny it, how do you demand that we debate instead according to the scriptures?"

Fortunatus said: "You claim that he was born according to the flesh as a descendant of David, though it is proclaimed that he was born of a virgin[12] and was glorified as the Son of God. It is necessary, after all, that what comes from spirit be regarded as spirit and that what comes from flesh be understood to be flesh. Against this there is the authority of the gospel in which it is said, *Flesh and blood shall not possess the kingdom of God, nor shall corruption possess incorruption* (1 Cor 15:50)."[13]

At this point an outburst was produced by those sitting there who wanted us to use rational arguments instead. For they saw that Fortunatus did not want to accept everything that was written in the book of the apostle. Then everyone everywhere began to argue as to the extent that he said that the word of God was held bound in the nation of darkness. Because those who were present were horrified at this, they left.

The Second Day's Debate

On the next day, again with the use of a stenographer, the proceedings continued as

Fortunatus said: "I say that almighty God brings forth no evil from himself and that what belongs to him remains without corruption, having sprung from and been born from one inviolable source, but that the other contrary things that

---

12. See Is 7:14.
13. Fortunatus attributes the authority of the gospel to this text from the apostle.

are found in the world do not flow from God and did not appear in this world with God as their principle, that is, that they do not take their origin from him. We have therefore accepted in faith that these evils are foreign to God."

20. Augustine said: "And this is our faith: God is not the father of evils, nor did he make any evil nature. But since each of us agrees that God cannot be corrupted and defiled, it is up to the prudent and faithful to judge which is the purer faith and the one more worthy of the majesty of God: that which claims that the power of God or some part of God or the Word of God can be changed, violated, corrupted, and bound, or that which says that almighty God and all of his nature and substance can never be corrupted in any respect, but that evils are due to the voluntary sin of the soul, to which God gave free choice. And if God had not given this free choice, there could be no just judgment in punishing, nor any merit in acting rightly, nor a divine command to do penance for sins, nor the forgiveness of sins, which God gave to us through our Lord Jesus Christ. For someone who does not sin by his will does not sin. I think that this is clear and obvious to everyone. Hence, it ought not to upset us if, in accord with our merits, we suffer some difficulties in the things that God has made. For, just as he is good in creating all things, so he is just in not sparing our sins. For, by way of example, if some of a person's limbs were bound by another person, and if something false were written by his hand apart from his own will, I ask whether, if this fact were revealed to the judge, he could condemn this man for criminal falsehood? Hence, if it is evident that there is no sin where there is no free choice of the will, I want to hear how the soul, which you say is a part or a power or a word or something else — whatever it might be — of God, did anything evil so that it might be punished by God or do penance for sin or deserve pardon, since it sinned in no way."

Fortunatus said: "I proposed that we discuss substances because God is considered to be the creator only of good things but the avenger of evils, for the reason that evils do not come from him. I am right, therefore, to hold that God avenges evils because they do not come from him. But if they came from him or he gave us the freedom to sin, since you say that God gave free choice, he would already be found to consent to my sin, because he would be the author of my sin or would be ignorant that I, whom he did not make worthy of himself, was going to sin. This, then, is what I proposed and what I now ask: Did God establish evils or not? And did he establish an end of evils? For it is evident from the facts themselves and from the gospel faith that the things that we said were made by him, that is, by God their maker, are considered incorruptible inasmuch as they were created by and arose from him.

"I set forth these ideas, which are both part of our faith and ones that you can approve in our confession, though they do not lack the authority of the Christian faith. And I can in no way show that my faith is correct unless I confirm the same faith by the authority of the scriptures. That, then, is what I have indicated; that is what I have said. If evils entered the world with God as their author, be so good as to say this yourself. Or if you are correct to believe that evils do not come from God, the mind of those present ought also to hear and learn this from you. I spoke of substances, not of the sin that is found in us. For, if our thoughts about doing evil did not have an origin, we would not be forced to come to sinning or wrongdoing. For we sin unwillingly and are forced by the contrary substance that is our enemy, and so we conform ourselves to this knowledge of the way things are. Instructed by that knowledge and restored to the memory of its pristine state, the soul recognizes the source from which it takes its origin, the evil in which it is situated, and the goods by which it can correct the sin it committed unwillingly. And thus, by correcting its wrongdoings for the sake of good works, it can place before God the merit of its reconciliation with the help of our savior, who teaches us both to perform good actions and to flee from evil ones. After all, it was suggested to us that a human being either serves righteousness or makes himself subject to sins not because of some opposing nature but of his own accord, and yet, if the soul — to which, as you say, God gave free choice — were situated in the body alone without any opposing nation, it would be without sin and would not make itself subject to sins."

21. Augustine said: "I say that there is no sin if we do not sin by our own will, and for this reason there is also a reward, because we act rightly by our own will. Or, if a person merits punishment who sins unwillingly, a person ought also to merit a reward who does good unwillingly. But who is there who would doubt that a reward is only given to someone who has done something with a good will? From this we understand that punishment too is imposed upon someone who did something with a bad will. But since you take me back to those earlier natures and substances, it is my faith that almighty God — a point that must especially be noted and fixed in the mind — that almighty God, who is just and good, made good things. But the things that he made cannot be the same as he himself is who made them. For it is unjust and foolish to believe that works are equal to those who wrought them or that creatures are equal to their creator. Hence, if devout faith holds that God made all things good, though he is nonetheless much better and far more excellent than they are, the origin and beginning of evil lies in sin. As the apostle says, *Covetousness is the root of all evils; certain persons have gone along with it, suffered shipwreck from the faith, and involved themselves in many sorrows* (1 Tm 6:10). For, if you are looking for the root of all evils, you have the apostle who says that covetousness is the root of all evils. I cannot look for the root of the root. Or, if there is another evil, whose root is not covetousness, covetousness will not be the root of all evils. If, however, it is true that covetousness is the root of all evils, in vain do we look for some other kind of evil.

"But, regarding the opposing nature, which you introduce, I ask you to be so good as to tell me, since I have already replied to your objections: If that opposing nature is the totality of evil and if sin can only come from it, ought it alone not to merit punishment and not the soul, from which sin does not come? But if you say that it alone merits punishment and that the soul does not merit it, I ask on whom the penance is imposed that it is ordered to do. If the soul is ordered to do penance, sin comes from it, and it sinned by the will. For, if the soul is forced to do evil, it is not the soul that does evil. Is it not foolish and utterly mad to say that the nation of darkness sinned and that I do penance for those sins? Is it not utterly mad to say that the nation of darkness sinned and that I receive forgiveness for those sins? For according to your faith I can say, 'What have I done? What have I committed? I was with you; I was whole; I was defiled by no corruption; you sent me here. You suffered under necessity; you were looking out for your kingdoms since a defilement and devastation threatened them. Since, then, you recognize the necessity by which I was overwhelmed, which did not allow me to breathe, which I could not resist, why do you accuse me as a sinner? Or why do you promise the forgiveness of sins?' Reply to this without ambiguity, please, as I replied to you without ambiguity."

Fortunatus said: "We say that the soul is forced to sin by the opposing nature. You do not want there to be a root for sin except for the evil that is found in us, though it is clear that, even apart from our bodies, there are evils in the whole world. For an evil root is not the source only of the evils that we have in our bodies but also of those that are found in the whole world and that have good names. For Your Reverence said that this covetousness, which is found in our bodies, is the root of evil, but, when the desire for evil does not come from our bodies, it appears in the whole world from that opposing nature as its source. After all, the apostle called covetousness, which you said was the root of all evils, the root of evils, not the sole evil. But covetousness, which you said is the root of all evils, is not understood in a single way as if it were found only in our bodies.[14]For it is clear that the evil that is found in us comes from an evil author and that this root, which you say exists, is a small portion of the evil. Thus the evil that is found in us is not itself the root but a portion of the evil — of the evil that is found everywhere. Our Lord also called that root the bad tree that never bears good fruit, the tree that his Father did not plant and that is rightly uprooted and cast into the fire.[15]For you say that sin ought to be attributed to the opposing nature. That nature is the nature of evil. And there is a sin of the soul if,[16]after the warning of our savior and his sound teaching, the soul does not separate itself from the contrary and hostile race and if the soul does not adorn itself with purer realities. Otherwise, it cannot be restored to its own substance. For it was said: *If*

---

14. I have not followed the CSEL text, which has *cordibus*, but PL, which has *corporibus*, as is also found above.

15. See Mt 15:13; 3:10.

16. I have conjectured *nisi* in place of *si*. The translator of the BA version comments that the passage is practically impossible to translate literally.

I had not come and spoken to them, they would not have sin. But now, after I have come and have spoken to them and after they have refused to believe me, *they shall not have pardon for their sin* (Jn 15:22). Hence, it is clear that it was right to do penance after the coming of the savior and after this knowledge of the way things are. By this knowledge the soul could again be presented to the kingdom of God, from which it went forth, after having been as if washed by the divine fountain of the filth and vices both of the whole world and of the bodies in which the same soul is found. For the apostle said, *The wisdom of the flesh is opposed to God. For it is not subject to the law of God, for it cannot be.* (Rom 8:7) It is clear from this that the good soul is seen to sin not of its own accord but because of the influence of the wisdom that is not subject to the law of God. For the same apostle goes on to say, *The flesh has desires opposed to the spirit and the spirit has desires opposed to the flesh, so that you do not do the things that you will* (Gal 5:17). He also says, *I see another law in my members that resists the law of my mind and leads me captive under the law of sin and death. Therefore, wretched man that I am, who will set me free from the body of this death if not the grace of God through our Lord Jesus Christ* (Rom 7:23-25), *through whom the world is crucified to me and I to the world?*" (Gal 6:14)

22. Augustine said: "I recognize and embrace the testimonies of the divine scriptures, and I shall explain in a few words, as God will graciously allow me, how they fit with my faith. I say that free choice of the will existed in the man who was created first. He was created in such a way that nothing at all would have resisted his will if he had chosen to keep the commandments of God. But, after he sinned by free will, we who are descended from his stock were cast down into necessity. Each of us can discover after a little reflection that what I say is true. For at present, before we become entangled in some habit, we have in our actions the free choice of doing or not doing something. But after we have done something with this freedom and the deadly sweetness and pleasure of the action has taken hold of the soul, the soul is so entangled in that same habit of its own making that afterwards it cannot conquer what it fashioned for itself by sinning. We see that many do not want to swear but, because their tongue has acquired the habit, they cannot hold back, and words fall from their lips that we cannot say have nothing to do with the source of evil. For I shall discuss with you the words that I wish you understood in your heart in the same way as they are always on your tongue. For you swear by the Paraclete. If, then, you want to learn by experience that I am speaking the truth, begin not to swear. You will see that your habit has its habitual effect. And this is what fights against the soul: a habit produced in the flesh. This is, of course, the wisdom of the flesh, which is the wisdom of the flesh as long as it cannot be subject to the law of God. But when the soul has been enlightened, it ceases to be the wisdom of the flesh. For scripture said that the wisdom of the flesh could not be subject to the law of God

in the same way as if someone said that icy snow could not be hot. For, as long as it is snow, it can by no means be hot. But snow is melted by heat and ceases to be snow so that it can become hot. In the same way, when our mind has been enlightened and God has subjected the whole person to the rule of the divine law, the wisdom of the flesh, that is, the habit produced in the flesh, becomes a good habit in place of the bad habit of the soul.

"As a result, the Lord said with perfect truth that the two trees which you mentioned, the good tree and the bad tree, have their own fruit; that is, the good tree cannot produce good fruit, nor can the bad tree produce good fruit, but only as long as it is bad. Let us take two human beings, one good and the other bad. As long as the one is good, he cannot produce bad fruit; as long as the other is bad, he cannot produce good fruit. But in order that you may understand that the Lord mentioned these two trees in order to signify free choice, and that those two trees are not our natures but our wills, he said in the gospel, *Either make the tree good, or make the tree bad* (Mt 12:33). Who is there who can make a nature? If, then, we are commanded to make a tree good or bad, it is up to us to choose what we want. Concerning this sin of man, then, and concerning this habit of the soul produced in the flesh, the apostle says, *Let no one mislead you* (Eph 5:6); *every creature that God has made is good* (1 Tm 4:4). The same apostle, whom you yourself mentioned, says, *Just as through the disobedience of the one many were made sinners, so through the obedience of the one many were made righteous* (Rom 5:19). For *death came through a man, and the resurrection of the dead came through a man* (1 Cor 15:21). As long as we bear the image of the earthly man,[17] then, that is, as long as we live according to the flesh, which is also called our old self,[18] we experience the necessity of our habit so that we do not do what we will. But the grace of God has poured the love of God into us and made us subject to his will, since he said to us, *You have been called to freedom* (Gal 5:13) and, *The grace of God has set me free from the law of sin and death* (Rom 8:2). But it is the law of sin that whoever sins shall die. From this law we are set free when we begin to be righteous. It is the law of death that said to the man, *You are earth, and you shall return to earth* (Gn 3:19). For we are all born from him in that way because we are earth, and we shall return to the earth because of the punishment of the first man's sin. But, because of the grace of God that sets us free from the law of sin and death, we have turned back to righteousness and are set free, so that afterwards the very same flesh that tormented us with punishments when we remained in sin might be made subject to us in the resurrection and might not afflict us with any opposition, so that we do not keep the law and commandments of God. Hence, since I have replied to your questions, be so

---

17. See 1 Cor 15:49.
18. See Rom 6:6.

good as to reply to what I desire: How is it possible that, if there is a nature opposed to God, sin is imputed to us who were sent into that nature not by our will but by God, whom nothing can harm?"

Fortunatus said: "It happens just as the Lord himself said to his disciples, *Look, I am sending you like sheep into the midst of wolves* (Mt 10:16). From this we should know that our savior would not have wanted, with a hostile mind, to send his lambs, that is, his disciples, into the midst of wolves if there had not been some opposing power, which he described by the comparison with wolves, where he had also sent his disciples in order that souls that could perhaps be deceived in the midst of wolves would be called back to their own substance.[19] From this, then, we see the antiquity of our times and of our years, which we are recalling. For before the creation of the world souls were sent in this way against the opposing nature in order that, in subjecting it by their suffering, they might win the victory for God. For the same apostle said that there was a struggle not only against flesh and blood but also against the principalities and powers and the spirits of wickedness and the dominion of darkness.[20] If, therefore, evils are found and wickedness exists in both places, evil does not now exist only in our bodies but in the whole world, where souls are seen to exist which dwell beneath this sky and are imprisoned there."

23. Augustine said: "The Lord sent his lambs into the midst of wolves, that is, righteous human beings into the midst of sinners, to preach the gospel at the time of the man who was assumed by the inestimable wisdom of God, in order to call us from sin to righteousness. But the apostle's assertion that we have a struggle not against flesh and blood but against principalities and powers and the other things he mentioned signifies that, just as we did, the devil and his angels fell by sin, are fallen, and have gained earthly possessions, that is, sinful human beings. We are under their yoke as long as we are sinners, just as, when we are righteous, we shall be under the yoke of righteousness. And we have a struggle against them in order that we may pass over to righteousness and be set free from their dominion. And so, please briefly answer for me the one question I ask: Was God able to be harmed or was he not? But, please, I beg you, answer me that he was not able to be."

Fortunatus said: "He was not able to be harmed."

24. Augustine said: "Why, then, according to your belief, did he send us here?"

Fortunatus said: "I profess that God could not be harmed and that God sent us here. But because that is opposed to your belief, tell me for what reason the soul appeared here, which our God now desires immediately to set free both by his commandments and by his own Son, whom he sent?"

---

19. That is, souls would be called back to the good substance that sent it into this world.
20. See Eph 6:12.

25. Augustine said: "Since I see that you have been unable to reply to my questions and have wanted to ask me something, look, I shall satisfy you, provided you remember that you did not reply to what I asked. I do not know how many times I said — not now, but a short while ago — why the soul is enveloped in miseries here in the world. The soul sinned and for this reason is unhappy. It received free choice; it used free choice as it wanted to; it fell; it was cast out of happiness and involved in misery. For this reason I read out for you the testimony of the apostle, who said, *Just as death came through one man, so the resurrection of the dead comes through one man* (1 Cor 15:21). What more do you ask? Hence, answer me: Why did he who could not be harmed send us here?"

Fortunatus said: "We must seek the reason why the soul came here or why God desires to set free from here the same soul, which lives in the midst of evils."

26. Augustine said: "I request this reason from you. In other words, if God could not be harmed, why did he send us here?"

Fortunatus said: "We are being asked, if evil could not harm God, why the soul was sent here or for what reason it was mingled with the world. This is evident from the words of the apostle: *Does the vessel say to the potter who made it: Why have you formed me in this way?* (Rom 9:20) If, then, this topic must be discussed, we must question him who sent the soul here under no compulsion from necessity. But if he was under some necessity to send the soul, it is right that he also has the will to set it free."

27. Augustine said: "Is God, then, pressured by necessity?"

Fortunatus said: "That is indeed the case. But do not stir up animosity over what was said, because we do not make God subject to necessity but say that he voluntarily sent the soul."

28. Augustine said: "Read what was said previously."

And it was read out: "But if he was under some necessity to send the soul, it is right that he also has the will to see it free."

Augustine said: "We heard: 'But if he was under some necessity to send the soul, it is right that he also has the will to see it free.' You said, therefore, that he was under some necessity to send the soul. But if you now want to speak of will, I also add this: He whom nothing could harm had a cruel will in sending the soul into such miseries. Since I say this for the sake of refuting you, I ask pardon from that one God in whom we have the hope of being delivered from all the errors of the heretics."

Fortunatus said: "You assert that we say that God is cruel in sending the soul, but you claim that God made man and breathed a soul into him, which he certainly foreknew would be involved in future misery[21] and could not be restored to its inheritance by reason of its evils. This is an act either of someone

---

21. I have followed the conjecture in PL rather than the text established in CSEL.

ignorant or of someone who hands the soul over to these evils that were mentioned previously. I have recalled this because you said not long ago that God adopted the soul for himself, not that the soul came from God. For adoption is something else."

29. Augustine said: "I remember that I spoke yesterday about our adoption according to the testimony of the apostle, who says that we have been called to adoption as children.[22] That answer, therefore, was not mine but the apostle's. And on this topic, that is, on this adoption, let us inquire, if you want, at the proper time, and I shall reply concerning that inbreathing of the soul when you reply to my objections."

Fortunatus said: "I say that the soul went forth against the opposing nature, and that that nature could not harm God in any way."

30. Augustine said: "What need was there for this going forth when God had nothing to watch out for, since nothing could harm him?"

Fortunatus said: "Is it certain in your mind that Christ came from God?"

31. Augustine said: "Again you question me; reply to my questions."

Fortunatus said: "I have accepted in faith that Christ[23] came here by the will of God."

32. Augustine said: "And I ask: Why did God, who is omnipotent, inviolable, and immutable, and whom nothing can harm, send the soul here to these miseries, to error, to these evils which we suffer?"

Fortunatus said: "After all, it was said: *I have the power to lay down my soul and the power to take it up again* (Jn 10:18). Now[24] he said that the soul went forth by the will of God."

33. Augustine said: "But I am asking for the reason, since nothing could harm God."

Fortunatus said: "We have already said that nothing harms God, and we have said that the soul was present in the opposing nature in order to place a limit upon the opposing nature. Once it has imposed a limit upon the opposing nature, God takes up the same soul. For he himself said, *I have the power to lay down my soul and the power to take it up again.* The Father gave me the power to lay down my soul and to take it up again. About which soul, therefore, would God, who was speaking in the Son, say this? It is clear that it is our soul that is found in these bodies because it came by the will of God and will be taken up again by his will."

34. Augustine said: "Everyone knows why our Lord said, *I have the power to lay down my soul and the power to take it up again.* For he was going to suffer

---

22. See Eph 1:5.

23. I have followed the CSEL reading of *ipse* rather than *ipsa*, which is found in PL. In the first case Christ is referred to; in the latter the soul.

24. The CSEL text has *non* instead of *nunc,* which is found in PL. I have chosen to follow the PL text, which fits better with what follows.

and rise. But I ask of you again and again: If nothing could harm God, why did he send the soul here?"

Fortunatus said: "To place a limit on the opposing nature."

35. Augustine said: "And in order to place a limit on the opposing nature, did God, who is omnipotent and most merciful toward all, want to make the opposing nature limited in order to make us free from every limit?"

Fortunatus said: "But for this reason he calls it back to himself."

36. Augustine said: "If he calls the soul back to himself from a lack of limit, from sin, from error, and from misery, what need was there for the soul to suffer such great evils for so long a time, up to the end of the world, since nothing could harm God, who you say sent the soul?"

Fortunatus said: "What am I going to say, then?"

37. Augustine said: "I too know that you do not have anything to say and that I never found anything to say on this question when I was one of your Hearers, and for this reason I was warned by God to abandon this error and convert to — or rather return to — the Catholic faith,[25]because of the mercy of him who did not allow me to cling to this error forever. But if you admit that you do not have anything to reply, I shall explain the Catholic faith to all who are listening and who recognize this fact, if they allow me and want me to do this, for they are believers."

Fortunatus said: "Without any prejudice to what I profess, I would say that, when I have gone over with my elders the objections that you raised, if they do not reply to my questions, which you are now likewise setting before me, I shall consider — for I too want my soul to be set free by the certain faith — coming to the investigation of this topic which you are offering me and which you promise that you will show me."

Augustine said: "Thanks be to God!"

---

25. See *Confessions* I, 11, 17.

Answer to Adimantus, a Disciple of Mani

(Contra Adminantum, Manichaei discipulum)

Introduction

Augustine tells us that, while he was still a priest, there came into his hands a work of Adimantus, who was a disciple of Mani. There is no reason not to take Augustine's use of the word "disciple" in the strict sense. Hence, Adimantus would most probably have been one of the twelve immediate disciples of Mani, the one whom Faustus of Milevis called "most learned" and "a man who should alone be studied after our blessed father, Mani." In his *Answer to an Enemy of the Law and the Prophets* Augustine tells us that Adimantus had the first name Addas. He was sent by Mani to Egypt to preach the Manichean religion, and from there it seems that his writing made its way to Augustine in Hippo Regius.

The basic theme of Adimantus' work is the incompatibility of the Old and the New Testaments, which he tries to establish by citing texts from both Testaments that were seemingly opposed to each other. The rejection of the Old Testament on the grounds that it was opposed to the New is standard gnostic teaching that goes back at least as far as Marcion in the second century. Augustine elsewhere speaks of interpreting scripture in terms of history, allegory, analogy, and etiology, and there he explains that the analogical interpretation of scripture demonstrates the harmony of the two Testaments. Augustine's *Answer to Adimantus*, like his *Answer to an Enemy of the Law and the Prophets*, is an extended illustration of the analogical interpretation of scripture. One by one, Augustine takes the allegedly contradictory passages cited by Adimatus, and he explains how they are not in fact contradictory. He mentions in his *Revisions* that he replied to certain questions twice because the answers he had written got lost but were found after he had written the second reply. He also mentions that he left some questions unanswered due to the press of more important tasks and also simply to forgetfulness. The work, as we have it, contains twenty-eight chapters, some very brief, others more lengthy. The chapters follow the order of the books of the Old Testament from which the objections were drawn.

Adimantus claimed first of all that Genesis had ascribed the creation of heaven and earth to God the Father, while John the evangelist ascribed the creation of all things to the Word. Augustine says that the Manicheans are refuted for three reasons. First, Christians understand that the God who created heaven and earth is the Trinity. Secondly, when Genesis says that God said, *Let there be made*, he obviously created by his Word. And thirdly, if one does not understand that the Son was at work with the Father in Genesis, though he is not mentioned, then one ought to exclude the Son from the activities of the Father that Christ mentions in the gospel without any mention of his own sharing in them. The Manicheans also point to a passage from the apostle in which creation is attributed to the Son without mention of the Father, and Augustine cites another passage from the apostle in which creation is attributed to the Father without mention of the Son (chapter 1).

Adimantus claimed that God's rest on the seventh day after the work of creation in Genesis was contrary to Christ's claim that his Father was still at work. Augustine points out that Genesis did not say that God rested from all his works but from all the works that he had made. Hence, he continued to govern the world and did not create another world. In addition, Augustine explains that the Jews observed the Sabbath in a carnal manner by abstaining even from actions that helped other people but that Christians understand the Sabbath, which they do not observe as the Jews did, in terms of hoping for the rest that Christ promised would be theirs at the end of the world (chapter 2).

The Manicheans claimed that, in uniting man and woman in marriage, the God of Genesis was opposed to Christ, who promised the kingdom of heaven to anyone who leaves wife and home for his sake. Augustine notes first that the New Testament also speaks about a man's loving his wife. He also observes that, when Christ was questioned by the Jews concerning divorce, he reaffirmed the position of the Old Testament. Augustine warns that, if the Manicheans claim that Christ's words are an interpolation, they are undermining the credibility of the whole gospel. Furthermore, he explains that the New Testament allows a man to leave his wife for the sake of the kingdom of heaven but does not allow him to abandon the kingdom of heaven for his wife. The apostle Paul also commands a man to love his wife, and he uses the union of man and wife to illustrate Christ's union with his Church. Finally, Augustine cites a text from Isaiah in which, even in the Old Testament, God made great promises to those who were eunuchs and kept his commandments (chapter 3).

Adimantus claimed that God's punishing Cain with the barrenness of the earth was opposed to Jesus's words to his disciples that they should not worry about what they were to eat or wear. Augustine argues that the Manicheans supposed that the murderous Cain should be compared to the disciples of Christ, although it was fitting that Cain was cursed with the earth's barrenness, while Christ's ministers experienced its fruitfulness. If the Manicheans are horrified at God's curse upon Cain, Augustine responds, they should be even more horrified at Christ's having cursed the barren fig tree. Furthermore, there are passages in the Old Testament that teach us not to worry about tomorrow just as there are in the New (chapter 4).

The Manicheans claimed that the words of Genesis — that God made human beings to his image and likeness — were opposed to the words of Christ, who called the Jews children of the devil and a brood of vipers. Augustine explains that Genesis spoke of human beings before they sinned, while Christ was speaking to sinners. He points out, too, that the scriptures speak of sons on the basis of nature, on the basis of teaching, and on the basis of imitation, and that the Jews were children of the devil either because he was their teacher or because they imitated him. The apostle Paul also teaches that human beings have been made to the image of God and that we have been so renewed to the image of God by Christ that we love our enemies (chapter 5).

The Manicheans opposed the Old Testament commandment about honoring one's parents to the words that Christ addressed to his prospective follower, who wanted first to bury his parents, when he said that he should allow the dead to bury the dead. Augustine explains that the apparent opposition can be resolved in the same way as he resolved the question about leaving one's wife. He also notes that Christ himself told another prospective disciple that he should keep the commandments, which included the commandment to honor one's parents (chapter 6).

Exodus speaks of a jealous God, who punishes children for the sins of their parents to the third and fourth generation. The Manicheans claimed that the Lord's words in the gospel, to the effect that his disciples should imitate the goodness of their heavenly Father and should forgive their brothers seven times seventy times, were opposed to the passage from Exodus. Augustine says that it is right that God punishes sinners, and he points out that the Manichean God punishes even his own members along with the nation of darkness. Moreover, God punishes the children of sinful parents when the children continue to live in the sins of their parents, and he punishes them out of justice, not out of cruelty. Augustine suggests that the children to the third and fourth generation signify the people who continued to sin in the ages from Abraham to David, from David to the Babylonian captivity, from the Babylonian captivity to the coming of Christ, and from the coming of Christ to the end of the world, as Matthew distinguished these ages in his genealogy of Jesus. There are, furthermore, many passages in the Old Testament that speak of God's goodness, just as there are many passages in the New that speak of his punishing sinners. Augustine explains that God is said to be jealous because, in keeping us from sinning, he is like a jealous husband who guards the chastity of his wife. Finally, he says that God will forgive a sinner seven times seventy times, but only if the sinner repents (chapter 7).

So too, the Manicheans pointed to the opposition between the law of Exodus, in which it said that one should exact an eye for an eye and a tooth for a tooth, and the teaching of Christ in the Sermon on the Mount. Augustine admits that the passages from Exodus and from Matthew show a difference between the two Testaments, but between two Testaments of one God. He explains that Exodus had set a limit to retaliation because people tended to exact a penalty far beyond the injury they suffered. In that way they learned a degree of leniency so that Christ could teach them even to forgive those who did them an injury (chapter 8).

In many passages of the Old Testament God is said to have spoken with human beings and to have been seen by them. The Manicheans contrasted with these passages the words of Christ, that no one had seen God save the Son who revealed him and that the Jews had neither heard his voice nor seen his face. Augustine says that the first of these words resolves the whole question. For the Son, that is, the Word of God, has made God known from the creation of the world, whether by speaking or by appearing either through an angel or through some other creature, when he willed and to whom he willed. If the Manicheans are disturbed because God spoke to sinners in the Old Testament, Augustine responds by saying that Christ spoke to sinners in the New Testament and that the truth speaks whenever anyone speaks the truth. Moreover, the Jews did not hear God's voice because they did not obey him, and they did not see his face because it was impossible (chapter 9).

The Manicheans found fault with the Old Testament directions for building a tabernacle for God to dwell in, and they contrasted with them Christ's words that heaven was God's throne and the earth was his footstool. Augustine's rejoinder is that it was the Old Testament that first spoke of heaven as God's throne and of the earth as his footstool, and he quotes the words of Jesus that the temple in Jerusalem was the house of his father (chapter 10).

In Exodus God forbade the worship of alien gods because he was, as he said, a jealous God. Augustine comments that the Manicheans do not like this prohibition because they have in fact many gods that they worship. They also complain that the Old Testament statement that God is jealous is contrary to the New Testament claim that God is just. Augustine explains that God's jealousy is simply his providence, by which he keeps a soul from committing fornication through the worship of alien gods, and that it does not signify mental anguish, as it can in a jealous human spouse. Scripture chose to use words in speaking about God that human beings regard as unworthy of him in order to teach us that even words that we might think worthy of God are unworthy of his majesty. Thus "mercy" is in its root meaning a term unworthy of God, though the scriptures again and again speak of his mercy (chapter 11).

In Deuteronomy God forbade the Jews to eat blood because blood was the soul. The Manicheans opposed to this Christ's teaching that we should not fear those who could kill the body but could not harm the soul. For, if our soul was our blood, they asked how human beings did not have power over their souls. The Manicheans also quoted the words of the apostle, that flesh and blood would not possess the kingdom of God, and they argued that, if our blood was our soul, then our soul would not possess the kingdom of God. Augustine first of all points out that the Old Testament never says that the human soul is blood and that, if animal souls are blood, it presents no problem. Even if it were true that the human soul was blood, the Jews who believed this would not be guilty of a crime if the blood of their parents were devoured by animals. But the Manicheans believe that human souls return in other living beings; hence, Adimantus has to be afraid of beating his father while beating a lazy animal. Furthermore, the Manicheans do not refrain from killing fleas and lice, though they cannot explain why human souls do not return in such tiny creatures. Augustine explains that he can also interpret the words about blood being the soul as a sign, just as Christ said that bread was his body. The apostle Paul's statement that flesh and blood would not possess the kingdom of God has to be understood in the context of the First Letter to the Corinthians, where the apostle clearly teaches that by flesh and blood he meant our present mortal and corruptible bodies. They will not possess the kingdom of God because they will be transformed into immortal and incorruptible bodies in the resurrection. Augustine explains that he has taken the present occasion to discuss the resurrection of the body because the Manicheans deny the resurrection of the body. The text from Deuteronomy, however, spoke about blood, not about the body, and Augustine claims that the Old Testament said that blood was the soul in figurative language, just as the apostle Paul said that Christ was a rock. But he does not explain this figure of speech, and he asserts that it is enough for the Manicheans to know that Catholics do not understand scripture as the Manicheans suppose (chapter 12).

Adimantus cited the words of Deuteronomy about not worshiping images because God is a devouring fire and a jealous God. Augustine says that he has already said enough about God's jealousy, but he notes that the Manicheans tie God's jealousy to the prohibition of idols in order to curry favor with the pagans. Then he reiterates that scripture uses language which is obviously unworthy of God in order to make us realize that all human words are unworthy of God. The Manicheans object to God's being a devouring fire, but Christ said in the New Testament that he came to cast fire upon the earth. This is the fire of love that devours our old selves and that had set afire the hearts of the disciples at Emmaus. Adimantus had tried to show that the God of the New Testament was good, as opposed to the God of the Old Testament, who was jealous. Augustine asserts that someone else could claim just the opposite by gathering the many passages from the Old Testament that speak of God's goodness and the passages from the New Testament where God might be seen as cruel (chapter 13).

Deuteronomy had permitted people to kill animals and to eat them according to the desire of their hearts. Adimantus claimed that the gospel and the apostle Paul were opposed to this. Augustine states that Deuteronomy was not permitting the Jewish people to eat to the point of overindulgence. Adimantus quoted the apostle's words about not eating meat and drinking wine. Augustine accuses him of taking a single verse out of its context and quotes all of Romans 14. For the apostle did not, like the Manicheans, think that meat and wine were unclean but clearly stated that all foods were clean, though he advocated abstinence in order to control concupiscence and to avoid giving scandal to a weaker brother.

Augustine is puzzled that Adimantus opposed the apostle's words about not partaking of the table of the Lord and of the table of demons to the passage in Deuteronomy about killing and eating animals, since the latter passage had nothing to do with sacrifices. He again quotes at length from the apostle, this time from the First Letter to the Corinthians, to show that Paul was speaking of meat offered to idols. Finally, he explains that the animals that were called unclean in the Old Testament could symbolize various kinds of unclean or sinful human beings (chapter 14).

Adimantus found that the prohibition in Leviticus against eating various unclean animals was contrary to the words of Jesus, that nothing entering a man's mouth defiled him. Augustine expresses his amazement that Adimantus would use these words of Jesus immediately after having claimed that meat and wine were unclean. Then Augustine argues that the unclean animals which the Jewish people were forbidden to eat symbolize the sorts of human conduct that the Church rejects as unclean and are not absorbed into her body. Adimantus claimed that Jesus had said to the crowds that nothing that entered a man's mouth defiled him, but that he forbade his disciples to eat meat. Augustine says that Adimantus tried to use this ploy because the Manicheans allow their Hearers to eat meat though they forbid their Elect to do so. Augustine points out that, when Peter took the Lord aside and asked him to explain his words, Jesus repeated the same idea to the future head of his Church. If a Manichean were to ask Augustine to explain what the unclean animals symbolized, he would decline to do so on the grounds that it would take too long, but he also argues that it is not necessary, since the apostle Paul said that all those observances of the Old Testament were symbols of the things to come, which Christ has fulfilled (chapter 15).

Adimantus quoted from Deuteronomy the law concerning the observance of the Sabbath and from Genesis the law concerning circumcision. He then tried to show that Jesus's words were opposed to these passages, because the Lord said that the scribes and Pharisees worked hard to make a single convert and then made him a son of hell, as if the convert became a son of hell because he observed the law regarding the Sabbath and circumcision. Augustine shows that the convert became a son of hell because he imitated the evil actions of the scribes and Pharisees, not because he observed the law, which Jesus in fact praised. Adimantus quoted the words of the apostle Paul, that neither circumcision nor the lack of circumcision was important, as if they were opposed to the law, but Augustine shows that they are clearly not against the law. Adimantus also quoted the apostle's words to the Galatians about their observances of days, the Sabbath, and solemnities. Augustine indicates that Adimantus misquoted Paul, and then he explains that Christians no longer observe the days that the Jews celebrated, because the Jewish observances were signs of the realities that have now been realized in Christ and the Church. Hence, Christians understand both circumcision and the Sabbath in a spiritual sense as referring to the circumcision of the heart and to the heavenly rest (chapter 16).

Adimantus opposed Christ's words about loving one's enemies to the passage in Exodus about the extermination of the peoples in the land promised to the Jews. Augustine says that Adimantus has added verses from Exodus about not worshiping the gods of these nations in order to curry favor with the pagans, and he suggests that the Manicheans understand Christ's command to love one's enemies to include not merely human beings but even demons and idols. With regard to the Jews' killing of their enemies Augustine first notes that what is important is the intention with which they did this. He also points to Saint Paul's handing a man over to Satan for the destruction of his flesh to show that one can impose punishment with love. He then turns against the Manicheans a story from the apocrypha about the apostle Thomas and argues that, when the Jews saw the punishment inflicted upon the peoples who worshiped idols, they would have a salutary fear of the punishment that they might receive if they abandoned God. Augustine insists that every parent punishes a child whom he loves if the child does wrong, though parents do not, of course, punish children with death. But God — who knows what punishment he should give and whom he should punish — punishes human beings at times even with death, for, though he loves them as human beings, he hates them as sinners. Augustine also cites a passage from Saint Paul to show how God corrects human beings with weakness, illness, and even death. He uses the parable of the unjust judge to show that God promised his elect that he would take vengeance on their enemies, and he claims that, as long as the Manicheans do not understand that vengeance does not have to involve hatred, they will not understand how the Old and New Testaments are not opposed to each other. Augustine shows from the Acts of the Apostles and from various apocryphal books which the Manicheans accepted that the apostles imposed punishments and exacted vengeance with love, and he asserts that both the Old and the New Testaments teach the severity and the mercy of God. Finally, Augustine points to the example of David, who showed mercy to his enemy, Saul, though God had handed Saul over into his power (chapter 17).

Adimantus said that the words of Jesus about renouncing the things of this world in order to be his follower were opposed to the promises of temporal blessings in Deuteronomy. Augustine replies that carnal and temporal blessings were appropriately promised to the Jewish people and that spiritual and eternal blessings are now appropriately promised to the Christian people. And he also points out that Jesus promised his followers many temporal blessings in this life while the books of the Old Testament also teach a contempt for temporal goods (chapter 18).

The Manicheans opposed the words of Jesus about the blessedness of the poor in spirit to God's promise in the Old Testament of riches to his friends and poverty to his enemies. Augustine wonders how the Manicheans could fail to see that Jesus also promised that the meek would inherit the earth. And the parable of Lazarus and the rich man show how the God of the New Testament reduced his enemies to poverty. Augustine adds a series of passages from the Old Testament in which riches are held in contempt and argues that, if the Manicheans paid attention to such texts, they would see how the two Testaments were in harmony with each other (chapter 19).

Adimantus claimed that the words of Christ to his apostles about not carrying gold and silver, two tunics, sandals, and a staff contradicted the promises of temporal blessings in Leviticus. Augustine observes that he has already said a great deal about the temporal blessings promised to the people of the Old Testament. From the teaching and example of the apostle Paul he shows that Jesus' words were not commands that he gave to his disciples but were what he permitted them to do. He cites the teaching in the First Letter to Timothy on how the rich of this world should place their hope not in their riches but in God, and he shows that it is wrong not to have riches but to place one's hope in them. The people of Israel, moreover, learned to love God because of the temporal blessings he gave them. The Manicheans also averred that the apostle's words, that God was pleased not by fighting and dissension but by peace, were opposed to the Old Testament. Augustine explains that the peace which God wants for us is a peace that no one can take away, not the sort of peace which Manicheans preach in their myth (chapter 20).

The Manicheans thought that Jesus' words about taking up one's cross and following him were opposed to the Deuteronomical curse upon anyone who was hanged upon a tree. Augustine indicates that Jesus did not literally mean that everyone ought to take up a cross. Rather, a Christian crucifies his flesh with its passions and desires so that his old self is put to death. Christ assumed our mortality, and by dying on the cross he put our death to death. Hence, it was not Christ but death that was cursed by the words of Deuteronomy, and, by undergoing for us the most ignominious form of death, Christ revealed to us his love for us (chapter 21).

The Manicheans viewed Jesus' action of healing a withered hand on the Sabbath as contrary to God's command that a man be stoned to death for gathering wood on the Sabbath. Augustine indicates a number of differences between Jesus' act of healing on the Sabbath and the man's act of gathering wood on the Sabbath, and he mentions that he has already said things about the carnal observance of the Sabbath, the punishment of death, and the times of God's severity and of God's mercy (chapter 22).

Augustine complains that the Manicheans do not understand that the blessings upon wife and children that God promised in Psalm 128 to the man who feared the Lord were signs of the Church. The Manicheans objected that Christ's words about those who became eunuchs for the kingdom of God were opposed to the words of the psalm (chapter 23).

The Manicheans thought that the words of the Lord about unconcern for the morrow contradicted the words of Solomon about imitating the diligence of the ant in storing up food for winter. Augustine says that they do not understand that the Lord's words have to do with our not loving temporal things and with fearing that we shall lack necessities. The words of Solomon, however, should be interpreted as referring to gathering the word of God in a time of tranquility and storing it away for a time of adversity (chapter 24).

Hosea had asked God to give certain people an empty belly, dry breasts, and lifeless seed. Augustine claims that the Manicheans do not understand that the words of the prophet are figurative, and he illustrates his point from the New Testament. Hence, the Manicheans are wrong to think that the words of Christ about not marrying or being given in marriage after the resurrection are opposed to Hosea's words (chapter 25).

Adimantus produced a passage from Amos which said that God caused evils. Augustine replies that we must understand the evils in that passage to be punishments of sin, but not sins. Just punishment is of course something good. Adimantus set opposite to the passage from Amos the words of Christ about the good tree producing only good fruit. Augustine points out that the good tree of which Christ spoke was not God but a good human being. He also says that Adimantus should have noticed that in the same chapter of the gospel Christ said that his Father was going to uproot the tree that he did not plant. Hence, the God of the New Testament also causes the evil of punishment (chapter 26).

In Isaiah God said that he created evils. To this Adimantus contrasted the beatitude about the peacemakers who will be called the children of God. Augustine resolves this objection in the same way as he had the previous one. He also points to the apostle's words about the mercy and severity of God in the New Testament, to Ezekiel's words about God's not wanting the death of the sinner, and to the words of Christ which he will speak to those damned to the fires of hell (chapter 27).

The final chapter deals with the supposed opposition between Isaiah's vision of God surrounded by the seraphim and the apostle's having said that God is invisible. Augustine remarks that invisible things can be seen by the eyes of the mind, even if they cannot be seen by the eyes of the body. He shows that the scriptures speak of three kinds of vision: by the eyes of the body, by spiritual sight in the imagination, and by the eyes of the mind. And he concludes by saying that the Manicheans seem to have overlooked Christ's promise that the clean of heart will see God (chapter 28).

Revisions I, 22 (21)

Answer to Adimantus, a Disciple of Mani

1. At the same time there came into my hands certain *Discussions of Adimantus*, who had been a disciple of Mani. He composed these *Discussions* against the law and the prophets, having tried to show that the gospel and the apostolic writings were as it were contrary to them. I replied to him, citing his words and giving my response. I completed the work in one volume, and in it I replied to certain questions not once but twice, because my first response had been lost and was then found after I had replied the second time. To be sure, I resolved some of the same questions in sermons addressed to the people of the Church.[1] I have still not replied to others. Some remained that were passed over because of other more urgent matters as well as through forgetfulness.

2. In this work I said, "For before the coming of the Lord the people that received the Old Testament were bound by certain definite shadows and figures of things in accord with the wondrous and most well-ordered arrangement of the times. In it, nonetheless, there is so great a proclamation and prediction of the New Testament that no commandment and promise is found in the teaching of the gospel and of the apostles, however difficult and godly, that is not present in those old books."[2] But I should have added "almost" and have said: "So that almost no commandment and promise is found in the teaching of the gospel and of the apostles, however difficult and godly, that is not present in those old books." What do the words of the Lord in the Sermon on the Mount, *You have heard that it was said to the people of old, but I say this to you* (Mt 5.21.22), mean, after all, if he did not command more than was commanded in the old books? Moreover, we do not read that the kingdom of heaven was promised to that people among those things that were promised in the law given through Moses on Mount Sinai, which is properly called the Old Testament, which the apostle says was prefigured by the maidservant of Sarah and her son.[3] Then, if the figures are examined, we find that everything was foretold in those books that Christ brought about or that we are waiting for him to bring about. On account of some commandments, nonetheless, that are presented in figures but that in their proper sense are not found in the Old Testament but in the New, it would have been more cautious and balanced to say "almost no" rather than "no commandments" are found in the New that are not also found in the Old Testa-

---

1. See Sermons 1, 50, 142, 153.
2. *Answer to Adimantus* 3,4.
3. See Gal 4:22-24.

ment, although the two commandments about the love of God and neighbor —
to which everything in the law, the prophets, the gospel, and the apostles refers
— are found in the Old Testament.

3. Also my words, "In the holy scriptures the term 'sons' is used in three
ways,"[4] were said without sufficient thought. For we certainly passed over some
other ways. For we find there *a son of hell* (Mt 23:15) or *an adopted son* (Rom
8:15; Gal 4:15), and these expressions are not said in terms of birth or in terms of
teaching or in terms of imitation. We gave examples of these three ways as if
they were the only ones. In that way the Jews were *sons of Abraham* (Jn 8:37) in
terms of birth. The apostle calls those to whom he taught the gospel his sons in
terms of teaching.[5] And he calls us sons in terms of imitation, *as we are sons of
Abraham* (Gal 3:7), whose faith we imitate. But I said, "When a person has
donned incorruption and immortality, he will no longer be flesh and blood."[6] I
meant that there will not be flesh in terms of carnal corruption, not in terms of its
substance, in accord with which the body of the Lord was still called flesh after
the resurrection.[7]

4. In another place I said, "Unless someone changes his will, he cannot do
what is good, and in another passage he teaches that this has been placed in our
power, where he says, *Either make the tree good and its fruit good, or make the
tree bad and its fruit bad* (Mt 12:33)."[8] This is not opposed to the grace that we
preach. It is certainly in the power of a human being to change his will for the
better, but that power only exists if it is given by God, of whom it was said, *He
gave them the power to become children of God* (Jn 1:12). Since it is in our
power to do something when we will to do it, nothing is so much in our power as
the will itself, *but the will is prepared by the Lord* (Prv 8:35 LXX). In that way,
then, he gives us the power. What I said later, "It lies in our power that we merit
either to be grafted on by the goodness of God or cut off by his severity,"[9] must
also be understood in this way. For nothing is in our power but that which
follows upon our will. And when the will is made strong and powerful by the
Lord, even an act of piety that was difficult and impossible becomes easy.

The book begins as follows: "On the words: *In the beginning God made
heaven and earth.*"

---

4. *Answer to Adimantus* 5, 1.
5. See 1 Cor 4:14-15.
6. *Answer to Adimantus* 12, 5; see 1 Cor 15:54.
7. See Lk 14:39.
8. *Answer to Adimantus* 26,1.
9. Ibid. 27,1.

Answer to Adimantus, a Disciple of Mani

1. On the words: *In the beginning God made heaven and earth*, up to the words, *And evening came and morning came, one day* (Gn 1:1-5). The utterly foolish Manicheans think that this chapter of the law is opposed to the gospel. They say that in Genesis it is written that God made heaven, earth, and light by himself, but in the gospel it says that the world was made by our Lord Jesus Christ, where it says, *And the world was made by him, and the world did not know him* (Jn 1:10). They are refuted in three ways. First, because when it says, *In the beginning God made heaven and earth*, a Christian sees the Trinity, whereby we understand not only the Father but also the Son and the Holy Spirit. We do not believe in three gods but in one God, the Father, the Son, and the Holy Spirit, although the Father is the Father, the Son is the Son, and the Holy Spirit is the Holy Spirit. It would take too long to discuss the unity of the Trinity here. Secondly, because where it says, *God said, Let there be made, and there was made* (Gn 1:3-24), it is necessary to understand that he made what he made by his Word. But the Word of the Father is the Son. This section of Genesis, therefore, where it says, *And God said, Let there be made, and there was made*, is not opposed to the passage of the gospel where it says, *And the world was made by him*, that is, by our Lord, because he is the Word of the Father by whom all things were made. Finally, if the Son is not understood in Genesis because it did not say there that God made anything by the Son, then God did not in the gospel also feed the birds and clothe the lilies by the Son,[10] along with the countless other things that the Lord himself says God the Father does, though he does not say that the Father does them by the Son.

But the Manicheans also add the testimony of the apostle. He says of our Lord Jesus Christ: *He is the firstborn of all creation, and all things were made by him in heaven and on earth, those that are visible and those that are invisible* (Col 1:15-16), and they say that this passage is opposed to Genesis, where God is said to have made the world without the Son's being specifically mentioned there. They are terribly mistaken and do not see that, if this is so, the apostle is opposed to himself, since in another passage he speaks of the one *from whom all things are, by whom all things are, and in whom all things are* (Rom 11:36) without mentioning the Son. But just as the Son is not mentioned here but is nonetheless understood, so he is in Genesis. And just as these two passages of Paul are not opposed to each other, neither is Genesis opposed to the gospel.

---

10. See Mt 6:26.30.

2, 1. On the words: *And God finished on the sixth day all the works that he made, and on the seventh day he rested from all the works that he had made* (Gn 2:2). The Manicheans also speak slanderously of this passage and say that what is written in Genesis, namely, that God rested on the seventh day from all the works he made, contradicts the New Testament, because the Lord says in the gospel, *My Father is working up to now* (Jn 5:17). In no way are these opposed. For the Lord is refuting the error of the Jews, who thought that God rested on the seventh day so that he did no work at all from that time on. But God rested from all the works that he made in such a way that afterward he did not make another world with all the things that are in it, but still not so that he also rested from the governance of the world. After all, it did not say, "God rested from all his works so that he did not work thereafter." Rather, it said, *God rested from all the works that he made*, so that thereafter he did not work in making the world, the work from which he ceased after its completion, but he did work in governing the world, the work in which the Lord taught that he was involved. Nor does that rest signify that God sought repose after his labor but that he ceased from creating the natures of things after their completion, though he works in governing them up to now.

2, 2. The Jews did not understand the observance of the Sabbath, however; they thought that one ought to cease even from works that contribute to the well-being of human beings. For this reason the Lord also refuted them in other passages by a remarkable comparison concerning the ox that fell into a pit and the beast that had to be untied to be led to water.[11] The Sabbath, which Christians did not repudiate but understood, of course ceased to be observed in a carnal manner, but it is retained by the saints, who understand the words of the Lord who calls us to rest and says, *Come to me, you who labor, and I shall refresh you. Take my yoke upon you, and learn from me that I am meek and humble of heart, and you will find rest for your souls. For my yoke is easy, and my burden light.* (Mt 11:29-30) That passage of scripture signifies this Sabbath, that is, this rest, which the Jews did not understand, and in accord with God's plan for the different times they followed its shadow, while the body producing that shadow, that is, the truth, was going to be given to us. But just as we are told of that rest of God's after the making of the world, so on the seventh day, that is, at the end of this age, we shall attain the rest that is promised to us after the works that we have in this life, if they are righteous works. It would take too long to discuss this. The Lord, then, did not rescind the scripture of the Old Testament, but he makes us understand it, nor did he undo the Sabbath so that what was prefigured would be lost, but rather he reveals it so that what was hidden might be seen.

3, 1. On the words in Genesis: *And God said, It is not good for the man to be alone; let us make a helper for him. And God sent a sleep upon Adam, and he fell*

---

11. See Lk 14:5; 13:15.

asleep, and he took one of his ribs, from which he formed Eve, whom he brought to Adam. And he said, And therefore a man shall leave his father and mother and shall cling to his wife. (Gn 2:18-20) Again, the Manicheans speak slanderously of this passage. They say that this statement, where it is written that God both formed the woman and united her to the man, is against the New Testament, because in the gospel the Lord says, *Everyone who leaves home or wife or parents or brothers or children for the sake of the kingdom of heaven will receive a hundred times as much in this time and will possess eternal life in the world to come* (Mt 19:29; Mk 10:29-30; Lk 18:29-30). In this slander I am surprised that they are so blinded, or rather I am not surprised. For, as scripture says, *Their malice has blinded them* (Wis 2:21). But still who does not see that there are forceful commandments in the New Testament about loving one's wife? Why, after all, do they also say that the Old Testament is opposed to the statement of the Lord in which he says that a man must leave his wife for the sake of the kingdom of heaven rather than that the New Testament is opposed to itself? And that is absolutely wrong to say. For it is necessary to understand and not rashly accuse the passages that seem contradictory to the ignorant.

3, 2. For even the Lord, when asked by the Jews whether he approved the dismissal of a wife after giving her a certificate of divorce, replied to them and said, *Have you not read that he who made them from the beginning made them male and female? And he said, On this account a man shall leave his father and mother and cling to his wife, and they shall be two in one flesh. And so they are not now two but one flesh. What God has made one, then, let man not divide. They said to him, Why, then, did Moses command that she be given a certificate of divorce and dismissed? Jesus said to them, On account of the hardness of your hearts Moses permitted you to dismiss your wives. From the beginning, however, it was not so. But I say to you, whoever dismisses his wife, except for a case of fornication, makes her commit adultery, and if he marries another, he himself commits adultery.* (Mt 19:3-9) There the Manicheans have the statement of the Old Testament reaffirmed by the Lord himself against the ignorance of the Jews. At the same time he also bore witness to Moses that on account of the hardness of their heart he allowed them to divorce their wives. Do they also say that the gospel is opposed to the gospel? But if they say that this section is not authentic and was added by those who corrupted the scriptures — for they often say this when they do not find anything to say in reply — what will they do if someone else says that what they cite as the Lord's words, *Everyone who leaves home or wife or parents or children for the sake of the kingdom of heaven,* and so on, is an interpolation and is not authentic? The poor wretches do not understand how they are trying to overthrow the whole Christian faith when they say that. But the true faith and the discipline of the Catholic Church affirms that both are true and were said by the Lord and are in no way contradictory, because the union of a husband and wife comes from the Lord and the leaving of a wife for the sake of the kingdom of heaven also comes from the Lord.

It does not follow that, because Jesus Christ raised the dead and gave them life, one should not give up life itself for the sake of the kingdom of heaven. So too, then, although the Lord gives a wife to a man, he should leave her, if necessary, for the sake of the kingdom of heaven. After all, this is not always necessary. For the apostle says, *If any believer has a non-believing wife and she agrees to live with him, he should not divorce her* (1 Cor 7:12). He indicates, of course, that, if she does not agree to live with him, that is, if she detests in him his faith in Christ and does not tolerate him because he is a Christian, he should leave her for the sake of the kingdom of heaven. In this vein the same apostle says in what follows: *But if a non-believing spouse departs, let him depart, for a brother or sister is not subject to servitude in such a case* (1 Cor 7:15). If anyone abandons the kingdom of heaven, therefore, because he is unwilling to leave a wife who cannot put up with a Christian husband, he is rebuked by the Lord, and likewise, if any man abandons his wife after giving her a certificate of divorce, when it is not either a case of fornication or of obtaining the kingdom of heaven, he is likewise rebuked by the Lord. Thus these two passages of the gospel are not found to be contrary to each other, nor is the gospel found to be contrary to the Old Testament, because a wife is united to her husband in order that they may together merit to possess the kingdom of heaven, and a man is commanded to leave his wife if she is preventing her husband from possessing the kingdom of heaven.

3, 3. And thus, when the apostle warns both sorts of Christians, that is, husbands and wives, does he not speak in this way: *Love your wives as Christ also loved the Church and handed himself over for her* (Eph 5:25), and, *Wives should be subject to their husbands as to the Lord* (Eph 5:22), because the Church is also subject to Christ? Does not the same apostle understand as a great mystery the passage which these wretches mock in the Old Testament, where it says, *And for this reason a man shall leave his father and mother and shall cling to his wife, and they shall be two in one flesh* (Gn 2:24)? For he says, *This is a great sacrament. I mean, however, in Christ and in the Church.* (Eph 5:32) Then he adds, *And yet, let each man love his wife as he loves himself, but let the wife fear her husband* (Eph 5:33). Does he not in another place show most clearly that both the nature and the union of both sexes were established by the Lord God, who created and arranged them, when he says, *And yet, in the Lord the wife is not without her husband, nor the husband without his wife. For as the woman came from the man, so a man also comes through a woman. But all things come from God* (1 Cor 11:11-12)? If these people were willing to consider this, they would not create a fog of confusion for the ignorant with certain passages that they have separated and placed in opposition to one another quite fraudulently, but they would realize that everything both in the Old and in the New Testament was written and entrusted to us by the one Holy Spirit.

3, 4. For even in the Old Testament, in Isaiah the prophet, they have the great promises made to eunuchs, lest the Manicheans think that they were praised by the Lord only in the New Testament, where he says that there are certain men who have castrated themselves for the sake of the kingdom of heaven, and added, *Let him who can accept this accept it* (Mt 19:12). For Isaiah also speaks in this way: *The Lord says to those eunuchs who will keep my commandments and choose for themselves what I want and will be capable of my covenant. I will give them in my house and within my walls a place most renowned, better by far than that of sons and daughters. I will give them an eternal name, nor shall it ever fail.* (Is 56: 4-5) For before the coming of the Lord the people that received the Old Testament were bound by certain definite shadows and figures of things in accord with the wondrous and most well-ordered arrangement of the times. In it, nonetheless, there is so great a proclamation and prediction of the New Testament that no commandment and promise is found in the teaching of the gospel and of the apostles, however difficult and godly, that is not present in those old books.[12] But the holy scriptures want not rash and proud accusers but diligent and pious readers.

4. On the words in Genesis: *And the Lord said to Cain, What have you done? The cry of your brother's blood cries out to me from the earth. Now you shall be cursed by the surface of the earth that has drunk and received the blood of your brother because of his murder at your hand. For you must work the earth, which will give you sterile produce.* (Gn 4:10-12) The Manicheans speak slanders against this passage of Genesis, in which Cain received the curse whereby he was punished by the barrenness of the earth. In their desire to prove that it is contrary to the gospel, it certainly seems to me that they do not think that they are dealing with human beings; instead they act as if those who listened to them or read their writings were animals. For that was the way in which they took advantage of their ignorance and slowness of wit, or rather their blindness of heart. They claimed, indeed, that what the Lord said to his disciples in the gospel was contrary to this passage. For he said, *Do not worry about the morrow, for the morrow will take care of itself. Look at the birds of the sky, for they do not sow or reap, nor do they gather food into barns.* (Mt 6:34.26) The Manicheans do this as if Cain, the murderer of his brother, should be compared with the disciples of Christ. They do this as if, because Cain merited the punishment of the earth's barrenness, it follows that the disciples — who, in following the Lord Jesus Christ, were being prepared for preaching the gospel — should suffer the same barrenness. On the contrary, even in those two passages, one of which they

---

12. *See Revisions* 1, 22 (21), 2.

quoted from Genesis and the other from the gospel as if they were contradictory, there is found such a great compatibility and harmony that none greater should be desired. What, after all, is more fitting, what is more appropriate than that barrenness should overtake that man, even as he labors on the earth, whose crime took the life of his brother, while the fruitful earth served those by whose ministry their brothers were being set free through their preaching of the word of God, though they did not worry even about the morrow?

But if the Manicheans are horrified that in the Old Testament the earth was rendered barren for a sinner by the curse of God, why are they not horrified that, at the curse of our Lord Jesus Christ, a tree was dried up without any sin on the part of its owner?[13] Likewise, if they are pleased by the statement of the Lord, when he says that his disciples should not worry about the morrow because God takes care of their sustenance, why are they not also pleased by the prophet's statement, when he sings and says, *Cast your cares upon the Lord, and he will feed you* (Ps 55:23)? In this way the poor wretches might understand, if they were capable, that the other things said about God which they detest in the Old Testament are so correct that they are also found in the New, and that the things which they praise and approve in the New are also found in the Old. From this the obvious harmony of the two Testaments might become clear for those who understand them correctly.

5, 1. On the words in Genesis: *Let us make man to our image and likeness* (Gn 1:26). The Manicheans say that this passage in Genesis, in which it says that man was made to the image and likeness of God, is contrary to the New Testament, because the Lord says to the Jews in the gospel, *You are from your father, the devil, and you want to carry out the wishes of your father; he was a murderer from the beginning and did not stand in the truth, because the truth is not in him* (Jn 8:44), and because in another passage the Jews are called a brood of vipers.[14] They do not understand that the former statement, that man was made to the image and likeness of God, was said of man before he sinned, but that the latter statement in the gospel, *You are from your father, the devil*, is said to sinners and unbelievers. For in the holy scriptures the term "sons" is understood in three ways.[15] It is understood in one way according to nature, as Isaac is the son of Abraham or as the other Jews who have the same origin are his sons. It is understood in another way according to teaching, as anyone is called the son of someone from whom he has learned something. In that way the apostle calls his sons those who have learned the gospel from him.[16] It is understood in a third way according to imitation, as the apostle calls sons of Abraham those who

13. See Mt 21:19.
14. See Mt 3:7; 23:33.
15. *See Revisions* 1, 22 (21), 3.
16. See 1 Cor 4:14-15.

imitate his faith.[17] The Lord, then, calls the sinful, unbelieving Jews sons of the devil in two ways. It is either because they learned from him their impiety, just as the apostle says of the devil himself, *who is now at work in the sons of unbelief* (Eph 2:2), or it is because they imitate him. This pertains instead to the statement that was made about him, *And he did not stand in the truth.* For the Jews also did not stand in the truth of the law that was given them, as the Lord testifies when he says, *If you believed Moses, you would also believe me. For he wrote about me.* (Jn 5:46) In terms of the venom of their sins they are also called broods of serpents and vipers.[18]

5, 2. Not only Genesis, however, but also the apostle cries out that man was made to the image of God when he says, *A man certainly ought not to veil his head since he is the image and glory of God, but a woman is the glory of her husband* (1 Cor 11:7). And in order that we might clearly understand that man was made to the image of God, not according to his old sinful condition that is subject to corruption but according to his spiritual formation, the same apostle admonishes us that, having stripped off the habit of sin, that is, our old self, we should put on the new life of Christ, which he calls our new self. And to teach that at one point we lost this, he calls it a renewal. For he speaks as follows: *Stripping off your old self with its actions, put on your new self that is being renewed in the knowledge of God in accord with the image of him who created it* (Col 3:9-10). People who have been renewed to his image are therefore sons, and they have been made like him even to the point of loving their enemy. As the Lord says, we ought to love our enemies in order that we might be like our Father who is in heaven.[19] Scripture teaches that God himself placed this in our power when it says, *He gave them the power to become sons of God* (Jn 1:12). But people are called sons of the devil when they imitate his impious pride, fall away from the light and the height of wisdom, and do not believe the truth. The Lord rebukes such people when he says, *You are from your father, the devil,* and so on. The prophet agrees with this passage of the gospel when he says, *I said, You are gods and all sons of the most high, but you shall die like men and you shall fall like one of the princes* (Ps 82:6-7).

6. On the words in Exodus: *Honor your father and your mother* (Ex 20:12). Likewise, the Manicheans say that the passage of the gospel, where, to someone who says, *I will first go to bury my father,* the Lord says, *Let the dead bury their dead, but you come and announce the kingdom of God* (Lk 9:59-60), is contrary to this passage, where God gave the commandment about honoring one's parents. This is resolved in the same way as was the previous one about leaving

---

17. See Gal 3:7.
18. See Mt 3:7, 12:34; 22:33.
19. See Mt 5:44-45.

one's wife for the sake of the kingdom of heaven.[20] For we ought to honor our parents, and we also ought — without any impiety — to consider them unimportant for the sake of the proclamation of the kingdom of God. If, after all, the gospel is contrary to the Old Testament on account of this statement, it is also going to be contrary to the apostle, who admonishes both children to honor their parents and parents to love their children.[21] Not only that, however, but even the Lord will be thought to be contradicting himself — something that it is wicked to believe — because in another passage he says to the man in search of eternal life, *If you wish to attain life, keep the commandments* (Mt 19:17), among which he also mentions that one: *Honor your father and your mother* (Mt 19:19). By carrying out these commandments one grows into the love of God, in which complete perfection is found. For love of one's neighbor is a sure step toward the love of God. And so, to the man who replies that he has observed all those commandments, he says that he lacks one thing if he wants to be perfect, namely, that he should sell all he has, give it to the poor, and follow him.[22] From this it is clear that we should honor our parents at the proper level but should certainly consider them unimportant in comparison with the love of God, especially if they hinder that love. For you have it written even in the old scriptures, *He who says to his father or mother, I do not know you, or he who does not acknowledge his own children, knows your testament* (Dt 33:9). And so, if love of one's parents is commended in the New Testament and if contempt for one's parents is commended in the Old, the two Testaments agree with each other on both matters.

7, 1. On the words in Exodus: *I am a jealous God, punishing children to the third and fourth generation for the sins of their parents who hated me* (Ex 20:5). The Manicheans say that the Lord's words in the gospel, *Be good like your heavenly Father, who makes his sun rise over the good and the bad* (Mt 5:45), and that other saying of the same Lord, *You must forgive your brother who sins not merely seven times but even seventy times seven times* (Mt 18:22), are contrary to this passage. Yet if I ask them whether God does not punish his enemies, they will undoubtedly be thrown into confusion. For they say that God is preparing an eternal prison for the nation of darkness, which they say is the enemy of God. And that is not enough: they do not hesitate to say that he will also punish his own members along with that nation.

But when the Manicheans come to passages of the Old and the New Testament, they pretend that they are extremely good, in order to deceive the ignorant and in order to charge that the Testaments are opposed to each other. But let them tell us to whom the Lord is going to say, *Enter into the eternal fire that was*

---

20. See above 3, 2.
21. See Eph 6:2-4; Col 3:20-21.
22. See Mt 19:20-21.

prepared for the devil and his angels (Mt 18:41), if he spares everyone and condemns no one. Hence, we must understand that it was correct to say that God punished children who hated him for the sins of their parents. For from the addition, *who hated me*,[23] it is understood that he punishes for the sins of their parents those who have chosen to continue in the same wickedness. Such people, after all, are punished not because of God's cruelty but because of his justice and their sinfulness, as the prophet says, *For the holy spirit of discipline will put to flight the insincere and will withdraw from minds that lack understanding, and a man will be rebuked when wickedness overtakes him* (Wis 1:5); that is, a man will be rebuked when his sinfulness overtakes him after the Holy Spirit has withdrawn from him. And in another passage it says, *They thought this, and they were mistaken, for their malice blinded them* (Wis 2:21). And in still another passage it says, *Each person is bound by the ropes of his own sins* (Prv 5:22). From the New Testament the apostle agrees with these testimonies from the Old, when he says, *God handed them over to the desires of their heart* (Rom 1:24). By this harmony of the two Testaments it is quite clear that God is not brutal but that each person is brutal to himself when he sins.

7, 2. But I think that the words of scripture — that punishment extends to the third and fourth generation — mean nothing else than that from the time when Abraham begins to be the father of the people of the Jews there are four ages, including this present age, which the evangelist Matthew distinguishes.[24] One age stretches from Abraham up to David; another from David up to the migration into Babylon; the third from the migration into Babylon up to the coming of the Lord. A fourth age runs from then up to the end — the old age, as it were, of the world, which is longer than the other ages. We believe that those ages represent those generations, although the individual ages are composed of many generations. The third age begins from the migration into Babylon when the Jews were taken captive, while in the fourth age, that is, after the coming of our Lord, the nation of the Jews was completely uprooted from their own land. From this we are made to understand the words of scripture, namely, that God will inflict punishment for the sins of parents upon the third and fourth generation, legitimately and deservedly, of course — upon those who have preferred to continue to hold onto the sins of their parents rather than to follow the righteousness of God. For the prophet Ezekiel most clearly showed that the sins of a father do not pertain to a son who lives righteously.[25]

7, 3. But the words of the gospel, *Be good like your heavenly Father, who makes his sun rise over the good and the bad*, are not contrary to the Old Testament. For God does this to invite them to repentance, as the apostle says, *Do you*

---

23. Augustine makes the relative clause modify "children," though it is difficult to see how this conforms to the text in Exodus.
24. See Mt 1:17.
25. See Ez 18:14-20.

not know that the patience of God invites you to repentance? (Rom 2:4) Nonetheless, we should not believe that God will not punish those people who, as the
same apostle says, *store up for themselves wrath on the day of wrath and of the
revelation of the just judgment of God, who will repay each person according to
his works* (Rom 2:5). After all, the prophet also predicts this patience and goodness of God when he says, *But you spare everyone because all things belong to
you who love souls* (Wis 11:27). And there are countless other passages from
which we understand that both Testaments preach the mercy and justice of God
in goodness and severity.

7, 4. But if they are troubled because it says, *I am jealous* (Ex 20:5), they
should also be troubled by what the apostle Paul says, *With the jealousy of God I
am jealous for you, for I have betrothed you to one man, to present you as a
chaste virgin to Christ* (2 Cor 11:2). For holy scripture, while speaking with our
words, also shows through these words that nothing can be said worthily of God.
After all, why should these words not also be said of that majesty of which whatever is said is said unworthily, because that majesty surpasses all the resources
of all languages by its ineffable loftiness? For, because husbands usually guard
the chastity of their wives jealously, the scriptures referred to the power and
discipline of God as the jealousy of God, by which he does not allow the soul to
commit fornication with impunity. But the soul's fornication is a turning away
from the fecundity of wisdom and a turning to the conception of temporal snares
and corruptions.

7, 5. But when he says that one should forgive one's brother not only seven
times but seventy times seven times,[26] he is of course speaking of a brother who
repents. God, however, says that he punishes the sins of those who hated him,
not of those who are reconciled to him through repentance. For even in the
prophet the Lord says, *I do not want the death of the sinner so much as that he
should return and live* (Ez 18:23; 23:11). From this it is easily seen that both
Testaments agree and are in harmony — inasmuch as they were both written by
one God — concerning the patience that invites to repentance, concerning the
forgiveness that pardons the repentant, and concerning the justice that punishes
those who refuse to be corrected.

8. On the words in Exodus: *An eye for an eye, a tooth for a tooth* (Ex 21:24),
and other passages of the sort. The Manicheans criticize this passage because the
old law permitted punishment equal to the crime and because it says that an eye
should be lost for an eye and a tooth for a tooth, as if the Lord showed in the
gospel that these two were in opposition and in contradiction to him. For he says,
*You have heard that it was said to the people of old: An eye for an eye, and a
tooth for a tooth. But I say to you: Do not resist a bad man, but if he strikes you on
the cheek, offer him the other as well. And if anyone wants to go to court with you*

---

26. See Mt 18:22.

and take your tunic, give him your coat as well. (Mt 5:38-40) In these two statements the difference between the two Testaments is really shown — both of
which, however, have been provided for by one God. For, because at first carnal
human beings burned to avenge themselves as if the injury about which they
complained were greater than it was, it was set down for them, as the first step
toward leniency, that the pain inflicted by the avenger should in no way exceed
the amount of the injury received. For in that way someone who had first learned
not to go beyond the injury he received might be able at some point to forgive it.
For this reason the Lord, now guiding the people to the highest peace through the
grace of the gospel, built another step upon this one, so that someone who had
already heard that he should not impose a punishment greater than the injury he
suffered would rejoice with a mind at peace in forgiving the whole injury.

In those old books as well a prophet foretold this when he said, *O Lord, my
God, if I did this, if there is injustice on my hands, if I repaid those who were
causing me evil* (Ps 7:4-5). And another prophet says of such a person who
suffers injuries and puts up with them most calmly, *He will offer his cheek to the
one who strikes him; he will be covered with insults* (Lam 3:30). From this it is
understood that a limit in taking vengeance was correctly established for carnal
persons and that the complete forgiveness of an injury was not only commanded
in the New Testament but foretold long before in the Old.

9, 1. On the words that God spoke with Adam and Eve, with the serpent, with
Cain, and with other persons of old;[27] it is recorded that he also appeared to some
of these and was seen by them not in one but in many passages of the scriptures
in which God is found to have spoken with human beings. The Manicheans,
therefore, lie in ambush and say that all of this is contrary to the New Testament,
because the Lord says, *No one has ever seen God except the only Son, who is in
the bosom of the Father; he has made him known to us* (Jn 1:18). And again he
says to the Jews, *You have never heard his voice or seen his face, nor do you
have his word remaining in you, because you have not believed him whom he
sent* (Jn 5:37-38). We reply to them that, with the words written in the gospel, *No
one has ever seen God except the only Son, who is in the bosom of the Father; he
has made him known to us*, the whole question is resolved. For the Son himself,
that is, the Word of God, not only in the last times when he deigned to appear in
the flesh but even earlier, from the creation of the world, made the Father known
to whom he willed, whether by speaking or by appearing, either through some
angelic power or through just any creature. He is, after all, the truth in all things;
all things exist for him, and all things obey the least sign from him and are
subject to him, so that he is seen by whom he chooses, when he wants to be seen,
through a visible creature, even with their eyes. And yet, according to his
divinity and insofar as he is the Word of the Father, coeternal with the Father and

---

27. See Gn 3, 4, 12, and so on.

immutable, through whom all things were made,[28] he is seen only by a heart that has been completely purified and is utterly simple.

And so in certain passages scripture itself testifies that an angel was seen when it says that God was seen.[29] So too, in that wrestling match with Jacob, he who appeared was called an angel.[30] And when he appeared to Moses in the bush,[31] and likewise in the desert when Moses received the law after he had led the people out of the land of Egypt, God spoke to him.[32] But whether it was in the bush when God sent him or later when he gave him the law, Stephen says in the Acts of the Apostles that an angel appeared to him.[33] We say this so that no one might suppose that the Word of God, by whom all things were made, can be limited as if by locality and can visibly appear to someone otherwise than through some visible creature. For, as the Word of God is in the prophet and it is correct to say, "The Lord spoke," because the Word of God, that is, Christ, speaks the truth in the prophet, so he himself speaks in the angel when the angel announces the truth and it is correct to say, "God spoke" and "God appeared." In the same way it is also correct to say, "The angel spoke" and "The angel appeared," though in the first case scripture spoke of God dwelling in the creature and in the second case of the creature acting in obedience to him. According to this rule the apostle also says, *Or do you want to experience Christ who speaks in me?* (2 Cor 13:3)

9, 2. But if it disturbs them that God speaks even to sinners in the Old Testament, to Adam or Eve or the serpent, let them notice that even in the New Testament the Lord provides an example of this in the Lord's words to a foolish and greedy man, *You fool, this night your life will be taken from you. To whom will these things which you have amassed belong?* (Lk 12:20) For, when the truth is spoken even to sinners, through whatever creature it is spoken, it is spoken by no one else but by him who alone is truthful. But, as for his words to the Jews, *You have never heard his voice* (Jn 5:37a), he says this because at least those with whom he was speaking did not obey him. He also says to them, *Nor have you seen his face* (Jn 5:37b), because it is impossible. But he says, *Nor do you have his word remaining in you* (Jn 5:38), because Christ remains in the person in whom the word of God remains, and those people rejected him. For, after the Lord had said, *Father, glorify me with that glory in which I was with you before the world was made* (Jn 17:5), a voice was heard from the sky: *I have glorified and I will glorify you* (Jn 12:28). Many of the Jews who were present heard this voice, but they should not for this reason be said to have heard his voice, because

---

28. See Jn 1:1.3.
29. See Gn 18:1-2.
30. See Gn 32:24-30.
31. See Ex 3:2.
32. See Ex 19:3.
33. See Acts 7:30.35.

they did not obey it and believe. Hence, it is not surprising that the Word of God, that is, the only Son of God, makes the Father known to whom he wishes through himself, to whom he wishes through some creature, either by words or by sight, though he himself is seen through himself only by a clean heart and the Father through him. *For blessed are the clean of heart because they shall see God* (Mt 5:8). If we should not be surprised at this, we should also not be surprised that all the testimonies from both Testaments agree.

10. On the words that God spoke to Moses when he said to him: *Say to the children of Israel, Take the first fruits from every man, and offer it to me, that is, gold, silver, bronze, purple, linen, scarlet wool, goat hides, red-dyed hides of lambs, whole timbers, oil for lighting, spices, and precious stones, that is, beryl, and construct a tabernacle in which I can dwell with you* (Ex 25:2-8). The Manicheans also raise a question about this, and they say that the words of the Lord in the gospel, *You shall swear neither by heaven, because it is the throne of God, nor by the earth, because it is his footstool* (Mt 5:34-35), are contrary to this passage. For they argue and they think that they are saying something important when they ask: "How does that God whose throne is heaven and whose footstool is the earth dwell in a tabernacle that was constructed from gold, silver, bronze, purple, and from the fur and hides of animals?" They also use the apostle Paul as a witness, because he says that God dwells in inaccessible light.[34]

We address a similar question to them, and we produce from the Old Testament what they produced from the New Testament. For in the Old Testament it was first written, *Heaven is my throne, but the earth is my footstool. What house will you build for me, or what will be the place of my repose? Has not my hand made all these things?* (Is 66:1-2) See, the books of the Old Testament have passages where they teach that God does not dwell in temples made by hand, and yet with a scourge made out of ropes the Son of our God drove from the temple those who were selling cattle and doves and overturned the tables of the money-changers.[35] And he said, *The house of my Father shall be called a house of prayer, but you have made it a den of thieves* (Mt 21:13).[36] If, then, someone wants to mislead the ignorant by these two passages set in opposition to each other and to say that God — whose throne is heaven and whose footstool is the earth, and who is said not to dwell in a house made by hand — is glorified in the Old Testament, while in the New Testament his house is said to have been constructed by human beings, will the Manicheans not at long last admit that God's dwelling place, made by the hands of human beings, is understood to signify something in both Testaments and that both Testaments teach that God does not dwell in places built by human beings?

---

34. See 1 Tm 6:16.
35. See Mt 21:12.
36. See Is 56:7; Jer 7:11.

11. On the words in Exodus: *You shall not worship strange gods* (Ex 20:5), and again, *Your God is called jealous for he is very jealous* (Ex 34:14). When the Manicheans speak slanderously against this passage, where scripture says, *You shall not worship strange gods*, they show quite clearly that they are pleased at the worship of many gods. Nor is this surprising, since in their sect they mention and teach a very numerous family of gods — those, that is, who came down even to these visible things that they venerate and worship instead of the light of the truth — and for this reason they are displeased at what is written in Exodus, *You shall not worship strange gods*. The Manicheans also add the reason why scripture said this: *Your God is called jealous for he is very jealous* — that is, in order that we would not love him inasmuch as he is a jealous God whose jealousy does not permit us to worship strange gods. And for this reason they say that these passages are contrary to the gospel, because the Lord says, *Just Father, the world has also not known you* (Jn 17:25), as if God ought not to be called just unless he allows us to worship strange gods. For they say that a just god and a jealous god are for all intents and purposes contrary to each other, and they mislead poor wretches who do not understand that the whole hope of our salvation is the jealousy of God.

This term, after all, signifies his providence, by which he does not allow any soul to commit fornication against him with impunity. In this sense the prophet says, *You will destroy all those who commit fornication against you* (Ps 73:27). For, just as what is called the wrath of God is not a disturbance of his mind but his power to punish, so the jealousy of God is not the anguish of mind by which a husband is often tormented over a wife or a wife over a husband, but the most tranquil and purest justice, which allows no soul to be happy if it is corrupted and in a sense weighed down by false opinions and evil desires. It is the people who have not yet seen that no words are adequate to that ineffable majesty who, after all, are horrified at these words. For in that way they suppose that they should refrain from these words as if they might say something worthy of God when they do not use them. For, when teaching human beings with understanding how ineffable the sovereign godhead is, the Holy Spirit chose to use even words that human beings regard as unworthy in order to warn them that even words that human beings think that they say in a somewhat worthy manner of God are unworthy of that majesty for which a respectful silence is more appropriate than any human word. I consider the jealousy of a human being and I find a disturbance that torments the heart. And yet, when I consider the cause, I find nothing but the fact that one does not tolerate adultery on the part of a spouse. For jealousy is usually said to exist mostly and in the proper sense between spouses. And so, if a husband were by himself happy, omnipotent, and just, he would avenge the sin of his wife without suffering any torment, with complete ease, and without any injustice. In a human manner of speaking, even if not in a proper but in a metaphorical one, I would still call this action jealousy. After all, did anyone criticize Tully, who certainly knew how to speak Latin, when he said to Caesar, "None of your virtues is either more admirable or more pleasing than your mercy"?[37] And yet they say that mercy is so called because it makes the heart miserable over the misery of someone else who is suffering. Does a virtue, then, make the heart miserable? What, then, would Tully say in response to those attackers but that he chose to refer to clemency by the term "mercy"? For we often speak correctly when we use not only the proper words but also ones that are close to them.

I wanted to mention that author since the question in this case concerns a word, not some reality. For, just as our authors, that is, the authors of the divine scriptures, have mainly had realities in mind, the concern of worldly authors is almost entirely about words. But I have the gospel and all the books of the New Testament in which the mercy of God is very frequently praised. If these wretches, then, dare to do so, let them raise the question from those books, and let them deny that God is merciful for fear that he be thought to have a heart full of misery. Just as God can have mercy without misery in his heart, then, so let us also not refuse to understand the jealousy of God without any loss or torment, and let us bear with the condition of human language in order that we might come to a divine silence.

But if they say that a jealous God and a just God are contrary to each other, what are they going to say when I find these words in the New Testament, *With the jealousy of God I am jealous for you* (2 Cor 11:2), and the testimony from the old books used in the gospel, *Jealousy for your house has consumed me* (Jn 2:17; Ps 69:10)? Again, when they read in the Old Testament, *The Lord is just and has loved justice; his face has seen equity* (Ps 11:8), will they not also admit that the two Testaments seem to the ignorant to be contrary to each other in such a way that we find the jealousy of God in the New and the justice of God in the Old? But for those who understand well, both passages in both Testaments are in harmony because of the great unity and peace that comes from the Holy Spirit.

12,1. On the words that one should not eat blood because blood is the soul of the flesh.[38] The Manicheans oppose to this statement of the old law the statement of the Lord in the gospel that we should not fear those who kill the body but cannot harm the soul.[39] And they argue, saying, "If blood is the soul, how can people fail to have power over it, since they do many things with blood, whether collecting it and setting it before dogs and birds as food or spilling it and mixing it with filth and mud?" After all, people can without difficulty do these and countless other things with blood. And so they ask insultingly how, if blood is the soul, a person's killer cannot harm the soul since he has such great power

---

37. Cicero, *In Defense of Ligarius (Pro Ligario)* 22.
38. See Dt 12:23.
39. See Mt 10:28.

over the person's blood. They also add the words of the apostle Paul, *For flesh and blood shall not possess the kingdom of God* (1 Cor 15:50), and they say, "If blood is the soul, as Moses says, no soul will be found to attain the kingdom of God."

To this slander the response ought to be that they should be obliged to show where it is written in the books of the old law that the human soul is blood. For they will nowhere find this in that scripture, which those wretches will never be permitted to understand as long as they try to tear it to shreds. But if nothing of the sort is said there about the human soul, why does it matter to us if the soul of an animal either can be slain by a killer or cannot possess the kingdom of God? But these men are too concerned about the souls of animals. For, though the souls of human beings are rational, these people still think that those souls return in animals. For this reason they think that the heavenly kingdoms have been closed to them if they agree that they have been closed to the souls of animals.

12, 2. Why is it that Adimantus, one of the disciples of Mani, whom they mention as a great teacher of that sect, has dared to insult the people of Israel? He has dared to insult the people of the Jews, then, because according to their idea that the soul is blood, the souls of their parents have partly been devoured by serpents, partly been consumed by fire, and partly dried up in deserts and on the most rugged mountains. But even if anyone granted that this was true, he would not prove that those whom he chose to insult were guilty of any crime. For they did not in some way harm the souls of their parents, to which he said all this happens in accord with their idea. Hence, they can feel grief over this, but not guilt.

But what will Adimantus himself do in keeping with his own opinion, according to which he believed that even rational souls, that is, the souls of human beings, can be stuffed into the bodies of wild animals? What, then, will he do about the great crime of wearing down a slow beast with blows or an excited one with reins, if his father's soul should happen to be in it? I do not want to mention that he could also kill his parents in the midst of lice and fleas, for they do not refrain from the slaying of these. What good does it do them, after all, that they sometimes deny that human souls return in these very tiny living things? For they deny this so that they will not be held guilty of so many killings or be forced to spare lice and fleas and bedbugs and to endure such annoyances from them without any freedom to kill them! After all, they have a lot to explain as to why a human soul can return in a little fox and cannot return in a weasel, though the cub of a little fox is perhaps even smaller than a large weasel. Then, if it can return in a weasel, why can it not return in a mouse? And if it can return in a mouse, why can it not return in a lizard? And if it can return in a lizard, why can it not return in a locust? Then in a bee, then in a fly, then in a bedbug, and finally even in a flea or in anything else that might be much smaller. They do not find anywhere to set a limit, and in this way their consciences are overwhelmed by countless crimes of murder on account of this silly belief.[40]

12, 3. For from the words of scripture that the blood of an animal is its soul,[41] apart from what I said above, namely, that it is no concern of mine what happens to the soul of an animal, I can also interpret that commandment as a sign that was given. After all, the Lord did not hesitate to say, *This is my body* (Mt 26:26), when he gave us a sign of his body.

12, 4. But as for the words of the apostle, *Flesh and blood shall not possess the kingdom of God*, it is also stated in the law: *My spirit will not remain in them because they are flesh* (Gn 6:3). And in the old books a future reward is promised many times to the souls of the righteous. But the apostle nonetheless wanted to convey what sort of body the righteous will have as a result of the change in the resurrection, because *they will not marry or take wives, but they will be like the angels in heaven* (Mt 22:30). Since he wanted to convey this future change of the bodies of the saints, then, the apostle said, *For I say to you, brothers, that flesh and blood shall not possess the kingdom of God.* This can be discovered not from one statement that has been singled out and quoted in order to deceive but from the study of the whole letter, or rather from just reading it, for the matter is not obscure. For in this sense, he says, *This corruptibility must don incorruptibility, and this mortality must don immortality* (1 Cor 15:53). That he says this of the body is very evident from what went before, when he says, *Not all flesh is the same; the flesh of human beings is other than that of animals; the flesh of birds and of fish is also different. And there are heavenly bodies and earthly bodies, but the glory of heavenly bodies is other than the glory of earthly ones. The glory of the sun is other than the glory of the moon and other than the glory of the stars. For star differs from star in glory. So too will be the resurrection of the dead. The body is sown in corruption; it will rise in incorruption. It is sown in ignominy; it will rise in glory. It is sown in weakness; it will rise in power. An animal body is sown; a spiritual body will rise. If the body is animal, it is also spiritual, as scripture says, The first man, Adam, became a living soul; the last Adam will become a life-giving spirit. But what is spiritual is not first, but what is animal; what is spiritual comes afterward. The first man is earthly from the earth; the second man is heavenly from heaven. The earthly are like the earthly man; the heavenly are like the heavenly man. And as we have donned the image of the earthly man, let us also don the image of him who is from heaven. But I say this, my brothers, because flesh and blood cannot possess the kingdom of God as their inheritance, nor can corruption possess incorruption as its inheritance* (1 Cor 15:39-50). Surely it is already clear why the apostle said this. Why, then,

---

40. I have followed the reading *credulitatem*, which is found in five manuscripts and in PL, rather than *crudelitatem*, which is found in the CSEL text.
41. See Dt 12:23.

does this fellow out of a shameful deceit cite only this last verse and pass over in silence the previous ones, by which people could correctly understand what the Manicheans misinterpret? For, because the body of the Lord was raised up to heaven after the resurrection in order to receive a heavenly transformation for that heavenly dwelling, and because we are commanded to hope for this also on the last day, the apostle said, *The earthly are like the earthly man*, that is, mortal, *and the heavenly are like the heavenly man*, that is, immortal not only in their souls but also in their bodies. Hence, he had also said above that the glory of heavenly bodies is other than the glory of earthly ones. But the fact that he said that the body will be spiritual in the resurrection should not lead us to think that it will not be a body but a spirit. Rather, he says that the body will be subject in every way to the spirit without any corruption or death. After all, we ought not to think that the body we now have is not a body but a soul, because he refers to the body as *animal*.[42] Therefore, just as it is now said to be an animal body because it is subject to the soul but cannot yet be called spiritual because it is not yet fully subject to the spirit as long as it can suffer corruption, so it will then be called spiritual when it will be unable to resist the spirit and eternity because of some corruption.

12, 5. Or if it still seems insufficiently proven that the apostle made this statement on account of the change that lies ahead, when he said, *Flesh and blood cannot possess the kingdom of God as an inheritance, nor will corruption possess incorruption as an inheritance* (1 Cor 15:50), pay attention to what he immediately adds: *See, I tell you a mystery. We shall all indeed arise, but we shall not all be changed, in an instant, in the blink of an eye, at the last trumpet. For the trumpet will sound, and the dead will rise incorruptible, and we shall be changed.* (1 Cor 15:51-52) Then he goes on to say what I quoted a little before to show the sort of change this will be. Indeed, he immediately says, *For it is necessary that this corruptible body put on incorruptibility and that this mortal body put on immortality* (1 Cor 15:53). From this, then, you see that flesh and blood will not possess the kingdom of God because, when it dons incorruptibility and immortality, it will no longer be flesh and blood but will be changed into a heavenly body.[43] We have taken the opportunity to comment on this, because the Manicheans also attack this statement very much, since they deny the resurrection of the body. For the present question was not posed concerning the body but concerning the soul, which they think is understood in the law in such a way that it is thought to be blood, though we do not understand it in that way at all. But though we are not concerned about the souls of animals, with which we do not share reason, we still say that what the law says — namely, that blood should be

---

42. The Pauline expression "animal body" is related to "soul" (*anima*).
43. See Dt 12:23-24.

poured out and not taken as food because the blood is the soul[44] — was stated there as a sign, like many other things. And almost all the sacraments of those scriptures are full of figures and signs of the future proclamation that has now been revealed through our Lord Jesus Christ. For blood is the soul just as the rock was Christ, as the apostle says, *For they drank from the spiritual rock that followed, but the rock was Christ* (1 Cor 10:4). But we know that, after the rock was struck, the children of Israel drank water in the desert.[45] The apostle was speaking about them when he said this, and yet he did not say, "The rock signi-fied Christ," but, *The rock was Christ*. And in order that the people would not interpret the rock in a carnal sense, he calls it spiritual, that is, he teaches that it is understood spiritually. It would take a long time, and it is not necessary here, to explain the sacraments of the same law, except when they can be explained briefly. It is enough, however, that those who speak slanderously of them know that we do not understand them in the sense that they often mock, but as the apostles, who understood all of them, explained a few of them in order that they might leave the others to be explained according to the same rules by their successors.

13, 1. On the words in Deuteronomy: *See that you do not forget the testament of your God, which he wrote down, and that you do not make for yourselves like-nesses and images*. It also adds and says: *Your God is a devouring fire and a jealous God*. (Dt 4:23-24) Adimantus set forth these words from the scriptures in this way. For we have undertaken to refute and to destroy his calumnies. But I think that I already gave an adequate response previously about the jealousy of God when he spoke slanderously of it.[46] Yet we recall not only there but also here that he attacked the scriptures with regard to God's jealousy in such a way that he also added what the Lord our God commands in those books about not worshiping idols, as if he blames God's jealousy for no other reason than that we are kept from the worship of idols by that very jealousy. Hence, he wants to be thought to be in favor of idols. The Manicheans do this in order to win over the good will of even the pagans for their most wretched and insane sect. But they also set against this passage of the law the passage from the gospel in which a certain man went up to the Lord and asked him, *Good teacher, what must I do to obtain eternal life?* Jesus replied to him, *Why do you ask me about the good? No one is good save the one God*. (Mk 10:17-18) They do this so that we might think that they are opposed to each other for the reason that in the law it says that *God is a devouring fire* and that *God is jealous*, whereas in the gospel it says that *no one is good save the one God*.

---

44. See Dt 12:23-24.
45. See Nm 20:11.
46. See above 7.

13, 2. And indeed we have already responded with regard to God's jealousy that these words were not used in the scriptures to signify some disturbance and anguish on God's part. But because nothing that is worthy of God can be said of him, scripture has on this account resorted to these terms, which people think are unworthy, in order to make them realize that even the terms that they think are appropriate to use of the ineffable divine excellence are unworthy of the majesty of God, whose wisdom first descended to human words when it was going to descend as far as a human body. See, I said "descended."[47] And if I begin to examine that word, I see that I have not said it in its proper sense. For only what can move from place to place can descend in the proper sense. After all, one who descends seems to leave a higher place and to move toward a lower place. But since the wisdom of God is wholly present everywhere, it can in no way move from place to place. Of this wisdom John speaks in the gospel, for he was a man close to the Lord's heart. He says, *He was in this world, and the world was made by him, and the world did not know him*, yet he also adds and says, *He came to his own, and his own did not receive him* (Jn 1:10-11). How was he here, and how did he come here, unless one admits that his ineffable sublimity had to be signified by human words in order that it might be suitable for human beings, but that it had to be understood in divine silence in order that it might make human beings gods?

A reason, then, can be given as to why it was said in this way; still nothing worthy of God can be said of God, since whatever is said of God is already unworthy because it can be said. Remove from jealousy the error and the pain, and what else will remain but the will to protect chastity and to punish marital corruption? What expression other than the jealousy of God, then, could better teach us that we are called to marriage with God, that he does not want us to be spoiled by a shameful love, and that he punishes our impurity and loves our chastity? It is not pointless that it is commonly said, "He who is not jealous is no lover."

13, 3. To this there also belongs the expression, *a devouring fire* (Dt 4:24), about which I need not argue; instead I should ask them: "What fire did the Lord say that he came to cast upon this world?" For he said this in the gospel, which they cannot attack, not because they want to show honor to Christ but because they want to deceive Christians. When they are reminded about how the Lord said, *I came to cast fire upon this world* (Lk 12:49), these wretches say, "But that is something else." To them we reply: Have no fear: this too is something else. For the same Christ who speaks in the Old Testament when he says, *I am a devouring fire* (Dt 4:24; 9:3), also says in the gospel that he came to cast fire upon this world; that is, it is the Word of God, which he is. For of course he explained the old scriptures to his disciples after the resurrection, beginning

---

47. The CSEL text omits this sentence, which is found in PL.

from Moses and all the prophets, and his disciples admitted that they were then set afire. For they said, *Was not our heart burning in us on the road when he explained the scriptures to us?* (Lk 24:32) He is a devouring fire, for the love of God consumes our old life and renews our being. Inasmuch as God is a devouring fire, he makes us love him, but inasmuch as he is a jealous God, he loves us. Do not fear the fire, therefore, because it is God. But fear the fire that God has prepared for heretics.

13, 4. Now, Adimantus chose from the gospel the passage where the Lord said, *No one is good save the one God* (Mk 10:18), in order to raise it as an objection for the ignorant, as if it were contrary to this passage of the law. But who can count how many times the goodness of God is found in the Old Testament? I shall cite one passage that is sung daily in the Church: *Praise the Lord because he is good, because his mercy endures forever* (Ps 118:1.29). Surely this passage too seems contrary to the jealous God, as the Manicheans think, and yet it is sung in the books of the Old Testament. Likewise, when he prepared a wedding for his son, that king found among the guests a man who was not dressed for a wedding, and, after first addressing him with the term "friend," he ordered that he be bound hands and feet and cast into the outer darkness.[48] That king does not seem good to those who have difficulty in understanding. And suppose that someone cited this passage of the gospel, as Adimantus cited that one from the Old Testament, and slanderously brought accusations against the gospel, and suppose that this person praised the books of the Old Testament instead, where it says, *Praise the Lord, because he is good, because his mercy endures forever,* and found fault with the New, because an invited guest is sent to such a great punishment on account of his attire. Suppose that with deceitful perversity he works hard to collect all the passages from the Old Testament that manifest gentleness and all the passages from the New that manifest severity and that he claims that these are opposed to each other, and that he praises the Old and finds fault with the New. He too would likewise find uneducated people miserably ignorant of the divine scriptures whom he might persuade to retain the Old Testament rather than the New. When the Manicheans do just the opposite, that is, find fault with the Old as if it were opposed to the New, I am surprised that it does not enter their minds that someone could at some time read both and praise both Testaments, having understood them by the help of God, and could either grieve over the deceit and malice of these people as human beings or avoid them as heretics or mock them as ignorant and proud.

14, 1. On the words in Deuteronomy: *Kill according to the desire of your soul, and eat every sort of meat in accord with the pleasure that the Lord has given you. But avoid eating blood; rather, pour it out like water upon the earth.* (Dt 12:15-16) Adimantus thinks that these words are contrary to the Lord's words in

---

48. See Mt 22:2-13.

the gospel, *Let not your hearts be weighed down by overeating and heavy drinking and worldly concerns* (Lk 21:34), and to the apostle's words, *It is good not to eat meat or to drink wine* (Rom 14:21), and again, *You cannot partake of the Lord's table and the table of demons* (1 Cor 10:21). We, however, say that all these things, which were written either in the Old or in the New Testament, were put there because particular reasons demanded them, and we show that they are not opposed to one another. And yet he too could have noticed in the words that he quotes from the Old Testament, namely, *Kill according to the desire of your soul, and eat every sort of meat,* did not have to do with immoderate eating, since there follows: *in accord with the pleasure that the Lord has given you* (Dt 12:15). For the Lord did not give you immoderate pleasure but enough to sustain nature and good health. But whoever goes after immoderate eating follows his own vice, not the pleasure that the Lord has given. And so the words of the gospel, *Let not your hearts be weighed down by overeating and heavy drinking and worldly concerns,* are not contrary to it. For, when each person attains only the pleasure that the Lord has given, that is, a moderate and natural pleasure, his heart is not weighed down *by overeating and heavy drinking and worldly concerns.*

14, 2. But with regard to what the apostle says about not eating meat and not drinking wine, he commands this not because they are unclean, as the Manicheans think in their error and as they hurl down into error those whom they have persuaded of such ideas. Rather, since he himself gave the reason why he said this, we do not have to interpret or explain this statement. After all, it is enough to add to these words the whole passage from the letter of the apostle in order to see clearly the reason why the apostle said this and to understand the deceit of those who select certain fragments from the scriptures in order to deceive the uneducated by them, because they do not connect up the parts that were written before and after, from which they could understand the purpose and intention of the writer. The apostle, then, speaks as follows: *Accept a person weak in faith without pronouncing judgment on the way he thinks. One person, of course, believes that he can eat everything. But one who is weak should eat vegetables. Let the one who eats not hold the one who does not eat in contempt, and let not the one who does not eat judge the one who eats. For God has accepted him. But who are you to judge another's servant? He stands or falls for his own master. But he will stand, for the Lord is able to make him stand. One person judges one day to be different from another; another person judges every day to be the same. Each person should be convinced in his own mind. One who observes a day observes it for the Lord, and he who eats eats for the Lord, for he gives thanks to God. And he who does not eat does not eat for the Lord and gives thanks to God. For none of us lives for himself, and none of us dies for himself. For, if we live, we live for the Lord, and if we die, we die for the Lord. Whether we live or die, then, we are the Lord's. After all, Christ died in order that he might be lord of the dead and of the living. But why do you judge your brother? Or why do you spurn your brother? For we shall all stand before the judgment seat of the Lord. For scripture says, As I live, says the Lord, every knee shall bend before me, and every tongue shall confess to God. Therefore, each of us will give an account on his own behalf. Let us, therefore, no longer judge one another, but rather judge so that you do not set a stumbling block or a scandal for your brothers. I know and am certain in the Lord Jesus that nothing is unclean in itself, except for someone who thinks that it is unclean. For him it is unclean. After all, if your brother is saddened on account of your eating, you are no longer living in accord with love. Do not, because of your food, destroy one for whom Christ has died. Let not, therefore, our good be blasphemed. For the kingdom of God is not food and drink but righteousness and peace and joy in the Holy Spirit. One who obeys Christ in this matter is pleasing to God and has the approval of men. And so, let us pursue what pertains to peace and to mutual edification. Do not destroy the work of God on account of food. For all things are clean, but it is bad for someone who eats and causes his brother to stumble. It is good not to eat meat and not to drink wine or anything that causes your brother to stumble. Have before God the faith that you have within yourself. Blessed is the man who does not condemn himself by what he approves. But he who has doubts is condemned if he eats, because he does not do so out of faith. Everything, however, that does not come from faith is sin.* (Rom 14:1-23)

Do we need anyone's interpretation in order for us to understand why the apostle said this and with what great malice these people pluck certain passages from the scripture so as to trick the ignorant? For the apostle also said that, according to our belief, all things are clean, but that they are unclean for the person who thinks them unclean, and that one must abstain from them when they are eaten so as to cause scandal, that is, when someone weak thinks that he must abstain from all meat, lest he chance upon meat offered to idols. And then he could think that the person who eats meat does it in honor of idols, and he could be seriously scandalized, though meat offered to idols defiles no one if it is taken in good faith by a person who does not know that. Hence, in another passage the same apostle forbids us to ask when something is bought from a butcher or when someone invited by a non-believer sees meat served to him at his table. The Manicheans think that such meat is unclean not on account of its having been offered in sacrifice but because it is meat, though the apostle cries out that all things are clean and that every creature of God is good and that all things are made holy by the words of prayer.[49] And yet he says that we should abstain from meat if a weak person is perhaps scandalized. In a certain passage he most clearly referred to these Manicheans when he said that in the last days there would be some persons who would forbid marriage and abstain from foods

---

49. See 1 Tm 4:4-5.

that God created.[50] For he quite properly designates who these people are who abstain from such foods not in order to bridle their concupiscence or to spare the weakness of someone else but because they think that meat is unclean and deny that God is its creator. Let us, for our part, maintain the apostolic teaching which says that all things are clean for the clean,[51] while preserving the moderation of the gospel, so that our hearts are not weighed down by overeating and heavy drinking and worldly concerns.

14, 3. For I do not see why the Manicheans believe that the words of the same apostle, *You cannot partake of the table of the Lord and the table of demons* (1 Cor 10:21), should be set over against this passage of the law as if it were contrary to it. After all, the law does not speak about sacrifices when it says in Deuteronomy, *Kill according to the desire of your soul, and eat every sort of meat in accord with the pleasure that the Lord has given you,* but about the foods that pertain to a person's nourishment. But because the Manicheans say that it is a sacrifice even when certain animals are prepared for a person's dinner, they thought that these passages were, in accord with their interpretation, contrary to each other. For this reason they also recalled the passage where the apostle said, *What the pagans sacrifice they sacrifice to demons and not to God* (1 Cor 10:20), where he was most clearly speaking about sacrificial victims that are offered to demons in a temple and not about the food that people prepare for themselves.

For this is what he says: *What then? Do I say that what is offered to demons is anything or that an idol is anything? Rather, what they sacrifice they sacrifice to demons and not to God. I do not want you to be associated with demons. You cannot drink the cup of the Lord and the cup of demons. You cannot partake of the table of the Lord and the table of demons. Or are we rivals of the Lord? Are we stronger than him? All things are permitted, but not all things are beneficial. Let no one seek his own advantage but that of the other person. Eat everything that comes from a butcher shop without asking any question on account of conscience. For the earth and its fullness belongs to the Lord. If anyone from among the non-believers invites you and you choose to go, eat everything that is set before you without excluding anything on account of conscience. But if someone says to you that this is meat offered to idols, do not eat it on account of the one who indicated this and on account of conscience. I do not mean your conscience but the conscience of the other person. After all, why is my freedom subject to the judgment of another person's conscience? If I partake with thanksgiving, why do I suffer abuse over that for which I give thanks? Whether, therefore, you eat or drink or whatever you do, do everything for the glory of God.* (1 Cor 10:19-31)

---

50. See 1 Tm 4:1-3.
51. See Ti 1:15.

Let the Manicheans pay attention to this and see how it was said in Deuteronomy: *Kill according to the desire of your soul, and eat every sort of meat in accord with the pleasure that the Lord has given you.* After all, the fact that the Jews were given a commandment about not eating certain meats that are called unclean can signify unclean human beings who were represented in the old scriptures by symbols. For, just as that ox whose mouth scripture forbids us to muzzle when it is grinding wheat signifies the evangelist, as the apostle explains with perfect clarity,[52] so those foods that were forbidden signify certain forms of uncleanness on the part of human beings, which are not admitted into the society of the body of Christ, that is, into the solid and everlasting Church. For it is as plain as can be that, with regard to food, absolutely nothing is unclean, but it is bad for a person who eats something and causes scandal.

15, 1. On the words in Leviticus: *Separate the unclean from the clean, and let no one eat the meat of a camel, a donkey, a rabbit, a pig, an eagle, a falcon, a crow, a vulture, and so forth.*[53] Nowhere can the soul of this man, who raises as objections passages from the two Testaments as if they were opposed and contrary to each other, be more clearly proved to be utterly full of deceit and fraud than in this passage, where he mentioned that one should abstain from the meats of some animals. For he believed that he should set over against this idea the passage in the gospel where the Lord says, *Nothing that enters into a man makes him unclean, but the things that come out of him make him unclean* (Mt 15:11). If he did this in ignorance, there is nothing more blind, but if he did it knowingly, there is nothing more wicked. Had he himself not a little before quoted the testimony of the apostle who said, *It is good, my brothers, not to eat meat or to drink wine* (Rom 14:21), when he wanted something from the New Testament to oppose the Old, where it said, *Kill according to the desire of your soul, and eat every sort of meat* (Dt 12:15)? How, then, is he now pleased at the statement of the Lord where he says that there is nothing that enters into a man that makes him unclean but that the things that come out of a man make him unclean? Where will he hide from this statement? Where will he flee? Let him tell me. For, out of a perverse and superstitious pretense at abstinence, he commands people to flee from the uncleanness of meat and to separate it from the foods of the holy. Surely, after all, if it is true that the things that enter into a man do not make him unclean, the Manicheans make a big mistake when they say that people eat unclean foods when they eat meat. But if such foods are unclean, what will they do about this testimony drawn from evangelical and divine authority, where the Lord says that a man is not made unclean by the things that enter into him but by those that come out of him? And will they perhaps say, as they are accustomed to say when the authority of the scriptures

---

52. See Dt 25:4; 1 Cor 9:7-8; 1 Tm 5:17-18.
53. See Lv 11.

puts pressure on them, that this passage was inserted into the gospel by those who corrupted the scriptures? Why, then, does Adimantus use this chapter as an authority and try to attack the Old Testament from a source by which he himself is knocked down? For any Catholic Christian, who reverences and understands both scriptures, will reply to him that these Testaments are not opposed, because the passages concerning the meat of certain animals, which God commanded a people who were still carnal not to eat, were put there to signify human conduct that the Church, which is the body of the Lord, cannot accept into the solid and everlasting bond of its unity. For she rejects them like unclean food and does not absorb them into her innermost parts.

Thus all those commandments imposed upon a carnal people foretold the future discipline of a spiritual people and, for this reason, do not contradict the statement of the Lord in which he says with compete truth that a man is not made unclean by the things that enter into him. For those words impose burdens upon slaves, while these words shake the yoke of slavery from those who are now free. Nonetheless, those words were uttered so that the burdens borne by slaves would foretell the faith of a free people. For, as the apostle says, *all these things happened to them as symbols on account of us, upon whom the end of the ages has come* (1 Cor 10:11). If, therefore, the things that they endured happened symbolically, they accepted symbolically what they were commanded.

15, 2. When, therefore, I give these answers and show in this way that these two passages from the individual Testaments are not contradictory once they are compared, what is this fellow going to do? For the witness that he has produced against his opponent speaks very weighty testimony against him. After all, he cited the testimony from the gospel where the Lord says that a man is not made unclean by the foods that enter into him, but he himself does not cease to warn and teach that we must abstain from meat as an unclean food. And yet he perceived the great wound he inflicted upon himself and the great blow by which he struck and injured himself. In order that no one might ask him and say, "How, then, do you forbid eating meat if the Lord says, as you mention, *Nothing that enters into a man makes him unclean, but the things that come out of him make him unclean* (Mt 15:11)?" he chose to apply a useless medicine to the deadly wound. In the gospel, he says, the Lord tells the crowd, *Listen and understand: Nothing that enters into a man makes him unclean* (Mt 15:10-11), and so on. The fact that he mentioned that the Lord said this to the crowd proves nothing but that Adimantus did what he did not out of ignorance but out of malice, in order that he might later say to his Hearers that the Lord spoke these words to the crowd and not to a few saints, such as they wanted themselves to be thought to be.

For the Manicheans permit their Hearers, as persons still unclean, to eat meat, but they think that for themselves, as persons already clean, it is criminal and wicked. Hence, Adimantus wanted people to think that the Lord also held this view because he taught this not to a few saints but to the crowd. O worst of men, confident of the negligence of the human race regarding the concealment of his own deceptions! For he did not believe that there was anyone who would take up the gospel and read the following lines and discover someone hiding traps for the careless and less provident in the meadows in which the Lord pastures his flocks. For his disciples were disturbed over these words, and they believed that the Lord had not spoken in plain language but in figures when he said that a man is not made unclean by the things that enter into him as food. His disciples, after all, were also Jews who had it drilled into them from childhood that they should abstain from eating certain meats. Approaching him, they said to him, *Do you realize that the Pharisees are scandalized at hearing these words? But he said in reply, Every field that my heavenly Father has not planted will be uprooted. Leave them alone; they are blind and leaders of the blind. If a blind man offers guidance to a blind man, both fall into the ditch.* (Mt 15:12-14) And so, though Jesus called the unbelief of the Jews the field that the heavenly Father did not plant, Peter still thought that it was a parable and that the Jews were blamed and called blind because they could not understand it. Hence, Peter said to him in reply, *Explain this parable to us* (Mt 15:15). And showing most clearly that it was not a parable but plain language, he said to them, *Are you still without understanding? Do you not understand that everything that enters the mouth goes to the belly and is passed into the toilet? But what comes out of the mouth comes from the heart, and those things make a man unclean. For from the heart come evil thoughts, murders, adulteries, fornications, thefts, false testimony, and blasphemies. These are what make a man unclean. To eat without washing one's hands does not make a man unclean.* (Mt 15:16-20)

The Jews raised the question about unwashed hands, and the Lord used that as an occasion to make a general statement about the things that enter the mouth and go to the belly and are passed into the toilet, that is, about our food. Although, then, scripture says that, after summoning the crowds to himself, he said, *It is not what enters into the mouth but what comes out of the mouth that makes a man unclean* (Mt 15:11), we nonetheless see quite clearly the fear that this fellow had when he added this to his words when citing such a testimony. It was, as we said a little before, in order that he would have something to answer to those who raised the question for him of why the first rank of Manicheans think it is wrong for themselves to eat meat, namely, that the Lord's words were understood to have granted this not to the Elect but only to the crowds. But the following verses make it clear that the Lord also replied to Peter — who questioned him apart from the crowd and in the hearing of his disciples, whom he certainly was training for the highest role in the Church — in such a way that he testified that he did not say this as a parable and showed that it pertained to everyone. Hence, these people do not have grounds for taking food from people's mouths and for binding them in the snare of superstition.

15, 3. Perhaps one of them might say: "Explain to us, then, what is signified by the meat of a pig, a camel, a rabbit, a hawk, a crow and the others, from which the law commanded us to abstain." I do not want to, because it would take too long. But suppose that I cannot. Does it follow then that no one can? And there are already countless volumes in which these things are explained. To refute these people it is enough for us that not I but the apostle says that those observances are a foreshadowing of what was to come. When he forbids their servile observance, he nonetheless declares that they signify something when he says, *Let no one, therefore, judge you in food or in drink or in respect to a feast day or the new moon or the Sabbath, which is a foreshadowing of what is to come* (Col 2:16-17). And so, after the things to come, which were signified by those observances, came to be through the Lord Jesus Christ, their servile observances were taken away, but the people who have been set free possess their interpretations. For whatever signified the Church to come is prophecy. You, however, have the same apostle saying, *Do not extinguish the Spirit; do not scorn prophecy; read everything; hold onto what is good* (1 Thes 5:19-20). We should, then, read the divine scripture, recognize the providential working of the Holy Spirit, see the prophecy, reject the servitude of the flesh, and retain the understanding of a free people.

16, 1. On the words in Deuteronomy: *Observe and make holy the day that the Lord commanded you. You shall labor on six days and do all your work. But on the seventh day of the Sabbath hold a feast for the Lord your God, doing no work, neither you yourself, nor your son, nor your daughter, nor your male or female slave, nor your ox, nor your ass, nor any of your animals, nor your tenant. Your manservant and maidservant shall rest just like you. Remember that you were a slave in Egypt and that the Lord your God rescued you with a mighty hand and an outstretched arm. For this reason the Lord has commanded you to observe the seventh day.* (Dt 5:12-15) And again it is written in Genesis how he spoke to Abraham concerning circumcision. He said, *Keep my covenant, you and your offspring that will come after you. This is my covenant that you shall keep between me and you along with your offspring: You shall circumcise every male in the flesh of his foreskin, and this shall be a sign of the covenant between me and you. But on the eighth day after his birth you shall circumcise every male in your people. You shall also circumcise a slave born in your house and one you have purchased, who is not of your people. And this shall be the covenant in your people. And every male who will not circumcise his foreskin shall lose his soul from the midst of the people, because he has broken my covenant.* (Gn 17:9-14)

Adimantus cites all these words of the Old Testament to set them against those from the New Testament, and he says that the words which the Lord speaks in the gospel concerning a convert are contrary to them: *Woe to you, scribes and Pharisees, hypocrites; you wander over sea and land in order to make one convert, and when you have done so, he will be a son of hell much more than you are* (Mt 23:15). They say this as if the Lord were saying that the convert was the son of hell because he is circumcised and observes the Sabbath and not rather because he is forced to imitate the corrupt morals and the evil way of life of the Jews, not that by which they observe the commandments of the law but that by which they act against the law. He says this about them most clearly in another passage, where he says that they reject the commandment of God in order to uphold their own tradition.[54] For, though the law commanded that they honor their father and mother, they themselves devised a way to dishonor their parents. And he likewise says to them, *Woe to you, scribes and Pharisees; you hold the keys to the kingdom of heaven, and you yourselves do not enter, nor do you allow others to enter* (Lk 11:52). And in another passage he commanded his hearers to obey what the scribes and Pharisees say but not to imitate what they do. For he said, *They sit upon the throne of Moses; do what they say, but do not do what they do* (Mt 23:2-3). In this passage the Lord reaffirms the authority of the law given through Moses yet shows most clearly that it is necessary to avoid and flee from the conduct of those who were not obeying the law they had received. But by these perversities of theirs they brought it about that, when a gentile came over to their law, that is, became a convert, he followed their conduct and became a son of hell much more than they themselves were. For they devoted a great effort to have a gentile become a Jew and forced him, once he became a Jew, to imitate their own worst practices.

16, 2. Nor was Adimantus the Manichean able to see that the words which he quotes from the apostle as contrary to this are not at all contrary, because all his attention was focused not on investigating but on finding fault with the scripture. For he quotes the apostle saying: *Has someone circumcised been called? He should not undo his circumcision. Has someone not circumcised been called? He should not be circumcised. For the lack of circumcision is not important, and circumcision is not important, but only the observance of the commandments of God.* (1 Cor 7:18-19) Now, what is more obvious than that the apostle commands that each person remain just as he was when called? For, since the realities had come of which those observances were the shadows, he did this in order to show that we should not put our hope in the shadows but in the realities which those shadows signified were going to come, that is, in Christ and the Church. And for this reason the observances were already all empty, but still the apostle did not teach that they were to be removed as something harmful but that they were to be considered unimportant as something superfluous. Hence, if a Jew had come to believe in Christ, he was not forbidden to maintain those superfluous observances lest he scandalize his own people, yet he should not suppose that his salvation was found in them. For it is not those signs but what

54. See Mt 15:3-6.

they signify that brings one to salvation. And so *the lack of circumcision is not important, and circumcision is not important, but only the observance of the commandments of God.* (1 Cor 7:19) And as for what the apostle says in another passage, *Would that those who are disturbing you were castrated* (Gal 5:12), he does not say this because circumcision is contrary to the gospel, as the Manicheans think. But it is contrary to the gospel that anyone should abandon the reality that the shadow symbolized and should follow the empty shadow. Those who were imposing the yoke of circumcision, as if it were necessary for salvation, upon the gentiles who believed in Christ wanted this, though the shadow was no longer to be a symbol in the flesh, but the reality itself was to be borne in the heart.

16, 3. And the words, "You observe the days and Sabbaths and solemnities. I fear for you that I have labored for you in vain," were not written as Adimantus cites them. For the apostle did not mention the Sabbath there. For he says, *You observe the days and years and seasons. I fear for you that I have labored for you in vain.* (Gal 4:10-11) But suppose that he said this of the Sabbath? Do we not also say that we should observe not these signs but rather the realities that they signify? For the Jews observed them in a servile manner, not understanding the realities that they signified and foretold. The apostle blames this in them and in all who serve a creature rather than the creator.[55] For we also celebrate as solemnities the Lord's Day and Easter and any number of other Christian feast days. But because we understand the reality to which they belong, we do not observe the seasons but what the seasons signify. The Manicheans, however, find fault with them as if they observe no days or seasons. But when they are asked the opinion of their sect about these matters, they try to explain them all in order that they may be thought to observe not the seasons but the realities of which they are the signs. Elsewhere we have shown that these realities are mythical and false. But now we have said this in order that they might be forced to say with their own lips that these observances can be reasonably celebrated, and in that way it is evident that circumcision of the flesh was both rightly imposed upon slaves and rightly understood by free persons.

We therefore reject that carnal circumcision along with the apostle and approve that spiritual circumcision along with the apostle. And we do not observe the Sabbath rest in time, but we understand the temporal sign and turn the gaze of our heart to the eternal rest which is signified by that sign. We therefore reject along with the apostle the observance of the times, and along with the apostle we hold onto the understanding of the temporal signs. We approve the difference of the two Testaments in such a way that in the Old Testament there are the burdens of slaves and in the New the joys of free people; in the Old we

55. See Rom 1:25.

recognize the prefiguring of what we possess, and in the New we have it as our possession. The apostle interprets the Sabbath for the Hebrews when he says, *There remains, therefore, a Sabbath rest for the people of God* (Heb 4:9). He also interprets circumcision when he says of Abraham, *And he received the sign of circumcision as a seal upon the righteousness of his faith* (Rom 4:11). And so, I spiritually hold to the apostolic interpretation; in freedom I disdain the carnal interpretation involving slavery, while I venerate God, the author of both Testaments. As Lord he set what he should fear before the old man who was fleeing, and as Father he disclosed to the new man who was returning what he should love.

17, 1. On the words in Exodus: *If you hear my voice with your ear and do whatever I command you, I will hate those who hate you and bring sorrow to those who bring you sorrow. My angel shall go before you and bring you to the Amorites, the Perizzites, the Canaanites, the Jebusites, and the Gergesites, and you shall kill them. You shall not worship their gods, nor shall you do their works. But you shall utterly destroy them and wipe out the memory of them.* (Ex 23:22-24) Against these words quoted in that way from the old books, Adimantus sets, as if contrary to them, the words of the gospel where the Lord says, *But I say to you, Love your enemies; bless those who curse you; do good to those who hate you; and pray for those who persecute you* (Mt 5:44). In the first place we must see what ought to have been enough for someone who wanted to show that these passages were contrary, namely, what Adimantus pointed out was written in the old law about killing enemies. For the Lord gave commands about loving enemies, that is, about loving human beings who can be brought to salvation by our patience and love. Everyone understands this, and it has been shown very often by examples. What, then, does it mean that Adimantus thought that the following verses should be added, where it was written, *You shall not worship their gods, nor shall you do their works. But you shall utterly destroy them and wipe out the memory of them* (Ex 23:24), except that the Manicheans force people to love even the gods of the pagans, and that they think that the Lord's words in the gospel, *Love your enemies* (Mt 5:44), refer not only to human beings but also to demons and even to idols? If that is so, who would not despise this insanity? But if they do not think this, this fellow was very mistaken who wanted to recall that the destruction of the superstitions of the pagans was commanded in the Old Testament, since he wanted to set over against it, as if contrary to it, what was written in the New Testament about loving one's enemies.

17, 2. But we do not say that what was said to that people in the old books about killing human enemies is contrary to this commandment of the gospel, by which the Lord orders us to love our enemies. For the slaughter of their enemies was appropriate to a people who were still carnal, for whom the law was given like a schoolmaster, as the apostle says.[56] But the intention with which those very few men in that people, like Moses and the prophets, who at that time were holy and spiritual men, carried out the slaughter of their enemies, and whether they loved those whom they killed, is very much hidden from the ignorant and the impious who love their own blindness. And since they are not capable of seeing these things, they must instead be compelled by the weight of authority. After all, what do the words of the apostle mean: *I am indeed absent in body, but I am present in spirit. And as if I were present, I have already pronounced judgment in the name of our Lord Jesus Christ upon the man who has acted in that way. When you have assembled and I am present in spirit, by the power of the Lord Jesus hand over this man to Satan for the destruction of the flesh in order that his spirit may be saved on the day of the Lord Jesus* (1 Cor 5:3-5)? And what does that slaughter that the Manicheans greatly exaggerate and hatefully spread about involve but the destruction of the flesh? But because the apostle explained the intention with which he did it, he made it sufficiently clear that one can inflict punishment on an enemy with love. And yet *destruction of the flesh* can here also perhaps be understood in another way as that which is brought about through penance.

The Manicheans, however, read the apocryphal scriptures, which they also say are completely uncorrupted, where it is written that the apostle Thomas cursed a man who struck him with the palm of his hand out of ignorance, not knowing who he was, and that that curse immediately took effect. For, after that man had gone out to a spring in order to bring in water, since he was a waiter at a banquet, he was killed and torn to pieces by a lion. In order that this would be made known and strike terror into the others, a dog brought his hand to the tables where the apostle was banqueting, And thus, when those who did not know it asked the reason for this and it was disclosed to them, they were converted, so that they had a great fear of the apostle and paid him great honor. And from this start he began to teach the gospel.[57]

If someone wanted to turn the teeth of the Manicheans against themselves, how bitingly he would criticize this story! But because the intention with which the apostle did this is not passed over there in silence, we see the love of the man who imposed the punishment. For we read in that writing that the apostle prayed for the man upon whom he imposed a temporal punishment in order that he would be spared at the judgment to come. If, then, in the time of the New Testament, when love is especially commended, God casts a fear of visible punishments over carnal people, how much more ought we to understand that this was appropriate in the time of the Old Testament for that people whom the fear of the law was restraining like a schoolmaster? For this is the briefest and clearest

---

56. See Gal 3:24.
57. See *The Acts of the Holy Apostle Thomas* 6-9.

difference between the two Testaments: fear and love; the former pertains to the Old, the latter to the New, but the two come from and are united by the most merciful dispensation of the one God. And in the old scripture the intention of those who imposed punishments is passed over because very few spiritual people knew from divine revelations what they were doing. After all, the people — for whom fear was useful — were subdued by a very severe command in order that, just as they saw that their wicked enemies and the worshipers of idols were given into their hands to be killed, they themselves might also fear that they would be given into the hands of their enemies if they scorned the command-ments of the true God and fell into the worship of idols and the impieties of the nations. For, when they sinned in a similar manner, they were punished in a similar manner. But all this temporal punishment strikes terror into weak souls in order to educate those nourished under discipline and to be able to turn them away from everlasting and indescribable punishments, because carnal human beings have more fear of the punishment that God imposes in the present time than of that which he threatens for the future.

17, 3. Love can therefore be found in one who imposes punishment. Every father experiences this with his own son when he restrains him by the harshest restrictions if he falls into a sinful way of life, and the more he loves him and thinks that he can be corrected in this way, the more he does so. But human beings do not kill the children they love when they want to correct them, because many consider this life as a great good, and everything for which they want to raise their children they look for in this life. But faithful and wise people, who believe that there is another better life and know it in part as much as they can, do not punish their children by killing them when they want to correct them, because they believe that they can be corrected in this life. But God, who knows what punishment to give to each person, punishes by death those he wants to, whether by means of human beings or by the hidden course of nature. He does not hate them insofar as they are human beings, after all, but insofar as they are sinners. For in these old books we read that it was said to God, *And you hate none of the things that you have made* (Wis 11:25), but God governs all things under the sway of justice either by punishments or by rewards. Was the apostle Paul not speaking to Christian believers when he said, *But let a man examine himself, and in that way let him eat the bread and drink from the cup. For anyone who eats and drinks unworthily eats and drinks judgment upon himself, because he does not recognize the body of the Lord. On this account there are among you many weak and sick persons, and a good many fall asleep. If, however, we judged ourselves, we would certainly not come under judgment. But when we are judged by the Lord, we are rebuked in order that we might not be condemned with this world* (1 Cor 11:28-32)? See, it is evident that God corrects lovingly, not only with weaknesses and sicknesses but also with temporal death, those whom he does not want to condemn with the world.

17, 4. Let the Manicheans pay heed to this and see how wicked nations could also be given into the hands of a people who, though still carnal, were nonetheless worshiping the one God, in order to be slain by them. And yet, if there were any spiritual persons among that people, they would understand that the plan of God does not include hatred for anyone and that what the Lord commands us in the gospel, namely, to love our enemies, is not opposed to this. He himself nonetheless promises vengeance when he introduces the parable concerning that judge who, though he was not just and neither feared God nor respected human beings, could not endure the daily pleas of the widow who asked that he grant her justice, and he granted her request in order that he would not be bothered any more. On the basis of a comparison with that judge, he said that for much better reasons God, who is most kind and just, takes vengeance on the enemies of his children.[58] Let the Manicheans dare, if they can, to raise the objection to him and ask: "Why is it that you commanded that we love our enemies, while you plan to take vengeance on our enemies?" Is God perhaps going to act against the will of his saints by punishing and condemning those whom they love? On the contrary, the Manicheans should instead turn toward God from this slanderous blindness, and they should understand his will in both Testaments so that they are not found on the left side, among those to whom the Lord is going to say, *Enter into the eternal fire that was prepared for the devil and his angels. For I was hungry and you did not give me anything to eat* (Mt 25:41-42), and so forth. For these wretches are displeased that God gave the enemies of his people into their hands to be killed, yet they themselves forbid bread to be given to a poor man who is not an enemy but a beggar. Let them understand, rather, that vengeance can exist without hatred, which is something that only a few understand, and nonetheless as long as it is not understood, whoever reads the books of both Testaments will certainly be buffeted by great labor and errors and think that the scriptures are contrary to each other.

17, 5. The apostles had not yet grasped in their mind that vengeance can exist without hatred when they were angry at those who did not welcome them with hospitality and asked the Lord whether he wanted them to call down fire from heaven, as Elijah had done, in order that the fire might devour those inhospitable people. Then the Lord answered them, saying that they did not know the Spirit whose sons they were and that he came to deliver and not to destroy people.[59] For in their hostile attitude they wanted to destroy the people whom they wanted the fire to devour. But afterwards, when they were filled with the Holy Spirit and had become perfect, so that they could now love their enemies, they received the power to exact vengeance, because they were now able to exact vengeance without hatred. The apostle Peter exercised that power in the book that the Mani-

---

58. See Lk 18:2-8.
59. See Lk 9:52-56.

cheans do not accept, because it clearly contains the coming of the Paraclete, that is, of the Holy Spirit, the comforter, whom he sent to them when they were grieving after he had ascended into heaven out of their sight.[60] For a comforter is sent to those who are in sorrow, in accord with the statement of the same Lord: *Blessed are they who mourn because they shall be comforted* (Mt 5:5). He also said, *The sons of the bridegroom will mourn when the bridegroom has been taken from them* (Mt 9:15).

In that book, therefore, in which it is most clearly stated that the Holy Spirit came,[61] whom the Lord promised as a comforter, we read that at the word of Peter human beings — a husband and wife who dared to lie to the Holy Spirit — fell over and died.[62] In their great blindness the Manicheans find fault with this, though in the apocryphal books they treat as something important what I mentioned about the apostle Thomas,[63] namely, that the daughter of Peter himself was made a paralytic by the prayers of her father,[64] and that the daughter of a gardener died at the prayers of Peter.[65] And they reply that it was good for them that the one suffered paralysis and that the other died. Yet they do not deny that this was done by the prayers of the apostle. But who told them, "It was not good for the impious nations to be killed" — those nations given over by God into the hands of the people of the Jews, at which they with their mockery pretend that they are surprised? But since the apostles did these things not out of hatred but with a good intention, how do the Manicheans prove that the minds of the spiritual men who existed in that people hated those whom divine justice commanded those men to remove from this life? Let them rather suppress their rashness and cease to mislead the ignorant, who either do not have time to read or refuse to read or read with the wrong attitude and fail to notice that both the mercy and the severity of God are taught by each Testament. For do we not read in the old books concerning the love of an enemy that evil is not to be repaid with evil: *O Lord, my God, if I have done this, if there is iniquity on my hands, if I have returned evil to those who did me wrong, may I rightly fall helpless to my enemies* (Ps 7:4-5)? Who would say this except someone who knew that God is pleased when no one repays evil with evil? But it is a mark of those who are perfect that in sinners they hate only the sins but love the human beings, and that when they impose punishment they do not impose punishment with the bitterness of severity but with the moderation of justice. Otherwise, treating the sin lightly might do more harm to the sinner than the penalty of the punishment.

---

60. Augustine is referring to the Acts of the Apostles, which the Manicheans did not accept because they held that Mani was the Holy Spirit whom Christ had promised.
61. See Acts 2:4.
62. See Acts 5:1-11.
63. See *The Acts of the Holy Apostle Thomas* 6-9; see above 17, 2.
64. See *The Acts of Peter*, Coptic Fragment.
65. See *The Acts of Peter*, The Gardener's Daughter.

And yet righteous human beings did not do this except by the authority of God, for fear that anyone might suppose that now and then he has permission to kill or to take to court or to afflict with punishments whomever he wants. At some times the authority of God is clearly stated in the scriptures, while at other times it is concealed in order that the reader may be instructed by clear passages and be exercised by those that are obscure.

17, 6. David certainly had King Saul — his enemy and pursuer, who was extremely ungrateful and extremely hostile — handed over into his power to do to him what he wanted, and he chose to spare him rather than to kill him. For he was not ordered to kill him, nor was he forbidden to do so. In fact, he had even heard from God that he could do with impunity whatever he wanted to do to his enemy, and yet he channeled that great power toward gentleness.[66] Tell me whom he feared when he refused to kill him. We cannot say that he feared the man who had been given over into his power, nor can we say that he feared God, who had given him over. Where, then, there was neither difficulty nor fear in killing, love spared the enemy. See, David the warrior fulfilled the commandment of Christ we have received, that we should love our enemies. And I wish that the Manicheans, who have distorted the human feeling of mercy to some sort of cruel insanities, would imitate this! For, as long as they believe that bread weeps, something that is impossible, they do not offer it to a human being whom they see weeping. They might perhaps say, as these blind men often toss about insane abuse, that David, who spared his enemy, was better than God, who had given him the power to kill him, as if God did not know the man to whom he had given this power. He certainly knew the will of his servant. But he wanted the love of his enemy in David's heart, which God already knew, to become known also to other human beings in order that they might imitate him. Hence, God gave over into David's power the enemy whom God did not want to be killed as yet, in accord with his providential governance of things, which had to be carried out by David. In that way the goodness of David is commended so that human beings might have something to love, and the wickedness of Saul is brought to a more fitting end so that human beings might have something to fear.

18, 1. On the words in Deuteronomy: *If with your ear you hear the voice of the Lord your God, blessed are you in your field, blessed in your meadow; blessed the fruit of your womb and the fruit of your land, and the offspring of your cattle, and the herd of your oxen, and the flock of your sheep; blessed are you in your going in and coming out* (Dt 28:1.3-4.6). They say that to this passage the words in the gospel are contrary: *If anyone wishes to follow me, let him deny himself and take up his cross and follow me. For what good does it do a man if he gains the whole world but suffers the loss of his soul? Or what will a man give in exchange for his soul?* (Mt 16:24.26) But we show that this passage is not

66. See 1 Sm 24:3-16; 26:7-16.

opposed to the other one on the basis of the rule by which it should be known by now that carnal and temporal rewards were suitably promised to a people that was still carnal, but they were promised by the one God, to whom every creature belongs, both higher and lower. In fact, after all, Adimantus himself has quoted the testimony from the gospel where the Lord says, *Do not swear either by heaven, because it is his throne, or by the earth, because it is his footstool* (Mt 5:35). This was, of course, written in the old books: *Heaven is my throne, and the earth is my footstool* (Is 66:1). Why, then, is it surprising if God gives the goods of his throne to those who serve him in a spiritual way and the goods of his footstool to those who serve him in a carnal way? For the spirit is higher and the flesh lower, just as the things of heaven are higher and the things of earth lower. And yet all those things, that is, the field, the meadow, the fruit of the womb, the fruit of the land and of cattle, the herd of oxen, and the flock of sheep, can be interpreted spiritually. But this consideration is not at present pertinent. In the New Testament, however, whose reward and inheritance belongs to the new man, the Lord still promises an increase in this world of those same things to those very people, whom he wants to hold temporal goods in contempt, in order that they may serve him in the gospel. For he says that they will receive a hundredfold in this world, but eternal life in the world to come,[67] just as it says in the old scripture, *A whole world of riches belongs to a faithful man* (Prv 17:16 LXX). The apostle exults over this when he says, *As if having nothing and yet possessing all things* (2 Cor 6:10). If, then, in the New Testament, besides the eternal good that is promised to the saints, an increase of these goods that will pass away is not withdrawn and becomes more ample the more it is possessed in contempt, how much more were such rewards of a carnal people owed to them in the Old Testament, when he who is the governor of all times, though still the one and true God, arranges and rules all things in accord with their time.

18, 2. But so that the Manicheans do not suppose that these things were held in contempt only in the books of the New Testament, let them listen to the prophet rejecting such happiness and chanting that we should take refuge in the one Lord God. For he speaks as follows: *Rescue me from the wicked sword, and snatch me from the hand of foreigners whose mouth has uttered vanity and whose right hand is the right hand of injustice. Their sons are like saplings strong in their youth. Their daughters are dressed and adorned like the temple. Their store-rooms are full, overflowing everywhere. Their sheep are fertile, becoming more numerous as they go out. There is no break in their wall, no passage, and no cry in their streets. They have called the people that has these things happy, but happy is the people whose God is the Lord.* (Ps 144:11-15) Let them pay heed, then, to how this happiness in wicked people is mocked and how complete happiness is fixed unshakeably in God alone. For wicked persons say that the

---

67. See Mt 19:29.

people that has them is happy, but that people is happy whose God is the Lord. The Manicheans, however, thought that the Lord's words, *If anyone is ashamed of me or of my words in this sinful and adulterous people, the Son of Man will also be ashamed of him when he comes in the glory of his Father and in the praise of his holy angels* (Mk 8:38), are contrary to this passage of the Old Testament. I fail to see that this pertains to the contempt of temporal possessions. But if it does pertain in the sense that someone terrified at the loss of such things might be either ashamed or frightened to confess Christ, what do they have to say? For we say that these are gifts of God, but that they are nonetheless the lowest gifts and should, in comparison with the salutary confession of Christ, not only be lost but freely thrown away. Yet it was useful that the Lord God promised them to a carnal people that loved them and was not yet capable of receiving the heavenly promises, in order that it would not seek them from idols and demons.

19,1. On what is written in the law: I am the one who gives riches to my friends and poverty to my enemies.[68] They oppose to these words what the Lord says: *Blessed are the poor in spirit because theirs is the kingdom of heaven* (Mt 5:3), and, *Woe to you who are rich because you have received your consolation* (Lk 6:24). But why do they refuse to look at other passages also in the gospel? For where it is written, *Blessed are the poor in spirit because theirs is the kingdom of heaven*, there follows, *Blessed are the meek because they shall possess the earth as their inheritance* (Mt 5:4). See, the scriptures say that the friends of God become rich by inheriting the earth. But when that rich man is reduced to such great need that he begs the poor man whom he had neglected to dip his finger into a little water and to let some moisture trickle onto his dry tongue,[69] they should understand how the enemies of God become poor, and they should recognize what is written in the law: I am the one who gives riches to my friends and poverty to my enemies.

19, 2. For I have shown above that these temporal riches are held in contempt even in the old scripture, and anyone who is willing to read them will find this in countless passages. Among them there is also this one: *The small portion of a righteous man is better than the many riches of sinners* (Ps 37:16). And this one: *The law from your lips is a good for me beyond thousands of pieces of gold and silver* (Ps 119:72). And there is also: *The judgments of God are true, righteous in themselves, more desirable than gold and many precious stones* (Ps 19: 9-10). And this one: *Blessed is the man who discovers wisdom, and immortal is he who sees prudence. For it is better to purchase her than a treasure of gold and silver. She is more precious than the finest stones. No evil stands up against her. She is*

---

68. The text is not a literal quotation from scripture but a composite of various passages such as 1 Kgs 3:13 and Prv 6:11.
69. See Lk 16:24.

well known to all who draw near to her and to those who consider her with care. Everything precious is unworthy of her. (Prv 3:13-15) And there is: *On this account I desired understanding, and she was given to me. I invited her, and the spirit of wisdom came to me. I set her above kingdoms and thrones, and I considered respectability nothing in comparison with her. I did not compare precious stones to her because all gold is in comparison with her a grain of sand, and silver will be counted like mud in comparison with her.* (Wis 7:7-9) If the Manicheans either read these texts or did not read them impiously, they would see that in the scriptures of the two Testaments all things are in harmony with one another and are ranked at their proper levels with regard both to what should be sought after and to what should be shunned, and both to what should be taken and to what should be rejected.

20, 1. On the words in the law: *If you walk in the law and keep my commandments, I will give rains in their season, and the earth shall produce its crops and the trees their fruits, and your vintages shall follow upon your harvests and your planting shall follow upon your vintages. And you shall be satisfied and shall sit in peace on your land, and you shall sleep, and there shall be no one to terrify you. I will destroy every wild animal from your land, and you shall pursue your enemies, and they shall fall before you by the sword. And five of you shall chase off a hundred, and a hundred of you shall chase off ten thousand. And your enemies shall fall before you by the sword, and I will come and bless you and make you many. You shall eat the previous harvest that has grown old, and you shall cast away the old to make room for the new.* (Lv 26:3-10) Now no one needs to ask us to show how fittingly God promised these things to that people. For we have said many things on this matter, and anyone for whom they are not enough is much too slow. But they also say that a passage from the New Testament is contrary to this one, that is, the passage where the Lord says, *Carry neither gold nor silver, nor coins in your belts, nor a bag for the road, nor two tunics, nor sandals, nor a staff, for the worker is worthy of his reward* (Mt 1-:9). Why is it surprising if he gave these directives to the preachers of the gospel? Were the Jewish people called to this ministry? All these directives, nonetheless, must be examined spiritually so that the Lord himself does not seem to impious people to have acted contrary to his own commandments. After all, he had a purse in which he carried money for necessary food.[70] Or are they perhaps going to say that to have money in belts is a sin, but to have it in purses is not a sin? It is understood that the apostles were not commanded but permitted to do these things from the fact that the apostle Paul worked with his own hands to earn his livelihood and did not use the power, as he himself says, that the Lord

---

70. See Jn 12:6.

gave to the preachers of the gospel.[71] It is also permissible not to do what the Lord permits, but it is a sin if one does not do what he commands.

20, 2. They also add the story about the rich man to whom the Lord said, *You fool, this night I shall require your soul of you. To whom will belong what you have amassed?* (Lk 12:20) and they say that it is no less contrary to this section of the law. For in this man, who regarded those uncertainties as certain, the emptiness of vain joy is mocked, but the omnipotence of the one who made the promise made that promise certain for the people of Israel. For this reason, in writing to Timothy, the apostle Paul speaks as follows concerning the rich of this world, who he knew had their place among the members of the Church: *Command the rich of this world not to think proud thoughts and not to put their hope in the uncertainty of riches but in the living God, who offers us all things in abundance to enjoy. Let them do good; let them be rich in good works; let them give readily, share, and store up for themselves a good foundation for the future in order that they may attain true life.* (1 Tm 6:17-19) Who would fail to understand here that it is blameworthy not to have these things but to love them, to place one's hope in them, and to prefer them or even to compare them to truth, justice, wisdom, faith, a good conscience, and the love of God and neighbor, which make every pious soul rich in its inner self before the eyes of God? But in order that people might love God, who gives all these invisible and eternal things to those who love him, that is, who gives himself full of all these to his lovers — in order, then, that people might love him, even at the time when the carnal soul, that is, one entangled in the loves of the flesh, knew how to desire only earthly and temporal goods, such a carnal soul had to be persuaded that God gives even these goods, because it is true, and it is very useful to believe it. These promises, which these wretched Manicheans most stupidly mock, brought it about that this people of Israel learned in whatever way they could how to love God, even in these lowest things, though fear achieved more in them. All those temporal gifts, nonetheless, are symbols of eternal gifts, and that victory over enemies prefigures victory over the devil and his angels.

20, 3. And as for what they add as if it were contrary to the Old Testament, namely, that the apostle said that God does not take delight in fighting and dissension but in peace,[72] let them know that those scriptures proclaim a God from whom no one can take away peace, not the sort whom they preach. For their god, fearing that war would invade his territories, sent his own members far away so that they endured wars at a great distance from home and afterwards, having been defeated and defiled, could not be set free and purified. But in our human nature, which has by sin flowed down to lower levels, God finds such delight in peace that he does not abandon the scales of justice. And he does not

---

71. See Acts 18:3; 1 Cor 4:12; 1 Thes 2:9; 2 Thes 3:8-9.
72. See 1 Cor 14:33.

want the peace he loves to be trampled on by sinners but to be loved by those who struggle and to be seized by those who conquer, and he wants to promise those things in figures to carnal people and to reveal them openly to those who are spiritual.

21. On the words in Deuteronomy: *Cursed is everyone who has been hanged upon a tree* (Dt 21:23). Though this question is often aired by the Manicheans, still I do not see what is contrary to the statement that Adimantus thought should be opposed to it from the gospel, where the Lord said, *If you wish to be perfect, sell everything that you possess, and distribute it to the poor, and take up your cross and follow me* (Mt 19:21; 16:24). Here, except for the fact that he mentions the cross, Adimantus notices nothing contrary to the words, *Cursed is everyone who has been hanged upon a tree.* As if just anyone could take up such a cross and follow the Lord! But when we follow the Lord we take up that cross of which the apostle says, *Those who belong to Jesus Christ have crucified their flesh with its passion and desires* (Gal 5:24). For by such a cross the old man, that is, the old way of life, is destroyed, which we contracted from Adam, so that what was voluntary in him has become natural in us. The apostle shows this when he says, *We too were once by nature children of wrath, just like the others* (Eph 2:3). If, then, the old way of life comes from Adam, because of whom the old way of life is also referred to as the old man, what absurdity is involved in the fact that a curse was pronounced against the old man, whom the Lord hanged upon the tree?

For he assumed mortality as a result of being born as an offspring of Adam. He was born of the Virgin as mortal, not having sinful flesh but bearing the likeness of sinful flesh,[73] because he was able to die, and death comes from sin. For this reason there is also that passage: *Knowing that our old man was nailed to the cross along with him in order that the body of sin might be destroyed* (Rom 6:6). It was not, therefore, the Lord but death itself that merited a curse from the tongue of Moses, the servant of God. In taking on death our Lord destroyed it. And so there was hanged upon the tree the death that came to the man through the woman by the persuasion of the devil. For this reason in the desert Moses also raised up the serpent on the branch of a tree to signify that death. And since we are healed of deadly desires through faith in the cross of the Lord, the cross by which death was hanged on the tree, those who were poisoned by the bites of the serpents were for this reason immediately healed when they looked at the serpent that was fixed to and raised up on the branch of a tree.[74] The Lord himself bore witness to this sacred sign when he said, *For, just as Moses raised up the serpent in the desert, so the Son of Man must be raised up* (Jn 3:14). By taking up the most ignominious kind of death in the eyes of human beings, that is, death on

---

73. See Rom 8:3.
74. See Nm 21:9.

the cross, our Lord Jesus Christ revealed to us his love, so that the apostle rightly said, in order to set us afire with love for him, *Christ redeemed us from the curse of the law, having become a curse for us. For it is written: Cursed is everyone who hangs on a tree.* (Gal 3:13) As a result, Christian freedom fears not only no death but not even any kind of death, as Jewish slavery did.

22. On the man whom God commanded to be stoned because he was found to gather wood on the Sabbath.[75] When in the gospel the Lord healed the withered hand of a man on the day of the Sabbath,[76] he did a divine and not a human deed, nor did he surrender his leisure. For he gave the command, and the action was done. And so this action was not like that of the man gathering wood, who, when he was discovered doing that on the day of the Sabbath, was stoned by the order of God. We have, however, already said many things about the servile observance of the Sabbath and the punishment of temporal death. For, just as the goodness of God is emphasized in the time of love, so his severity is in the time of fear. And since before the coming of Christ it was not yet necessary to lay bare to the people the mysteries in the symbols found in the law, those people were not invited to understand what they signified, but they were forced to carry out what was commanded. For they did not as yet cling to God by the spirit but served the law by the flesh. I am surprised, however, that these people deplore the stoning of a human being by the commandment of God, because the man gathered wood against the commandment of the law, and that they do not deplore the withering — by the word of Christ — of a tree that did nothing against any commandment,[77] though they believe that a tree has the same kind of soul as a human being.

23. On the words: *Your wife is like a flourishing vine, and your sons are like saplings of olive trees around your table, and you shall see your children's children, and you shall know that a man who fears the Lord is blessed in this way* (Ps 128:2-4). This was expressed in figurative language by the prophet, and the Manicheans do not understand that it has to do with signifying the Church. And they think that it is contrary to what the Lord said in the gospel about eunuchs who make themselves eunuchs for the sake of the kingdom of heaven.[78] But we have already sufficiently discussed husband and wife and eunuchs in the third chapter.

24. On the words in Solomon: *Imitate the ant and observe its diligence, because from summertime up to winter it gathers food for itself* (Prv 6:6.8). The Manicheans also do not understand that this has to be interpreted spiritually, and they think that we were commanded to store up things on earth or that we should also be concerned about the barns that men generally rush to fill apart from any

---

75. See Nm 15:35.
76. See Mt 12:10-13.
77. See Mt 21:19.
78. See Mt 19:12.

commandment. And for this reason Adimantus says that that passage is opposed to this sentence from the gospel where the Lord says, *Do not worry about the morrow* (Mt 6:34). But they also do not understand that this has to do with our not loving temporal things, and with our not fearing that we might lack things that are necessary, and with our not serving either God or man for the sake of acquiring them. For, if this was said in order that we would not keep bread for tomorrow, the vagrants of Rome — whom people call *passivi*,[79] who, once their belly is full from the daily dole, either immediately give away or throw away what remains — would fulfill this commandment better than the disciples of the Lord or than Paul the apostle. For, even when they walked the earth with the Lord of heaven and earth, the disciples had money belts, and Paul, who scorned all earthly things, still managed those things that were necessary for this life in such a way that he even gave a command with regard to widows. He said, *If any believer has widows in his family, he should give to them in a sufficient amount so that the Church is not burdened by them, in order that she can provide sufficiently for genuine widows* (1 Tm 5:16). But what was said about the ant means that, just as an ant gathers its food for the winter during the summer, so each Christian should gather the word of God in a time of tranquility, which summer signifies, in order that in adversity and tribulations, which are signified by the term "winter," he may have the means to live spiritually. After all, a person does not live by bread alone but by every word of God.[80] But if it bothers them that the ant hides what it gathers in the earth, those people should also be angry over the treasure which the Lord says was found in the field.[81]

25. On the words in Hosea: *Give them an empty belly and dry breasts; make lifeless the seed of their womb so that they are barren* (Hos 9:14). This prophetic utterance is of course also figurative. For neither in the gospel do they understand a belly of flesh when they read: *Streams of living water will flow from his belly* (Jn 7:38). And the apostle had breasts of sorts when he said, *I gave you milk to drink, not solid food* (1 Cor 3:2). And again he said, *I have become a little child in your midst, just like a nurse hugging her children* (1 Thes 2:7). And he was in labor with the Galatians who had returned to their carnal practices until Christ would be formed in them.[82] And so what Adimantus quotes from the gospel, namely, *In the resurrection from the dead people will neither marry nor be given in marriage, and they will not die, but they will be like the angels of God* (Mt 22:30), is not opposed to these words of the prophet. For this is, of course, what those eunuchs receive concerning whom Isaiah speaks. He says, *I will give them a place of renown, much better than that of sons and daughters, an eternal*

---

79. *Passivi* were, in African Latin parlance, according to a note in PL, a wandering, unstable, low class of men.
80. See Dt 8:3; Mt 4:4.
81. See Mt 13:44.
82. See Gal 4:19.

name (Is 56:5). Let the Manicheans, therefore, not suppose that such a reward is promised to the saints only in the New Testament, and let them understand that an empty belly, dry breasts, and seed that is lifeless, so that they do not bear children, was said of the people of whom the apostle says, *For, just as Jamnes and Mambres resisted Moses, so these people resist the truth, men corrupt of mind, reprobates in terms of the faith, but they will not go further. For their madness will be evident to all, just as that of those former men was.* (2 Tm 3:8-9) And so, when they go no further, then they will have an empty belly, dry breasts, and lifeless seed. And in those words the Manicheans should deign to see themselves as in a mirror.

26. On the words in the prophet Amos: *Is it possible that two men walking on a road would not know each other? Does a lion return to its cub without food? Does a bird fall to the earth without a trap? Do they set a snare for no reason in order to catch nothing? Does a trumpet sound in the city in order not to frighten the people? So too, is there some evil perpetrated in the city that the Lord will not cause?* (Am 3:3-4) In this passage *evil* should be understood not as sin but as punishment. For we speak of two kinds of evil: one that human beings do, another that they suffer. The evil that they do is sin; the evil that they suffer is punishment. The prophet, therefore, was speaking of punishments when he said this. For under divine providence, which rules and governs all things, human beings do the evil that they will with the result that they suffer the evil that they do not will. But the Manicheans accuse the prophet who says these things as if they did not read in the gospel, *Are not two sparrows sold for a penny, and does one of them fall to the earth apart from the will of your Father?* (Mt 10:29) Thus God causes the evil that is not evil for God himself but for those whom he punishes. And so, insofar as it pertains to him, he causes something good, because everything just is good, and that punishment is just. Hence, Adimantus' objection that the Lord said, *A good tree produces good fruit, but a bad tree produces bad fruit* (Mt 7:17), is not contrary to this. For, though hell is evil for someone damned, the justice of God is good, and this fruit comes from a good tree. By the evils of his sins, however, Adimantus has stored up for himself wrath on the day of wrath and of the revelation of the just judgment of God, who will repay each person according to his works.[83] And yet these two trees were most clearly presented as a likeness of two human beings, that is, of someone just and of someone unjust, because, unless someone changes his will, he cannot do what is good. In another passage the Lord teaches that this is placed in our power, where he says, *Either make the tree good and its fruit good, or make the tree bad and its fruit bad* (Mt 12:33).[84] For he says this to the people who thought that they could speak what was good, though they were bad, that is, who thought

---

83. See Rom 2:5-6.
84. *See Revisions* 1, 22 (21), 4.

that they could produce good fruit, though they were bad trees. For he goes on as follows: *You hypocrites, how can you speak what is good since you are bad?* (Mt 12:34) A bad tree, therefore, cannot produce good fruit, but it can become a good tree from a bad one in order that it might bear good fruit. The apostle says, *For you were once darkness, but now you are light in the Lord* (Eph 5:8), as if he had said, "You were once bad trees and for that reason you were able to produce only bad fruit. *But now you are light in the Lord*, that is, now that you have become good trees, bear good fruit." He says the following: *Walk like children of the light, for the fruit of the light is found in all righteousness and truth. Give your approval to what is pleasing to the Lord.* (Eph 5:8-10) For, if Adimantus were not intentionally malevolent, he could have noticed in the passage from the gospel how God is said to produce evil. For the Lord says there what Adimantus also quoted: *Every tree that does not bear good fruit will be cut down and cast into the fire* (Mt 7:19). These are the evils that God produces, that is, punishments for sinners, because he casts into the fire the trees that persevered in their wickedness and refused to become good, although this is evil for the trees themselves. But God, as I have often said, does not bear evil fruit, because the punishment of sin is the fruit of justice.

27. On the words in the prophet Isaiah: *I am God: I make peace and I create evils* (Is 45:7). This passage is also handled by the same rule. For Adimantus does not find fault with God's having said, *I make peace*, but with his having said, *I create evils.* Paul the apostle treats these two in a similar fashion in one passage where he says, *You see, therefore, the goodness and the severity of God — his severity, of course, toward those who have fallen, but his mercy toward you if you continue in goodness. Otherwise you will be cut off, and they will be grafted on if they do not continue in their unbelief. For God is able to graft them on again.* (Rom 11:22-23) In these words of the apostle we see quite clearly the goodness of God in accord with which Isaiah said, *I am God: I make peace*, and the severity of God in accord with which Isaiah said, *I create evils.* At the same time he also showed that it lies in our power that we merit either to be grafted on by his goodness or cut off by his severity.[85] Hence, the gospel where the Lord says, *Blessed are the peacemakers because they shall be called the children of God* (Mt 5:9), is not contrary to Isaiah, as Adimantus thinks or rather wants others to think. For from the one part at least he ought to have recognized that Isaiah knew that peacemakers are the children of God, because God said through him, *I am God: I make peace.* But when he fixed his eye on the second part in order to interpret it wrongly, he blinded himself to the first part. It is as if someone else equally blind would want to say that the Old Testament is good, where God says, *I do not want the death of the sinner as much as that he should return and live* (Ez 33:11), and that the New Testament is bad, where Christ

---

85. *See Revisions* 1, 22 (21), 4.

says, *Enter into the eternal fire that was prepared for the devil and his angels* (Mt 25:41). Will he not fall into the pit and hurl down with himself all those uneducated people who are ignorant of the scriptures, who follow him into the blindness of ignorance out of a similar malice? But someone who reads them with a believing eye finds both in the New Testament what they accuse in the Old and in the Old what they praise in the New.

28, 1. On the words in Isaiah, *And it happened in the year in which King Oziah died that I saw the Lord sitting on a very high throne, and the temple was full of his glory, and round about there stood the seraphim, who had six wings, and with two they covered their face, but with two they covered their feet* (Is 6:1-2). Adimantus opposes to this passage the words of the apostle, *But to the king of the ages, who is invisible, be honor and praise forever* (1 Tm 1:17). On this question we must ask him why in that vision of Isaiah he decided to pass over the two wings by which the seraphim flew, saying, *Holy, holy, holy Lord God of hosts* (Is 6:3), and why in the words of the apostle he decided not to quote the whole passage. For the apostle spoke as follows: *But to the king of the ages, the only God, who is invisible and incorruptible, be honor and glory for ages upon ages* (1 Tm 1:17). Did he perhaps fear that the reference to the Trinity would commend the prophet to the reader and make him suspect that something important was hidden there? For it is said three times: *Holy, holy, holy Lord God of hosts*. But in the apostle he perhaps saw that, if he mentioned *God who is incorruptible*, he would receive the reply that we now give to the Manicheans: "What, then, was the nation of darkness going to do to the incorruptible God if God refused to fight with it?" Either he perhaps read faulty manuscripts, or perhaps the manuscript in which we are reading Adimantus is faulty. If that is the case, we should no longer debate with him on a doubtful issue. But we should now ask him in what sense the prophet said that he saw God on a very high throne and the apostle Paul said that the true God is invisible. I ask these Manicheans, then, whether invisible things can be seen. If they say that they can be, why, then, do they speak so critically of the prophet if he saw the invisible God? But if they say that they cannot be seen, let them criticize the apostle instead, if they dare. For he says, *For, from the creation of the world, the invisible things of God are intellectually grasped through the things that have been made* (Rom 1:20). Now he himself said *invisible things*, and he himself again says *are grasped*. Are the Manicheans not forced here to admit that these things are invisible to bodily eyes but visible to the mind? In that way, then, the prophet saw God, who is invisible in a bodily way, not in a bodily way but in a spiritual way.

28, 2. For many kinds of vision are found in the holy scriptures. One of them is according to the eyes, as Abraham saw three men under the oak of Mamre,[86] and

---

86. See Gn 18:1.

as Moses saw the fire in the bush,[87] and as the disciples saw the Lord transfigured on the mountain between Moses and Elijah,[88] and other visions of this sort. There is a second kind of vision, according to the spirit, by which we imagine those things that we sense through the body. For, when this part of us is taken up by God, many things are revealed to it not through the eyes of the body or the ears or any other carnal sense, but they are still things like these. In this way Peter saw that sheet being lowered from the sky with various animals.[89] The vision of Isaiah that the wicked criticize with great ignorance is also of this kind. For a bodily shape does not circumscribe God, but, just as many things are said in figurative and not proper language, so many things are revealed in figures. But the third kind of vision is according to the gaze of the mind, by which truth and wisdom are seen when they are understood. Without this last kind those two kinds that I explained earlier either are useless or even lead to error. For, when the things that God shows to the senses of the body or to that part of the mind which grasps the images of bodily things are not only perceived in these ways but are also understood by the mind, then their revelation is complete. To this third kind belongs the vision that I mentioned, where the apostle says, *For, from the creation of the world, the invisible things of God are intellectually grasped through the things that have been made.*

In order that God might be seen by way of that vision, hearts of the loftiest morals are purified by the piety of faith and by the knowledge[90] of God. After all, what good did it do King Belshazzar that he saw before his eyes the hand that wrote on the wall? Because he could not bring to that vision the gaze of his mind, he still sought to see what he had seen. Endowed with the sort of ray of light by which these visions are understood, Daniel, however, saw with his mind what the king saw with his body.[91] Again, King Nebuchadnezzar saw a dream with the part of the mind that grasps images of things, and because he did not have an eye of the mind suited for seeing what he had seen in a better way, that is, for understanding what he had seen, he therefore sought the gaze of another, namely, Daniel, to interpret his vision. And yet, in order that he might have a certain faith in Daniel as he explained the vision, the king demanded that Daniel also tell him his dream. But when the Holy Spirit revealed it, Daniel saw what the king had seen in his dreams with the part of the mind that grasps bodily images, and he saw with his mind what it meant.[92] But he is not a prophet of the true and highest God who sees visions given by God only with the body, or even

---

87. See Ex 3:2.
88. See Mt 17:2-3.
89. See Acts 11:5-6.
90. I have followed the reading *agnitionem,* found in five manuscripts and PL, instead of *actionem,* which the CSEL text has.
91. See Dn 5.
92. See Dn 2.

with that part of the spirit by which the images of bodies are grasped, but does not see them with the mind. Generally, however, we find that the scriptures set forth how visions are seen but not how they are understood, in order that the vision of the mind, in which their whole fruit is found, might be left to the readers to provide them with exercise. But from many things that are written plainly we are shown how those authors understood the things that they set forth in their books as they were shown to them in figures. For what is shown in figures pertains to those two kinds of vision. But to the vision of the mind, that is, of the intelligence, there pertains the simple and proper revelation of things that have been understood and are certain. The Holy Spirit of the highest and immutable wisdom nonetheless manifests and adapts all these kinds by distributing them in marvelous and ineffable ways. But these Manicheans are wretched who speak slanderously of the prophet when he says that he saw God and who raise as an objection the passage from the apostle in which he says that he is invisible. For, if someone else should raise as an objection to these words of the apostle the words of the gospel where the Lord says, *Blessed are the clean of heart because they will see God* (Mt 5:8), how will they reply that the invisible God can be seen? They pressure the ignorant with the word "invisible," and, even if they know in what way God is said to be invisible, they are afraid to have it known. So great is the destruction of minds that are conquered by error when they want to conquer a human being.

Answer to the Letter of Mani known as *The Foundation*

(Contra epistulam Manichaei quam vocant Fundamenti)

Introduction

Augustine's *Revisions* lists his *Answer to the Letter of Mani Known as The Foundation* as the second work he wrote after his consecration as a bishop late in 395. Hence, it is quite probable that he wrote this work in 396. Mani's letter known as *The Foundation* was one of the most important of the Manichean scriptures, though it now survives only in fragments quoted by Augustine and his friend Evodius. Besides the fragments contained in the present work, there are others in Augustine's *Answer to Felix, a Manichean* 1, 16 and 19; in his *The Nature of the Good* 42 and 46; and in Evodius' *The Faith in Answer to the Manicheans* 5, 7, and 11. As Augustine mentions in the *Revisions*, the present work deals only with the beginning of Mani's letter. He tells us that he had written some notes with a view to answering the whole letter but that he never found the time to carry out what he had planned. The book focuses on only a few points. First, Augustine argues against Mani's claim to be an apostle of Jesus Christ, and he stresses the unreasonableness of Mani's demand that we believe this about him after he has promised us knowledge rather than faith. Secondly, Augustine objects to Mani's saying that one side or part of the land of light faces the land of darkness. Here he argues that Mani's language necessarily implies that God or the land of light, as well as the land of darkness, is corporeal, and he emphasizes the ugliness of the wedge of darkness that has been thrust into the land of light. Thirdly, he attacks the five natures and their inhabitants that Mani located in the land of darkness, and he points out the inconsistencies that are present in this fantasy world of Mani's making and insists that Mani located many good features in the land of darkness, which he claimed was the greatest evil. Here Augustine presents his own account of the nature of evil and answers the Manichean question about where evils come from. The work, in sum, represents one of several pleas to Augustine's Manichean friends to come to their senses and enter the Catholic Church.

Augustine begins his work by praying that God will help him to correct the Manicheans by gently consoling, by benevolently exhorting, and by calmly arguing with them (section 1). He refuses to become angry at the Manicheans, for only someone who does not understand how difficult it is to rise up to see the light of the truth could be angry and rage at them (section 2). Augustine recalls his own struggle to come to the truth, and now he wants to be patient with the Manicheans as others were patient with him when he was in error (section 3). He asks the Manicheans to put aside with him any arrogant claim that either of them has the truth. At least they should regard him as someone who is hearing them for the first time and seeking instruction from them (section 4). He will ignore, then, the fact that there are some in the Catholic Church who have attained wisdom. In any case the vast majority in the Church are simple believers, and he points to the many reasons why the authority of the Catholic Church now possesses him as a believer (section 5).

Augustine turns, therefore, to the *Letter of the Foundation* for instruction about the truth. Its beginning declares Mani to be an apostle of Jesus Christ. Augustine asks why he should believe that Mani was an apostle of Jesus Christ. The Manicheans promised knowledge of the truth, but now they demand belief in the apostleship of Mani. Augustine argues that the Manicheans cannot appeal to the authority of the gospel as the reason for believing that Mani was an apostle, since he himself only believes in the gospel because of the authority of the Catholic Church, which also tells him not to believe Mani. Furthermore, the New Testament mentions the names of the apostles but never mentions Mani — unless the Manicheans are going to appeal to the passage in which Christ promised the Paraclete, since they claim that Mani was the Paraclete (section 6). Augustine wonders why Mani did not call himself an apostle of the Paraclete rather than an apostle of Jesus Christ, and he suggests that Mani wanted his followers to think that he was not sent by the Paraclete but was assumed by the Paraclete, just as the man Jesus Christ was assumed by the Word of God (section 7). He asks the Manicheans why they object to the birth of Christ from the womb of the Virgin Mary when they do not object to Mani's having been born as the result of his parents' having sexual intercourse, although they believe that he was the Holy Spirit (section 8). When Mani adds the words, "by the providence of God the Father," he implies, Augustine claims, that he himself is the Holy Spirit, or perhaps he indicates that he wanted to be worshiped instead of Jesus Christ. Augustine recalls that the Manicheans celebrate the Bema, a feast commemorating Mani's death, instead of the Passion of Christ, for the Manichean Christ, who did not have a real body, could not have suffered and died (section 9). If the Manicheans ask when the Paraclete came, Augustine quotes for them the passage from the Acts of the Apostles in which Christ promised to send the Holy Spirit and also the passage that described the coming of the Holy Spirit on Pentecost (section 10). According to the Gospel of John the Holy Spirit could not come until Jesus was glorified, that is, until his resurrection and ascension, and the Holy Spirit was given to the disciples after the resurrection and again on Pentecost after the ascension. But the Manicheans do not accept the Acts of the Apostles. Hence, Augustine returns to his proposal on seeking the truth and resumes his examination of Mani's *Letter of the Foundation* (section 11).

The lines from Mani's work that follow promise a knowledge of the truth, but they do not present such knowledge (section 12). Further lines add a pious wish for God's peace and the knowledge of the truth, with which Augustine finds no fault (section 13). Still further lines promise a knowledge of the birth of Adam and Eve, which is once again only a promise of knowledge — and a promise of knowledge without any ambiguity (section 14). But then Mani begins to speak about the origin of the battle between light and darkness before the creation of the world, and here Augustine insists that Mani is saying things that not only cannot be known but that cannot even be believed (section 15). Mani continues with a description of the two substances of light and of darkness (section 16). Augustine asks how Mani is going to prove the existence of these two substances and how he even knows it. If Mani is going to demand that we believe, Augustine claims that he has better reason to believe the Catholic scriptures in which we read of the promise and the coming of the Holy Spirit. He insists that Mani has to prove either that what he says is true or that he is the Holy Spirit. According to Augustine, however, Mani can do neither (section 17). Augustine asks how Mani could have come to know what he says that he knows. If he claims that the Holy Spirit revealed it to him, he still asks us to believe him. Hence, he should not have promised us knowledge (section 18). But what Mani says is not only uncertain but false, for he describes the bright and holy land as having one part or side opposite the land of darkness (section 19). In saying this he implies that this bright and holy land, which is the nature of God, is extended in space and is bodily. Any body is smaller in a small part and larger in a large part, as Augustine illustrates with examples. But even the nature of the soul is non-bodily. From the way in which the soul becomes aware of what is happening in its body, Augustine argues that the soul is present as a whole in each part of the body. He then argues for the incorporeality of the soul from the way in which memory stores images of things we have perceived and from the way in which our intelligence grasps the truth and rejects bodily images as the truth (section 20). If the soul, which is subject to change, is not extended in space, then one should certainly not suppose that the immutable God is extended in space (section 21).

Since, however, it is difficult for many to grasp the incorporeal nature of God and of the soul, Augustine descends to the level of such people in his examination of Mani's claim that the bright and holy land has one side and part opposite the land of darkness. He points out that no one speaks of "one side and part" unless there is another side and part. Furthermore, the land of darkness is certainly corporeal and could not touch the bright and holy land unless it too were corporeal (section 22). Augustine develops the imagery that the Manicheans use in speaking about the juxtaposition of the two lands and shows that the land of darkness is touched by the land of light on two sides (section 23). For the land of darkness cuts into the land of light like a dark wedge that penetrates it from beneath (section 24). Augustine argues that the anthropomorphism of many simple believers in the Catholic Church is less reprehensible than the

Manichean images of their God, whom the dark wedge of the land of darkness splits open from below. Furthermore, the little ones in the Catholic Church will become adults and will come to understand the scriptures spiritually (section 25).

Augustine asks the Manicheans whether God the Father and the bright and holy land are one and the same substance and nature or whether this land is another nature like a divine body. If they say that God and this land and God's kingdoms are different natures, they end up with at least four substances instead of two. If they say that this land belonged to God because of its nearness, why did the land of darkness not also belong to him, for it too was near (section 26)?

According to the Catholic faith the almighty God created all natures that he made out of nothing, made them all good, and arranged them in their ranks from highest to lowest. Whatever is is good insofar as it is, and, insofar as it fails, it shows that it is not what God is. If the Manicheans claim that the bright and holy land is the same nature as God, they are left with its being penetrated by the dark wedge. The only escape that the Manicheans have is to admit that God created the land of light out of nothing (section 27). However the Manicheans may try to picture the relation of the two lands, they cannot escape Mani's words about the land of light's having one side and part next to the land of darkness. Augustine explores three ways in which one might picture the sides of the two lands, each with straight sides, each with curved sides, and one with a straight side and the other with a curved side. He points out problems with each hypothesis (section 28). For example, if the land of darkness has a straight side, one has to admit that its straightness is something beautiful that it shares with the straightness of the side of the land of light. Furthermore, if one were to take away its straightness, one would not take away its substance, though one would make the side crooked. In that way the Manicheans could learn that evil is not a substance (section 29). Furthermore, if the land of darkness has a straight side, there is something good in it, which it would lose if it became crooked (section 30).

Mani described the land of darkness with its five elements and each of their inhabitants. From the exterior to the interior the natures are darkness, waters, winds, fire, and smoke, and their respective inhabitants are serpents, fishes, birds, quadrupeds, and bipeds (section 31). Augustine points out the number, qualities, forms, and life that are present in the evil land and insists that these are all good and can only have come from God (section 32). The Manicheans claim that the inhabitants of the land of darkness are savage and deadly. Augustine agrees that their savagery and deadliness are blameworthy, but he asks the Manicheans to notice all their good features and to praise them along with him (section 33). With the exception of darkness, which is not a nature, the natures that Mani mentions are good, though they are not the highest good like God nor higher goods like the angels but lower goods like the earthly goods from which they derive their names (section 34). Mani has arranged these natures in his phantasms, as they supposedly were in the land of darkness. But he is refuted in many ways. Darkness, after all, which is simply an absence of light, cannot beget anything. If Mani tries to claim that the darkness there is not like the darkness on this earth, Augustine asks how he knows this and indicates other ways in which he was in error about the five natures and their inhabitants (section 35). Augustine agrees with the Manicheans in blaming the evils they find in the land of darkness, but he asks them to notice all the goods that he also finds there. If one removed all those evils, there would still remain the natures, which are good insofar as they are natures. But if one removed all the goods from those natures, nothing would remain at all (section 36). If the Manicheans object that those evils cannot be removed from those natures, Augustine says that the good features cannot be removed from them either (section 37). The Manicheans ask where the evils in the land of darkness come from. Augustine points out that the evils that they find in their imagined land of darkness have blinded them to the goods that are there (section 38).

Many things can be said to be evil, but the evil of all things is nothing other than corruption. Corruption, furthermore, is not a nature but is opposed to nature (section 39). Everything that is corrupted loses some good. Therefore, incorruption or incorruptibility is good. Hence, the natures that Mani puts in the land of darkness are either corruptible or incorruptible. If they are incorruptible, they are supremely good, but if they are corruptible, they have some good that they can lose (section 40).

Having asked what evil is and having found that it is not a nature but is opposed to nature, Augustine turns to the question of the source of evil, that is, of corruption. His answer is that evil comes from the fact that corruptible natures were not begotten from God but made out of nothing. And since God, the highest good, made them, they are all good (section 41). The objection that God should have made supremely good the natures he created out of nothing amounts to a demand that they should have been made equal to the only-begotten Son of the Father (section 42). So too, the objection that God should not have made the good things that he made because they are less than the highest good overlooks the fact that the rational soul is so good that only God is better than it. Furthermore, if the rational soul had remained obedient to God, all other things would have obeyed it and not have caused it pain and difficulties. But, as a result of Adam's sin, we justly suffer the rebellion of lower creatures (section 43). Hence, corruption is evil, and it does not come from God, the creator of natures, but from the fact that they were made out of nothing. But God rules and governs everything, and he orders corruption so that it harms lower natures as the just punishment of the condemned and as the testing and admonition of those who are turning back to God, the highest good (section 44). Augustine shows from the New Testament how God adds the punishment of corruption to the voluntary corruption of sin (section 45). He argues that, since to be corrupted is to tend toward non-being, what is corruptible in any nature does not come from God, who is being, but from the fact that the nature was made out of nothing (section 46). The coming to be and ceasing to be of temporal things under which we suffer is a just punishment of our sins and an admonition that we should love eternal realities instead (section 47). Hence, we should not seek in the beauty of the temporal order what it does not admit, but we should praise God for the goodness that the temporal order contains and hasten to the vision of the highest good, which is not contained in places and does not pass away in time (section 48). The phantasms that we derive from the senses are obstacles to that vision. Hence, we should especially detest the phantasms of the Manichean heresy that picture God as spatially extended and as limited on one side in order to find a place for evil. And with that Augustine brings the present book to an end, promising to write others against Manicheanism, if God permits and helps him to do so (section 49).

Revisions I, 21 (22)

Answer to the Letter of Mani Known as *The Foundation*, One Book

The book in answer to the letter of Mani known as *The Foundation* refutes only its beginning, but for the other parts of it notes have been added — where it seemed good — by which the whole of it might be destroyed and by which I would have been helped if I ever had time to write against the whole letter.

This book begins as follows: "I have asked and I now ask the one, true, almighty God."

Answer to the Letter of Mani Known as *The Foundation*

1, 1. I have asked and I now ask the one, true, almighty God, from whom all things are, through whom all things are, and in whom all things are,[1] that, in refuting and restraining the heresy to which you Manicheans have adhered perhaps more unwisely than maliciously, he might give me a mind that is peaceful and tranquil and that thinks more of your correction than of your overthrow. For, although the Lord overthrows the kingdoms of error by means of his servants, he commands that human beings, insofar as they are human beings, be corrected rather than destroyed. And whatever punishment God exacts before that last judgment — whether by means of wicked persons or of righteous ones, whether by means of persons without knowledge or of ones with knowledge, and whether openly or hiddenly — we should believe that it is aimed not at the destruction of human beings but at their healing, and that those who reject this healing are being prepared for final punishment. Hence, in this universe of things there are some that are capable of causing bodily punishment, such as fire, poison, illness, and other such things, and others by which the mind is punished in itself not by the troubles of its body but by the snares of its desires, such as losses, exiles, the death of loved ones, insults, and things like that. But certain other things do not torment but comfort and soothe, as it were, those who are languishing, such as consolations, exhortations, conversations, and other things of that sort. The sovereign justice of God brings about some of all of these by means of evil persons who do not know it, but some others by means of good persons who do know it. And so it is up to us to choose and to desire the better means in order that we may have a way to approach your correction not in contention and jealousy and persecutions but by gently consoling, by benevolently exhorting, and by calmly arguing. Thus scripture says, *But a servant of the Lord should not be quarrelsome but gentle toward all, docile, patient, and rebuking with modesty those who think differently* (2 Tm 2:24-25). It was up to us, therefore, to want to seek these roles, but it is up to God to grant what is good to those who are willing and who ask him.

2, 2. Let those rage against you who do not know the labor by which the truth is found and how difficult it is to avoid errors. Let those rage against you who do not know how rare and arduous it is to overcome carnal phantasms by the

---

1. See Rom 11:36.

serenity of a pious mind. Let those rage against you who do not know the great difficulty with which the eye of the inner self is healed in order that it may be able to see its own sun — not this sun with its heavenly body, which you worship and which is bright and radiant for the carnal eyes of both human beings and animals, but that sun of which the prophet wrote, *The sun of justice has risen for me* (Mal 2:4), and of which the gospel said, *He was the true light that enlightens every person coming into this world* (Jn 1:9). Let those rage against you who do not know with what sighs and groans it comes about that God can be understood to some small degree. Finally, let those rage against you who have never been deceived by the sort of error by which they see that you have been deceived.

3, 3. But I was tossed about greatly and at length and was at last able to see what that pure truth was which is perceived without the recounting of an empty myth. In my wretched condition I barely merited, with the help of the Lord, to conquer the vain images of my mind that had been gathered from various opinions and errors. I made myself subject very slowly to the most merciful physician who called me and coddled me in order to wipe away the fog of my mind. I wept at length in order that the immutable and inviolable substance might interiorly win me over to those divine books that harmoniously sing of him. Finally, I sought with curiosity, listened to with attention, believed with rashness all those fictions that hold you ensnared and bound by long-standing habit, and I persistently tried to convince those whom I could of them and defended them stubbornly and spiritedly against others. I can therefore not rage against you at all, for I ought to support you now as I needed support at that time, and I ought to deal with you with as much patience as those closest to me dealt with me when I was in error, maddened and blinded by your teaching.

3, 4. But in order that you might more readily be made docile and might not oppose me with an attitude that is hostile and destructive for you, I must, as anyone would agree, obtain from you that both sides renounce any arrogance. Let neither of us say that he has found the truth. Let us seek it in such a way as if neither of us knows it. For it is thus that we shall be able to seek it with diligence and harmony, if without any rash presumption we do not believe that we have found it and know it. Or, if I cannot obtain this from you, at least grant that I may now listen to you for the first time and speak with you now for the first time as if I did not know you. I think that what I ask for is fair, namely, that I observe this rule — that I do not pray with you, do not frequent your meetings, do not accept the name "Manichean," if you do not give me a clear account, without any obfuscation, of all those things that pertain to the salvation of the soul.

4, 5. For in the Catholic Church — to say nothing of the most pure wisdom whose knowledge a few spiritual persons attain in this life, so that they know it at least to a very small degree, since they are human beings, but know it nonetheless without any doubt — the remaining crowds are, of course, made completely secure not by the liveliness of their understanding but by the simplicity of their belief. To say nothing, then, of the wisdom that you do not believe exists in the Catholic Church, there are many other things that most rightfully hold me in her bosom. The agreement of peoples and nations holds me. The authority begun with miracles, nourished with hope, increased with love, and strengthened with age holds me in the Catholic Church. The succession of priests from the very see of the apostle Peter, to whom after his resurrection the Lord entrusted the feeding of his sheep,[2] right up to the present episcopacy holds me in the Catholic Church. Finally, the name "Catholic" holds me in the Catholic Church. It was not without reason that this Church alone, among so many heresies, obtained this name so that, though all heretics want to be called Catholic, no heretic would dare to point out his own basilica or house to some stranger who asked where the Catholic Church was to be found. These many and great and very dear links to the Christian name hold a believer in the Catholic Church, even if, on account of the slowness of our intelligence or the merit of our life, the truth does not yet reveal itself in full clarity. But among you, where there are none of these things to invite and to hold me, only the promise of truth is heard. To be sure, if the truth is revealed so clearly that it cannot come into doubt, it ought to be preferred to all the things by which I am held in the Catholic Church. But if it is only promised and not revealed, no one will move me from that faith which binds my mind to the Christian religion by such great bonds.

5, 6. Let us see, then, what Mani teaches me, and let us especially consider the book that you call *The Letter of the Foundation*, in which almost the whole of what you believe is contained. When it was read to us poor wretches at that time, you said that we were enlightened. It begins of course as follows: "Mani, an apostle of Jesus Christ, by the providence of God the Father. These are the words of salvation from the enduring and living fountain." Pay careful heed, please, to what I ask. I do not believe that Mani is an apostle of Christ. I ask you not to get angry and begin to curse. For you know that I decided not to believe rashly anything you say. I ask, then, who this Mani is. You will reply: "an apostle of Christ." I do not believe it. You no longer have anything that you can say or do. For you promised the knowledge of the truth, and now you force me to believe what I do not know. You are perhaps going to read the gospel to me and try to defend the person of Mani from there. If, then, you have found someone who does not yet believe the gospel, what would you say to him if he said to you, "I do not believe"? In fact I would not believe the gospel if the authority of the Catholic Church did not move me.[3] Why should I not believe the people whom I obeyed when they told me, "Believe the gospel," when they now tell me, "Do not believe the Manicheans"? Choose which you want. If you say, "Believe the

---

2. See Jn 21:15-16.
3. These words of Augustine are frequently cited because of their implications for the relation between scripture and the Church.

Catholics," they warn me not to place any faith in you. Hence, while believing them, I cannot do anything but not believe you. If you say, "Do not believe the Catholics," you will not succeed in forcing me into the Manichean faith by means of the gospel, since I believed the gospel because the Catholics preached it. But if you say, "You were correct to believe the Catholics when they praised the gospel, but you were not correct to believe them when they disparaged Mani," do you think that I am so foolish as to believe what you want me to believe and not to believe what you do not want me to believe without your having given me any reason? I act much more justly and cautiously if, because I have already believed the Catholics, I do not cross over to you unless you do not order me to believe but make me know something with complete clarity and evidence. Hence, if you are going to give me a reason, leave the gospel aside. If you stick with the gospel, I will stick with those whom I believed when they taught me the gospel, and at their orders I will absolutely not believe you. If, however, you can perhaps find something perfectly clear in the gospel about the apostleship of Mani, you will weaken for me the authority of the Catholics who command me not to believe you. But if that authority is weakened, I shall not be able to believe the gospel either, since I believed it because of the Catholics. Thus, whatever you produce from the gospel will accomplish nothing with me. Hence, if nothing clear is found in the gospel about the apostleship of Mani, I shall believe the Catholics rather than you. But if in the gospel you read something clearly in favor of Mani, I shall believe neither the Catholics nor you. I shall not believe them because they lied to me about you, but I shall not believe you because you bring forth for me the scripture that I believed because of the people who lied to me. But God forbid that I should not believe the gospel. For, because I believe it, I do not see how I can also believe you. After all, the names of the apostles that we read in it do not include among them the name of Mani.[4] In the Acts of the Apostles we read who took the place of Christ's betrayer,[5] and I must believe that book if I believe the gospel because the Catholic authority likewise commends both writings to me. In the same book we have the very well-known story of the calling and apostleship of Paul.[6] Read for me now, if you can, in the gospel or in some other book which I admit that I have already believed, a passage where Mani is said to be an apostle. Or are you perhaps going to read the passage where the Lord promised the Holy Spirit, the Paraclete,[7] to his disciples? With regard to that passage see how many and how weighty are the reasons that call me back and that deter me from believing Mani.

6, 7. Why, I ask, after all, does the beginning of this letter read: "Mani, an apostle of Jesus Christ," and not say instead: "The Paraclete, an apostle of Jesus

---

4. See Mt 10:2-4; Mk 3:16-19; Lk 6:13-16.
5. See Acts 1:26.
6. See Acts 9:1-19.
7. See Jn 16:7.

Christ"? If, however, the Paraclete, who was sent by Christ, sent Mani, why do I read: "Mani, an apostle of Jesus Christ," and not rather: "Mani, an apostle of the Paraclete"?[8] If you say that Christ himself is the Holy Spirit, you contradict the scripture where the Lord says, *I shall send you another Paraclete* (Jn 14:16). But if you think that Mani correctly used the name of Christ there — not because Christ is the Paraclete but because both are of the same substance, that is, not because they are one person but because they are of one nature — Paul could also have said, "Paul, an apostle of God the Father," because the Lord said, *The Father and I are one* (Jn 10:30).[9] Never does he say this, and neither do any of the apostles write that he is an apostle of God the Father. What, then, does this novelty mean? Does it not seem to you to smack of some sort of error? For, if Paul thought that it made no difference, why does he not call himself in various ways an apostle of Christ in some letters and in others an apostle of the Paraclete? But I have always heard "an apostle of Christ" as often as I have heard it, but I have never heard "an apostle of the Paraclete." What do we suppose is the cause of this action of Mani if not that pride, the mother of all heretics, drove the man to the point that he wanted to be thought not to have been sent but to have been assumed by the Paraclete in such a way that he himself would have been said to be the Paraclete. The man Jesus Christ was not sent by the Son of God, that is, by the power and wisdom of God, but was, according to the Catholic faith, assumed in such a way that he himself was the Son of God, that is, in such a way that the wisdom of God appeared in that very man in order to heal sinners. In the same way Mani wanted to be thought to have been assumed by the Holy Spirit, whom Christ promised, so that, when we hear "Mani, the Holy Spirit," we understand an apostle of Jesus Christ, that is, someone sent by Jesus Christ, who promised that he would send him. What a singular audacity and unspeakable sacrilege this is!

7, 8. But I still ask why, since the Father and the Son and the Holy Spirit are united in the same nature, as you also admit, you do not think it shameful to preach that Mani, a man assumed by the Holy Spirit, was born from the union of the two sexes, yet you are afraid to believe that the man assumed by the only-begotten wisdom of God was born of a virgin? If human flesh, if intercourse with a man, and if the womb of a woman could not defile the Holy Spirit, how could the womb of a virgin defile the wisdom of God? You must grant, then, that this Mani, who boasts of the Holy Spirit and of his evangelical authority, was either sent or assumed by the Holy Spirit. If he was sent, let him call himself an apostle of the Paraclete. If he was assumed, let him grant a human mother to the man whom the only-begotten Son of God assumed, if he also

---

8. "Apostle" comes from a Greek word meaning "sent."

9. Augustine is using "person" and "nature" as technical terms in the theology of the Trinity, in which there are three persons in the one divine nature.

grants a father to the one whom the Holy Spirit assumed. Let Mani believe that the Word of God was not polluted by the virginity of Mary if he exhorts us to believe that the Holy Spirit could not be polluted by the intercourse of his parents. But if you say that Mani was assumed by the Holy Spirit, not in the womb or before he was in the womb but when he was already born, it is enough if you admit that he had flesh procreated by a man and a woman. For, since you do not fear the bowels and blood of Mani coming from human intercourse and his intestines filled with the excrement which that flesh carried about, and since you do not believe that the Holy Spirit, by whom you believe that that man was assumed, was contaminated by all of this, why should I fear the virgin's womb and her intact genitals and not rather believe that the wisdom of God remained immaculate and undefiled in the organs of his mother after the man was assumed? Whether your Mani claims that he was sent or that he was assumed by the Paraclete, neither of these could be true. Hence, I shall be more cautious and not believe that he was either sent or assumed.

8, 9. For, in adding the words, "by the providence of God the Father," what else was he aiming at in having mentioned Jesus Christ, whose apostle he says he is, and God the Father, under whose providence he says that he was sent by the Son, but that we should believe that he himself is the third, namely, the Holy Spirit? For he writes as follows: "Mani, an apostle of Jesus Christ, by the providence of God the Father." He did not mention the Holy Spirit, whom he ought most of all to have mentioned, since he commends to us his status as an apostle by the promise of the Paraclete so that he may bring pressure to bear on the ignorant by the authority of the gospel. When we ask you this, you reply that of course the Holy Spirit, the Paraclete, was mentioned when Mani was called an apostle because the Holy Spirit chose to come in Mani. I ask, therefore, as I asked above, why you are horrified when the Catholic Church says that he in whom the divine wisdom came was born of a virgin, though you are not at all horrified that he in whom you preach that the Holy Spirit came was born of a woman who had intercourse with a man. I do not know what else I should suspect but that this Mani, who seeks access to the hearts of the ignorant by means of the name of Christ, wants to be worshiped instead of Christ. I will state in a few words my grounds for making this conjecture.

I often used to ask you at that period, when I was one of your Hearers, why you generally did not celebrate the paschal feast of the Lord or at times celebrated it without fervor and with only a few people, with no vigils, with no longer fasts imposed upon the Hearers, and, finally, without a more festive solemnity, though you celebrate with great honors your Bema, that is, the day on which Mani was killed, with the lectern raised up by five steps, adorned with precious cloths, placed in the midst and facing toward the worshipers. When, therefore, I used to ask you this, the reply was that we had to celebrate the day of the suffering of the one who really suffered, but that Christ, who was not born and who presented to human eyes not real but simulated flesh, did not endure any suffering but pretended to. Who would not bemoan the fact that people who want to be called Christians are afraid that the truth might be polluted by the womb of a virgin and are not afraid that it might be polluted by a lie? But to return to the point, who would not suspect, when he pays careful attention, that Mani denied that Christ was born of a woman and had a human body in order that Christ's Passion, which is now the greatest solemnity throughout the world, would not be celebrated by those who believed in Mani, and in order that the solemnity which Mani wanted would honor the day of his death with such great devotion? After all, what we found most pleasing in that celebration of the Bema was that it was celebrated in place of the paschal feast. For we strongly desired that feast day, once the other that used to be most sweet to us had been withdrawn.

9, 10. Perhaps you will ask me, "When did the Paraclete promised by the Lord come?" Here, if I did not have something else that I believed, I would find it easier to look forward to his coming in the future than to grant that he has come by means of Mani. But now, since the coming of the Holy Spirit is most clearly proclaimed in the Acts of the Apostles, what necessity forces me to believe heretics so perilously and so readily? For in the book I mentioned it is recorded as follows: *We have given, O Theophilus, our first account of all the things that Jesus began to do and to teach on the day he chose the apostles through the Holy Spirit and commanded them to preach the gospel. To these men he showed himself alive after his suffering by many proofs over the course of days. He was seen by them for forty days. He also taught them about the kingdom of God as he lived with them, and he commanded them not to leave Jerusalem but to await the promise of the Father, of which you have heard, he said, from my lips. For John, to be sure, baptized with water, but you will begin to be baptized by the Holy Spirit, whom you are going to receive after these few days that come before Pentecost. But when they came, they asked him, saying, Lord, will you be revealed at this time, and when will the kingdom of Israel be revealed? But he said, No one can know the time that the Father has placed in his own control, but you will receive the power of the Spirit coming over you and you will be witnesses to me in Jerusalem and in all of Judea and Samaria and as far as the whole world.* (Acts 1:1-8) There you have where he told his disciples about the promise of the Father, which they heard from his lips concerning the Holy Spirit who was going to come. Now let us see when he was sent.

For a little later he goes on and says, *At that time, when the day of Pentecost came, they were together in one place with the same attitude, and suddenly there was produced a noise from heaven, as if a strong wind were blowing, and it filled that whole place in which they were sitting. And they saw tongues as it were of fire that were divided and rested upon each of them. And they were all filled with the Holy Spirit and began to speak in tongues as the Holy Spirit gave them to speak. There were Jews, however, dwelling in Jerusalem, people from every nation under heaven. And when the noise was produced, a crowd gathered and was confused, because each heard them speaking in his own language and dialect. They were astonished and amazed, saying to one another, Are not all these men who are speaking from the people of Galilee? And how do we recognize in them the language to which we were born? They were Parthians, Medes, Elamites, and people who inhabit Mesopotamia, Armenia and Cappadocia, Asia, Phrygia and Pamphilia, Egypt and the territories of Africa near Cyrene, and some who had come from Rome, Jews who lived there, and Cretans and Arabs. All heard them speaking the praises of God in their own tongues. They were astonished and fearful because of what had happened, saying, What does this mean? But others mocked them, saying, These men are full of new wine.* (Acts 2:1-13) There you see when the Holy Spirit came. What more do you want? If we should believe the scriptures, why should I not believe those that are supported by the strongest authority? For they have merited along with the gospel, in which we likewise believe that the Holy Spirit was promised, to become known to peoples and to be handed on and preached to future generations. When, therefore, I read these Acts of the Apostles that are linked to the gospel with equal authority, I find not only that the Holy Spirit was promised to those genuine apostles but also that he was so clearly sent that no room is left for errors about this matter.

10, 11. For his resurrection from the dead and his ascension into heaven are our Lord's glorification. But it is written in the Gospel according to John, *The Spirit, however, had not yet been given because Jesus had not yet been glorified* (Jn 7:39). If, then, he had not yet been given because Jesus had not yet been glorified, he must have been given as soon as Jesus was glorified. And because of his twofold glorification, as man and as God, the Holy Spirit was also given twice — once, after he rose from the dead, when he breathed into the face of his disciples, saying, *Receive the Holy Spirit* (Jn 20:22), and again, after he ascended into heaven after ten days had passed. This number signifies perfection, since to the number seven, which is the number of the days of creation, there is added the trinity of the creator. Among spiritual men many things are piously and carefully written on these topics, but I shall not swerve from my goal. For I have undertaken to deal with you not in such a way as to teach you — something that you might regard as proud — but as if I myself desired to learn from you what I could not learn over nine years. Hence, I have the writings that I should believe about the coming of the Holy Spirit. If you forbid me to believe them for fear that I might rashly believe what I do not know — for that is what you usually warn — much less should I believe your writings. Hence, either remove all books from our midst and disclose by argument the truth about which I cannot be in doubt, or bring forth the sort of books that do not arrogantly impose on me what I should believe but that show me without any deceit what I should learn. Perhaps you are going to say, "This letter is such a book." I do not want to delay longer on its threshold, then. Let us look within.

11, 12. "These are," it says, "salutary words from the everlasting and living fountain. He who hears them and first has believed them and secondly has observed what they teach will never be subject to death but will enjoy eternal and glorious life. For he is certainly to be judged happy who has been instructed by this divine knowledge, and having been set free by it he will remain in ever-lasting life." This, as you see, is a promise of the truth, not yet its revelation. And even you can notice very easily that any sort of errors can be hidden under this veil so that they might sneak unnoticed into the minds of the ignorant through this ornate doorway. Now suppose it said, "These are deadly words from a poisoned fountain. He who hears them and first has believed them and secondly has observed what they teach will never be restored to life but will be afflicted with a punishing and bitter death. For he certainly should be judged unhappy who is enveloped in this infernal ignorance, into which he will sink and in which he will remain in everlasting torments." If, then, it said this, it would be speaking the truth, but it would not only not have won over any reader to this book but would have stirred up the deepest hatred in all those into whose hands it had come. Hence, let us turn to the following words, and let those previous words not mislead us, which can be words shared by good people and bad ones, by learned people and ignorant ones. What, then, follows?

11, 13. It says, "May the peace of the invisible God and the knowledge of the truth be with the holy and most dear brothers who believe and likewise observe the heavenly commandments." May it be as it says. For this too is a good and most acceptable prayer. Only we should remember that these words can be spoken by good teachers and by deceivers. And so, if the letter said only such things, I would grant that everyone should read it and embrace it. Nor would I disapprove of the words that follow after this. For it adds: "But may the right hand of the light protect us and rescue us from every evil incursion and from the snares of the world." And I do not want to find fault with anything at all that is written at the beginning of this letter until we come to the subject matter. Other-wise, much effort would be used up on minor points. Now, then, let us see the man's perfectly clear promise.

12, 14. "And so," it says, "concerning what you, dearest brother Patticius,[10] indicated to me that you wanted to know when you said, 'Of what sort was the birth of Adam and Eve? Were they brought forth by a word or were they begotten by a body?' you shall receive an answer, as is fitting. For in various writings and revelations many have inserted and mentioned things about them in different ways. Hence, how the truth stands about this matter is unknown by almost all peoples and even by all those who have argued long and extensively

---

10. Patticius seems to be the person to whom the *Letter of the Foundation* was addressed.

about it. For, if they had attained to a clear knowledge of the generation of Adam and Eve, they would never be subject to corruption and death." It promises us clear knowledge of this matter, therefore, in order that we may not be subject to corruption and death. And if this is not enough, see what follows. "Many things," it says, "must necessarily be mentioned first in order that one may be able to arrive at this mystery without any ambiguity." This is what I said, namely, that the truth should be revealed to me so that I may arrive at it without any ambiguity. And if he did not promise this, I ought nonetheless to require and demand it so that, for the sake of the great reward of most evident and most certain knowledge, I would not be ashamed of becoming a Manichean instead of being a Catholic Christian, despite anyone's arguments to the contrary. Now let us hear what it tells us.

12, 15. It says, "Hence, if it seems good to you, first hear what existed before the creation of the world and how a battle was incited in order that you may be able to distinguish the nature of light and of darkness." Now it has set forth things that are incredible and absolutely false. For who would believe that before the creation of the world any battle was initiated? Even if it were believable, nonetheless now we would like not to believe but to know this. For someone who says that the Persians and Scythians warred with each other many years ago says something believable, something that we can believe after having either read or heard about it, but not something that we could know from having experienced or seized upon it. Since, therefore, I would reject this man if he said something of the sort — after all, he did not promise things that I would have to believe but things that I could know without any ambiguity — how shall I not reject him when he says things that are not only uncertain but also unbelievable? But what if he makes those things clear and known by some arguments? Let us, then, listen, if we can, with complete patience and calmness to what follows.

13, 16. It says, "In the beginning these two substances were divided from each other. And God the Father — everlasting in his holy origin, magnificent in his power, true in his nature, always exulting in the eternity that is his own, containing within himself wisdom and the living senses by which he grasps the twelve members of his light, that is, the abundant riches of his kingdom — controlled the empire of light. But in each of his members there were hidden thousands of countless and immense treasures. The Father himself, however, outstanding in his praise and incomprehensible in his greatness, has, joined to himself, the blessed and glorious worlds that are inestimable in number and extent, with whom the same holy and illustrious Father and progenitor lives, while no one in his remarkable kingdoms is either needy or weak. But his most splendid kingdoms were founded upon the bright and blessed land so that they could never either be moved or shaken by anything."

13, 17. How is he going to prove these things to me, or how has he come to know them? Do not frighten me with the name of the Paraclete. For, first of all you yourselves have made me wary, and I have come to you not to believe things that are not known but to know things that are certain. After all, you know how fiercely you are accustomed to attack those who believe rashly, especially since Mani himself, who has now begun to tell an uncertain story, promised full and solid knowledge shortly before.

14, 17. Secondly, if faith is to be demanded of me, that scripture would have more of a hold[11] on me where I read that the Holy Spirit came and inspired the apostles[12] to whom the Lord had promised that he would send him.[13] Hence, either prove to me that what Mani says is true, so as to show me those things that I cannot believe, or prove to me that he who says them is the Holy Spirit, so that I may believe what you cannot prove. For I profess the Catholic faith, and I am confident that through it I shall come to certain knowledge. But you who try to shake my faith, give me, if you can, certain knowledge in order to convince me that I rashly believed what I believed.

There are two claims that you bring forth: one, when you say that he who speaks is the Holy Spirit, and a second, when you say that what he says is evident. I ought to have learned both of them from you, but I am not greedy: teach me just one of them. Show me that this man is the Holy Spirit and I shall believe that what he says is true. Or show me that what he says is true and I shall believe that he is the Holy Spirit, even if I do not know this. Could I do anything with you that is fairer or that manifests more good will? But you can show me neither the one nor the other. You have chosen nothing else but to praise what you believe and to mock what I believe. When I in turn praise what I believe and mock what you believe, then, what do you think should be our judgment? Or what do you think that we should do but abandon those who invite us to certain knowledge and afterward command us to believe uncertainties? We should instead follow those who invite us first to believe what we cannot as yet see in order that, having been strengthened by faith, we may merit to understand what we believe, when it is no longer human beings but God himself who interiorly enlightens and strengthens our mind.

14, 18. And since I have asked how he would prove this, I now ask how he has come to know it. If he says that it was revealed to him by the Holy Spirit and that his mind was enlightened by God, so that he might know as certain and evident the things that he says, he himself indicates the difference between knowing and believing. After all, he to whom these things are most clearly shown has knowledge, but in those to whom he recounts these things he does not convey knowledge but urges belief. And whoever rashly agrees with him becomes a Manichean not by knowing what is certain but by believing what is uncertain,

---

11. I have followed the reading *teneret* found in PL rather than *terreret* found in CSEL.
12. See Acts 2:1-13.
13. See Jn 14:16-17.

like the sort of ignorant youngsters we were, whom Mani once deceived. He ought not, then, to have promised us knowledge or clear insight or the attainment without any ambiguity of what we are seeking, but he should instead have said that these things were shown to him, while those to whom he recounts them ought to believe him concerning what they do not know. But if he said this, who would not reply to him, "If I am going to believe what I do not know, then, why should I not rather believe the things that are praised by the agreement of the learned and the unlearned and confirmed among all peoples by the weightiest authority?" In his fear that someone might say this to him, he befogs the ignorant, first promising them knowledge of certainties and afterward asking for belief in uncertainties. Yet if someone were to say to him that he should at least demonstrate to us that these things were shown to him, he fails here too and orders us to believe this as well. Who would put up with so great a lie and such great pride?

15, 19. But if I show, with the help of our Lord and God, that what he says is not only uncertain but also false, what can be found more unfortunate than this superstition, which not only does not disclose the knowledge and truth that it promises but says things that are strongly opposed to knowledge and truth? This will be seen more clearly in what follows. For he speaks in this way: "But next to one part and side of that bright and holy land there was the land of darkness with its deep and immense greatness, in which dwell fiery bodies, that is, deadly beings. Here there was endless and incalculable darkness flowing from that same nature along with its own offspring. Beyond them there were foul and murky waters with their denizens. Within them there were horrible and mighty winds along with their prince and forebears. Again there was a fiery and corruptible region with its leaders and nations. In the same way there was within this region a people full of fog and smoke in which there dwelled the cruel prince and leader of all, who was surrounded by countless princes. Of all of these he was the mind and origin. These were the five natures of the deadly land."

15, 20. If Mani said that the nature of God was an airy or ethereal body, he would certainly be mocked by all who are able to see by some sort of gaze of a clearer mind that the nature of wisdom and truth is not distended and spread out through any stretches of space but is great and magnificent without any mass and is not smaller in one part and larger in another but equal to the highest Father in all respects, not having one part here and another there but being whole everywhere and present everywhere.

16, 20. But why should I speak about the truth and wisdom that surpasses all the powers of the soul, when the nature of the soul itself, which is found to be mutable, does not in any way occupy stretches of space with any mass of its own? For whatever has any mass can only be diminished by parts because it has one part here and another there. A finger, after all, is smaller than the whole hand, and one finger is smaller than two, and this finger is in one place, the other in another, and the rest of the hand still elsewhere. We see this not only in the masses of bodies with their different members, but this piece of the earth is not where that piece is, because each has its own place. And a smaller part of a liquid is in a smaller place and a larger part in a larger place, and one part is toward the bottom and another around the rim of the cup. Similarly, parts of air each fill their own places, and it is impossible that the air which fills this house also have simultaneously within itself the air that the neighboring houses have. One part of the light is poured in through this window, another through that window, and a larger amount of light through a larger window and a smaller amount of light through a smaller window. And there cannot be any body whatsoever, whether heavenly or earthly, whether airy or liquid, that is not smaller in a part than in the whole. Nor can it in any way have another part in this part's place at the same time, but, having one part here and another there, it is extended through any stretches of space by a mass that is spread out and divided or rather — so to speak — capable of being cut.

But even if we do not consider the power of the soul by which it understands the truth, but the lower power by which it holds the body together and has sensation in the body, the nature of the soul is in no way found to be extended by any mass in stretches of space. For it is present as a whole to the individual small parts of its body, nor is there a smaller part of it in a finger and a larger part in an arm, as the finger itself is smaller than the arm, but it is just as great everywhere because it is whole everywhere. For, when a finger is touched, the soul does not sense through the whole body, and yet the whole soul senses. For that touching does not escape the awareness of the whole soul,[14] and this would not happen if the whole soul were not present. Nor is the whole soul present so that, when a finger is touched and the soul senses in the finger, the soul abandons the rest of the body and crowds itself into that one place where it senses. But when the whole soul senses in a finger of the hand, if another place is touched on the foot, the whole soul does not cease to sense in the finger. And in that way the whole soul is present at the same time in individual places at a distance from each other, not abandoning one place in order to be whole in another, nor occupying both so that it has one part here and another there. But, being able to manifest its whole self at the same time in individual places, it shows well enough that it is not contained in stretches of space because the whole soul senses in the individual places.

17, 20. What then if we think of its memory — not of intelligible things but of these bodily ones, a memory that we see the other animals have? For farm animals wander through familiar places without going astray. Wild animals seek their own dens. And dogs recognize the bodies of their masters, and while sleeping they often whimper and at times burst out barking; in no way could they do this if in

---

14. See *The Magnitude of the Soul* 25, 48, where Augustine defines sensation as "a change in the body that of itself does not escape the awareness of the soul."

their memory there were not present images of things they saw or sensed somehow or other through the body. Who would adequately think of where these images are received, where they are carried, or where they are formed? After all, if these images could not be larger than what the size of our body can hold, someone might say that the soul forms and preserves these images within the space of its own body, by which the soul itself is enclosed. But now, although the body occupies a small part of the earth, the mind contains images of immense regions of both heaven and earth, and, as clusters of them come and go, the mind does not become crowded. And from this the mind shows that it is not spread out through space, because it is not, so to speak, taken in by those images of very great places but rather takes them in — not in some pocket but by the ineffable might and power that allows it to add anything to them, to subtract it from them, to contract them into a small space, to expand and spread them out through immense spaces, to put them in order, as it chooses, to disrupt their order, to multiply them, and to reduce them to a few or to a single individual.

18, 20. What shall I say now about that power by which the truth is known? By this power we resist with great energy these very images that are derived and framed from the senses of the body and offer themselves in place of the truth. By it we see, for example, that the true Carthage is distinct from the one that the mind frames in thought and changes at will with complete ease, and that from the same capacity there come the countless worlds in which the thought of Epicurus journeyed in countless ways. And — not to run on at length — from that same capacity there comes this land of light spread out through endless space and the five caverns of the nation of darkness with their denizens, in which the phantasms of Mani have dared to lay claim for themselves to the name of truth. What, then, is this power that distinguishes these? Certainly, however great it may be, it is greater than all these, and it is thought of without any such picturing of things. Find a place for this, if you can; spread it out through space; extend it by the swelling of an endless mass. Surely, you cannot do so if you are thinking aright. For whatever of the sort comes to your mind, you judge that it can be cut by thought into parts, and there you make one part smaller and another larger to the extent that you want. But you see that power by which you pronounce judgment on these things is above them not by the loftiness of its position but by the dignity of its power.

19, 21. Hence, if you see that the soul is so often subject to change, whether because of the crowd of various desires, or because of dispositions that change in accord with the abundance or lack of things, or because of the play of countless phantasms, or because of forgetfulness and remembering or of learning and ignorance — if, then, as I said, you see that the soul, which is so often subject to change because of these and other such motions, is not spread out and extended through space but transcends all spaces by the liveliness of its power, what ought one to think or judge about God who, while remaining unshakable and immutable above all rational minds, gives what should be given to each? The soul more readily dares to speak of him than to see him, and it speaks less of him the more clearly it can see him. If, nonetheless, as the Manichean phantasms shout out, he were spread out in an area of space that was bounded on one side but was limitless on the others, particles in him of any size and countless pieces, some larger, others smaller, would be measured off in accord with the choice of the person thinking of them. In that way, for example, a two-foot part in him would be eight parts less than a ten-foot part. For all natures that are spread out through such spaces and cannot be whole everywhere are necessarily subject to this. This extension is not found in the soul, and those who cannot grasp these ideas have ugly and shameful ideas about the soul.

20, 22. Perhaps, however, we should not deal with carnal minds in this way but should rather come down to the level of thought of those souls that either do not dare or are not yet able to follow along by thinking of an incorporeal and spiritual nature. Thus they do not consider their own thought itself by that same thinking and do not find that it judges concerning stretches of space without any stretch of space. Let us, therefore, come down to their minds and ask them next to what part or next to what side, as Mani says, of the bright and holy land the land of darkness was. For he says "next to one part and side," and he does not say which part and which side, the right or the left. But whichever side they choose, it is certainly clear that we speak of one side only where there is another side. Where there are three or more sides, we either understand the area of a figure bounded on all sides, or, if in one part it is without limit, it must be limited in those parts that are called sides.

Let them, therefore, say what touched the land of light on the other side or on the other sides, if on the one side there was the land of darkness. They do not tell us, but, when they are pressed to tell us, they say that the other sides of that land, which they call the land of light, are unlimited, that is, are stretched out through endless space and bounded by no limit. They do not understand that there are no longer sides, something that is perfectly evident to any slow minds. There would, after all, be sides if they were bounded by their limits. He says, "What difference does it make to me if there are no sides?" But because you said "next to one part and side," you were forced to understand another part or other parts and another side or other sides. For, if there was only one side, he ought only to have said "next to the side," not "next to one side," just as in the case of our body we correctly say that something is next to one eye because there is another eye or next to one nipple because there is another nipple. But if we say "next to one nose" or "next to one navel," although there is no other, we shall be laughed at by both the learned and the ignorant. I am not going to press you over words, however. After all, perhaps you wanted to use "one" in the sense of "only."

21, 22. But what, then, was next to the side of the land that you call bright and holy? Mani says that it was "the land of darkness." What is that? You at least concede that that land is bodily. You must say this since you say that all bodies derive their origin from it. What follows, then? Though you are slow, though you are carnal human beings, I ask, "Do you not at last see that these two lands could not touch each other by their sides if both were not bodily?" Why, then, did you say to us, who were misled by I know not what kind of blindness, that only the land of darkness is or was bodily, but that it is necessary to believe that the land that is called the land of light is non-bodily and spiritual? At long last let us good people wake up, at least when admonished. Let us see — something that is most easy to see — that the two lands cannot touch each other with their sides unless both are bodies.

21, 23. Or if we are even too thick-headed and slow-minded for this, I ask whether the land of darkness itself had one side, while the others were unbounded, like the land of light. The Manicheans do not believe that it is so. For they are afraid that it would be thought equal to God. They say, therefore, that it is limitless in depth and length, but they maintain that above and beyond it there are stretches of endless emptiness. And so that the land of darkness would not seem to contain one part, while the land of light had twice as much, they limit the land of darkness on two sides. Take, for example, one loaf of bread — for in this way one can picture more easily what they say — that is formed into four sections, three of which are white and one black. Now remove the distinction from the three white parts and make them endless on the top, below, and around back. For they think about the land of light in this way. But make that dark quarter endless downward and backward, but with a limitless emptiness above it. They suppose that the land of darkness is like that. But they reveal these things as secrets to people who are zealous inquirers and very attentive.

22, 23. If it is so, in any event, we see that the land of darkness is touched by the land of light on two sides, and, if it is touched on two sides, it of course also touches on two sides. Indeed, "next to one side there was the land of darkness."

22, 24. Then, how ugly the shape of the land of light appears, like a cloven hoof with a kind of black wedge inserted from below, limited only where it is cloven, while also gaping and lying open above with a void interposed and whatever extends limitlessly upward from the surface of the land of darkness. How much better, then, is the shape of the land of darkness shown to be, since the land of darkness cleaves, while the land of light is cloven, and the land of darkness is inserted, while the land of light lies open. The land of darkness admits into itself no room for emptiness, while the land of light is defined only on the lower side where it is penetrated by the enemy wedge. Ignorant and greedy human beings attribute greater honor to a multiplicity of parts than to unity, and so they assign six parts to the land of light, three on the bottom and three on the top, and they have preferred that the land of light be penetrated rather than that it penetrate. For, even if because of such a shape they deny that it is mingled with the land of darkness, they cannot deny that it is penetrated.

23, 25. Do not compare now the spiritual men of the Catholic faith, in whom the mind, as much as it can in this life, sees that the divine substance and nature is not extended over any areas of space and is not shaped by dimensions of members. Compare instead our carnal and little ones who often, when they hear of certain members of our body in an allegory, such as when the eyes of God or the ears of God are mentioned, picture God for themselves with the freedom of the imagination in the shape of the human body. Compare these latter with those Manicheans who often describe those bits of nonsense of theirs as great secrets to interested and curious human beings, and consider which of them thinks in a more tolerable and better way about God. Is it those who think of him in a human shape endowed with the highest dignity of its own kind or those who think of him as spread out with an endless mass, yet not in every direction but endless and solid in three quarters, while in one quarter cloven, lying open, gaping, undefined because of emptiness above, but split by the wedge of the land of darkness below — or, if it is better to say this — open above in its own nature but entered from below by another nature.

See, along with you I mock the carnal human beings who cannot yet grasp spiritual realities and think of God in a human form. And, if you can, mock along with me those who in their very pitiful thinking imagine so ugly and shameful a fissure or cut in God, so emptily gaping above, so badly blocked from below. And yet, there is also this difference — that, if those carnal persons who think of God in human form are content to be nourished with milk in the bosom of the Catholic Church, they do not thrust themselves into rash opinions. Rather, they nourish there a pious desire for seeking; they ask there in order that they may receive; they knock there in order that it may be opened for them.[15] They begin to understand spiritually the allegories and parables of the scriptures and gradually come to know that God's powers are appropriately mentioned as ears in one place, in another as eyes, elsewhere as hands or feet, or even as wings or feathers, also as a shield, a sword, a helmet, and countless other such things. The more they make progress in such understanding, the more they are confirmed in being Catholics. But when the Manicheans abandon their imagining of that shape, they cannot be Manicheans. For they ascribe it to the praises of their founder as something proper and excellent when they say that the divine mysteries which the ancient writers set forth in figures in the scriptures were left to be resolved and revealed by this man who was going to come last. And they say that no teacher will come from God after him precisely for the reason that Mani said nothing in figures and allegories. For he had made clear what the ancients had said in that way and plainly and openly revealed his own thoughts. The Manicheans, therefore, do not have any interpretations to which they can have recourse when it is read to them from their founder: "But next to one part

---

15. See Mt 7:7.

and side of that bright and holy land was the land of darkness." Wherever they turn, hemmed in by their pitiful phantasms, they inevitably come upon clefts or abrupt divisions and junctures or splits[16] of the most shameful sort, and it is most pitiful to believe these things — I will not say of the immutable nature of God but of every non-bodily nature, even though subject to change, such as is the soul. And yet, if I cannot turn myself to higher things and direct my thoughts away from false imagery (which I carry about fixed in my memory by means of the senses of the body) to the freedom and purity of a spiritual nature, how much better would I do to think of God in the form of the human body than to insert that black wedge into his lower fissure and, not finding in that higher and most vast indefiniteness the means to shut it up, to leave it lying and gaping open with its limitless emptiness? What is uglier than this opinion? What can be said or imagined that is darker than this error?

24, 26. Next I wish that he would tell me, since I read that "God the Father and his kingdoms were founded upon the bright and happy land," whether the Father and his kingdoms and land are of one and the same substance and nature. If that is the case, that wedge of the nation of darkness does not any longer split open and penetrate another nature, as it were, which would be like the body of God — something that would be utterly shameful because of its unspeakable ugliness — but that wedge of the land of darkness splits open and penetrates the very nature of God. I beg you; consider these ideas; you are human beings. I beg you; consider these ideas and flee from them. Tearing open your hearts, if it is possible, root out and drive off the sacrileges of such images from your faith.

Or are you going to say that those three are not of one and the same nature but that the Father has one nature, the kingdoms another, and the land still another, so that they have their own different natures and substances arranged in levels of excellence? If that is true, Mani ought to have preached not two but four natures. But if the Father and the kingdoms have one nature and the land alone has a different nature, he should have preached three natures. Or if he preferred to say two because the land of darkness does not belong to God, I ask how the land of light belongs to God. For, if it has a different nature and if God did not beget or make it, it does not belong to him, and his kingdoms are located in another's territory. Or if it belongs to him because it is nearby, the land of darkness, which not merely touches the land of light by its nearness but tears into it by penetration, should also belong to him. But if he begot it, we should not believe that it has a different nature. For we ought to believe that what God begot is the same nature as God, as the Catholic Church believes about the only-begotten Son. And so, you are necessarily brought back to that shamefulness which must be fled from and detested, namely, that the black wedge does not split open that land, as if it were another and different nature, but splits open the very nature of

---

16. I have followed PL in reading *fissuras* instead of *fulturas.*

God. But if God did not beget it but made it, I ask what he made it out of. If out of himself, what else is this but to have begotten it? If out of some other nature, I ask whether it was good or evil. If it was good, there was some other good nature, then, that did not belong to God. In no way will you dare to say this. But if it was evil, that nation of darkness was not the only evil nature. Or had God perhaps taken up some part of it in order to turn it into the land of light and to establish his kingdoms upon it? He would have done this with the whole of it, then, in order that at some point there would be no evil nature. But if he did not made the land of light out of some other substance, it remains that he made it out of nothing.

25, 27. Hence, if we have now persuaded you that almighty God can make something good out of nothing, enter into the Catholic Church and learn that all the natures that God made and created, arranged in levels of excellence from the highest down to the lowest, are all good, but that some are better than others, and that they were made out of nothing. For God their maker worked mightily, so to speak, through his wisdom in order that what was not would be able to be and in order that it would be good, insofar as it was, but would show, insofar as it was lacking, that it is not born of God but made by him out of nothing. If you consider this, you do not find anything to hold you back. For you cannot say that the land of light, as you describe it, is either the same nature as God, lest the ugliness of that fourth part be inserted into the nature of God, or that it is born of God, lest you be forced to understand that it is nonetheless the same nature as God and would be reduced to that same deformity. You cannot say that it is a nature other than God, lest you be forced to say that God locates his kingdoms in someone else's territory and that there are not two but three natures. Nor can you say that God made it out of some other substance, lest there be some other good besides God or some evil besides the nation of darkness. What is left, then, is for you to admit that God made the land of light out of nothing, and you do not want to believe this. But if God could make out of nothing some great good, which would nonetheless be inferior to him, he could also, because he is good and is not grudging toward any good, make another good that would be inferior to that first good. He could also make a third good, to which the second would be preferred, and carry on from there the order of created natures to the lowest good. Thus the totality of them would not flow off uncertainly because of their indefinite number but would stay as they were, limited by a definite number. Or, if you are unwilling to admit that God made this land of light out of nothing, there will be no way out by which to avoid such great shamefulness and such sacrilegious opinions.

25, 28. At least see that carnal thinking is free to entertain the sort of images it wants on the chance that you might be able to find some other form for the joining of the two lands, so that such a despicable and repulsive appearance of things does not come to mind. I mean that the land of God — whether it is of the same nature as God or of another nature, in which the kingdoms of God have nonetheless been established — lies there immense with such a huge mass that it lies with its members stretched out and spread endlessly, and in them it most foully and shamefully receives from underneath that very wedge of the land of darkness as something of huge greatness that has been inserted into it. But whatever other shape you find by which these two lands might be joined to each other, you certainly cannot delete the words of Mani. I do not mean other words by which he described these things more explicitly. For, because fewer persons know them, they are perhaps thought to entail less danger. But I mean the very words from the *Letter of the Foundation* which we are now discussing and which all of you who are called "Enlightened" know very well. Here, in fact, is how it is written: "But next to one part or side of that bright and holy land there was the land of darkness with its deep and immense size."

26, 28. What more do we want? After all, we know that it was next to a side. Imagine, however you want, the shapes, and describe the lines. Surely that immense mass of the land of darkness is joined to the land of light by either a straight side or a bent and curved side. But if it is joined to it by a curved side, that holy land also has a curved side. For, if it has a straight side and touches this curved side, there lie between them certain deep caverns endlessly empty, and there is no longer an emptiness merely above the land of darkness, as we often heard. If that is the case, how much better would it have been for the land of light to be somewhat further removed and for that great emptiness to come between them so that it could not be touched at all by the land of darkness! In fact, such a great space of empty depth would open up that, if any wrongdoing arose on the part of that nation, even if the princes of darkness wanted to leap across into the land of light — after all, bodies cannot fly unless they are supported by bodily air — they would be hurled down into that void. And because it would be without end in a downward direction, they would never come to the bottom. Even if they were able to live forever, they would nonetheless be unable to do any harm while being forever carried downward.

But if the land of darkness is joined to the land of light by a curved side, the land of light also receives it in a curved hollow in an ugly manner. If the land of darkness was curved inward in the shape of a theater, it embraced the curved part of the land of light that it received in a union that is no less ugly. And if the land of darkness had a curved side and the land of light a straight side, it did not touch it as a whole. And it would certainly have been better, as I said above, that it touch it nowhere and that there be in between so great a void that it would separate the two lands by a fair distance and would not permit any of the rash and wicked to do any harm while falling headlong without end.

But if it touched a straight side with a straight side, I do not see any openings or gaps. Rather, I see clearly such great peace and such a great harmony of the two lands with each other that there could not be a greater union. After all, what is more beautiful, what is more suitable, than that a straight side be joined to a straight side, so that nowhere does some hollow or bend break or destroy that natural and stable union through an endless area of space and from endless eternity? Even if they were separated by an intervening void, those straight sides of the two lands would not only be beautiful in themselves because they are so straight, but, even with the interposition of a distance, they would still be suited to each other, so that on one side and on the other the two equally straight sides, even if they did not touch, would still, thanks to their likeness, fit together in a single beauty. But when this union is added, what could be more harmonious and peaceful than these two lands? I also do not find anything more beautiful that could be said or thought than this union of the two straight sides.

27, 29. What shall I do with those most wretched souls who have been perverted by error and longstanding habit? For these people do not know what they are saying when they say these things, for they are not paying attention. I beg you: no one is pressuring you; no one is pushing you into conflict; no one is mocking your past errors except someone who has not experienced God's mercy so that he may be free from errors. We aim only at bringing them to an end. Pay attention for a little while without animosity or bitterness. We are all human beings; we hate not you but your errors and lies. I beseech you: give heed for a little while. O God of mercies, help those who pay attention, and kindle the interior light for those who seek the truth. For what do we understand if we do not understand that straight is better than crooked? I ask you, then, if you peacefully and modestly listen to this: If someone made crocked the straight side of the land of darkness that is joined to the straight side of the land of light, would he take no beauty from it? You must admit, if you do not want to bark like dogs, that, if he makes it crooked, he takes from it not only that beauty but also the beauty that it was able to have in common with the straight side of the land of light. In taking away this beauty, then, and making it crooked instead of straight, so that what was harmonious is discordant and what was suitable is repugnant, he did not take from it any substance, did he? In this way, then, learn that evil is not a substance. Rather, just as in a body beauty is lost or is rather diminished by a change for the worse in shape, and what was previously said to be beautiful is now said to be ugly, and a body that was previously pleasing is now displeasing, so in a soul the beauty of a correct will, by which one lives piously and righteously, is spoiled when the will is changed for the worse. And by that sin the soul that was gaining happiness by the goodness of a correct will is made unhappy without the addition or subtraction of any substance.

27, 30. Next, consider this as well. Even if we concede that the side of the land of darkness is evil for other reasons, because it can be said to be obscure or dark or anything else, it is still not evil insofar as it is straight. Just as I concede that there is something evil in its color, then, so you must also concede that there is something good in its straightness. It is wrong, therefore, to separate this good, however great it is, from God its maker. For, unless we believe that every good that is in any nature comes from him, we are in error in a most dangerous manner. How, then, does Mani say that this land is the greatest evil, though I find in the straightness of its side a good of no small beauty in terms of the body? And how does he want it to be completely separate from the almighty and all-good God? For we do not find anyone else to whom this good that we find in it should be attributed but to the author of all goods. But, he says, that side was evil. Suppose that it was evil. It would certainly be worse if it were not straight but twisted. How, then, is it the greatest evil if we can think of something worse than it? Secondly, that must be something good by whose lack anything becomes worse. But that side would become worse by lacking straightness. There is, therefore, some good in it, namely, the straightness. And you will never tell me the source from which it is present there unless you turn to him from whom we say that all goods, whether great or small, nonetheless come. But now let us pass from a consideration of this side to other topics.

28, 31. Mani says, "In that land dwell fiery bodies, that is, deadly beings." When he says "dwell" he of course wants us to understand that they have souls and are living. But lest we be thought to want to attack him over a word, let us consider all the inhabitants of that land as he distributes them over five living kinds. "Here there was endless and incalculable darkness flowing from that same nature along with its own offspring. Beyond them there were foul and murky waters with their denizens. Within them there were horrible and mighty winds along with their prince and forebears. Again, there was a fiery and corruptible region with its leaders and nations. In the same way there was within this region a people full of fog and smoke, in which there dwelled the cruel prince and leader of all, surrounded by countless princes. Of all of these he was the mind and origin. These were the five natures of the deadly land."

We see five natures like parts of one nature that he calls the deadly land. These are darkness, waters, winds, fire, and smoke. He arranges these five natures so that darkness, from which he begins his count, is external to the others. Within darkness he places waters, within waters winds, within winds fire, and within fire smoke. And each of these five natures has certain kinds of their own inhabitants, which are nonetheless five. For I ask whether there was one kind of inhabitant in all five natures or different kinds, just as the natures themselves are different. The Manicheans answer that there were different kinds, and thus they teach from other books that the darkness had serpents; the waters swimming things, such as fish; the winds flying things, such as birds; the fire quadrupeds, such as horses, lions, and other such animals; and the smoke bipeds, such as human beings.

29, 32. Who, then, arranged these? Who distributed and distinguished them? Who gave them number, quality, form, and life? For these things are all good in themselves, nor do we find a source from which they are given to each nature apart from God, the source of all goods. For the Manicheans do not try to portray this land, which they call the land of darkness, in the way that poets are also accustomed to describe or somehow to portray chaos as a certain formless matter without beauty, without quality, without measurements, without number and weight, something or other that is confused, without order and distinction, and utterly lacking every quality. For this reason certain Greek teachers call it ἄποιον. It is not in this way that the Manicheans attempt to present this land which they call the land of darkness. Rather they join and align one side to the opposite side in another far different and contrary way. They count, distinguish, and put in order five natures, endow them with their own qualities, and do not permit them to be alone and barren but fill them with their own inhabitants, and they ascribe to them forms, which are suited to them and appropriate for their inhabitants, and also life, which surpasses everything. To enumerate these great goods and to say that they are separate from God, the source of all goods, is to fail to recognize the great good of order in things and the great evil of error in oneself.

30, 33. "But," Mani says, "these five kinds which inhabit those natures were savage and deadly." He says this as if I would praise in them their savagery and deadliness. Look, I deplore along with you the evils that you attack in them. Praise along with me the goods that you yourself mention in them. In that way you will see that you want to establish goods mixed with evils as the greatest and ultimate evil. I deplore along with you their deadliness; praise along with me their well-being. After all, those kinds could not have been born, been nourished, or have inhabited that land without well-being.

I deplore there along with you the darkness; praise there along with me the fertility. For you call the darkness "incalculable" and add "along with its offspring," although darkness is not bodily and has this whole name from the absence of light, just as nakedness means to lack clothes and emptiness means to be without bodily fullness. And for this reason darkness could not beget anything, although the dark land, that is, the land lacking light, could beget something. But let us omit this for now. Where offspring come to be, though, there is balance suited for well-being, and a certain mathematical harmony sets in order and builds into unity the members of those who are born and who fit together with one another in a peace coming from moderation. Who would not understand that all these things deserve greater praise than darkness deserves blame?

I deplore there along with you the muddy murkiness of the waters; praise there along with me the form and quality of the waters and the suitable members of their swimming denizens, the life that maintains and rules their body, and all the balance suited to the well-being of their kind. For, however much you may find fault with the muddy and turbid waters, yet, since you say that the waters are such that they can both beget and maintain their own living beings, you cannot take from them the form of some sort of body and the likeness of parts by which they are formed and are at peace in a single quality. For, if you take that away, there will be no body. If you are human, you see that all those things are praiseworthy. And however much you exaggerate the savagery of their denizens and their impulse to injure and destroy one another, you still do not take away from them the numerical limits of their forms, by which their individual bodies are at peace with themselves because of the equality of their members. Nor do you take from them the balance of well-being and the governance of the soul, which brings the parts of its body into the unity of friendship and harmony. If you observe these with a human mind, you see that these features should be praised more than those that you find displeasing should be deplored.

I deplore there along with you the horror of the winds; praise there along with me the nature of the same winds, which provides breath and nourishment and the form of a body that is continuous and spread out by the suitability of its parts. Thanks to all these the winds were able to beget, nourish, and maintain in well-being those who inhabited them. Praise there along with me both the other things that were praised in all living beings by the previous argument and what is proper to them, namely, the quick and easy passage of their inhabitants from where they want and to where they want and the harmonious effort and equal movement of their wings in flight.

I deplore there along with you the destructiveness of fire; praise there along with me the fire that generates and bestows life and its opportune tempering in those that are born, so that they come together and are brought to perfection with their own numbers and members and so that they can live and dwell there. You recognize that all these things deserve admiration and praise not merely in the habitat of fire but in its inhabitants as well.

I deplore there along with you the obscurity of smoke and the cruelty of the prince who, as you say, dwells in it; praise there along with me the fact that in smoke itself you find no part unlike the rest, because it preserves in its kind the harmony and moderation of its parts with one another, so that it is what it is because of a certain unity. No one who seriously considers these facts fails to praise them in admiration. Why is it that you even give to smoke the force and power to generate inasmuch as you even attribute to it princely inhabitants, so that smoke is fertile there and offers to its inhabitants a healthful place to dwell, which is something we have never seen here?

31, 34. In the prince of smoke you have also noticed only his cruelty, which you blamed. Ought you not to have noticed the other features that would make you praise his nature? For he had a soul and a body, the former giving life, the latter filled with life, with the soul ruling and the body obeying, with the soul leading and the body following, with the soul holding the body together and the body not breaking down, with the soul moving harmoniously and the body made stable by the harmonious framework of its members. Does not the ordered peace or peaceful order in this one prince move you to praise? What we have said about the one, however, may be understood about the others. But he was, after all, savage and cruel to the others. I do not praise this, but I praise those great qualities that you do not want to notice. If anyone who has rashly believed Mani looks at and considers them, at least after he has been admonished, he undoubtedly recognizes that, when he speaks of these natures, he is speaking of certain goods, not of the highest and uncreated goods, such as God, the one Trinity, nor of created goods that have received a lofty position, such as the holy angels and the most blessed powers, but of the lowest goods that have received a position at the lowest level of reality in accord with the limitation of their own kind. When these natures are compared with the higher, the ignorant consider them blameworthy, and when they consider how much good that is present in the higher natures is lacking in these lower natures, they call the absence of this good evil. I am arguing about these natures in this way, to be sure, because they have the names of things that we are familiar with in this world. For we know darkness, waters, winds, fire, and smoke. We also know animals that crawl, that swim, that fly, that have four legs, and that have two legs. In all of these the exception is darkness, which, as I said, is nothing but the absence of light, which is discerned by the eyes when they do not see, just as silence is perceived by the ears when they do not hear. It is not that darkness is something but that there is no light, just as silence is not something but that there is no sound. With the exception of darkness, then, the others in this list are natures and are familiar to all of us, and no one who is wise separates from God, the author of all goods, their form, because it is praiseworthy and good insofar as it is.

32, 35. For, when that infamous Mani chose to arrange in his phantasms, as if in the nation of darkness, the natures that he came to know in this world, he is proven to be a complete liar, first, because darkness can beget nothing, as was said. But he says, "That darkness was not like the darkness you know in this world." How, then, are you going to teach me about it? Are you, who so verbosely promise learning, perhaps going to force me to believe? Go ahead, make me believe. Yet there is one thing that I know: If that darkness does not have form, as this darkness does not, it could not have begotten anything. But if it does, it was a better darkness. But when you say that it was not like the darkness in this world, you want us to believe that it was some worse darkness. You could have also said that silence — which is to the ears what darkness is to the eyes — begot there some deaf or mute animals, so that, when someone tells you that silence is not a nature, you might reply, "But the silence is not like the silence you know in this world." In that way you could say whatever you wanted to those whom you had first deceived into believing you.

And yet, what led him to imagine that serpents were born in darkness could well have been something he noticed in the very beginnings of those serpents after their birth. But there are serpents that see very keenly, and they exult in the presence of light in such a way that they seem to speak very weighty testimony against him.

Secondly, it was easy for Mani to observe those beings swimming here in waters and to transfer them to those phantasms. It was the same with those beings flying in the winds, because the movement of this thicker air in which birds fly is called wind. But I do not know how it entered his mind to imagine four-footed animals in fire. And yet he did not say this without a reason but paid insufficient attention and erred greatly. After all, the reason the Manicheans usually give is that quadrupeds are big eaters and are in much heat during intercourse. But in their eating many human beings outdo any quadruped, and humans are certainly bipeds, whom he calls the offspring not of fire but of smoke. It is not easy to find any beings with a greater appetite than geese, and whether he puts them in the smoke because they are two-footed or in the waters because they love to swim or in the winds because they are winged and sometimes fly, they certainly do not belong to fire, according to his classification. But with regard to heat in coupling I suspect that he has noticed that horses whinny, often bite through their reins, and rush to mares. Having noticed this, since he wants to write quickly, he failed to observe the common sparrow, in comparison with which any stallion is found to be very cold.

But when we ask them why Mani located bipeds in smoke, they answer that the two-footed kind is haughty and proud, for they say that human beings derive their origin from this kind. And because smoke rises up in balls and swells, as it were, into the air, it was not unreasonable that they noticed that smoke is like proud persons. This observation ought to have sufficed to provide some likeness to proud human beings either to form or to understand some allegory, but still not so that we should believe that for this reason two-footed animals are born in smoke and from smoke. For they also ought to have been born from the dust, because it often rises to the sky with no less swirling and height. And they ought to have been born in clouds that the earth often exhales, so as to make those who see them from a distance uncertain whether they are smoke or clouds.

Finally, why in the case of waters and winds did Mani draw an argument from their tolerance of the place that they inhabited to their inhabitants, because we see both that those that swim live in waters and that those that fly live in the winds? But fire and smoke did not deter this liar of a man so that he was ashamed to put such inhabitants in fire and in smoke. What could he have put there more absurd than these? After all, fire burns and destroys quadrupeds, and smoke suffocates and kills bipeds. At least Mani is surely forced by this to admit that he says that these natures were better in the nation of darkness, where he wants us to believe that everything was worse. For there fire begot quadrupeds, nourished them, and maintained them without harm or even quite comfortably. Similarly, smoke also reared and maintained its bipeds, which were born in its most gentle bosom, not only without any difficulty but even giving them life and indulging them for that princedom. Thus we see that these lies — which were conceived by the observation of things seen in this world, but by a carnal mind that is less diligent and careful, and which were brought to birth by phantasms and were thoughtlessly written down and published — have added to the number of the heretics.

33, 36. But the Manicheans must be pressured more in that kind of way so that they may understand, if they can, how truly God is said, in the Catholic Church, to be the author of all natures. I was acting in that kind of way when I said: I deplore along with you the disease, the blindness, the murky foulness, the horrible violence, the corruptibility, and the cruelty of the princes, and other things of this sort. Praise along with me the form, the distinction, the order, the peace, the unity of forms, the suitableness of members, the numerical equalities, the vital spirits and nourishment, the balance of well-being, the soul's rule and governance, the obedience of bodies, the likeness and harmony of parts in the individual natures either of those that dwell there or of those in which they dwell, and other such things. For in that way they understand, at least if they were willing to pay attention without stubbornness, that goods and evils are already intermingled when they speak of the land where they believed that only the greatest evil existed. And therefore, if the evils that I mentioned were removed, the goods that were praised would remain without any blame, but, if those goods are taken away, no nature remains. From this someone who can see already sees that every nature is good insofar as it is a nature. For, if the things that are good are taken away from one and the same nature, in which I find things to praise and he finds things to blame, there will be no nature left. But if the things that are displeasing are taken away, a nature will remain free of corruption.

Take away from the waters their foulness and turbidity, and pure and tranquil waters remain. Take away from the waters their harmony of parts, and there will be no waters. If, then, when that evil has been removed, the nature remains in a purer state, but, when that good has been removed, no nature remains, the good that it has causes a nature to be there, but the evil that it has is not a nature but is contrary to nature. Take away from the winds their horror and excessive force, which displease you, and you can think of gentle and moderate winds. Take away from the winds the likeness of their parts, by which their body is joined into a unity and is at peace with itself so that it is a body, and no nature will be left for you to think of. It would take a long time to run through the others. But it is clear to those who judge without bias that, when these natures are spoken of, certain displeasing features are added to them, and that, when we remove these, better natures remain. From this it is understood that they are good insofar as they are natures, since, when in turn you take away from them all the good they have, there will be no natures. Pay attention also, you who want to judge correctly, to that cruel prince. If you take away his cruelty, notice the great praiseworthy features that remain: the frame of his body, the harmony of his members on this side and that, the unity of form and the peace of parts joined to one another, and the order and disposition of the soul that rules and gives life and of the body that obeys and receives life. If all these and any that I have not listed are taken away, no nature at all remains.

34, 37. But you may perhaps say that those evils cannot be removed from such natures and therefore must be accepted as natural. The present question is not what can or cannot be removed, but it is surely no small enlightenment for our understanding that all natures, insofar as they are natures, are good, because we can think of those goods without those evils but can think of no nature without those goods. For I can think of waters without their being disturbed by mud, but no form of a body enters the mind or can in any way be perceived without the peace of continuous parts. And for this reason those muddy waters could not have existed without this good, a good that makes it possible for a bodily nature to exist. For, when you say that those evils cannot be removed from such natures, we reply that neither can those goods be removed from such natures. Why, then, do you want to call those things natural evils on account of the evils that you think cannot be removed, but do not want to call them natural goods on account of those goods that you are convinced cannot be removed?

34, 38. It remains for you to ask — for this is usually your last question — where those evils come from, which I said are displeasing to me as well. I shall perhaps reply if you first tell me where those goods come from, which you also are forced to praise if you do not want to have a heart filled with contradictions. But why should I ask this, since we both admit that all good things, whatever they are and however great they are, come from the one God who is supremely good? Resist Mani himself, then, who thought that so many and such great goods — which we have mentioned and rightly praised, such as the peace and harmony of parts in each nature, the well-being and strength of living beings, and the other things that I do not want to repeat now — exist in that fictitious land of darkness. It is thus that he tries to separate them from the God whom he admits to be the author of all goods. For he does not see those goods as long as he pays attention only to what displeases him. He is like someone terrified by the roar of a lion, when he sees it carrying off and tearing to pieces the bodies of animals and of human beings that it had captured, and because of a certain childish weakness of mind he is stricken with such a great fear that he sees only the ferocity and savagery of the lion. And, completely overlooking and passing over its other qualities, he cries out that the nature of that animal is not only evil but a great evil, with greater exaggeration in proportion to his greater fear. But if he saw a tame lion being led along, whose ferocity had been subdued, especially if he had never previously been frightened by that beast, he would then be free to consider and praise the beauty of the lion without worry or fear.

I shall say nothing about this except what is most pertinent to the issue: It is possible that a nature gives offense in some respect and that one develops a hatred for the whole nature, although it is clear that the beauty of the real and living animal is much better, even when it causes fear in the forest, than that of an imitation and simulation of an animal when it is praised in a mural. Do not, therefore, let Mani deceive you by this error and make you blind with respect to the beauty of natures, when he faults some things in them in such a way as to make you find displeasing in every respect what he cannot criticize in every respect. And in this way let us dispose our mind for a fair judgment, and let us now ask where the evils (of which I said that I too disapprove) along with those goods come from. We shall see this more easily if we are able to group all the evils under one rubric.

35, 39. After all, who has any doubt that everything that is called evil is nothing other than corruption? Different evils can of course be called by different names, but that which is the evil in all the things in which we can find some evil is corruption. But the corruption of a learned soul is called ignorance; the corruption of a prudent soul is called imprudence; the corruption of a just soul is called injustice; the corruption of a brave soul is called cowardice; the corruption of a peaceful and quiet soul is called desire, fear, sadness, or pride. Then, in a living body the corruption of health is called pain and disease; the corruption of strength is called weakness; the corruption of rest is called labor. Then, in a mere body itself the corruption of beauty is called ugliness; the corruption of straightness is called crookedness; the corruption of order is called disorder; the corruption of wholeness is called division, fracture, or diminishment. It would be long and difficult to mention by name all the corruptions of the things that I have mentioned and of countless others, since many that are said of the body can also be said of the soul, and there are countless things in which corruption has special names. Still it is easy to see that corruption does no harm unless it undermines the natural condition and that it is therefore not a nature but is contrary to nature. But if we do not find in things any evil but corruption, and if corruption is not a nature, then no nature is an evil.

35, 40. But if you are perhaps unable to understand this, consider the fact that everything that is corrupted is diminished in terms of some good, for, if it were not corrupted, it would be incorrupt. But if it also could not be corrupted at all, it would be incorruptible. Either incorruption or incorruptibility must be good, however, if corruption is evil. But there is now no question about an incorruptible nature. We are dealing with natures that can be corrupted and which, as long as they are not corrupted, can be said to be incorrupt but cannot be said to be incorruptible. For that alone is said to be incorruptible in the proper sense which not only is not corrupted but also cannot be corrupted in any respect. All things, therefore, that are incorrupt but that can nonetheless be corrupted are, when they begin to be corrupted, diminished in terms of that very good with respect to which they were incorrupt, and that is a great good, because corruption is a great evil. And as long as corruption can be increased in them, they have some good in terms of which they may be diminished. Hence, those natures that Mani pretends existed in the land of darkness either could have been corrupted or could not have been corrupted. If they could not have been, they were incorruptible — a good than which there is none higher. If they could have been, either they were corrupted or they were not corrupted. If they were not corrupted, they were incorrupt, which is something that we see can only be said with great praise. But if they were corrupted, they were diminished in terms of that great good. If they were diminished in terms of any good, they had some good in terms of which they were diminished. But if they had some good, those natures were not the greatest evil, and Mani's whole myth is false.

36, 41. But because we have asked what evil is and have come to know that it is not a nature but is contrary to nature, we must next ask where evil comes from. If Mani had done this, he perhaps would not have fallen into the difficulties of so great an error. He asked in the wrong order and with excessive haste where evil came from because he had not first asked what evil was. And for this reason, when he asked this question, he could only come up with vain phantasms, which a mind that has been fed too much by the senses of the flesh strips away only with difficulty. Someone, then, who wants not to fight but to avoid error will ask: Where does this corruption come from, which we have found is like a generic evil in things that are good but nonetheless corruptible? Such a person, who seeks with great ardor and piously knocks with constant perseverance, quickly finds the truth. For people can produce some reminder by means of verbal signs. But the one true teacher, the incorruptible truth, the sole interior teacher, does the teaching. He also became exterior in order to call us back from exterior things to interior ones, and, taking the form of a servant[17] in order that his loftiness might become known to those who are rising up, he deigned to be seen as lowly by those who were lying prostrate. In his name let us make humble entreaty, and, begging for mercy through him, let us ask these questions. For, first of all, one can answer in very few words those asking where corruption comes from, when we say, "From the fact that these natures that can be corrupted were not begotten from God, but were made by him from nothing." Because the previous argumentation proved that they are good, no one can correctly say, "God ought not to have made them." But if he says, "He ought to have made them supremely good," he must understand that he who made these goods is himself the highest good.

37, 42. "What evil," you ask, "would result if these things were also made supremely good?" And yet, if anyone asked us, who have accepted and believed that God the Father is the highest good, where one might piously think some-

---

17. See Phil 2:7.

thing else supremely good came from, if it existed, we would only correctly respond, "From God the Father, who is supremely good." We shall remember, therefore, that what comes from him is born of him, not made by him from nothing, and for this reason is supremely, that is, incorruptibly good. And we see that it is not right to demand that the things that he made from nothing be as supremely good as he is supremely good whom he begot from himself. And if he had not begotten only one, he would not have begotten that which he himself is, because he himself is one. Hence, it is ignorant and impious to seek brothers for that only Son, through whom all good things were made by the Father from nothing, except insofar as he deigned to appear as a man. For in the scriptures he is said to be the only-begotten of the Father and the firstborn from the dead, and scripture says, *We have seen his glory like the glory of the only-begotten of the Father, full of grace and of truth* (Jn 1:14), and Paul says, *That he might be the firstborn among many brothers* (Rom 8:29).

37, 43. But if we say, "These goods that were made from nothing should not exist, but only the nature of God should exist," we shall be grudging toward such great goods, and it is an impious idea to think it an injustice not to be what God is and not to want some good to exist because God is placed above it. I beg you, O nature of the rational soul, accept that you are somewhat less than God is, and less to the degree that, after him, there is nothing better than you. Accept it, I say, and be humble, for fear that he may drive you off into the lowest regions, where the good that you are may become more and more worthless to you because of the pains of punishment. You are being proud toward God if you are indignant because he ranks above you, and you are thinking very contemptuously of him if you are not inexpressibly thankful that you are so great a good that only he is more excellent. After this has been established and confirmed, do not say, "God ought to have made me the only nature. I would not want anything good to come after me." For the good that comes after God ought not to have been the last good. And from this especially we see how great a dignity God has bestowed upon you — that he, who alone has dominion over you by nature, has made other goods over which you might also have dominion. Do not be surprised that they do not obey you in every way and that at times they even torment you. For your Lord has greater power than you yourself have over those things that obey you — as over the servants of his servants. Why, then, is it surprising if, when you sinned, that is, when you did not obey your Lord, they became for you a source of punishment by which you are dominated? For what is as just as this, and what is more just than God? Human nature merited this in Adam, whom there is no time now to discuss, but he who exercises dominion justly both by just rewards and by just punishments is revealed by the happiness of those who live rightly and by the punishment of sinners. And yet you are not left without mercy, for certain events and times call you to return. In that way the correct governance of the most high creator extends to earthly goods, which are corrupted and formed again. Thus you have consolations mingled with punishment so that you may praise God when you are delighted by the order of good things and have recourse to him when you are tried by the experience of evil ones. In that way, insofar as earthly things obey you, they teach that you are their lord, but insofar as they are troublesome to you, they teach you to obey your Lord.

38, 44. Hence, though corruption is evil, and though it does not come from the creator of natures but comes from the fact that they were made out of nothing, yet all the things that God made are set in order under his rule and governance so that corruption harms only the lowest natures. For it punishes the damned, and it tests and admonishes those who are returning in order that they may cling to the incorruptible God and remain incorrupt. For he is our one good, as the prophet said, *It is good for me to cling to God* (Ps 73:28). Do not say, "God should not have made corruptible natures." For, insofar as they are natures, God made them; insofar as they are corruptible, however, God did not make them. After all, corruption does not come from him who is alone incorruptible.

If you grasp this, give thanks to God; if you do not grasp it, be still and do not rashly condemn what you do not understand. And, as a suppliant before him who is the light of the mind, pay attention in order that you may understand. For when one says "corruptible nature," one says not one but two things. So too, when one says, "God made from nothing," we hear not one but two things. Ascribe those individual terms to individual things, therefore, so that, when you hear "nature," it goes with "God" and when you hear "corruption," it goes with "nothing." Thus, though these corruptions do not come from God's handiwork, they are still to be placed in his power in accord with the order of reality and the merits of souls. And so we are correct to say that reward and punishment come from him. For he did not make corruption, but he can deliver to corruption one who merits to suffer corruption, that is, one who has begun to corrupt himself by sinning, in order that against his will he may feel the corruption that torments him who willingly brought about the corruption that attracted him.

39, 45. After all, it was not written in the Old Testament alone, *I make good things and create evil ones* (Is 45:7), but it is more clear in the New Testament, where the Lord says, *Do not fear those who kill the body and have nothing more that they can do, but fear him who, after he has killed the body, has the power to send the soul to hell* (Mt 10:28; Lk 12:4). But the apostle Paul bears witness that penal corruption is added to voluntary corruption by the judgment of God when he says, *For the temple of God, which you are, is holy; if anyone corrupts the temple of God, God will corrupt him* (1 Cor 3:17). If this were said in the old law, with what great invectives would these people attack it, accusing God as a cause of corruption! Because they feared this term, many Latin translators did not want to say, *God will corrupt him*, but said, *God will destroy him*. Without avoiding the reality itself, they avoided the offending term, although these Manicheans would not attack any the less the God who was a source of destruction if they found this in the old law or the prophets. But they are refuted by the Greek copies in which it is written with perfect clarity, *If anyone corrupts the temple of God, God will corrupt him.* But if anyone asks the Manicheans in what sense this was said, so that God is not thought to be a source of corruption, they immediately explain that *will corrupt* was said in the sense of "will hand over to corruption," or in any other sense they can find. If they approached the old law with this attitude, they would also understand many marvelous things in it, and they would not tear to shreds with hatred what they did not understand but would respectfully postpone their judgment.

40, 46. If anyone does not believe that corruption comes from nothing, however, let him set before himself these two, being and non-being, as if on two sides for the sake of understanding, so that we may walk more slowly with those who are slow. Then let him put something in the middle, such as the body of a living being. Let him ask himself this question: When that body is shaped and is born, when its form increases, when it is nourished, becomes healthy, grows strong, becomes beautiful, and gains solidity, toward which side does it tend insofar as it lasts and insofar as it is made stable — toward being or toward non-being? He will have no doubt that something exists even in those first beginnings, but that it is made to be more the more it is stabilized and strengthened by form, beauty, and power, and that it tends toward the side on which being was placed. Now, then, let it begin to be corrupted. Let that whole condition be weakened; let its powers waste away; let its strength fade; let its form be spoiled; let the framework of the members break down; let the harmony of its parts decrease and disappear. Let him also now ask where it is tending by this corruption. Is it toward being or toward non-being? I do not think that he is so blind and slow as to doubt what answer he should give to himself and as not to perceive that the more anything is corrupted the more it tends toward destruction, but that everything that tends toward destruction tends toward non-being. Since, therefore, we must believe that God exists immutably and incorruptibly, but that what is called nothing clearly does not exist at all, and since you set before yourself being and non-being, and know that form is increased the more anything tends to be, while corruption is increased the more it tends not to be, why do you hesitate to say what comes from God in each corruptible nature and what comes from nothing, since form is according to nature, while corruption is contrary to nature? When form is increased, it makes something to be, and we admit that God *is* in the highest way. But when corruption is increased, it makes something not to be, and what is not is clearly nothing. Hence, I ask, why do you hesitate to state what in a corruptible nature, which you say is both a nature and corruptible, comes from God and what comes from nothing? And why do you seek a nature contrary to God since, if you admit that he *is* in the highest way, you see that he does not have any contrary?

41, 47. Why then, you ask, does corruption remove what God gave to nature? It does not remove it except where God permits. But he permits it where he judges it most well-ordered and most just in accord with the levels of beings and the merits of souls. For the form of the spoken word passes away and is replaced by silence, and yet our speech is achieved by the coming and going of passing words and is properly and pleasingly differentiated by measured intervals of silence. The lowest beauty of temporal natures also exists in this way, so that it is achieved and differentiated by the passing of things and by the death of those that are born. If our mind and memory were able to grasp the order and measure of its beauty, we would be so pleased with it that we would not dare to call the losses by which it is differentiated corruptions, but because we labor on the side of that beauty when fleeting temporal things that we love abandon us, we pay the punishment for our sins and are taught to love everlasting things.

42, 48. Let us, therefore, not seek in this beauty what it does not admit; it is the lowest beauty precisely because it does not admit what we are seeking. And in what it does admit let us praise God because he has given such a great good even to this beauty, though it is the least. Yet let us not cling to it as lovers of it, but let us pass beyond it as lovers of God, in order that, situated above it, we may judge concerning it and may not be entangled in it and judged with it. And let us hasten to the good that is not spread out in space, and does not pass in time, and from which all natures in places and times receive beauty and form. In order to see that good, let us cleanse our heart by faith in the Lord Jesus Christ, who said, *Blessed are the clean of heart because they shall see God* (Mt 5:8). For, in order to see that good, it is not necessary to prepare these eyes by which we see this light, which is spread out in space and is not whole everywhere but has one part here and another there. But let us cleanse that gaze and sight by which, to the extent that it is permitted in this life, we see what is just, what is pious, and what is the beauty of wisdom. Whoever sees these prefers them by far to the fullness of all stretches of space and perceives that they are not poured out through stretches of space but are made stable by incorporeal power.

43, 49. Since phantasms drawn from the senses of the flesh, which our thought considers and holds in imagination, are very inimical to this gaze, let us detest this heresy that has pursued a belief in its own phantasms and has hurled down and spread out the divine substance over areas of space — though bound-less — like a formless mass. It truncated it on one side in order to find a place for evil, which it could not see was not a nature but was contrary to nature, and it adorned evil with great beauty, with forms, and with the peace of its parts thriving in individual natures. For without these goods it was not able to think of any nature. As a result, those evils that it criticizes in that evil are buried under an abundance of goods.

But let this be the end of this volume; in others other insane ideas of this heresy will be refuted if God permits and gives his help.

Answer to Felix, a Manichean

(Contra Felicem Manichaeum)

Introduction

In the first line of the present work Augustine tells us that his debate with Felix, a Manichean, began on December 7, 404. He also indicates that the first day of the debate was a Wednesday, since Felix asked for a five days' adjournment, until Monday (which would have been December 12, 404), at the end of the first day.[1] The debate was held in Hippo and, at least on the second day, in the Church of Peace. Although the debate was recorded in the form of ecclesiastical proceedings, it was counted as one of Augustine's works and listed as such in his *Revisions*. Augustine tells us that Felix was a teacher among the Manicheans and was more clever than Fortunatus, whom Augustine had debated a dozen years earlier, though he was not a man learned in the liberal arts. He was therefore most probably one of the Elect. He may have been the same Felix who, according to Possidius, Augustine's friend and first biographer, became a convert to the Catholic Church.[2] He may also have been the recipient of Letter 79, in which Augustine challenges an unnamed Manichean to reply to a difficulty that Fortunatus was unable to handle — about what the nation of darkness was going to do if God refused to do battle with it; for the recipient of Letter 79, like Felix, was ready to die for his faith.

The first day of the debate moves along with brief questions and answers until one of Augustine's questions — about whether the nation of darkness could or could not harm God — stumps Felix, who then asks for an adjournment. The debate on the second day contains longer interventions on the part of both men. Augustine's statements provide interesting insights into his christology and soteriology as well as into the distinction between creation, generation, and making. Felix tries to defend Mani's dualism on the basis of the mission and teaching of Christ, and he shows a singular inability to understand how the soul can be from God and pertain to God but not be a part of God or of the same nature as God.

---

1. Some scholars have proposed an earlier year for the debate on the grounds that in his *Revisions* Augustine lists the present work before several others that were written before 404. Hence, they have emended the year to 398 by reversing the letters for the sixth consulate to those for the fourth. While this move resolves the problem of the order of the works in his *Revisions*, it leaves one with the problem that December 7th in 398 was not a Wednesday. Hence, I have followed the lead of the editors of the Bibliothèque Augustinienne volume and accepted the year of 404 as that of the work's composition.

2. See Possidius, *The Life of Augustine* 16.

Book One

At the beginning of the debate Felix declares his readiness to defend his faith if he is provided with the books of Mani, which had been confiscated in accord with the imperial laws and were being held by the civil authorities. Augustine has Mani's letter known as *The Foundation* brought forth, and Felix reads out the opening lines. Augustine asks him to prove that Mani was an apostle of Jesus Christ as Mani claims to have been (section 1). Felix asks Augustine to prove how Christ sent the Holy Spirit, the Paraclete, whom he promised to send in John's gospel. Augustine offers to show him where Christ's promise of the Holy Spirit was fulfilled (section 2). Hence, he reads from the Gospel of Luke of Christ's promise of the Spirit (section 3), and from the Acts of the Apostles he reads of the apostles' choice of Matthias as a replacement for Judas (section 4) and of the fulfillment of Christ's promise of the Holy Spirit on Pentecost. He therefore demands that Felix reject the writings of Mani, which aim to deceive their readers under the name of the Holy Spirit (section 5). Felix replies that, when he has been shown that the Holy Spirit has taught the whole truth that he seeks, he will abandon the writings of Mani; but he is looking among the apostles for someone to teach him about the beginning, the middle, and the end, that is, about the time before good and evil were mingled, about the present time in which they are mingled, and about the end times in which they will again be separated, at least to a large extent. Augustine points out that Christ did not promise that the Holy Spirit would teach us about the beginning, the middle, and the end. Felix insists that, since Augustine claims that the apostles received the Holy Spirit, one of them should either teach him what Mani taught him or destroy the teaching of Mani. To this Augustine replies that the teaching of the apostles is a far cry from the sacrilegious teaching of Mani, and he promises that he will destroy the teaching of Mani when more of Mani's letter is read out. Since Felix has been allowed to speak without fear of reprisal, he cites the words of scripture to call Augustine a liar (section 6). Augustine claims that the facts will soon show that Felix is a liar and observes that, since the apostles died long before the error of Mani arose, we do not find anything in the writings of the apostles that is obviously directed against Mani, though Paul, in the First Letter to Timothy, seems to have foreseen the Manichean heresy when he mentioned that some people would withdraw from the faith, turn their attention to the teachings of demons, forbid marriage, and declare various foods unclean (section 7). Felix asks that the passage from the First Letter to Timothy be read out again and then insists that Mani did not abandon the faith as those people did whom Paul described. Augustine replies that perhaps Mani did not abandon the faith because he never had the faith, but that the Manicheans persuade many uneducated Catholic Christians to abandon the faith when they forbid marriage and declare various foods unclean. He then asks once more that Felix either prove that Mani was an apostle of Jesus Christ or allow him to destroy his teaching (section 8). Felix says that the Holy Spirit came in the apostle Paul. Augustine replies that he did not come in Paul alone. Felix points out that Paul said that we know in part and prophesy in part, but that when what is perfect has come, what is in part will be done away with. He claims that in Mani what is perfect has come, for he has taught us about the beginning, the middle, and the end, and about the making of this world. For this reason the followers of Mani believe that he was the Holy Spirit, the Paraclete (section 9). Augustine says that he will explain why Paul said that we know in part and that he will show that we do not read in the gospel that Christ promised that the Holy Spirit would teach us the sort of things which Mani taught. The Holy Spirit came to produce Christians, not astronomers. The sort of things that Mani teaches about the making of the world do not pertain to Christian doctrine. The promise that the Holy Spirit would lead us into all the truth did not mean that he would teach us about how the world was made (section 10). The rest of the passage from the apostle clearly shows that, while our knowledge is partial in this life, it will be complete in the next, when we shall see God face to face (section 11).

Felix admits that he cannot stand up to the power of Augustine or to the imperial laws. He asks Augustine to teach him the truth so that it will be clear that what he holds is a lie. Augustine summarizes the course of the debate to this point and shows how Felix has failed to reply again and again to his questions. He insists that his power, which Felix says that he cannot stand up to, is the power of all believers in Christ, and that Felix fears the imperial laws because he does not have the Holy Spirit whom Christ promised. Felix claims that the apostles were afraid. Augustine replies that the apostles' fear made them wary but did not cause them to doubt their faith. Felix, however, had just the day before claimed that he was ready to be burned with the books of Mani if anything evil was found in them (section 12).

Felix says that he will not flee from the truth. Augustine asks whether Felix now sees God face to face in accord with the apostle's promise. Felix admits that he is seeking the truth and says that he will not abandon his religion unless Augustine first gives him a better one. Augustine insists that one must empty a vessel before putting something else into it, and he promises to show Felix how sacrilegious his Manichean faith really is. Felix misinterprets Augustine's metaphor about emptying a vessel, but Augustine insists that Felix must show that Mani is an apostle of Christ (section 13).

Felix again points to Christ's promise to send the Holy Spirit, who will lead us into all the truth. Augustine replies that, if Felix has the Holy Spirit and if various forms of worldly knowledge pertain to his teaching, he should tell him how many stars there are. Felix again demands that, if the Holy Spirit spoke through the apostles, Augustine show him what he asked. Augustine asks Felix to admit that he cannot answer his question. Felix claims that, if he is given the writings of Mani, he will answer. Augustine says that he has *The Foundation* and asks him to prove that Mani was an apostle of Jesus Christ. Felix says that he will prove this from another text of Mani's known as *The Treasury*. Augustine refuses to accept a proof from *The Treasury* because Mani is a liar. Felix asks for Mani's other writings, but Augustine insists that *The Foundation* should be enough (section 14). Felix asks to have many Manicheans present as judges of the debate and complains that the people present are opposed to him. Augustine says that those present are not opposed to the truth (section 15). Felix reads further in *The Foundation*. Augustine admits that he has so far found nothing objectionable apart from Mani's claim to be an apostle of Jesus Christ and asks Felix to read still further. Felix wonders how he will be able to believe Augustine if he admits that the beginning of the letter is good and the later parts are bad. Augustine corrects him and says that he did not say that the beginning of the letter was good but that he found only one bad idea. They agree to read more of the letter (section 16).

Felix reads from *The Foundation* up to the passage where Mani speaks of God's most splendid kingdoms founded upon the bright and blessed land. Augustine asks where God got this land, that is, whether he made it or begot it or it was equal to and coeternal with God. Felix appeals to the first verse of Genesis, which he interprets to mean that the earth already existed when God made heaven and earth. Augustine says that it is now up to him to explain to Felix what the verse from Genesis means. He does so and repeats his question about the bright and blessed land. Felix says that Manichean scripture interprets itself but that the answer Augustine wants is found not in *The Foundation* but in another of Mani's writings. Augustine and Felix accuse each other of not answering each other's questions (section 17).

Felix finally responds that, since God is eternal and there is nothing made in him, everything is eternal. He explains that God did not beget the bright and blessed land because what is born comes to an end. Augustine asks Felix why God is called a father if he did not beget anything. Felix replies that God generated other things, which are coeternal with him. Augustine suggests that Felix, therefore, was mistaken in saying that what is born comes to an end. Felix admits his mistake and says that he was thinking of birth in the flesh. Augustine persuades Felix to admit that God, what he generated, and the bright and blessed land are all equal and of one substance. He further points out that God is not the father of this land but its inhabitant, and he wonders how the land, which God neither made nor begot, belongs to him except in terms of its proximity. He asks whether this one substance is so well founded, as Mani had said, that it cannot be moved or shaken. After some quibbling, Felix agrees that it cannot be moved or shaken (section 18).

Augustine reads further from *The Foundation,* up to where Mani says, "But along one part and side of that bright and holy land," and he asks which side it is, the right or the left. Felix again appeals to his principle that Manichean scripture interprets itself. More of the letter of Mani is read out, in which Mani says that the father of the most blessed light foresaw the devastation that would arise from the darkness unless he sent some powerful deity to overcome and destroy the race of darkness. Here Augustine asks what the nation of darkness was going to do to God, whose kingdoms were so well founded that they could be moved or shaken by nothing. He asks whether the nation of darkness could harm him or not. Felix then asks why, if there was nothing opposed to God, Christ was sent here to free us from the snare of this death. Why, he asks, are we baptized? Why do we have the eucharist? Why are we Christians if there is nothing opposed to God? Augustine accuses Felix of not answering his question, but he explains the Catholic teaching on why Christ was sent, namely, to free us from our sins. For we, who are not born of God but made by him, are able to change. But Felix had claimed that God, what he generated, and the bright land were all one substance. Hence, Augustine asks again whether the nation of darkness could or could not harm God (section 19).

At this point Felix asks for an adjournment until the following Monday. Augustine agrees on the condition that, if Felix cannot respond to his question on Monday, he will admit defeat. Felix promises not to flee and agrees to stay with one of the men in the audience. Both Augustine and Felix then sign the proceedings and depart (section 20).

Book Two

The following Monday the debate resumes in the Church of Peace. Augustine repeats the question that had led to the adjournment five days previously. He asks Felix why God fought a war with the nation of darkness if nothing could harm him. For, if the nation of darkness could harm him, God was not incorruptible, as the truth and the teaching of the apostles testify that he is. Felix complains that he did not have at hand any of the writings of Mani by which he might have become instructed and insists that he cannot reply without his scriptures. Augustine accuses Felix of having just thought up this evasion and insists that he should have requested his books when he asked for the adjournment. Felix nonetheless asks for the books and also for a further delay. Augustine says that the Manichean writings are being held in public custody, and he asks Felix to admit that he cannot at present answer Augustine's objections. Felix requests all the Manichean writings, but Augustine insists that *The Foundation* contains the teaching about the war between God and the nation of darkness that resulted in the mingling of a part of God with the nation of darkness and its captivity and defilement. Augustine asks Felix to defend this teaching if he can and again poses his question about whether anything can or cannot harm God (section 1). Felix complains that Mani is being blamed because he said that there were two natures, though Christ had said that there were two trees, a good one and a bad one, and that an enemy of God had sown the weeds in the field. So too, the gospel speaks of the judgment at which the goats will be sent into the kingdom prepared for them from the beginning of the world. Furthermore, Saint Paul says that the wisdom of the flesh is opposed to God and that he was given an angel of Satan to buffet him. Hence, Felix concludes from the gospel and from Saint Paul that there is an enemy against whom God fought, just as Mani said (section 2). Augustine replies that Felix could not show from these scripture passages that God wanted to repel an enemy nature from his kingdom and that he mingled a part of himself with the opposing nature to be bound there and defiled by it. Felix has tried to interpret what scripture says about sinners as evidence for an evil nature, whereas the truth teaches that all natures are good and that God has given rational creatures free choice, by which they were able to sin if they willed to (section 3). Augustine explains that Christ was speaking of free choice when he spoke of the two trees, for he said that we should make the tree good and its fruit good or make the tree bad and its fruit bad. Clearly he was not speaking of natures but of wills (section 4). Augustine quotes from *The Treasury* in order to show how Mani made himself in a sense equal to God when he introduced the other nature, but he insists that Mani admitted free choice when he said that some souls refused to obey the law of God (section 5). Augustine appeals to the apocryphal *Acts of Leutius*, which the Manicheans accept, in which the devil is seen to be a sinner by his will, so that he now tries to seduce human beings to sin by their wills (section 6).

Having replied to Felix's questions, Augustine returns to the question of why God sent a part of himself to be polluted and held captive by demons if nothing could harm him. The apostle Paul, after all, had said that God was incorruptible and dwelled in inaccessible light. Hence, how could that nation of darkness approach the inaccessible light in which God dwelled, unless God permitted this? But if God had permitted the nation of darkness to approach him, he would not have permitted it to approach him as an enemy. Augustine points out the shameful way in which Mani holds that the parts of God that were captured by the enemy nation are released, and he emphasizes the impotence of God to secure the deliverance of all of his members from their captivity, so that some part of himself is destined for eternal captivity. Again, Augustine asks Felix why God mingled part of himself with the enemy nation if it could not have harmed him (section 7).

Felix says that the Manichean God is no more cruel than Christ, who will condemn some souls to eternal fire. Augustine explains that Christ will punish sinners who do not repent and who do not repent because they are unwilling to. Felix cannot understand why souls should be unwilling to be healed and insists that Christ, who condemns sinners to eternal fire, is more cruel than God, who could not purify souls and who bound them in the sphere of darkness. Augustine replies that he has shown from the scriptures that rational creatures were given free choice, by which they could sin and by which they could repent of their sins. He stresses the fact that repentance makes no sense if one has not sinned and that it is impossible to sin without free choice. We find, as Paul says, a law of sin in our members that resists the law of our mind because we have inherited the punishment of Adam's sin and also have built up habits of sin, which reduce our freedom. Just as we shall be rewarded if we use our free choice to obey God, so we shall be justly punished if we do not. Then Augustine returns to his question as to why God sent us here if nothing could have harmed him (section 8).

Felix asks in turn why God sent Christ here if nothing could harm God. Augustine complains that Felix once again has not answered what he has asked, but he agrees to answer what Felix has asked. He explains that God sent his Son, the Word of God, to assume flesh and to be seen by human beings in order to heal sinners. In his nature as the Word he could not suffer, but in the flesh he assumed for us he could suffer. But the Manichean God did not assume flesh and was bound and polluted in his very nature as God. Hence, Augustine again asks why God's substance was sent here to suffer in itself, not in flesh, since he had not assumed any flesh (section 9).

Felix asks to what nature Christ came in order to set us free. If Christ came to set us free from captivity, who held us captive? If we were in the power of God, we did not need to be set free. But the apostle Paul says that Christ came to set us free from the curse of the law (section 10). Augustine explains that Christ redeems from the devil those whom the devil held captive because they sinned through their free will. The devil first became a sinner by his free choice and then persuaded Adam to sin by his free choice. Christ came to set us free from the curse of the law, that is, from our condition of mortality, which is the punishment of sin. By taking on death, Christ killed death. In his suffering and death he gave us an example to strengthen our repentance, and in his resurrection he gave us an example to arouse our hope. The law was given in order that sin might be seen as sin and might humble sinners and thus bring them to repentance. Again Augustine asks Felix why God allowed a part of himself to be sent here (section 11).

Felix says that, if he possesses the power of free choice, he will be a Christian when he wills to be one. Augustine agrees but warns that God, who is the creator of our natures, is the judge of our wills. He invites Felix to see whether he has not failed in his defense of Mani and whether he should not choose to be what he is not as yet (section 12). Felix asks Augustine to show him the truth in order that he may hold it. Augustine tells him that it is already clear that what Felix holds is not the truth, and he repeats the points where he has demonstrated the error of Mani (section 13). Felix claims that Mani's error is still not apparent. Augustine asks him whether the error that says that God is corruptible should be condemned or not. Though Felix says that he is unsure whether Mani said that God was corruptible, he agrees that anyone who said that should be condemned (section 14). Then Augustine persuades him to admit that the part that was mingled with the nation of darkness is a part of the nature of God and that that part of God was bound and defiled by the nation of darkness (section 15). In an effort to make it sound more acceptable, Felix corrects Augustine' statement of Mani's position on the eternal punishment of the part of God that cannot be set free, but Augustine steers the discussion back to the pollution of God's substance. Felix asks what Christ delivers us from, since our souls, according to the Manicheans, are parts of God. But Augustine insists that we are not a part of God but are creatures of God that he has made (section 16). Felix argues that, unless our soul is from God, Christ had no reason to be crucified for it. Augustine then explains that all creatures are from God, but he distinguishes between what is from God by being created from nothing by him and what is from God by being generated from him and what is from God by being made from something that God created.

Once more Augustine returns to his question as to why the nature of God came here to be polluted so that it needed to be purified (section 17). Felix again insists that, if the soul is from God, it is a part of God, while Augustine repeats that the soul is from God, but as a creature that God has made. For the soul is mutable, while God, its creator, is immutable. Through its free choice the soul can sin and be polluted, and through God's mercy it can be set free (section 18). Felix tries to maintain that what God has made is equal to God, but Augustine again emphasizes the difference between what God begot from himself and what he created from nothing. He asserts that what the Father begot from himself can never be corrupted or polluted but that what he made from nothing can be (section 19). Again Felix tries to equate Mani's statement that a part of God was polluted with Christ's statement that the soul was polluted. And again Augustine insists that the soul is not a part of God, but he points out that Felix has admitted that Mani said that a part of God was polluted but that he had earlier said that anyone who claimed that a part of God was polluted should be condemned. Felix reiterates his emphasis on the similarity between what Mani said and what Christ taught, while Augustine continues to insist that the soul is not a part of God (section 20). Felix asks whether the soul belongs to God or not, and Augustine admits that the soul does indeed belong to God, but not as a part of God. Felix still fails to see why Mani is blamed for saying that a part of God was polluted and is being purified by Christ. Augustine returns to the admissions by Felix that Mani said that a part of God was polluted and that anyone who said that should be condemned (section 21).

At this point Felix yields and agrees to condemn Mani and the spirit that was in him. Augustine and Felix both sign the proceedings, and the debate ends.

Revisions II, 8 (35)

Answer to Felix, Two Books

I debated over the course of two days in the church in the presence of the people against a certain Manichean by the name of Felix. In fact he had come to Hippo to spread his error. For he was a learned man among them; though uneducated in the liberal arts, he was still more clever than Fortunatus.[1] These are ecclesiastical proceedings, but they are counted among my books. There are therefore two books. In the second of them there is a discussion of the free choice of the will either to do evil or to do good, but I was compelled by no need to discuss more carefully the grace by which they of whom scripture says, *If the Son has set you free, then you will be truly free* (Jn 8:36), become truly free.

This work begins, "On the seventh day before the Ides of December, in the sixth consulate of Honorius Augustus."

---

1. See *Confessions* V, 6, 11.

Book One

1. On the seventh day before the Ides of December, in the sixth consulate of Honorius Augustus, Augustine, the bishop of the Catholic Church of the territories of Hippo, said: "You know that you said yesterday that you could defend the writings of Mani and maintain that they contain the truth. If you are willing to do this today as well, or if you are confident that you can, say so."

Felix the Manichean said: "I do not deny that I said that I could defend my law if the authors of my law are brought before us."

And after Bishop Augustine had brought forth the letter of Mani known as *The Foundation*, he said: "If I read from this book, which you see that I am carrying, the letter of Mani that you call *The Foundation*, can you recognize whether this is it?"

Felix said: "I recognize it."

Augustine said: "Take it yourself and read."

And after Felix had taken the book, he read: "Mani, an apostle of Jesus Christ, by the providence of God the Father. These are the words of salvation from the everlasting and living fountain. Whoever hears them and first believes them and then observes what they teach shall never be subject to death but shall enjoy an eternal and glorious life. For he should certainly be judged happy who has been instructed by this divine knowledge, by which he will be set free and enjoy everlasting life."[2]

Bishop Augustine asked: "Have you recognized the letter of Mani with certitude?"

Felix said: "I have."

Augustine said: "Show us, then, how this Mani is an apostle of Jesus Christ. For we have never read in the gospel that he was among the apostles, and we know who was ordained in place of Judas the betrayer, that is, Saint Matthias,[3] and everyone recognizes who was called by the voice of the Lord from heaven, that is, Paul the apostle.[4] Prove to us, then, that this Mani is an apostle of Christ, which he dared to put at the beginning of his letter."

2. Felix said: "And Your Holiness should prove to me what is written in the gospel where Christ says, *I am going to the Father, and I am sending you the Holy Spirit, the Paraclete, to lead you into all the truth* (Jn 16:13). Prove to me

---

2. See *Answer to the Letter of Mani Known as The Foundation* 5, 6; 11, 12.
3. See Acts 1:26.
4. See Acts 9:17.

apart from this scripture that this is the scripture of the Holy Spirit, as Christ promised, where all the truth may be found. And if I find the truth in other books that do not belong to Mani, and if Christ also handed them down — for Christ said in that way that the Holy Spirit, the Paraclete, will himself lead us into all the truth — I shall, in accord with the words of Christ, reject the writings of Mani."

Augustine said: "You have not been able to show how Mani is an apostle of Christ, and you demand that I show how he sent the Holy Spirit, the Paraclete, whom he promised, in order that you may then reject the writings of Mani if you find the promise of Christ fulfilled apart from the writings of Mani. Although you ought first to respond to my questions, look, I nonetheless respond to you first, and I show you when the Holy Spirit, whom Christ promised, was sent."

And Augustine stepped up to the gospel and to the Acts of the Apostles.

3. And when he had taken the gospel book, he read: "*While they were saying these things, Jesus stood in their midst and said to them, Peace be to you; it is I; do not be afraid (Lk 24:36)*." And after he read it, he said: "This was after the resurrection." And after he had said this, he read: "*But, disturbed and frightened, they thought that they had seen a spirit. And he said to them, Touch, and see, because a spirit does not have flesh and bones as you see that I have. And after he said that, he showed them his hands and feet. But since they still did not believe and were in a state of wonder because of joy, he said, Do you have something here to eat? And they offered him a piece of baked fish and a cone of honey. And after he had eaten before their eyes, he took the remnants and gave them to them and said to them, These are the words that I spoke to you when I was still with you, because everything that was written about me in the law of Moses and the prophets and psalms had to be fulfilled. Then he opened up for them their meaning in order that they might understand the scriptures, and he said to them, In that way it was written, and in that way it was necessary that Christ suffer and rise from the dead on the third day and that in his name the forgiveness of sins be preached to all the nations, beginning from Jerusalem. But you are witnesses of these events, and I will send the promise of my Father to you. Remain in the city, however, until you are clothed from on high with power.*" (Lk 24:37-49)

And when he had returned the gospel book, he took the Acts of the Apostles and said: "In the gospel we have heard the holy evangelist recall the promise of Christ that is found in the Gospel according to John, which Felix, who is present here, has mentioned. For John the evangelist wrote where the Lord said, *I am sending you the Holy Spirit, the Paraclete (Jn 16:7)*. But Luke the evangelist testified to what I have just read, and he is in agreement with the truth that is found in John the apostle. Let us also see how what the Lord promised was brought about and how it was realized. Thus, since the fulfillment of the Lord's promise has been set forth in the canonical books of the holy Church, we shall not look for another Holy Spirit, the Paraclete, lest we fall into the snare of deceivers."

4. And he read out from the Acts of the Apostles: "*I composed the first discourse, O Theophilus, concerning all the things that Jesus began to do and to teach on the day when he chose the apostles through the Holy Spirit and commanded them to preach the gospel. He showed himself alive to them after his passion in many discussions over the course of days, appearing to them for forty days. He taught them about the kingdom of God and lived with them. And he commanded them not to leave Jerusalem but to wait for the promise of the Father, of which you have heard, he said, from my lips. For John baptized with water, but you shall begin to be baptized with the Holy Spirit, whom you shall also receive after not many days at Pentecost. But they came together and asked him saying, Lord, are you going to restore the kingdom of Israel at this time? But he said, No one can know the time that the Father has placed in his own power, but you shall receive the power of the Holy Spirit coming over you, and you shall be my witnesses in Jerusalem and in all of Judea and Samaria and even to the whole earth. After he said this, the clouds took him and he was carried off from them. And as they were looking on while he went to heaven, behold, two men were standing there in white garments, and they said to them, Men of Galilee, why do you stand there looking up to heaven? This Jesus who has been taken from you up to heaven will come just as you saw him going into heaven.*

"*Then they returned to Jerusalem from the mount called Olivet, which is a Sabbath day's journey from Jerusalem. And when they entered the city, they went into the upper room where there were living Peter and John, James and Andrew, Bartholomew and Matthew, James the son of Alphaeus, Simon the zealot, and Jude the son of James. And they all persevered together with one heart in prayer along with the women, Mary, who was the mother of Jesus, and his brothers. In those days Peter stood up in their midst while they listened; there was a crowd of about one hundred and twenty men in the one place. He said, Brothers, the scripture had to be fulfilled that the Holy Spirit foretold by the lips of the holy David concerning Judas, who was the leader of those who arrested Jesus, because he who had been counted among us had been given this ministry. He therefore bought a field with the payment for his injustice, and he tied a rope around his neck and, having thrown himself over a cliff, he burst open, and all his innards were poured out. And this became known to all who are inhabitants of Jerusalem, so that this field was called in their language Akeldama, that is, the field of blood. For it is written in the Book of Psalms: Let his farm be abandoned, and let there be no one to dwell on it, and let another take his episcopacy.*

"*And so it is necessary that one of these men who were together with us during all the time that the Lord Jesus Christ lived with us, beginning from his baptism by John up to that day on which he was taken from us, be a witness with us to his resurrection. And he presented two men, Joseph, who was called Barsabas as well as Justus, and Matthias. And Peter prayed and said, You, O*

Lord, who know the hearts of all, show us which of these two you have chosen to undertake the role of this ministry and preaching, which Judas abandoned to go to his own destiny. And they cast lots, and the lot fell to Matthias, and he was counted as the twelfth along with the eleven apostles." (Acts 1:1-26)

And after he had read it, he said: "We have now heard who was ordained in place of Judas the traitor — I mentioned this a little before — in order that no one may enter into the number of the apostles by fraud and deceive the ignorant by the title of apostle.

5. "Now let us see what we promised, namely, how Christ's promise about the Holy Spirit was fulfilled." And after he had said this, he read the passage: *"When the day of Pentecost came, they were all together in one place. And suddenly a noise was produced from heaven as if a strong wind were blowing, and it filled the whole house in which they were seated, and divided tongues like fire were seen, which rested upon each of them. And they were all filled with the Holy Spirit and began to speak in various tongues as the Spirit gave them to speak. But in Jerusalem there were inhabitants of Judea, men from every nation under heaven, and when the sound was produced, a crowd gathered and was thrown into confusion because everyone heard them speaking in his own language and dialect. They were filled with awe and were amazed, saying to one another, Are not all these men who are speaking Galileans by nationality? And how do we recognize in them the language of our birth? Parthians, Medes, Elamites, inhabitants of Mesopotamia, Judea and Cappadocia, Pontus, Asia, Phrygia and Pamphylia, Egypt and parts of Libya near Cyrene, visitors from Rome, both Jews and proselytes, Cretans and Arabs, all of them heard them speaking of the marvelous deeds of God in their own language."* (Acts 2:1-11)

And after he had read this, he said: "Have you now heard about the Holy Spirit and how he was sent? I have proved what you asked of me; it remains for you also to do what you promised. Because we have discovered when he sent the Holy Spirit whom he promised, you should reject the writing that aimed at deceiving the reader or listener under the name of the Holy Spirit."

6. Felix said: "I do not deny what I said, namely, that, when it has been proved to me that the Holy Spirit taught the truth that I seek, I shall reject that writing. After all, Your Holiness has read the passage to me where the apostles received the Holy Spirit, and in those apostles I look for one who will teach me about the beginning, the middle, and the end."

Augustine said: "If you have read that the Lord said, 'I am sending you the Holy Spirit who will teach you the beginning, the middle, and the end,' you surely force me to show you whom the Holy Spirit taught about this."

Felix said: "Because Your Holiness says that the apostles themselves received the Holy Spirit, the Paraclete, I say again, Let anyone you want from among the apostles teach me what Mani taught me, or let anyone you want of the twelve destroy his teaching."

Augustine said: "Far be it from the faith of the apostles that they should teach the faith of the sacrilegious Mani. But since you say that one of them ought to destroy the teaching of Mani, though the holy apostles are no longer in the body, I, who am not only the least of all the apostles but even of all the bishops — for when would I aspire to the merits of the apostles? — shall destroy the teaching of Mani, to the extent that the Lord deigns to give me a share of his Spirit, when the following parts of that letter, which you do not deny is Mani's, have begun to be read."

Felix said: "You said that the apostles have departed from their bodies but that their writings hold true even now. Your Holiness spoke, and you gave us the power to say what we want without any fear. You said, 'I will destroy the teaching of Mani,' and I say, '*Every human being is a liar* (Ps 116:11). God alone is truthful.'[5] The writings of God have spoken."

7. Augustine said: "You are, to be sure, both a human being and, as the facts themselves will now show, a liar. And since you have said what you wanted, not from the scripture of God, I too must say what I want. After all, if the teaching of your Mani is the truth, it cannot be destroyed even by me. If it is false, what difference does it make by whom it is destroyed? And yet you said of the writings of the apostles that, even though they are not in the body, their writings are still here. Now the apostles were taken from us before the error of Mani came into this world. For this reason we do not find that the writings of the apostles clearly argue against Mani. And yet, because the apostle Paul foresaw in this Holy Spirit, the Paraclete, whom he had received, the sort of person that Mani was and the sort of persons that you also are, I shall read this out so that you may recognize it."

And having taken the apostle Paul's Letter to Timothy, he read: "*But the Spirit clearly says that in the last times some will withdraw from the faith, paying attention to deceitful spirits, to the teachings of demons lying in their hypocrisy. Having their conscience seared and forbidding marriage, they will abstain from food that God created to be received with thanksgiving by those who believe and have come to know the truth. For every creature of God is good, and nothing that is received with thanksgiving should be rejected. For it is made holy by the word of God and prayer. In giving these commands to the brethren, you will be a good minister of Jesus Christ.*" (1 Tm 4:1-6)

And after he read this, he said: "I say that the Spirit of prophecy stated and expressed this concerning you and concerning the sort of persons who say that some creature of God is unclean and who say that all intercourse, even that with one's wife, is fornication. For this is what it means by the words *forbidding marriage*. But if you deny that all intercourse is fornication or if you say that all human food that is permissible and given to human beings to eat is clean, you do

---

5. See Rm 3:4.

not belong to those whom the apostle spoke of and foretold. But if you are found in these errors which I have mentioned, see, you have the apostle Paul who disproves and destroys the teaching of Mani, who was still to come. And so, reply to what I ask: Is all intercourse fornication, or is intercourse with one's wife not a sin?"

8. Felix said: "Let what the apostle said be read out for me once more." And there was read out: "*But the Spirit clearly says that in the last times some will withdraw from the faith, paying attention to deceitful spirits, to the teachings of demons lying in their hypocrisy. Having their conscience seared and forbidding marriage, they will abstain from food that God created to be received with thanksgiving by those who believe and have come to know the truth. For every creature of God is good, and nothing that is received with thanksgiving should be rejected. For it is made holy by the word of God and prayer. In giving these commands to the brethren, you will be a good minister of Jesus Christ.*" (1 Tm 4:1-6)

Felix said: "Mani did not withdraw from the faith, as Paul says, in the way that others have withdrawn from the faith as if into their own sect. But Mani withdrew from no sect so that one might say that he withdrew from the faith."

Augustine said: "Since I see that you do not want to reply to what you are being asked for fear that you may be found either not to have the Holy Spirit, whom we have already proved was sent to the apostles, or to be in the number of those whom the apostle indicated would come, where he also foretold you, I briefly reply to you: In accord with your understanding I shall accept what you said about the words, *They will withdraw from the faith.* This means that only those withdraw from the faith who were in some faith; Mani, however, was in no faith from which he withdrew but remained in the faith in which he was. I ask you whether Mani, or rather the teaching of lying demons that was present in Mani, did not lead any Catholic Christians astray, so that they withdrew from the faith. For many are led astray by you and through you and through that teaching, so that they withdraw from the faith and pay attention to deceiving spirits of the sort that was in Mani, and they begin to say that all intercourse is fornication. For this reason the apostle said, *They forbid marriage.* And they begin to say that meat which human beings eat is not a creature of God but a product of demons and is unclean. If that it so, it is clear that the Holy Spirit, the Paraclete, who was present in Paul, foretold concerning these people that, paying attention to deceiving spirits of the sort that was in Mani, they would withdraw from the faith.

"Now then, since I have replied, it is only fair that you reply to what I have asked. Do you do not say that all intercourse is fornication? Or, if you do not want to reply to this either, reply to what I first asked of you, namely, to prove that Mani is an apostle of Christ. Or if you do not want to do this either, allow me to destroy his teaching, as I promised, when his letter called *The Foundation* is read."

9. Felix said: "And I reply to the words of Your Holiness that the Holy Spirit, the Paraclete, came in Paul."

Augustine said: "Not in him alone."

Felix said: "I am referring to him because, if the Holy Spirit came in him, he also came to all. And if he came in Paul, he says in another letter, *We know in part and we prophesy in part. But when that which is perfect has come, those things that were said to be partial will be done away with.* (1 Cor 13:9) We hear that Paul says this. Mani came with his preaching, and we accepted him in accord with Christ's words, *I am sending you the Holy Spirit* (Jn 16:7). And Paul came and said that the Holy Spirit himself would also come, and afterward no one came. And so we accepted Mani because Mani came and by his preaching taught us about the beginning, the middle, and the end. He taught us about the making of the world, why it was made and whence it was made and who made it. He taught us why there is day and why there is night. He taught us about the course of the sun and the moon. Because we have not heard this in Paul or in the writings of the other apostles, we believe that Mani is the Paraclete. And so I repeat what I said above: If I hear in another writing where the Paraclete speaks, that is, the Holy Spirit, about whom I want to ask questions, and if you teach me, I shall believe you and renounce Mani."

10. Augustine said: "You say, therefore, that you do not believe that the Holy Spirit, the Paraclete, was present in the apostle Paul because Paul said, *We know in part and we prophesy in part* (1 Cor 13:9), and from this you think that by these words the apostle as much as said that someone else would come after him who would teach all the things that he himself could not teach because he spoke only in part. And you believe that this other person is Mani. First of all, then, I shall show from this very passage from the apostle why the apostle said this. Then you said that Mani taught you about the beginning, the middle, and the end and how and why the world was made, about the course of the sun and moon, and about the other things you mentioned. But we do not read in the gospel that the Lord said: I am sending you the Paraclete to teach you about the course of the sun and the moon. After all, he wanted to make Christians, not astronomers. But it is enough for human purposes that people know about these matters as much as they have learned in school. Christ said that the Paraclete would come to lead them into all the truth,[6] but he did not mention there the beginning, the middle, and the end. He did not mention there the courses of the sun and the moon. Or if you think that this teaching pertains to the truth that Christ promised through the Holy Spirit, I ask you how many stars there are. If you received that Spirit of which you speak, to whom it pertains to teach the things that I say do not pertain to Christian discipline and doctrine, it is necessary that you say so and answer me.

---

6. See Jn 16:13.

"For I have put you in my debt. Hence, if I ask you something about such matters and you do not reply, it is evident that that Spirit is not present in you of whom Christ said, *He will lead you into all the truth* (Jn 16:13), if that truth is the truth that includes these matters. And so, choose for yourself whether you are willing and ready to reply to me on these matters like a man who has received the Spirit who leads one into all the truth, and like a man who says that it pertains to the truth to know these facts about the world. I can then tell you those things that pertain to Christian doctrine, but since you think that how the world was made and what is happening in the world pertains to that doctrine, you must answer me about all those things. When you reply, you will clearly prove your case. But before you begin to speak, if you perhaps have what Mani, whom you follow, made up, let me first explain what I promised, namely, why the apostle said, *We know in part and we prophesy in part.*

11. "For, as the passage will soon indicate, he said that when someone is in this life he cannot attain all things, but he attains things in part in this life. But the Holy Spirit, who teaches us in part in this life, will bring us into all the truth after this life. To see that he taught this very clearly, listen to the apostle."

And when he said this, he read from the apostle: "*But prophecies will be done away with, and tongues will cease, and knowledge will be done away with. For we know in part and we prophesy in part. But when that which is perfect comes, that which is in part will be done away with. When I was a child, I spoke like a child, I had the wisdom of a child, and I thought like a child. But when I became a man, I did away with the things of a child. For we see now in a mirror in an enigma, but then we shall see face to face.*" (1 Cor 13:8-1 2)

And after he read this, he said: "Now tell me whether, if the apostle was speaking about the coming time of Mani, you now see God face to face."

12. Felix said: "I cannot do much against your power, for the position of a bishop is an awesome power, nor, secondly, against the emperors' laws. And I asked previously by way of a shortcut that you explain to me what the truth is. And if you do explain to me what the truth is, it will be clear that I do not hold it to be a lie."

Augustine said: "It has become apparent that you could not prove that Mani is an apostle of Christ. But I shall briefly explain why you could not. You said that you proved that Mani was an apostle of Christ because Christ promised that the Holy Spirit, the Paraclete, would come, and, because you did not see when the one whom Christ promised came, you therefore believed that Mani was the Holy Spirit. But I have proved through the holy canonical scriptures of the Church when the Holy Spirit, whom Christ the Lord promised would come, most obviously came. You then took a different tack and said that I ought to show you what he taught and whether he did away with the teaching of Mani. Although I replied, therefore, that Mani lived after the apostles, but that the apostles proclaimed their teaching before Mani was born, nonetheless I said that one of them, the apostle Paul, also prophesied through the Holy Spirit, who had come to all the apostles, that this teaching of yours was going to come, and he called it the teaching of lying demons. Thereupon I showed that the ideas that Paul said would be found in this teaching pertained to what you profess, that is, the prohibition of marriage. For you say that all intercourse, even with one's wife, is fornication. And you teach abstinence from foods that God has created. For I know that you say that some foods are unclean, though Paul goes on and says, *Every creature of God is good* (1 Tm 4:1).

"When at this point I asked you to reply, you said that Mani taught you the beginning, the middle, and the end, the course of the sun and the moon, and other things of the sort. When I showed that these things do not pertain to Christian doctrine, you replied that the apostle said that he knows in part and prophesies in part. I said that we cannot know the things of God when we are in this life and that we see here in a glass and in an enigma but shall then see face to face. And I asked you whether, if you think that the apostle Paul said that Mani was going to come to teach what Paul himself could not teach, it pertains to you, who say that you have received the Spirit, to see God at present face to face. Because you cannot do this, it is evident that the apostle Paul was speaking about the life of which John also says, *Beloved, we are the children of God, and it has not yet appeared what we shall be. For we know that, when he appears, we shall be like him because we shall see him as he is.* (1 Jn 3:3)

"When you heard this, you said that you could not stand up against my power. This power is not mine. Rather, if there is any power, it was given to me for the refutation of errors by him who is the power of all those who believe in him and wholeheartedly put their trust in him. You also said that my episcopal authority frightens you, though you see how peaceably we deal with each other, the great tranquility with which we discuss things, how the people present here do you no violence and cause you no fear but listen with complete tranquility, as is fitting for Christians. You also said that you feared the laws of the emperors. A man whom the Holy Spirit has filled would not fear this for the sake of the true faith. For during the Lord's passion the apostle Peter was afraid, and he denied him three times.[7] But when the Holy Spirit, the Paraclete, whom Christ had promised, filled him, he was crucified for his faith in the Lord. He who had first denied him out of fear afterward underwent a most glorious martyrdom for the sake of his confession. And so, from the very fact that you said that you feared the laws of the emperors, it is apparent that you have not found the Spirit of the truth, the Paraclete, though this is also apparent from other evidence. For even if you were not afraid, you would be refuted by other evidence."

Felix said: "The apostles were also afraid."

---

7. See Mt 26:69-75; Mk 14:66-72; Lk 22:55-62; Jn 18:16.25.

Augustine said: "They were afraid so that they were wary, but not so that they hesitated to confess their faith once they were arrested. You ought to have feared earlier that we would find you here. Now you are in our midst. Why are you afraid except that you do not have anything to say? For, if you had been afraid of the emperors, you would have been silent before. But now, since yesterday you gave a statement of your faith to the curator and publicly cried out that you were ready to be burned along with your books if anything evil were found in them, why did you appeal to the laws like a brave man yesterday while today you flee from them like a coward?"

13. Felix said: "I am not fleeing from the truth."

Augustine said: "Say, then, that you see God face to face in accord with your promise. For you said that the apostle Paul had said of you that you were going to receive so complete a truth that we would understand or believe that the apostle had the truth in part and that you have the whole of it."

Felix said: "I am not fleeing from the truth, but I am seeking the truth. Since I do not hold what you are saying, prove it to me by the divine scriptures. This is what I now ask."

Augustine said: "First state that you could not prove that Mani was an apostle of Jesus Christ, and to the extent that I can, after everything contrary to it has been removed from your heart by my ministry, by the Lord's gift I shall tell you what the knowledge of the truth is that leads to God, beginning from faith."

Felix said: "Since you say that I should deny my law and accept another one, though a better one, which is something that I too seek, I reply that I shall not deny my law before I receive another."

Augustine said: "But someone first pours out from a vessel what is bad, and in that way he fills it with what is good. Or if you still hesitate to pour it out, defend that with which you are full. For I shall show you, to the extent that the Lord helps me, how many uncleannesses and blasphemies the teaching of Mani is full of, if you permit us to read the letter whose beginning we have already considered, though you could not prove that Mani was an apostle of Christ. But you are creating delays in order that the rest might not be read out, where your sacrileges are clearly discernable. Or if you permit it, let the rest be read."

Felix said: "I permit it, since you said that I should pour out everything unclean and in that way put in good things. For this is the statement of Your Holiness. To it I reply: No one pours out water unless someone else has filled the vessel."

Augustine said: "See how thoughtlessly you said this. I am putting it more gently and am not saying: 'How insanely you said this.' To be sure, I offered you a comparison with a vessel. No one can put anything into a full vessel unless what it was full of has been poured out."

Felix said: "You spoke of one vessel, and I spoke of two."

Augustine said: "If you spoke of two vessels, do you want us to empty and then fill that vessel like yours so that you can pour out what you have?"

Felix said: "We both have one water."

Augustine said: "Since, then, you are both full of your water, what are we going to fill in order that we may teach you, unless one of you pours out what he has? Or, if it is good and for that reason ought to be kept, let that letter be read in order that it may be defended. Let us see whether you can defend the other things if you have failed in the beginning. Or, if you say that you did not fail in the beginning, prove to us how Mani is an apostle of Christ."

14. Felix said: "Christ said that he would send the Holy Spirit to lead us into all the truth."

Augustine said: "If you have that Spirit, pay attention to what I have long asked you. After all, you said that it pertains to Mani's teaching to know worldly matters too. Tell me how many stars there are if you have been led into all this truth."

Felix said: "And I say that, if the Paraclete spoke through the apostles, he also spoke through Paul, and I ask Your Holiness to show me the things that I have already mentioned."

Augustine said: "Admit that you could not show me what I asked, and I shall show you in accord with the scriptures what pertains to the Christian faith."

Felix said: "And I shall prove to you whatever you ask if you bring me the writings of Mani — the five authorities that I mentioned to you."[8]

Augustine said: "This letter whose beginning we have discussed and in which we have found it written, 'Mani, an apostle of Jesus Christ,' comes from these five authorities, and I see that you are not explaining that very beginning because you are not proving how Mani is an apostle of Jesus Christ."

Felix said: "If I do not prove these things in this work, I shall prove them in the second."

Augustine said: "In which second work?"

Felix said: "In *The Treasury*."

Augustine said: "Who wrote this *Treasury*, which you call by a name like that in order to mislead poor wretches? Mani! I do not want you to prove it from him since Mani himself lies when he says that he is what he is not."

Felix said: "Prove it to me yourself by someone else."

Augustine said: "What do you want me to prove to you?"

Felix said: "That Mani is lying."

Augustine said: "Because you cannot prove that Mani speaks the truth, must I prove that Mani lied?"

---

8. The writings of Mani are frequently said to be five, though a fragment of a sixth work is extant as well as the whole of a seventh in Coptic.

Felix said: "Why was I unable to prove it? Were the writings that I asked for brought forth, and I did not prove it?"

Augustine said: "But you ask for the writings of Mani, in which we do not have any faith. Prove it from elsewhere. But I prove to you from the very writing of Mani that Mani lied and that Mani blasphemed."

Felix said: "Let the books be brought out."

Augustine said: "The letter of Mani is present here, which you call *The Foundation*. There is no beginning in a building apart from its foundation. If I show that there is a collapse in the very foundation, why should we examine the rest of its construction?"

15. Felix said: "You say this in order to show that there is a collapse in it, and I say: Give me as many judges as you have, and I shall prove to you that Mani is not lying."

Augustine said: "Far be it from us and from the human race that you should see here as many Manicheans as you see people."

Felix said: "Give me, I said, what I asked of you."

Augustine said: "Whom, then, do you want me to give you?"

Felix said: "Those whom you want."

Augustine said: "I give you these people; if you have better ones, ask for them."

Felix said: "How are you giving me these people?"

Augustine said: "As the people who are present and are listening to us."

Felix said: "These people are not on my side."

Augustine said: "Do you ask for judges, then, who are on your side, not on the side of the truth?"

Felix said: "I want those who will listen to me — and not only to me but also to scripture itself, in order that it may be proved whether Mani speaks the truth or lies."

Augustine said: "You see, then, that they are listening. Let us read the rest, since you have admitted that this letter is Mani's."

Felix said: "I do not deny it."

Augustine said: "Let it therefore be read."

16. Felix said: "I do not have judges." And he added: "Let its beginning be read."

And when it was read we came to the place where the same letter has it in writing: "May the invisible peace and knowledge of the Truth be yours along with his brothers and most dear ones who believe and also obey the heavenly commandments. But may the right hand of the Light protect and rescue you from every evil attack and from the snare of the world. And may the piety of the Holy Spirit open the inmost parts of your heart in order that you may see your souls with those eyes."

Felix said: "Provide the scripture that refutes these ideas."

Augustine said: "Up to now we have heard nothing evil except that Mani dared to call himself an apostle of Christ. For the things that he said still pertain to the concealment of his deceitfulness and to the sheep's clothing[9] by which he first says good things in order to be able to introduce bad ones. But let us see what he wants to introduce by means of these words. For, if he introduces something evil, these words will also be evil and misleading. But if he says something good and true in what follows, we shall certainly grasp it. Permit, then, that the following passages be read."

Felix said: "If, then, you claim that good things are set forth first and that evil ones are introduced later, how can I believe you when you say to me that there are good things at first."

Augustine said: "I have not as yet said that they are either good or evil. Up to now we have heard nothing evil. I did not say that we have already heard something good. For I said that only the fact that he dared to say that he was an apostle of Christ was evil. But the words he spoke in what follows will turn out to be evil if they introduce something evil, and they will turn out to be good if they introduce something good. Permit, therefore, that the rest be read. Why are you afraid?"

Felix said: "I am not afraid."

Augustine said: "Permit, therefore, that they be read."

Felix said: "Let them be read."

17. And when they were read and we came to the passage where it has in writing, "But his most splendid kingdoms were founded upon the bright and blessed land, so that they could neither be moved nor shaken by anything,"

Augustine said: "From where did God have this land that Mani speaks of? Did God make it? Or did he beget it? Or was it equal to and coeternal with him? I am speaking of this land that Mani calls bright and blessed."

Felix said: "It is just as scripture says: *In the beginning God made heaven and earth, and the earth was invisible and subject to defilement and without form* (Gn 1:1-2).[10] I understand the words, *In the beginning God made the heaven and the earth, and the earth was,* in the sense that there seem to me to be two earths in accord with Mani's statement that there are two kingdoms."

Augustine said: "Because you quoted our scripture, against which you usually blaspheme, it falls to me to explain that scripture and to show you that it was written without blasphemy, both with the truth and not in agreement with Mani, in order that, at least in what follows, you may answer for me the question I asked."

Felix said: "I shall answer."

---

9. See Mt 7:15.
10. Felix introduces into the text from Genesis "and subject to defilement." Oddly, Augustine does not call this to his attention.

Augustine said: "In the words of scripture, *In the beginning God made heaven and earth*, scripture has summed up briefly what God made. Then, because this earth, which he had made, was not yet seen before he differentiated and adorned it, scripture went on to explain what sort of earth God made and of what sort of earth it had said, *In the beginning God made heaven and earth*, as if, after we had heard, *In the beginning God made heaven and earth*, we asked: What sort of earth? And he added, *But the earth*, that is, the earth God had made, *was invisible and without form*. God therefore did not speak of two earths but explained the sort of earth that there was. And so you answer me now what I asked in a few words: Was this bright and blessed earth, of which Mani speaks, upon which were founded the kingdoms of God, made by God himself, or was it begotten of him, or was it coeternal with him? If it is not a problem, answer that it is one of the three, without being evasive."

Felix said: "Scripture interprets itself."

Augustine said: "If, then, you know that there is some passage where scripture says that God either begot or made this earth or that it was coeternal to him, open to the passage you know, and read it to me."

Felix said: "It is not in this scripture but in another."

Augustine said: "I believe, therefore, that, if there is any such scripture, you remember what it said there. And so, answer me, you who know that scripture. And if I say that it is not so, you will prove me wrong. But if I recognize that it is so, I shall argue in accord with what you reply. State, then, whether God made this earth or begot it or it was coeternal with him, since you have read it in some book or other where you say that this is written."

Felix said: "Since Your Holiness has interpreted your scripture as you wished and since I have accepted it, accept in the same way whatever I say to you."

Augustine said: "As for what I asked, for the time being I accept what you say, provided that nothing moves me to the contrary, but if something moves me to the contrary, I shall indicate my problem to you so that you may reply to it."

Felix said: "I have not replied to what you said."

Augustine said: "The first thing is that you should give me an answer to what I asked, yet I myself acted so as to answer you first. Perhaps it does not bother you, and for this reason you have not replied. Perhaps it will not bother me when you reply. Reply, then, to what I have asked."

18. Felix said: "I am replying." And he added: "You have asked, then, about the earth where God dwells — whether it was made by him or whether he begot it or whether it is coeternal with him. And I say that, as God is eternal and there is nothing made in him, the whole is eternal."

Augustine said: "He did not, then, either beget it or make it?"

Felix said: "He did not; it is coeternal with him."

Augustine said: "But if he had begotten it, would it not be coeternal with him?"[11]

Felix said: "What is born has an end; what is unborn does not have an end."

Augustine said: "To what things, then, was he a father, or whose father was he, whom Mani now called a father? For, if he had not begotten anything, he could not have been a father."

Felix said: "There are other things that he has begotten."

Augustine said: "Are the things that he has begotten, then, coeternal with him, or are they not coeternal?"

Felix said: "Whatever God has begotten is coeternal with him."

Augustine said: "Therefore you were wrong when you said previously: 'Everything that is born has an end.'"

Felix said: "At the time I was wrong because I was speaking of begetting in terms of the flesh."

Augustine said: "Because you have very modestly admitted your error, may you merit to understand the truth."

Felix said: "May God bring that about."

Augustine said: "Now pay attention, therefore, in order that you may begin to recognize the error of this writing. If the things that God has begotten are not coeternal with him, the land that God did not beget, where all the things dwell that God has begotten, is better, for you say that that land was not begotten of him."

Felix said: "They are all equal to one another — both the things that he has begotten and those that he did not beget, that is, the land in which he dwelled."

Augustine said: "What? Is he who begot them equal to all of them or greater than they?"

Felix said: "Both he who begot them and those he begot and where he placed them are all equal."

Augustine said: "Are they, then, of one substance?"

Felix said: "They are."

Augustine said: "Are his children and is this land the same thing as God the Father?"

Felix said: "They are all this same thing."

Augustine said: "Is he, therefore, not the father of this land but its inhabitant?"

Felix said: "That is right."

Augustine said: "If he has neither begotten it nor made it, I do not see how it belongs to him except by proximity alone, just as if someone has a good neighbor, and then there will be two unborn realities: the land and the Father."

---

11. Contrary to PL and CSEL, I take this sentence as a question.

Felix said: "There are in fact three: the unborn Father, the unborn land, and the unborn air."

Augustine said: "And all this is one substance."

Felix said: "One."

Augustine said: "And has it been founded so that it can never be moved or shaken by anything?"

Felix said: "Motion and shaking imply a difference."

Augustine said: "Granted. But were these things still such that they could never be moved or shaken by anything?"

Felix said: "There is a difference between being moved and being shaken."

Augustine said: "I am not asking you about that."

Felix said: "But you want to trap me with that."

Augustine said: "Take 'being moved' however you wish. Was it unable to be moved?"

Felix said: "I do not say that it was unable to be moved but that motion is different."

Augustine said: "But I said 'neither moved nor shaken.' I did not say: 'It can certainly be moved, but it cannot be shaken,' or, 'It can certainly be shaken, but it cannot be moved.' Rather, I said both of these: 'It can be neither moved nor shaken.'"

Felix said: "Regarding the two things, there is a difference between 'being moved' and 'being shaken.'"

19. Augustine said: "Let us therefore read what follows; let us see whether this God who has kingdoms founded upon the bright and blessed land — kingdoms that can never be moved or shaken by anything — feared no one, since he whose kingdoms were founded so that they could be moved or shaken by no one necessarily feared no one."

And he read what follows: "But along one part and side of that bright and holy land."

And after he read it, Augustine asked: "Which side? The right or the left?"

Felix said: "I cannot interpret the scripture for you and explain what is not there. It is its own interpreter. I cannot speak lest perhaps I fall into sin."

Augustine said: "Let what follows, therefore, be read."

And then he read it and came to the place where it has: "But the Father of the most blessed light, knowing that the great ruin and devastation which was going to arise from the darkness would threaten his holy worlds if he did not set against it some outstanding and illustrious deity powerful in might, by which he could at the same time overcome and destroy the race of darkness so that, once it was wiped out, endless peace would be prepared for the inhabitants of the light."

Augustine said: "Now, since the clear blasphemies have begun, if you think that they should be defended, tell me what harm this nation of darkness, which God is seen to have feared lest a great ruin and devastation invade his kingdoms, could have done to God, especially since he said that his kingdoms were so founded that they could be neither moved nor shaken by anything. What, therefore, was this nation going to do to God? Could it do him harm or could it not? Give one answer or the other."

Felix said: "And I answer: If there is nothing opposed to God in the sense that the writings of Mani said that there is another kingdom, for what reason was Christ sent to deliver us from the snare of this death? To whom does this snare and death belong? If there is no enemy in opposition to God, why are we baptized? Why is there the eucharist? Why is there Christianity if there is nothing opposed to God?"

Augustine said: "I see that you do not want to reply to what I asked you and that you are asking that I reply to you, and I do not refuse to do so, provided that you nonetheless remember that I am replying to your question but that you were unwilling to reply to my question. But because you have asked me, listen to what you asked for. To be sure, we say that Christ came to set us free, and we say that we are set free from our sins, for we are not born of the substance of God but made by the Word of God. There is, however, a great difference between what is born of the substance of God and what has been made by God but is not of the substance of God. Whatever God has made, then, can be subject to change. But God himself is not mutable because his works cannot be equal to their maker and creator. You, however, who a little before said to my question, 'The Father who begot there the children of light and the air and the land itself and the children themselves are one substance and are all equal,' must tell me how the nation of darkness could have done harm to this substance, which was of course incorruptible. If it could do it harm, after all, it was not an incorruptible nature. If, however, it could not have, there was no reason why God should start a war and send here what he calls 'that deity.'"

Felix said: "I ask for a postponement in order that I may reply."

Augustine said: "When? Will skipping tomorrow be enough?"

20. Felix said: "Skip three days, that is, today and tomorrow and the next day, or up to the day after the Lord's Day, that is, a day before the Ides of December."

Augustine said: "I see that you have sought a postponement in order to reply. It is only human to grant it to you. But if you are unable to reply at the appointed time, what will happen?"

Felix said: "I shall lose."

Augustine said: "What if you flee?"

Felix said: "I shall be guilty in respect to this city and everywhere and in respect to my law."

Augustine said: "Rather, say this: If I flee, let me be considered to have condemned Mani."

Felix said: "I cannot say that."

Augustine said: "Therefore, tell us openly that you are thinking of fleeing, and no one will hold you here."

Felix said: "I am not going to flee."

Augustine said: "As I see it, you do not want to depart as someone who has been defeated, but at least say this: If I flee, I have been defeated."

Felix said: "I have said that."

Augustine said: "And how will it be seen that you have fled on account of these proceedings?"

Felix said: "Order that I stay with the person whom I shall choose."

Augustine said: "Choose for yourself someone from the brothers present here who are standing in the cancel."

Felix said: "I shall stay with the one who is in the middle."

Augustine said: "As you have chosen him, you shall stay with him until that day.

Felix said: "All right, and I agree to this."

Boniface said: "Christ will grant that, if I come with him, he will be a Christian."

I, Augustine, bishop of the Catholic Church of Hippo Regius, have signed these proceedings in the church in the presence of the people.

I, Felix, a Christian, a worshiper of the law of Mani, have signed these proceedings in the church in the presence of the people.

Book Two

1. When the appointed day arrived, that is, the day before the Ides of December, the debate began thus in the Church of Peace.

Augustine, the bishop of the Catholic Church of the territories of Hippo Regius, said: "When we were having our earlier debate, you remember that you asked for a delay, since you were unable to reply at the moment to the questions I had asked. If, then, after so long a stretch of time, that is, after five days, you have thought of something, answer me. For I had asked you this question then: If nothing was able to do God any harm, why did he wage a war with the nation that you call the nation of darkness — a war in which he mingled his own substance, which is identical with him, with the nature of demons, as you said when questioned? But if that nation was able to do him harm, you worship a God who is not incorruptible, as the truth and as the teaching of the apostles testify that he is."

Felix said: "We have come to the day on which it was agreed, when I left Your Holiness, that I would return to answer whatever questions you might want to ask. And I have had in my hands no scriptures, since none were given to me by which I might derive instruction. After all, no one goes off to battle unless he has first weighed the situation,[12] and no lawyer can plead his case without his notes. Neither can I reply without my scriptures."

Augustine said: "This is the evasion that you have thought up over so many days! And in a lost case and a sacrilegious error it will be unable to help you in any way if you have no answer to make. For all who were present — and I see that they are present now as well — know that you only asked for a delay of so many days. But you ought also to have asked for the books when you asked for the delay, if you thought that you could have derived instruction from them for your reply. Yet you did not do that. I know that you asked to look at your books. This was not in order that you might derive instruction but was long before you asked for a delay. But when you asked for a delay, you made no mention of returning the books to you and of looking at them so that you might be better instructed."

Felix said: "I am asking for them now; let the books be restored to me, and I shall come for the debate after a period of two days. And if I am defeated, I shall face whatever you decide."

---

12. I have followed the reading in CSEL of *meditatus*, though PL has *munitus* ("protected") and the BA edition has *militatus* ("fought"), all of which have some plausibility.

Augustine said: "I do not think that you are someone untrained in this wicked sect, as you yourself admit. Everyone already sees that you do not have any answer to make, even if you do not admit it. But since you are asking for your books, which are kept under public seal, and you say that you will come instructed after two days, once you have looked at them, recall that it is now clear that you could not reply to the questions that were posed for you. But take your books, and state which of them you want to be brought forth, so that you may look at them now and reply."

Felix said: "All the writings that were taken away from me. For there is the *Letter of the Foundation*, which Your Holiness knows well. I also said that it contains the beginning, the middle, and the end. I want it to be read, and I want you to prove whatever evil objections are raised against my law. I shall deny my law if the crimes that are raised as objections to my law are proved."

Augustine said: "You said that this is the letter that contains the beginning, the middle, and the end of your teaching. How sacrilegious this beginning is! In it you say that God fought against the nation of darkness and mingled a part of himself, which is identical with himself, with the nature of demons, so that it would be polluted and bound. This is so sacrilegious that those who hear it can scarcely endure it. This is the first objection to your sect. I do not care much whether you call it the beginning, the middle, or the end. Yet you do not deny that this was read from this letter, which you admit is Mani's. This is raised as an objection against you; defend it if you can so that we may go on to other points. Hence, I ask you again: If you worship an incorruptible God, what harm could some opposing nation of darkness, which you invent, have done to him? If it could have done him no harm, there was no reason why he should mingle a part of himself with the nature of demons. But if it could have done him some harm, you do not worship an incorruptible God."

2. Felix said: "Mani says that there are two natures, and now he is blamed because he said that there are two, a good nature and a evil nature. In the gospel Christ says that there are two trees: *The good tree never produces bad fruit, and the bad tree never produces good fruit* (Mt 7:17). There you have two natures. Again, it is recorded in the gospel: *Did you not sow good seed in the field? Where have the weeds come from? An enemy did this.* (Mt 13:27-28) If this enemy is not external to God, let it be proved to me. But if this enemy belongs to God, what sort of seed did he sow? Likewise, it is written in the gospel — it is Christ who is speaking — that in the last times he will set his throne in the middle of the world, send his angels to the east and the west, to the north and the south, gather all the nations before himself, and separate them, as a shepherd separates the sheep from the goats.[13] And, to state it briefly, he will say to the sheep, *Enter into the kingdom that has been prepared for you from the beginning of the world* (Mt

---

13. See Mt 25:31-32.

25:34), and he will say to the goats, who are on the left side, *Depart from me, you who have acted wickedly* (Mt 25:41a). For you had my name, but you did not do my works. *Enter into the eternal fire that was prepared for the devil and his angels* (Mt 25:41b). Who are they who have the name of Christ and are sent into eternal fire with the devil and his angels, and to what side do they pertain, with whom Christ is not mingled, though they bear his name? For Mani says that those whom Christ condemns do not belong to him.

"Now, Paul the apostle says, *The wisdom of the flesh is an enemy of God, for it is not subject to the law of God and it cannot be* (Rom 8:7). Mani says that what is an enemy of God does not belong to God, but Mani does not say that, if it belongs to God, he made an enemy for himself. Again Paul says, *The god of this world has blinded the minds of non-believers in order that they may not look upon the glory of the gospel of Christ, who is the image of God* (2 Cor 4:4). Paul himself again says, *A goad in my flesh was given to me, an angel of Satan who struck me day and night. On its account I asked the Lord that it might depart from me, and he said to me, My grace is enough for you, for virtue is tested in weakness.* (2 Cor 12:7-8) See what the apostle said; see what the evangelist said. Mani said that he who wages war against God is external to God. And Christ was crucified as well as all the apostles for the sake of God's commandment. Let Your Holiness tell me whether he who crucified them, who was displeased with God's commandment, belongs to God."

3. Augustine said: "You wanted to quote the holy scriptures, as if to invoke their patronage for your foolish ideas, though, because you do not understand them, you wander far from the truth. Nonetheless, amid all those passages that you quote, some as they were actually written and some otherwise than they were written, you were never able to show that, in wanting to repel a hostile nature, which was threatening his kingdoms, in order that he might have peace, God mingled a part of himself, which is identical with him, with the opposing nature of demons and caused it to be imprisoned and defiled by them. But this is the objection raised against you. Hence, not finding any reply to make, you quoted passages from the divine scriptures where it was said of sinners that they do not belong to the happy life that God grants to the good and the faithful. And you wanted these to be understood as two natures in accord with the ravings of Mani.

"But the truth says that all these things that we see and those that we do not see, which subsist as natures, were made by God. The truth says that among these the rational creature, which was also made, whether in the angels or in human beings, received free choice. If the rational creature chose to serve God by that free choice, it would, according to the will and law of God, have eternal happiness with him. But if it refused to be subject to his law and used its power against the rule of God, it would be subject to due punishment according to the justice of God. This is the omnipotence of God in creating all things; this is the justice of God in repaying sinners. But I shall prove not only from the divine scriptures, which you do not understand, but also from the words of your Mani himself, that free choice exists and that by free choice someone sins if he wills to and does not sin if he does not will to. For, once he is cornered, Mani sees the power of the truth, against which he had tried to introduce — not by the solid truth but by an empty phantasm — another nature, which God had not made, in opposition to God. And yet, for admitting the truth about free choice, the human nature in which God made him had more power over him than the sacrilegious myth that he himself concocted.

4. "Listen first, then, to the Lord himself concerning free choice, where he speaks of the two trees, of which you yourself made mention. Listen to him as he says, *Either make the tree good and its fruit good, or make the tree bad and its fruit bad* (Mt 12:33). When, therefore, he says, "Either do this or do that," he indicates a power, not a nature. After all, only God can make a tree. But each person has it in his will either to choose what is good and to be a good tree or to choose what is evil and to be a bad tree, not because the evils that we choose have some substance in themselves but because God created all the things that he created in their different ranks and distinguished them in their kinds. He created heavenly things and earthly things, immortal things and mortal things, all good, each in its own kind, and he placed the soul that has free choice under himself and above other things. In that way, if the soul served what was above it, it would rule what was beneath it. But if it offended what was above it, it would experience punishment from what was beneath it. And so, when the Lord said, "Either do this or do that," he showed that what they would do was in their power, while he was secure and certain in himself as God, and that, if they chose the good, they would receive a reward from him, while if they chose evil, they would feel punishment from him. But God is always just, whether he rewards or condemns.

5. "Listen, then, to how Mani himself — who is so perverse and so proud that, in introducing another nature, he makes himself equal to God and brings God down to his own level — admitted nonetheless that there is free choice. In your *Treasury*, to which you have given a name like that so as to deceive human beings, he certainly speaks in this way, as you yourself also recognize: 'But because of their negligence these souls did not permit themselves to be purified from the defilement of the previously mentioned spirits and did not obey the commandments of God in their entirety and were unwilling to observe fully the law given them by their deliverer and did not govern themselves as they ought to have,' and so on. You see that in these words he maintained free choice, though he did not know what he was saying. One who is unwilling to observe the law has it in his power to do so, if he wills. After all, he did not say, 'They could not,' but, 'They were unwilling.' Surely they are not forced by the nation of darkness if they are unwilling to observe the law. For, if they are forced, they are not unwilling but are unable to observe the law. But if they are unwilling, they are of

course not forced not to observe the law, but they are by their own will unwilling to observe it. What lies, then, in their own will — namely, that they are unwilling to observe the law — is a sin without any compulsion from the nation of darkness. Recognize that this is a sin without any compulsion from the nation of darkness, and from this you will see the source from which all sins come, from which all meriting of punishment comes, and from which all the assigning of punishment comes.

6. "You have this also in the apocryphal writings, which the Catholic canon does not admit but which are taken more seriously by you the further removed they are from the Catholic canon. Let me quote something from there; though I am not bound by its authority, you are refuted by it. In the *Acts* written by Leutius,[14] which he writes like the Acts of the Apostles, you have it expressed as follows: 'For specious lies and false displays and the seduction of visible things do not come from some nature of their own but from that man who by himself became worse through seduction.' You see how he said 'by himself' and 'through seduction.' For the devil was the seducer of the man. The devil was not a sinner by nature; rather, he first became a sinner by his will. But that it was in the power of the man not to consent to the seducer was expressed in the phrases 'by himself' and 'through seduction,' so that in the words 'by himself' you understand free choice and in the words 'through seduction' you understand the devil — not as oppressing someone against his will but as tempting someone who is willing.

7. "I have replied and proved, to the extent that I could, that the things which were written in the holy books concerning sinners and the righteous do not have to do with a diversity of natures but with a difference in merits. And in those merits nature does not produce a necessity, but the will commits a sin. Hence, reply to the question I asked. If nothing was able to do harm to God, why did God mingle a part of himself — his own substance, that which he is — with demons so that it might be polluted and bound in them? This is something that you cannot find in any of the divine and canonical scriptures. But if something was able to do him harm, you do not worship the incorruptible God, of whom the apostle says, *But to the king of the ages, to the immortal, invisible, incorruptible God alone be honor and glory forever and ever* (1 Tm 1:17). Secondly, he likewise says, *God dwells in unapproachable light* (1 Tm 6:16). Do the saints not approach that light? Scripture says of them, *Approach him, and be enlightened* (Ps 34:6). Do not the saints approach that light, for it is said of them, *Blessed are the clean of heart because they shall see God* (Mt 5:8)? But because only someone to whom God grants that he may approach that light can approach it,

---

14. *The Acts of Leutius*, an apocryphal work probably from the second century, are no longer extant.

the light is in itself unapproachable. No one, after all, can approach it whom God does not want to approach it. But one to whom God grants this will approach it.

"How, then, was that nation of darkness able to approach the dwelling of God, where there is unapproachable light, which no one approaches except him to whom God has granted it? Or if that nation of darkness had received from God the gift that it might approach it, God would not have granted it in order that the nation of darkness might attack the kingdom of God, and he would not have feared it. But if he had not given such a gift, so that it would be able to approach it, and if, secure in his kingdom, God was dwelling in unapproachable light, what could he have feared from the nation of darkness so that he mingled a part of himself — his own substance, that which he is — to be bound, oppressed, and defiled in it, where he would be not only miserably confined but also purified in a shameful way? For, in order that he might be purified from it, you say something that it is wicked even to hear, but, in order to refute you and perhaps to save you, we cannot keep silence. You say that, in order for a part of God to be purified from it, in a ship of light, which you call the sun (here you do injury to the creator of the sun and to the sun itself, which you say was made in order that such shamefulness might be carried out) — you say that, when located in the sun, God changed his powers into male demons to stimulate the passions of female demons and into female demons to stimulate the passions of male demons. In that way, when the demons are aroused, they pour out their lust upon the forms made by God, and the tension of their members is eased so that the part of God that was imprisoned there escapes. You have dared to believe so great an insult, so great a sacrilege, and you do not hesitate to preach it.

"These are the middle points of your teaching. But what is the end? What is it but that God could not purify his whole self? And because he could not, you say that he will make a cover, as it were, for the nation of darkness, in order that there may be condemned there for eternity that which could not be purified and which committed no sin of its own accord. In that way it turns out that your God — not the true God but a false one, not located somewhere in reality but pictured in your heart — unhappily mingles, shamefully purifies, and cruelly condemns a part of himself. Reply, therefore, to these points, and begin from the question I asked: Why did God, whom nothing could have harmed, mingle this part of himself with demons? Or if something could have harmed him, how is he incorruptible?"

8. Felix said: "You claim that, when Mani says these things, he is cruel. What are we to say of Christ who says, *Enter into eternal fire* (Mt 25:41)?"

Augustine said: "He said this to sinners."

Felix said: "Why were these sinners not purified?"

Augustine said: "Because they did not want to be."

Felix said: "Did you say, 'Because they did not want to be'?"

Augustine said: "I said, 'Because they did not want to be.'"

Felix said: "Why did they not want to be? Is there anyone who does not want to be cured? Is there anyone who does not want to be purified? Is there anyone ill who does not want to return to health? If what Mani says — namely, that some part of God which could not purify itself has been imprisoned in that sphere — is cruel, is it not cruel that Christ, who said, 'I have come for the sake of sinners,'[15] now sends into eternal fire those who bore his name? But, I think, they were not able to carry out his commandments. If what Mani says is cruel, what Christ said is even more cruel. If it was rather cruel that God could not purify them and bound them in the sphere of darkness, it seems even more cruel to send into eternal fire those whom Christ could not purify. Your Holiness must explain this cruelty to me."

Augustine said: "You would not say this if you either understood or admitted that you understood what I have already said. After all, you perhaps pretended that you did not understand what is obvious because you had nothing to say. For we have already stated and proved from the divine scriptures that there is free choice but that God is the just judge of free choice. He rewards the faithful who are obedient to him and willing to be healed, but he condemns the proud and the wicked. Because, therefore, he came to heal sinners, he of course heals those who have confessed their sins; he heals those who have repented. But no one repents when someone else sins. Rather, if there is just and truthful repentance, because of which the Lord says, *I have come to call to repentance not the righteous but sinners* (Mt 9:13), repentance itself indicates that it does not come from another nature but from our own will if we perhaps commit some sin. For, if one person repents when another sins, this is not a wise but an insane repentance.

"According to you, however, there are no sins. After all, the nation of darkness does not sin because it acts according to its nature. The nature of light does not sin because it is forced to do what it does. Consequently you find no sin that God might condemn; you find no sin that could be healed by repentance. But if there is repentance, there is also sin. If there is sin, there is also will. If there is will when one sins, it is not nature that forces one. But those who cannot do what they will to do are suffering some weakness. On account of this weakness the apostle says, *I see another law in my members that resists the law of my mind and holds me captive in the law of sin that is in my members* (Rom 7:23). It is clear that this weakness came by way of inheritance from the first sin of Adam and from bad habits. For even today people develop bad habits by free will, and, when they have developed them, they cannot easily overcome them. They themselves, therefore, have brought it about for themselves by themselves that a law dwells in their members in opposition to them. But those who begin to have a fear of God and by free choice submit themselves in order to be healed by the

---

15. See Mt 9:13.

very best physician, who is their merciful creator just as he is their good healer, are healed by the humility of confession and repentance. But the proud, who say that they are righteous or say that they themselves do not sin but that something else sins in them and that another nature sins regarding them, become incurable because of their pride, and they experience the just judgment of God, who resists the proud but gives grace to the humble.[16] It is not inappropriate, therefore, that God should say, *Enter into the eternal fire* (Mt 25:41), to those who rejected his mercy through free choice, and that he should say, *Come, blessed of my Father, receive the kingdom* (Mt 25:34), to those who received faith in him through free choice, confessed their sins, did penance, were displeased with the sort of persons they were, and pleased God as the sort of persons they became through him.

"Now, then, reply to the question I have asked. But I beg you that we should not create needless delays. If nothing was able to harm God, why did he send us here? If something was able to harm him, God was not incorruptible."

9. Felix said: "If nothing was able to harm God, why did he send his Son here?"

Augustine said: "See how you are always asking questions and refusing to answer questions. Listen to what you have asked, yet remember that you are not answering the questions I am asking but that I am answering yours. Nothing can harm God. But he sent his Son to be clothed in flesh and to be seen by human beings, to heal sinners, and to suffer for us in the flesh that he assumed from us. In his own nature, of course, he was not able to suffer anything because he was *the Word in the beginning, and the Word was with God, and the Word was God* (Jn 1:1-2). In this nature he was not able to suffer anything because *the Word was God*. But in order that he might be able to suffer for us, *the Word became flesh and dwelled among us* (Jn 1:14) by assuming flesh, not by having been changed into flesh. For he assumed humanity; he did not lose divinity. And so he is God and he is man, equal to the Father in the nature of God, having become mortal in the nature of man among us, on behalf of us, from us, remaining what he was while taking up what he was not, in order that he might set free what he had made, not what he was. The suffering of Christ does not come from indigence but from mercy. For he offered an example of suffering to us from us, that is, to humans from a human, to flesh from flesh. Yet he did not become worse in that flesh, but in him flesh was made better.

"A part of your God, on the other hand, without assuming any flesh — for there was none in the nation of darkness for which he might suffer — came down so that it was held captive, bound, polluted, and was purified in a more shameful manner than it was bound. Now, I have already spoken of its purification. The more disgraceful all these things are, the more easy it surely is to

16. See Jas 4:6.

understand that they do not happen to the nature of God. And far be it from a devout and believing mind to think such things of God, the good God, the true God, as you believe of the god whom you did not find but have made up.

"And so answer me now: If nothing could have harmed God, why according to your silly ideas was that pure substance sent here? For, since it did not assume any flesh, if it was going to suffer anything, it would have to suffer in itself, not in a flesh that it had not taken up."

10. Felix said: "If nothing from the opposing side could have harmed God and if nothing from the opposing nature could have harmed Christ, to what nature did Christ come in order to set it free? For, as you say, he came for the sake of our deliverance. Hence, we were in captivity. If we were being held in captivity and if Christ came in order to set us free from captivity, he who held us captive either was exterior to God or was the power of God. If it was the power of God that held us captive, why did he who held us captive send Christ? If it was a matter of his choice when he wanted to release us, why was Christ crucified? But everyone knows that Christ was crucified. Why did they crucify him? If it was the power of God, it was not harming us. If it was the power of God, we were not held captive in him, but we were as if with our prince, like a child with his parents, but not like Romans with barbarians. Since we were dwelling with the power of God, it was therefore not necessary that God send his Son so that he would be said to have come as our deliverer. If, then, it is clear that we were dwelling with the power of God, why did the apostle say, *Christ set us free from the curse of the law, for scripture says, Cursed is everyone who is hanged upon a tree* (Gal 3:13; Dt 21:23)? For the apostle says this. If he who curses everyone who is hanged upon a tree is the power of God — for Christ was hanged upon a tree, as well as all his apostles who were brought to trial for the sake of his commandment — who, then, is he who curses everyone who is hanged upon a tree?"

11. Augustine said: "Those whom Christ redeemed from the devil were held captive by the devil because of their consent and were placed by the just judgment of God under the sway of him to whose seduction they had consented through free choice. But just as it was in the power of man to consent to the devil so that he would be taken captive, so it was, when he was an angel, in the power of the devil to sin so that he would be changed for the worse. The angel, therefore, who was a sinner by free choice, urged man who had free choice to sin. Thus, if the devil had not willed to sin, he would not have sinned, and if man had not willed to sin, he would not have consented. But man was held captive by the devil, to whom he had consented, not because the devil had some power but because it was the just judgment of God to surrender man, who scorned the power of God above him and was unwilling to obey his law, into the devil's power. In that way, then, Christ found sinners under the power of sin, though sin

was a matter of free choice. Finding sinners under the power of sin, he redeemed those who confessed their sins from the power of the proud one."

"Yet the statement in the law, *Cursed is everyone who is hanged upon a tree* (Dt 21:23), because of which the apostle said, *Christ redeemed us from the curse of the law, for scripture says, Cursed is everyone who is hanged upon a tree* (Gal 3:13), does not blame the law but commends the mercy of the Lord. For Adam had sinned and all that mass and progeny of sin was cursed. But the Lord chose to take up flesh from that mass in order that by taking up mortality, which had come from punishment, he might bring about the destruction of death, which comes from grace. Hence, the law said, *Cursed is everyone who is hanged upon a tree.* For death itself was hanged upon the tree — death that came from the curse. Just as by taking up death he killed death, then, so by taking up the curse he destroyed the curse. Hence, the apostle also says, *We know that our old self is nailed to the cross together with him* (Rom 6:6), because from our old self, that is, from our mortal condition, which came as the penalty of sin, he deigned to take up mortal flesh from the Virgin Mary. In that flesh he offered us an example of both suffering and rising — of suffering in order to strengthen our readiness to suffer, of rising in order to stimulate our hope. In that way he showed us in the flesh that he took up from our mortal life two lives: one life filled with toil and the other the happy life, the life filled with toil that we must endure and the happy life that we must hope for. But we endure this life filled with toil because of the merit of sin. He manifested this life of toil in his flesh not by reason of his sinfulness, however, but out of an act of his mercy.

"For, so that you might know that the law is good, which you wanted to blame, the apostle Paul said in a certain passage, *The law entered in in order that sin might abound* (Rom 5:20). He still seems to blame it, but listen to what follows. He says, *But where sin abounded, grace was even more abundant* (Rom 5:20). The law, after all, was given to people who were proud and attributed everything to their own strength in order that, when they could not observe the law that they were given, they might be found to be transgressors and, having become guilty under the law, they might seek mercy from the author of the law. Hence, the same apostle says a little later, *And so the law is holy and the commandment is holy, just, and good* (Rom 7:12). But in order that you might not say that he is speaking of some other commandment, in order to show that he is speaking of the commandment of which he had said a little before, *The law entered in in order that sin might abound*, he immediately posed for himself the question, *Has what was good, then, become death for me? Of course not! Rather, in order that sin might be seen as sin, it produced death for me.* (Rom 7:13) For sin existed, but it was not seen as sin. The law was given to proud man; he acted against the law, and sin, which existed but was not seen as sin, was then seen as sin. But when seen as sin, it humbled proud man, and, once humbled, proud man became repentant. And by his repentance he won mercy.

"You have heard, then, what you were asking for; reply to what I am asking for. The nation of darkness was unable to harm God. Why did he send here a part of himself to be mingled with and polluted by the nature of demons?"

12. Felix said: "If we are free, let no one force anyone. When I want to, I shall be a Christian. The will either to be or not to be a Christian is up to us."

Augustine said: "It is evident that our will is in our power, and I have proved this from the divine scriptures. Even Mani, even he who led you into this error, was reluctantly obliged to say this. But as for what you say, 'Let no one force anyone. When I want to, I shall be a Christian,' clearly no one is forcing you. Be a Christian when you want to, for you have come here of your own will and you have debated these issues of your own will. And woe to a bad will if it is bad. Peace to a good will if it is good. For, whether it is bad or it is good, it is a will. The crown of a reward follows upon a good will, but punishment follows upon a bad will. God is the judge of wills but the creator of natures. If, then, you think that you are being forced to be a Christian, hear it from us that you are absolutely not being forced. Rather, think of what you hear; weigh it: you are free. Examine wisely, if you have any wisdom, even human wisdom, whether the truth supports what we have said and whether you yourself have failed in the defense of your Mani, as is apparent. And when you want to, be what you are not as yet, and stop being what you are."

13. Felix said: "Let us be brief, as Your Holiness said, so that we do not create a pile of documents. Here is what I asked on the first day, if it is all right with you. I came here: show me the truth so that it may be seen that what I hold is not the truth, and you will have me ready to believe."

Augustine said: "It is already quite apparent that what you hold is not the truth. Far be it from the hearts of those seeking or holding the truth to believe that God was forced by necessity to plunge his own substance into the nature of demons to be imprisoned and polluted. Far be it from the faithful to believe that, in order to set free his own substance, God transformed himself into males for the females and into females for the males in order to arouse their passions. Far be it from the faithful to believe that God afterward condemned his own substance, which he himself plunged into demons. It is evident that this is not the truth. But because you want to discover the truth in place of this error that has been driven out and refuted, you can, if something still bothers you about the knowledge of the Catholic faith, be instructed about the faith from the beginning. For devout faith makes a person suited for the perception of the immutable truth. Anyone who refuses to begin from this faith will remain outside in his pride and will not be able to be brought where he is tending or where he wants to arrive. But since that error is already evident, condemn the error so that you can begin to be fit to know the truth."

14. Felix said: "When it is apparent to me; because it is not apparent to me, since the other has not been shown to me, I cannot anathematize."

Augustine said: "Should the error that says that God is corruptible be anathematized or should it not be anathematized?"

Felix said: "Say that again."

Augustine said: "Should the error that says that God is corruptible be anathematized or should it not be anathematized?"

Felix said: "Let us see whether Mani says this."

Augustine said: "My question is: Should one who says that God is corruptible be anathematized or not?"

Felix said: "One who says that God is corruptible should be anathematized. Is this what you are asking me?"

Augustine said: "That is my question."

Felix said: "Are you saying that God is corruptible but not what you first said, namely, that he gave a part of himself to his enemies?"

Augustine said: "For now, answer what I am asking. Should one who says that God is corruptible be anathematized or not?"

Felix said: "Certainly."

Augustine said: "Should one who says that the nature and substance of God is corruptible be anathematized or not?"

Felix said: "I did not understand what you said."

Augustine said: "I am saying what everyone understands who does not pretend that he does not understand. Should one who says that the nature and substance of God — that very being, whatever it is, which is God — is corruptible be anathematized or not?"

Felix said: "Yes, he should be anathematized if it is proved that it is true."

Augustine said: "I have not yet said to you that Mani says that the nature of God is corruptible. Rather, I said that whoever says this should be anathematized."

Felix said: "And I replied: 'Yes.'"

15. Augustine said: "The part that was mingled with the nation of darkness: is it of the nature of God or of some other nature?"

Felix said: "Of the nature of God."

Augustine said: "Is that which is of the nature of God identical with God or is it something else that is not God?"

Felix said: "It is this way: what is of God is God in accord with the words of scripture, *The light shined in the darkness, and the darkness did not grasp it* (Jn 1:5), *for God is light, and there is no darkness in him* (1 Jn 1:5)."

Augustine said: "You have replied well that whatever is of the nature of God is God, that God is light, that there is no darkness in him, and that such a light shined in the darkness and the darkness did not grasp it. Let us see whether Mani does not say that a part of God was grasped by the darkness, whether he does not also say that it was held bound, whether he does not also say that it was defiled and polluted in such a way that it needs the mercy of someone to deliver and purify it. But if he says this, he should also be anathematized, according to you and according to your true admissions, because he says that a part of God and the nature of God, which is God himself, was grasped by the darkness, bound, and polluted. Speaking in accord with the gospel, you were not able to say this, but you stated the truth, namely, that *the light shined in the darkness, and the darkness did not grasp it.* Mani should be anathematized, therefore, because he said that the light became dark in the darkness and the darkness grasped it."

Felix said: "But both he who is polluted and he who is held captive are set free, and if we were polluted, we are purified."

Augustine said: "But it is not correct to say this of the nature of God. Rather, it is correct to say of that nature which can be polluted that it is polluted and is purified. But you see how very sacrilegiously it is said of that nature which cannot be polluted, 'It is polluted and is purified,' especially since you say that a certain part of God was polluted and that it was imprisoned for eternity in the sphere of darkness because it could not be purified. He who is not anathematizing this replied falsely a little before that everyone who says that God is corruptible should be anathematized."

16. Felix said: "As for what Your Holiness said, namely, that there is a part that did not purify itself from the defilement of the nation of darkness, Mani puts it this way: they were not admitted to the kingdom of God. For you state that they were condemned, but Mani says that they were not condemned but were placed under the custody of that nation of darkness."

Augustine said: "My discussion with you concerns the part that you say is purified after having been polluted. Afterwards, if necessary, I shall discuss the part that is confined in its sphere. Meanwhile, the part that is being purified had been polluted."

Felix said: "The part that is polluted is also being purified."

Augustine said: "Should not one, then, who says that the nature of God and the substance of God and that which God is can be polluted, bound, and defiled by the nation of darkness, be anathematized?"

Felix said: "From what has Christ purified us? From what has he set us free?"

Augustine said: "Christ did not set free a part of God, the nature of God, but set free by his mercy a creature that he made and that fell into sin by free choice. He purified a being that had been able to be polluted; he set free a being that had been able to be taken captive; he healed a being that had been able to become ill. But now we are speaking about God, about the nature of God, about the substance of God, about what God is. Was it able to be polluted or not?"

17. Felix said: "Is our soul that was polluted from God? If it was not from God, why was Christ crucified for it? If, then, it is clear that Christ was crucified

for the sake of our soul, it is clear that it is from God and had been polluted and that he has purified it."

Augustine said: "I say that not only our soul but also our body and every creature, both spiritual and corporeal, is from God, because the Catholic faith holds this. But that which God has begotten from himself and which is what he is is one thing, but that which God has made is something else. That which God has begotten is equal to the Father; that which God has made is something created, not equal to the creator. But we say that it is one thing to be from God, which is better expressed as 'of God,' because it is what God is, such as his only-begotten Son, such as his Word, by which all things were made.[17] But we say that other things are from God because he spoke and they were made, because he commanded and they were created.[18] Hence, the soul is one of those things that God has made, not something that he has begotten of himself. For this reason the Word that he has begotten was not able and is not able and will not be able to be polluted. But the soul which God has made as the ruler of the body — in order that it might serve what is above it and govern what is beneath it, that is, in order that it might serve God and govern its body — was polluted by sin when it held the law of God in contempt. But so as to offer mercy to those whom he made, God sent his Son, through whom he made them, and he remade them through him. When that which did not exist was to be created, it was created through the Word; when that which had become sinful was to be remade, a creature was assumed from the Virgin Mary in order that, by the fact that he was a man, he might show to man both what we are to endure and what we are to hope for.

"And so the nature of the Word, the substance of the only-begotten Son, did not suffer anything either from the Jews who persecuted him or from the devil, a bad angel, who persecuted him. But because the Word clothed himself with flesh, he clothed himself with something mortal, something able to suffer, something mutable. In that with which he clothed himself he suffered whatever he chose to suffer as an example of patience, and he refashioned it as an example of righteousness. Now, concerning the part of God, concerning that which is God, tell me whether it can or cannot be polluted. If it can, God is not immutable, and someone who says this should be anathematized. But if it cannot, you see that Mani must be anathematized, since he says that a part of God, the nature of God, that which God is, came here as pure to the nation of darkness and was bound and polluted, so that it needs to be released and purified."

18. Felix said: "Did you say that the soul is not from God?"

Augustine said: "I did not say that, but I said that it is from God, yet as something made by God, not as something born from God."

---

17. See Jn 1:3.
18. See Ps 148:5.

Felix said: "You said that the soul is not from God but is a creature of God because without God there is nothing. For that is what you are saying, and you do not want to state that the soul is from God."

Augustine said: "It is from God, but made by God."

Felix said: "Whether made or sent or given, it is from God. If, then, it is from God and if it was polluted and if Christ came to set it free from pollution, why do you find fault with Mani?"

Augustine said: "Because I say that the soul is not the nature of God but that it was made by God, sinned by free choice, was polluted by sin, and was set free by the mercy of God through repentance. But you say that the nature of God, that which God is, God from God, was captured and polluted in the nation of darkness. And there is a big difference between what God begot of himself and what he made not of himself but from nothing. That is, when it did not exist at all, it received from God its existence, so that it would begin to be."

Felix said: "It is therefore a part of God."

Augustine said: "I already told you: it is not a part of God. Listen to how you should understand that God is the almighty creator. All the things that come to be and what anyone makes is either of the agent or from something or from nothing. A human being, because he is not almighty, makes a son of himself. He makes something from something else, as a craftsman makes a chest from wood or makes a cup from silver. He was, after all, able to make the cup, but he was not able to make the silver. He was able to make the chest, but he was not able to make the wood. But no human being is able to make something to be from nothing, that is, from what does not exist at all. But because God is omnipotent, he both begot the Son of himself and made the world from nothing and formed man from the earth, in order to reveal by these three exercises of his power his causality, which is capable of all things. For he should not be said to have made but to have begotten what he made of himself. But as for what he made from something, as he made man of the earth, he did not make man of the earth in such a way that someone else made for him the earth whence he made the man, as God made for the silversmith the silver whence the silversmith made the cup. Rather, he himself both made to exist what did not exist and made to exist what was going to come to be out of what he himself had already created from nothing so that it existed. In this way, then, the soul, in this way the body, in this way every creature is understood to have been made by God, not to have been begotten of God so that it is what God is.

"And so now perhaps you will choose what you will hold and what you will reject. Choose what is better. We see that there are many mutable things and that they are still good, though mutable. We see that there are many mortal things and that they are still good, though mortal. But the absolutely immutable good is God himself. Choose what is better for you to hold: that God is mutable or that what God has made is mutable. For you must pick one of the two. If you are unwilling to admit that what God has made is mutable, it remains for you to say that God is mutable. But in order to free yourself from this sacrilege and from this blasphemy, so that you do not say that the substance of God is mutable, why do you not grant that God — who truly is and is immutable, because he also said, *I am who I am* (Ex 3:14) — has made all things good but not equal to himself? Hence, since he is immutable, it is not surprising if what he has made is not immutable but mutable, because it is not equal to him. And so, it could sin by free choice and be polluted and set free by his mercy."

19. Felix said: "You have said that a man makes a son for himself. There is no difference between a father and his son. Because, then, Your Holiness has said this, I also reply that God and what God has made are equal to each other."

Augustine said: "You have refused to understand that, when a man makes a son, he is not properly said to make but is properly said to generate. In that way I said that God begot and did not make his only Son. But he has made that which is not equal to him. What he has begotten, however, is equal to him. And so, choose for yourself whether you want to say that what God has made is mutable or that the nature of God is mutable."

Felix said: "As God is immutable, he whom he has begotten is likewise immutable, and if what he has made is of his nature, it is not changed."

Augustine said: "But I have already told you that what he has made is not of his nature. Rather, because he is omnipotent, he made it from nothing. It was not, and he made it not of himself, not of something that he had not made, but from nothing." Felix said: "I did not say that. Rather, I said that God is immutable and that what he has begotten is immutable and that what he has made is immutable. I did not say whence he made it. I did not ask whence he made it."

Augustine said: "But you heard from me what you did not ask so that you would stop saying stupid things. Almighty God was able to generate of himself and to make of nothing and to form something from what he had already made: of himself the Son equal to him, of nothing the world and all creation, and from something the man of the earth. For he is omnipotent. What, therefore, is of him can never be polluted as he himself cannot. But what has been made by him, not of him, can be polluted by free choice and can be purified by his mercy if it condemns its sin and acknowledges its creator.

"But you said a little before that one who says that a part of God can be corrupted and defiled should be anathematized, and you cannot deny that Mani said that a part of God was captured and polluted in the nation of darkness, and from these words it is clear that he blasphemed in such a way that he could probably not blaspheme in a worse way. So either anathematize him for saying such things, or you will be anathematized and rejected along with him."

20. Felix said: "Mani says that a part of God was polluted, and Christ says that the soul was polluted and that he came to deliver it from pollution."

Augustine said: "But the soul is not a part of God. For you already admitted that Mani said that a part of God was polluted. We, however, say that the soul was polluted because of the will to sin, but that the soul is not a part of God, was not begotten of God, but was made by God. The soul is said to be from God in the same way as some product of a carpenter is said to be from his art or to have been made by him yet has not been begotten of him, like his offspring.

"Because, then, you have already admitted that Mani said that a part of God was polluted, and since you have some time ago said that one who says that God or his nature is able to be corrupted or defiled should be anathematized, you have already anathematized Mani, though you do not want to admit it. For you said that God is polluted and that he is purified. By the very fact that you say 'He is purified' you have shown that he is polluted, and you have no way to escape. Both Mani and you have said that part of God is polluted. Therefore, anathematize Mani or you must be anathematized along with Mani."

Felix said: "I did not learn from Mani that a part of God was polluted, but I have learned from Christ that he came for the sake of the soul, because it was polluted."

Augustine said: "You did not learn from Christ that the soul is a part of God."

Felix said: "I have learned from Christ that the soul is from God."

Augustine said: "We have also learned that the soul is from God, but not that it is a part of God. For the soul is from God as a product is from an artisan, not of God as a son is of a father."

Felix said: "We are discussing pollution. If the soul, which is from God, was polluted and can be purified by Christ, who came for its sake, that part of God, of which Mani is speaking, can also be polluted and purified by the command of God himself."

Augustine said: "See, again you are saying that a part of God that has been polluted is purified, and a little before you had said that anyone who says that this part of God is corruptible should be anathematized. Now you say that it was able to be polluted, and you say that it can be purified in order to confirm that it was able to be polluted. We do not say this about a part of God, but we say this about the soul, which is from him as his work, not of him as his offspring. Return, then, to what you are saying, and distinguish from it what we are saying, namely, that the soul is neither God nor a part of God. But you say that Mani said that a part of God is polluted, and he says that it is purified in order to confirm that it is polluted. It remains, then, for you to anathematize him or to be anathematized if you hold these views."

21. Felix said: "Does the soul that has been defiled by sin belong to God or not?"

Augustine said: "It belongs to him, but it is not a part of God."

Felix said: "I did not ask that."

Augustine said: "And what did you ask?"

Felix said: "Does it or does it not belong to God?"

Augustine said: "I have already said both that it belongs to him and how it belongs to him."

Felix said: "But I am asking whether it is from God."

Augustine said: "It is from God, not of God."

Felix said: "If there is no sin because the soul is from God and was polluted, and if Christ both came to set it free and has set it free from sin, why do we blame Mani, who says that a part of God was polluted and is again purified?"

Augustine said: "You have already admitted that Mani said that a part of God was polluted, and you say that it is not a sin to pour out such blasphemy on God, but we say that the soul did in fact sin through free choice and is purified through repentance by the mercy of its creator. For it is not from God as part of him or as his offspring, but it is from God and has been made by God as his work. Hence, it is evident to all what the difference is between our faith and your perfidy. And so, according to your previous words, since you have conceded that one who says that the nature of God is corruptible — which it is evident that both Mani and you say — should be anathematized, you will be anathematized along with him since you have been unwilling to anathematize him."

22. After this there was considerable discussion between them, and Felix said, "Tell me now what you want me to do."

Augustine said: "To anathematize Mani, from whom such great blasphemies stem. But if you do it from your heart, then do it. For no one is forcing you against your will."

Felix said: "God sees whether I do it from my heart. For a human being cannot see that. But I ask that you give me your support."

Augustine said: "In what way do you want me to support you?"

Felix said: "Anathematize him first so that I may anathematize him afterwards."

Augustine said: "See, I am writing it with my own hand. For I want you also to write it with your own hand."

Felix said: "But anathematize him in such a way that you anathematize the spirit that was in Mani and that spoke these things through him."

Augustine took the paper and wrote these words: "I, Augustine, a bishop of the Catholic Church, have anathematized Mani and his teaching and the spirit that spoke such indescribable blasphemies through him, because it was a seductive spirit, not the Spirit of the truth but of wicked error. And I now anathematize the aforementioned Mani and the spirit of his error."

And after he had given the same paper to Felix, Felix also wrote these words by his own hand: "I, Felix, who had believed Mani, now anathematize him and his teaching and the seductive spirit that was in him, for he said that God mingled a part of himself with the nation of darkness and sets it free so shamefully that he transformed his powers into female demons before male demons and again into male demons before female demons in such a way that afterwards he confined for eternity a remnant of that part of himself in the sphere of darkness. I condemn all these things and the other blasphemies of Mani."

I, Bishop Augustine, have signed these proceedings in the church in the presence of the people.

I, Felix, have signed these proceedings.

The Nature of the Good

(De natura boni)

Introduction

Augustine lists *The Nature of the Good* in his *Revisions* between the *Answer to Felix, a Manichean* and the *Answer to Secundinus*. Hence, he began *The Nature of the Good* no sooner than the end of 404. The work does not seem to have been occasioned by any particular person or event and contains little that Augustine had not said elsewhere, though it has preserved a long quotation from Mani's *Treasury* as well as three quotations from his letter known as *The Foundation*.

The work can be divided into two main parts. The first part explains the Catholic and Manichean accounts of good and evil by appeal to rational arguments (paragraphs 1 to 23) and then by appeal to scripture (paragraphs 24 to 40). The second and much shorter part explains and refutes the Manichean doctrine of the two principles of good and evil (paragraphs 41-47).

Augustine begins by asserting that God, the highest good, is the immutable good, who has created out of nothing all natures, whether spirits or bodies, and has made them all good, though some are higher goods and others are lower goods. Creatures, which he made from nothing, are mutable, but what God begot of himself is immutable and equal to him (paragraph 1). There are some people, namely, the Manicheans, who introduce another nature that God did not make in order to account for the wickedness of spirits and the mortality of bodies. But since they admit that every good can only come from the highest good, Augustine believes that he can bring them to understand his position (paragraph 2). Catholics worship God from whom come all goods, great or small. Everything that is has some limit, form, and order (in Latin, *modus*, *species*, and *ordo*). A great good has a great limit, form, and order, while a small good has a small limit, form, and order. But where there is no limit, form, or order, there is no nature and nothing at all (paragraph 3). One should ask what evil is before asking where it comes from. Evil is nothing but the corruption of limit, form, and order. A corrupted nature is still good as a nature, though evil as corrupted (paragraph 4). A nature that has received more limit, form, and order remains better when it has been corrupted than a nature that has received less limit, form, and order and has not been corrupted. Thus corrupted gold is better than uncorrupted iron, and a sinful human soul is better than any body that is uncorrupted (paragraph 5). The incorruptible nature, which is God, is the highest good, and every corruptible nature is something good, because it could not be corrupted if it did not have some good to lose (paragraph 6). God granted to rational creatures that they could not be corrupted if they were unwilling to be corrupted. But if they willed to be corrupted by sinning, they are corrupted by punishment, even against their will, for God puts sinners in their proper order by his just punishment (paragraph 7). Lesser creatures are capable neither of happiness nor of unhappiness, but they are all good in their various degrees. In their coming to be and ceasing to be they manifest a certain beauty and do not disturb the limit, form, and order of the created universe (paragraph 8). God determines the proper punishment for each sin. When he forgives a sin, it is a sign of his goodness, and when he punishes a sin, it is a sign of his justice (paragraph 9). Corruptible natures would not be natures if they were not made by God, and they would not be corruptible if they were made of God (paragraph 10). Hence, nothing at all can harm the nature of God, and nothing can unjustly harm a nature under God (paragraph 11).

If the Manicheans paid attention to these ideas, they would not introduce another nature that God did not make and would not locate such great evils in God and such great goods in the greatest evil. It is enough for their correction that they admit that all goods, great and small, come from God (paragraph 12). Augustine lists many goods that are found in various natures, especially the universal goods of limit, form, and order. He points out that, if all these goods were removed, nothing at all would remain (paragraph 13). In comparison with the beauty of higher beings, lesser beings are judged deformed, and some people are misled into thinking of them as evil rather than as lesser goods (paragraph 14). Augustine observes that lesser beings could not be corrupted at all unless they had some limit, form, and order, and, if all limit, form, and order were removed, there would be nothing whatsoever, just as, if all sound were removed, there would be silence (paragraph 15). Privations of sound and of light can add beauty to the universe of natures. We know how to add beauty to our speech by moments of silence, and Augustine says that God, the perfect artist, knows even better how to produce beauty by use of privations (paragraph 16). No nature as a nature is evil, and evil for any nature is merely diminishment in good. But if no good remains, there is no nature remaining either (paragraph 17). Matter, or *hyle*, which the ancient philosophers spoke of, is the absence of all form, but as a capacity for form it is something good. It should not be confused with what the Manicheans call Hyle, namely, what fashions bodies, according to their myth (paragraph 18). God said to Moses, *I am who I am*, thus indicating that he *is* truly, that is, that he is immutable. He who *is* in the highest way can have no contrary except that which is not at all. Hence, every nature comes from him, and every nature is good (paragraph 19). Mental or bodily pain, which some people regard as especially evil, can only exist in a nature that is good. There are worse evils that involve no pain, such as rejoicing over sinfulness. As long as there remains something for corruption to destroy, there remains some good nature (paragraph 20). Small things are said to be modest in size, but if they lacked all limit (*modus*) they would not exist at all. Excessive things become immoderate and are blamed, but under God they are restrained by some limit (paragraph 21). God cannot be said to have a limit lest he be thought to have a boundary, nor can he be said to be immoderate since he gives a limit to all other things. Perhaps, Augustine suggests, God should be called the highest limit, as he is called the highest good (paragraph 22). Augustine explains how we sometimes speak of limit, form, and order as bad when they are less than they should be or are not suitable for the things for which they ought to be suitable. But where there is no limit, form, or order, there is nothing at all (paragraph 23).

Augustine then turns to a proof that the Catholic faith holds what reason has established. Some people, after all, cannot grasp what reason has shown, and others need to be shown that what they can grasp by their intellect is contained in the scriptures. Augustine therefore cites passages of scripture to show that God is immutable and incorruptible and that the Son of God is equal to the Father (paragraph 24). He explains that the words in the Gospel of John, *Without him nothing was made*, are not to be understood in the sense that nothing is something inasmuch as it was said to have been made (paragraph 25). God made all the things that he did not beget, but by his Word he made them from what did not exist at all. Augustine cites a text from 2 Maccabees as well as one from the apostle Paul in support of this (paragraph 26). He distinguishes the Latin pronouns, *ex* ("from") and *de* ("of"), to show that not everything that comes from God is begotten of God (paragraph 27). All natures come from God, but sins, which do not preserve natures but damage them, do not come from him. Scripture shows that sins come from the wills of sinners (paragraph 28). Though all things that God created are in him, sins do not defile God, since he is incorruptible and immutable, as Augustine shows from the Book of Wisdom (paragraph 29). Augustine also demonstrates from scripture that all bodily things come from God (paragraph 30). So too, the apostle Paul says that God alone is the judge of the punishment due to any sin, that the goodness of God forgives the sins of those who turn to him, and that God punishes sinners without any injustice (paragraph 31). Scripture explains that God gives some people the power to harm others, and in that way he tests the patience of good people and punishes the sinfulness of the evil (paragraph 32). Scripture asserts as well that the bad angels or devils were created good but became evil by their sinning. They have already received this lower heaven as their place of punishment but are destined for the eternal fires of hell after the judgment (paragraph 33). According to scripture, every creature of God is good. Hence, sin is not the desire for an evil nature but the abandonment of better goods for lesser ones against the command of the creator (paragraph 34). God did not forbid Adam to touch the fruit of the tree in paradise because it was evil but in order to teach the man that he ought to be subject to God (paragraph 35). Even the thorns and thistles, which the earth brought forth as punishment for sin, have their limit, form, and order, though they are bad for the nature that needs to be restrained by them. Sin is the misuse of a good nature, not the use of a bad one (paragraph 36). Even by sinning we do not defeat the will of God, for he knows how to put sinners in their proper order through punishment if they become disordered through sin (paragraph 37). The eternal fire of hell itself is a good nature, though it is evil for those who merit punishment in it (paragraph 38). Though the fire of hell is eternal, it is not eternal in the same way in which God is eternal, for his eternity is true immortality and the highest immutability (paragraph 39). Augustine insists that everything that he has said is in accord with the Catholic faith. Hence, no one can harm the nature of God, nor can the nature of God harm anyone unjustly or allow anyone to do harm with impunity (paragraph 40).

If the Manicheans were willing to consider these points, they would not in their blasphemy introduce the two natures, one good and the other evil. But they are so insane that in their myths they locate in the evil nature many great goods, as Augustine amply illustrates by examples, and in the good nature of God they locate many great evils, as Augustine also shows (paragraph 41). Furthermore, the Manicheans hold that some souls, which are a part of God's nature and which did not sin of their own accord, were sent to make war against the nation of darkness. And, having come down at the Father's command, they were taken prisoner by the enemy. God, moreover, was unable to set all of these souls free, and some of them will be confined forever in the sphere of darkness. Augustine quotes from *The Foundation* to show that, according to Mani, God feared ruin and devastation for his kingdoms, though they could not, he had said, be moved or shaken by anything. Though these souls did not sin by their will, they will be confined in the sphere of darkness for all eternity. And yet Mani also says quite inconsistently that these souls are confined there because they loved the darkness (paragraph 42).

According to the Manichean myth there were great evils in the nature of the light or of God before the mingling of the two natures. For, even before the conflict, the nature of the light was under the harsh necessity of having to fight. Or, if there was no such necessity, the nature of light went to war willingly. Hence, there was in the nature of God the will to do himself such great harm that he mingled himself with the darkness, was purified so shamefully, and was eternally condemned in part. Thus, before he had been mingled with evil, there was in God the evil of a wicked and destructive will. Or, if he was ignorant of what was going to happen, there was the great evil of such ignorance. Hence, Augustine insists that there was great evil in the nature of the good before it was in any way mingled with evil (paragraph 43). The Manicheans say that a part of the nature of God is mingled everywhere in the heavens, on the earth, and under the earth, in all bodies and in all seeds. The nature of God is not merely present there by the power of the divinity but is bound, oppressed, and polluted there. In order to purify and set free the parts of God held captive, the powers of God transformed themselves into handsome youths and fair virgins in order to arouse the passions of their opposite numbers in the nation of darkness and cause the emission of the divine substance "in order that the divine majesty may find ways of emerging through the genitals of demons," as Evodius puts it quite bluntly in his work entitled *Faith* (paragraph 44). The Manicheans also say that the part of God that was mingled with evil is set free by the Elect when they eat and drink bright foods and liquids and when they subsequently belch. Since the Manicheans hold that a part of God is held bound in all seeds, Augustine argues that the Elect, if they act consistently with their belief, must do what they read in their *Treasury* was done by the power of the heavens and the princes and princesses of darkness. For their own bodies also have the vital divine substance bound in them (paragraph 45). Augustine quotes another long passage from *The Foundation*, in which Mani describes how the princes of darkness created the first man in order to retain the light and prevent its escaping from them (paragraph 46). Augustine points out that, if a part of God is bound in human flesh by sexual intercourse and conception, and if the Elect are to purify parts of God by eating and drinking, it follows that they should set their God free not only by eating bread and vegetables and fruits but also by eating that by which a part of God is bound in the womb. Augustine claims to have heard that this sort of thing was done in various places, though he admits that the Manicheans deny it. In any case he insists that, regardless of their practice, the Manichean belief should force them to purify the light from whatever seeds they can (paragraph 47). Finally, Augustine prays that through his ministry God may set other Manicheans free from their terrible error just as he has already set some free (paragraph 48).

Revisions II, 9 (36)

The Nature of the Good, One Book

The book, *The Nature of the Good*, is against the Manicheans. In it I show that God is the immutable nature and the highest good; that other natures, whether spiritual or corporeal, come from him; and that they are all good insofar as they are natures; as well as what evil is and where it comes from; and the great evils that the Manicheans locate in the nature of the good and the great goods that they locate in the nature of evil — natures that their error has invented.

This book begins as follows: "The highest good, than which there is none higher, is God."

The Nature of the Good

1. The highest good, than which there is none higher, is God, and for this reason he is the immutable good and therefore truly eternal and truly immortal. All other goods are made only *by* him but are not made *of* him. For that which is of him is what he is, but those things which have been made by him are not what he is. And for this reason he alone is immutable, while all the things that he has made are mutable because he has made them from nothing. For he is so almighty that he can make good things, great and small, heavenly and earthly, spiritual and corporeal, of nothing, that is, of what does not exist at all. But because he is just, he did not make the things which he made of nothing equal to that which he begot of himself. Because, therefore, all goods, whether great or small, through any levels of reality, can only be made by God, but every nature insofar as it is a nature is something good, no nature can be made except by the highest and true God. For all goods, even though not the highest goods but close to the highest good, and — again — all goods, even the last, which are far from the highest good, can be made only by the highest good. Every spirit, therefore, even though a mutable one, and every body is made by God. These are all the natures that have been made. Every nature is, indeed, either a spirit or a body. God is an immutable spirit; a mutable spirit is a nature that has been made, but one better than a body. But a body is not a spirit, except when the wind is said to be a spirit in a certain sense, because it is invisible to us and we still feel its great force.

2. But there are those who cannot understand that every nature, that is, every spirit and every body, is naturally something good. They are disturbed by the wickedness of the spirit and the mortality of the body and, for this reason, try to introduce another nature for the evil spirit and the mortal body, which God has not made. We think that in what follows we can bring them to understand what we are saying. After all, they say that everything good can only come from the highest and true God, and this is both true and sufficient for correcting them, if they are willing to pay attention.

3. For we Catholic Christians worship God, from whom all goods come, whether great or small, from whom all limit comes, whether great or small, from whom all form comes, whether great or small, and from whom all order comes, whether great or small. For it is certainly the case that all things are better to the extent that they are more limited, formed, and ordered. But they are less good to the extent that they are less limited, less formed, and less ordered. These three, then, limit, form, and order — to pass over in silence countless features that are shown to pertain to these three — these three, then, limit, form, and order, are

like universal goods in the things made by God, whether in a spirit or in a body. God is therefore above every limit of a creature, above every form, above every order. He is not above them by spatial distance but by his ineffable and singular power, for from him comes all limit, all form, and all order. Where these three are great, there are great goods; where they are small, there are small goods; where they are not at all, there is no good. And again, where these three are great, there are great natures; where they are small, there are small natures; where they are not at all, there is no nature. Every nature, therefore, is good.

4. Hence, when the question arises where evil comes from, one should first ask what evil is. For it is nothing but the corruption of either a natural limit or form or order. A nature that has been corrupted, then, is said to be evil. For an uncorrupted nature is certainly good. But even a corrupted nature is good insofar as it is a nature, while it is evil insofar as it has been corrupted.

5. But it is possible that a certain nature that has received a more excellent order by its natural limit and form is still better, even when corrupted, than another uncorrupted nature that has received a lower order with a lesser natural limit and form. For example, in the judgment of human beings, in terms of the quality that is exposed to their eyes, gold, even when corrupted, is certainly better than uncorrupted silver, and silver, even when corrupted, is better than uncorrupted lead. In that way, in natures that are more powerful and spiritual, a rational spirit, even when corrupted by an evil will, is better than an uncorrupted non-rational spirit. And any spirit, even when corrupted, is better than any uncorrupted body. For a nature that, when it is present to a body, gives it life is better than the nature to which life is given. But, however corrupt may be the spirit of life that has been made, it can give life to the body, and, for this reason, even when it has been corrupted it is better than an uncorrupted body.

6. But if corruption takes away all limit, all form, and all order from corruptible things, no nature will remain. And for this reason every nature that cannot be corrupted is the highest good, as God is. But every nature that can be corrupted is itself also something good. For corruption could harm it only by taking away or lessening what is good.

7. To the most excellent creatures, that is, to rational spirits, God has granted that they cannot be corrupted if they are unwilling, that is, if they preserve obedience under the Lord, their God, and in that way cling to his incorruptible beauty. But if they are unwilling to preserve obedience, they are corrupted by punishment against their will, because they were willingly corrupted by sins. God is of course such a good that no one who abandons him is well off, and, among the things that God has made, the rational nature is so great a good that there is no good but God by which it may be happy. Sinners, therefore, are put in order by punishments, and because their being put in order is not in accord with their nature, it is punishment, but because it is in accord with their sin, it is justice.

8. But the other things that have been made of nothing, which are of course lower than the rational spirit, can be neither happy nor unhappy. But since in accord with their own limit and form they are good, and since, though they are lesser and the least goods, they could not come except from God, the highest good, they are set in order in such a way that the less stable yield to the more stable, the less strong to the stronger, and the less powerful to the more powerful, and in that way earthly things are in harmony with heavenly ones as subject to those that are more excellent. But as things withdraw and others take their place, there is produced a certain temporal beauty of its own kind, so that not even those that die or cease to be what they were defile and disturb the limit, form, and order of the whole of creation. In the same way a well-structured speech is certainly beautiful, though all the syllables and sounds in it pass on as if by being born and dying.

9. It is up to God's judgment, not to human judgment, what kind of and how much punishment is due to each sin. When this punishment is remitted for those who turn to him, there is great goodness on the part of God, and, when the due punishment is exacted, there is no injustice on the part of God. For it is better that a nature be set in order so that it may grieve in punishment rather than rejoice with impunity in sin. This nature, nonetheless, which has some limit, form, and order in however small an amount, is still something good. And if these are completely removed or entirely consumed, there will then be no good, because no nature will remain.

10. All corruptible natures, therefore, would not be natures at all if they were not made by God, and they would not be corruptible if they were made of him, because they would be what he is. And so they exist with whatever limit, whatever form, whatever order they have, because it is God who has made them. But they are not immutable, because that whence they have been made is nothing. For it would be an act of sacrilegious daring to set God and nothing on a par if we wanted that which has been made of nothing by him to be the same as that which has been born of him.

11. Hence, the nature of God cannot be harmed at all, and no nature under God can be harmed unjustly. For, when some people do harm unjustly by sinning, an unjust will is imputed to them, but the power by which they are permitted to do harm comes only from God, who, even though they do not know it, knows what those whom he permits them to harm deserve to suffer.

12. If those who introduce another nature that God did not make were willing to pay attention to all these points, which are so clear and so certain, they would not be filled with such great blasphemies that they locate such great goods in the greatest evil and such great evils in God. For, as I said above, what the truth forces them to admit against their will, namely, that all goods certainly come only from God, suffices for their correction, if they would pay attention. The great goods, then, do not come from someone other than the one from whom the

small goods come, but the great and the small goods come only from the highest good, which is God.

13. Let us recall as many goods as we can, which it is right that we should attribute to God as their creator, and, once these have been removed, let us see whether any nature remains. All life, both great and small, all power, both great and small, all health, both great and small, all memory, both great and small, all understanding, both great and small, all tranquility, both great and small, all strength, both great and small, all abundance, both great and small, all aware-ness, both great and small, all light, both great and small, all pleasantness, both great and small, all measure, both great and small, all beauty, both great and small, all peace, both great and small, and anything else of the sort that can come to mind, especially those things that are found in everything, whether spiritual or corporeal, that is, all limit, all form, and all order, both great and small, come from the Lord God. And whoever chooses to make bad use of all these goods will pay the penalty under God's judgment. But where none of these is at all, no nature will remain.

14. In all these things those that are small are, in comparison with greater ones, called by their opposite names. In that way, because there is greater beauty in the form of a human being, the beauty of an ape is said to be deformed in comparison with it. And this deceives those who lack wisdom into supposing that the former is good and the latter evil. In the body of the ape they do not notice its proper limit, the equality of its members on either side, the harmony of its parts, the preservation of its soundness, and the other things that it would take too long to run through.

15. But so that what we are saying may be understood and be satisfactory for those who are very slow, or so that even those who are stubborn and quite openly resist the truth may be forced to admit what is true, let them be asked whether corruption can do harm to the body of an ape. If it can, so that it becomes more ugly, what does it diminish but the good of beauty? Some of it will remain as long as the nature of the body exists. Hence, if the nature is destroyed when the good is removed, the nature is therefore good. In the same way we say that slow is contrary to fast, but someone who does not move at all cannot be said even to be slow. In the same way we say that a low sound is contrary to a high one and a rough sound to a smooth one. But if we remove all the form of a sound, there is a silence where there is no sound at all. This silence, nonetheless, is often counted as the contrary to sound because of the very fact that it is no sound. In that way light and dark are also spoken of as two contraries. Obscure things, nonetheless, have some light, and if they completely lack light, darkness exists because of the absence of light, just as silence exists because of the absence of sound.

16. Yet even these privations of things have such an order in the world of nature that those who consider them wisely see that they occur in a fitting manner. For, by not giving light to certain places and times, God also made dark-

ness just as appropriately as daylight. After all, if by holding back our voice we fittingly inject a silence in our speaking, how much more did he as the perfect artisan of all things fittingly produce privations of certain things? For this reason light and darkness also praise God in that hymn of the three boys;[1] that is, they bring forth his praise in the hearts of those who consider them well.

17. No nature, therefore, is evil insofar as it is a nature, but for any nature there is no evil except to be diminished in good. And if the good were completely removed by being diminished, just as no good would be left, neither would any nature be left — not merely the sort of nature that the Manicheans introduce, in which we find such great goods that their excessive blindness is amazing, but also the sort of nature that anyone might introduce.

18. Nor, after all, should even the matter that the ancients called *hyle* be said to be an evil. I do not mean what Mani, not knowing what he is saying, calls Hyle in his utterly insane folly, namely, the fashioner of bodies. For this reason we are correct to say to him that he introduces another God, since no one but God can fashion and create bodies. For they are only created when they have limit, form, and order, features that I think even the Manicheans admit are good and can only come from God. Rather, I mean by *hyle* a certain utterly formless and quality-less matter, from which these qualities that we perceive are formed, as the ancients said. Hence, wood too is called ὕλε in Greek because it is suited for workers, not in order that it might make something but in order that something might be made out of it. Nor should we, therefore, call an evil this *hyle*, which cannot be perceived through some form but can scarcely be thought of on account of its complete privation of form. For it itself also has a capacity for forms. After all, if it could not receive a form imposed on it by an artisan, it would not even be called matter. But if form is something good, for which reason those who excel in it are called well-formed, just as the beautiful are so called by reason of beauty, the capacity for form is undoubtedly also something good. In the same way, because wisdom is something good, no one doubts that to be capable of wisdom is something good. And because every good comes from God, no one ought to doubt that this matter, if there is any such thing, comes only from God.

19. Our God, therefore, said in a magnificent and divine manner to his servant, *I am who I am*, and, *You shall say to the children of Israel, He who is sent me to you* (Ex 3:14). For he truly is because he is immutable. Every change, after all, makes that which was not to be. He who is immutable, then, truly is. Other things, which have been made by him, have received being from him according to their limit. To him, therefore, who truly is there cannot be anything contrary except that which is not, and, for this reason, just as everything that is good comes from him, so everything that is natural comes from him, because

---

1. See Dn 3:51.72.

everything that exists naturally is something good. Every nature, therefore, is good, and everything good comes from God. Every nature, therefore, comes from God.

20. Even pain, however, which some persons consider especially evil, whether it is in the mind or in the body, cannot exist except in good natures. For that which resists, so that in some way it feels pain, refuses to cease to be what it was because it was something good. But when it is forced to something better, pain is beneficial; when it is forced to something worse, it is harmful. When the will resists a greater power, therefore, it produces pain in the mind. When the senses resist a more powerful body, they produce pain in the body. But there are worse evils that are without pain. For it is worse to rejoice over wickedness than to feel pain from corruption. Such joy, nonetheless, can only exist as the result of the acquisition of lower goods, but wickedness is the abandonment of better goods. Likewise, in the body a wound with pain is better than decay without pain, which is what is specifically called corruption. The dead body of the Lord did not see, that is, did not suffer, this corruption, as was foretold in the prophecy: *You will not allow your holy one to see corruption* (Ps 15:10). For who would deny that his body was wounded by the hammering in of the nails and pierced by the lance?[2] But if that which everyone calls the corruption of the body in the proper sense, that is, decay, still has something further to consume, the corruption increases by diminishing the good. And if it completely removes it, just as no good will remain, neither will any nature remain, because there will not be anything for corruption to corrupt. And so the decay will not exist either, because there will be nowhere for it to be.

21. Small and even tiny things are, of course, said to be modest in our common way of speaking because some limit remains in them; without it they are no longer modest but non-existent. But things that are called immoderate on account of their excessive increase are blamed for this very excess. Under God, nonetheless, even they must be restrained by some limit, because he arranged *all things in measure and in number and weight* (Wis 11:21).

22. God should not be said to have a limit, lest anyone think that this limit is his end. Nor should he be thought to be unlimited who gives a limit to all things so that they may exist in some way. On the other hand, God should not be said to be limited as if he received a limit from something. But if we say that he is the highest limit, we perhaps say something, at least if we understand the highest good in that which we call the highest limit. Every limit, after all, is good insofar as it is a limit; hence, all things that are limited, observe a limit, or are made limited can only be spoken of with praise, although with another understanding we may speak of a limit instead of an end, and we may say that there is no limit where there is no end. At times this is said as praise, as when we say, *And his*

---

2. See Jn 19:34; 20:25.

kingdom will have no end (Lk 1:33). For it could also be said, "It will have no limit," so that "limit" would be understood to have been said instead of *end*. For one who in no way reigns certainly does not reign.

23. Limit or form or order, then, are said to be bad either because they are less than they ought to be or because they are not suitable for the things for which they should be suited. Thus they are said to be bad because they are strange or unsuitable — for example, if someone is said not to have acted in a good way because he did less than he ought to have, or because he acted in such a way as he ought not to have acted in such and such a matter, or because he did more than he ought to have done or did it unsuitably. As a result, that which is blamed as having been done in a bad way is blamed only because the limit was not preserved in that case. Likewise, form is said to be bad either in comparison with something better formed or more beautiful, because one form is less and another greater not in mass but in beauty, or because it does not fit with the particular thing to which it is applied — so that it would seem strange and unsuitable, for example, if a man were to walk about naked in the forum, which is something that would cause no offense in the baths. Similarly, order is also said to be bad when the order itself is less observed. Hence, in that case not the order but rather the disorder is bad. Still, where there is some limit, some form, and some order, there is some good and some nature. But where there is no limit, no form, and no order, there is no good and no nature.

24. These truths, which our faith contains and reason has to some extent investigated, must be defended by the testimonies of the divine scriptures so that those who cannot attain them because of their weaker intellect may believe in the divine authority and in that way merit to understand. Those who do understand, however, but are less learned in the writings of the Church should not suppose that we produce these truths from our own intellect rather than that they are present in those books. And so it is written thus in the Psalms that God is immutable: *You will change them, and they shall be changed. But you are the self-same* (Ps 101:27-28), and in the Book of Wisdom it says of wisdom itself: *Remaining in itself, it renews all things* (Wis 7:27). Hence, the apostle Paul also says, *To the invisible, incorruptible God alone* (1 Tm 1:17), and the apostle James says, *Every best gift and every perfect gift is from above, coming down from the Father of lights, in whom there is no variation or shadow of change* (Jas 1:17). Likewise, the Son says in a few words that what the Father begot of himself is the same as he is: *The Father and I are one* (Jn 10:30). But because the Son was not made, although all things were of course made through him, scripture says, *In the beginning was the Word, and the Word was with God, and the Word was God. He was in the beginning with God. All things were made through him, and without him there was made nothing* (Jn 1:1-3), that is, nothing was made without him.

25. Now we should not listen to the ravings of human beings who think that we should understand *nothing* in this passage to mean "something," and who think that a person is forced into such vanity because *nothing* is placed at the end of the sentence. "Therefore," they say, "it was made, and because it was made, it is something; the nothing is something." For they have lost their mind out of their desire to contradict, and they do not understand that there is no difference whether one says, *Without him there was made nothing,* or, "Without him nothing was made." After all, even if it were said in that order, "Without him nothing was made," they could still say that the nothing was something because it was made. In the case of something that really exists, what difference is there whether one says, "Without him there was made a house," or, "Without him a house was made," provided it is understood that something was made without him and that the something is a house? And so, because it says, *Without him there was made nothing,* and because nothing is certainly not something when it is said in its true and proper sense, nothing is different whether one says, *Without him there was made nothing,* or, "Without him nothing was made." But who would want to speak with people who can say of what I said, "Nothing is different," "Therefore, something is different, because nothing is itself something"? But those who have a sound mind see the perfectly plain fact that the same thing was understood when I said, "Nothing is different," as would be understood if I said, "Different is nothing." But if they say to someone, "What did you do?" and he replies that he did nothing, it follows that they should attack him, saying, "Therefore you did something because you did nothing. For nothing is something." But they have the Lord himself as well, when he puts this word at the end of the sentence, where he says, *And in secret I have said nothing* (Jn 18:20). Let them read, then, and be silent.

26. Consequently, because all the things that God did not beget of himself but made through his Word he made not of things that were already existing but of things that did not exist at all — that is, of nothing — the apostle speaks as follows: *He calls those things that do not exist as well as those that do* (Rom 4:17). But it is expressed more clearly in the Book of Maccabees: *I beg you, my son, look at the heavens and the earth and all the things that are in them. See and realize that the things from which the Lord God made us did not exist.* (2 Mac 7:28) And from what is written in the psalm, *He spoke, and they were made* (Ps 148:5), it is evident that he did not beget them of himself but made them by his word and command. But what he did not beget of himself he certainly made of nothing. For there was nothing else whence to make them. The apostle speaks most clearly about this: *For from him and through him and in him are all things* (Rom 11:36).

27. "From him" does not means the same thing as "of him." After all, what is of him can be said to be from him, but not everything that is from him can correctly be said to be of him. For the heavens and the earth are from him,

because they were made by him, but not of him, because they are not of his substance. In the same way, if a man begets a son and builds a house, the son comes from him and the house comes from him, but the son is of him, while the house is of earth and wood. But this is because he is a human being who cannot make something of nothing. But God, from whom all things are, through whom all things are, and in whom all things are, did not need some matter that he had not made to help his omnipotence.

28. When, however, we hear, *From him and through him and in him are all things* (Rom 11:36), we ought surely to understand all the natures that exist naturally. After all, sins, which do not preserve but damage a nature, do not come from him. Holy scripture testifies in many ways that sins come from the wills of sinners, especially in that passage where the apostle says, *Do you, a human being who judges those who do such actions, though you yourself also do them, think that you will escape the judgment of God? Or do you hold in contempt the riches of his kindness and patience and forbearance, unaware that the patience of God is leading you to repentance? But, in keeping with the hardness of your heart and your impenitent heart, you store up wrath for yourself on the day of wrath and of the revelation of the just judgment of God, who will repay each one according to his works.* (Rom 2:3-6)

29. And yet, although all the things that God created are in him, those who sin do not defile him. Of his wisdom it is said, *But it reaches all things on account of its purity, and nothing defiled enters into it* (Wis 7:24-25). For, just as we believe that God is incorruptible and immutable, so must we believe as a consequence that he cannot be defiled.

30. But that he made even the least goods, that is, earthly and mortal ones, is undoubtedly signified in that passage of the apostle where, in speaking of the members of our flesh, he says, *If one member is honored, all the members rejoice along with it, and if one member suffers, all the members suffer along with it* (1 Cor 12:26). He also says there, *God put each of the members in the body as he wanted* (1 Cor 12:18), and, *God balanced things in the body, giving greater honor to that which lacked it, so that there would not be a division in the body but so that each of the members might have the same care for one another* (1 Cor 12:24-25). But what the apostle praises in that way in the limit, form, and order of the members of the flesh, you find in the flesh of all animals, both the largest and the smallest, though all flesh is reckoned to be among earthly goods and for this reason among the least goods.

31. Likewise, because the kind and amount of punishment that any sin deserves is up to God's and not man's judgment, scripture says, *O the depth of the riches of the wisdom and knowledge of God! How inscrutable are his judgments and unsearchable his ways!* (Rom 11:33) Likewise, the very fact that Christ was sent shows clearly enough that the goodness of God forgives the sins of those who turn to him. He died for us, not in his own nature, by which he was

God, but in our nature, which he assumed from a woman. The apostle proclaims the goodness of God in our regard and his love for us as follows. He says, *God shows his love for us in that, while we were still sinners, Christ died for us. For much better reason, having been made righteous in his blood, we shall be saved from wrath through him. After all, if when we were enemies we were reconciled to God through the death of his Son, for much better reason, after having been reconciled, we shall be saved in his life.* (Rom 5:8-10) But because even sinners receive the punishment they deserve and there is no injustice in God, he says, *What shall we say? Is God unjust in showing his wrath?* (Rom 3:5) In one passage, however, he warned that both goodness and severity come from him, where he says, *You see, therefore, the goodness and the severity of God, his severity toward those who have fallen, but his goodness toward you if you remain in goodness* (Rom 11:22).

32. So too, the power of those who do harm comes only from God. For, in the words of Wisdom, scripture says, *By me kings reign, and tyrants possess the earth through me* (Prv 8:15-16). And the apostle says, *There is no power save from God* (Rom 13:1). But in the Book of Job it says that this happens in accord with what the people deserve: *He makes a hypocrite reign on account of the perversity of the people* (Jb 1:12). And God says of the people of Israel, *I gave them a king in my anger* (Hos 13:11). For it is not unjust that the patience of good persons is tested and that the wickedness of evil is punished when wicked persons receive the power to do harm. Job, after all, was tested by the power given to the devil in order that he would be seen as righteous,[3] and Peter was tempted in order that he would not place his trust in himself,[4] and Paul was struck in order that he would not be filled with pride,[5] and Judas was condemned in order that he would hang himself.[6] Therefore, although God did all things justly through the power he gave to the devil, he will be punished in the end, not for the actions that were done justly but for the wicked will to do harm, which the devil had. Then God will say to the wicked, who continued to consent to the wickedness of the devil, *Enter into the eternal fire that my Father has prepared for the devil and his angels* (Mt 25:41).

33. But, because even the bad angels were not created by God as evil but became evil by sinning, this is what Peter says in his letter, *For God did not spare the angels when they sinned, but he thrust them into the prisons of the lower darkness and handed them over to be kept there in order to be punished at the judgment* (2 Pt 2:4). Here Peter showed that they still have coming to them the punishment of the last judgment, of which the Lord says, *Enter into the eternal fire that has been prepared for the devil and his angels* (Mt 25:41).

---

3. See Jb 1:6-2:10.
4. See Mt 26:31-35.69-75.
5. See 2 Cor 12:7.
6. See Mt 27:5.

Though even now they have received this lower world in punishment, that is, the lower dark air, as a prison, it is nonetheless called heaven — not that heaven in which the stars are found but this lower heaven whose clouds are formed out of fog and in which the birds fly. For we speak of the cloudy heaven and the birds of heaven. In this sense the apostle Paul calls those same wicked angels *the spirits of wickedness in the heavens* (Eph 6:12), who are envious of us and against whom we fight by living pious lives. So that we might not understand this as referring to the higher heavens, he clearly says elsewhere, *In accord with the prince of the power of this air, who is now at work in the children of unbelief* (Eph 2:2).

34. Likewise, since sin or wickedness is not to desire evil natures but to abandon better ones, we find it stated in the scriptures, *Every creature of God is good* (1 Tm 4:4), and for this reason every tree that God planted in paradise is certainly good. The man, then, did not desire an evil nature when he touched the forbidden tree, but he himself committed an evil act by abandoning what was better. The creator is, of course, better than any creature he created. His commandment ought not to have been abandoned in order that Adam might touch what was forbidden, though good. For, by abandoning what was better, he sought the good of a creature, which he touched contrary to the commandment of the creator. God, then, did not plant an evil tree in paradise, but he himself, who forbade that it be touched, was better.

35. For he had forbidden this in order to show that the nature of the rational soul was not in its own power but ought to be subject to God, and that it preserves the order of its own well-being through obedience but destroys it through disobedience. For this reason he called the tree that he forbade the man to touch *the tree of the knowledge of good and evil* (Gn 2:9), because, when he touched it contrary to the prohibition, he would experience the punishment of sin, and in that way he would learn the difference between the good of obedience and the evil of disobedience.

36. For who is so foolish as to think that he should find fault with a creature of God, especially one planted in paradise? After all, it is not right to find fault even with the thorns and thistles that, in accord with the sentence of God's judgment, the earth brought forth in order to wear out[7] the sinner in his labor. For such plants have their own limit, form, and order, and whoever considers them seriously will find them praiseworthy. But they are evil for that nature that needed to be restrained because of the merit of sin. As I said, to sin, then, is not to desire an evil nature but to abandon a better one, and so the act itself is evil, not the nature of which one makes bad use in sinning. Evil is making bad use of a good thing. Hence, the apostle blames certain persons who were condemned by God's judg-

---

7. I have followed the reading *conterendo*, found in four manuscripts, rather than *conterendos*, which the CSEL edition has.

ment because *they worshiped and served a creature rather than the creator* (Rom 1:25). For he does not blame the creature — since one who does that does injury to God — but blames those who have made bad use of a good thing by abandoning something better.

37. Hence, if all natures would preserve their own limit, form, and order, there will be no evil. But even if anyone chooses to make bad use of these goods, he does not in this way defeat the will of God, who knows how to justly set in order even the unjust. Thus, if through the wickedness of their will they make a bad use of his goods, through the justice of his power he makes good use of their evils, setting in correct order through punishments those who have set themselves in a perverse order through sins.

38. For even the eternal fire that will torment the wicked is not an evil nature, since it has its own limit, form, and order, which have not been ruined by any wickedness. But its torment is evil for the damned whose sins deserve it. After all, this daylight is not an evil nature because it torments inflamed eyes.

39. But the eternal fire is not eternal in the way that God is because, though it is without end, it is nonetheless not without a beginning. God, however, is also without a beginning. Secondly, because, though perpetual fire is applied for the punishment of sins, it is still a mutable nature. But true eternity is true immortality, that is, that supreme immutability that God alone has, who cannot change in any way. For it is one thing not to change though one is able to change, and it is something else not to be able to change. Just as, therefore, a man is said to be good, but still not in the same way as God, of whom scripture says, *No one is good but the one God* (Mk 10:18), so the soul is said to be immortal, but not in the same way as God, of whom scripture says, *He alone has immortality* (1 Tm 6:16). And just as a man is said to be wise, but not in the same way as God, of whom scripture says, *To God who alone is wise* (Rom 16:27), so fire is said to be eternal, but not in the same way as God, whose immortality alone is true eternity.

40. Since this is the way things are, in accord with the Catholic faith and sound doctrine and the truth, which is evident to those with understanding, no one can do harm to the nature of God, and the nature of God cannot do harm to anyone unjustly and does not permit anyone to do harm with impunity. *For*, the apostle says, *one who does harm will suffer the harm he has done, and God shows no partiality* (Col 3:25).

41. If the Manicheans were willing to bear this in mind without a destructive desire to defend their error and with a fear of God, they would not blaspheme in a most criminal way by introducing two natures — a good one, which they call God, and another, an evil one, which God did not make. They are so mistaken, so out of their minds, so raving mad, in fact, that they do not see that they are attributing great goods to that which they call the nature of the greatest evil when they are attributing to it life, power, health, memory, understanding, balance, strength, abundance, awareness, light, pleasantness, measures, numbers, peace,

limit, form, and order, while to that which they call the highest good they are attributing great evils — death, sickness, forgetfulness, folly, turmoil, weakness, need, insensitivity, blindness, pain, injustice, disgrace, war, lack of moderation, ugliness, and perversity.

They say that the princes of darkness both lived in their own nature and were safe in their kingdom and that they both remembered and understood. For they say that the prince of darkness delivered a speech of the sort that without memory and understanding he could not have delivered and those to whom he spoke could not have heard. They say that the princes of darkness had a balance suited to their body and mind and that they reigned in virtue of their power, had an abundance of their elements and of fecundity, were aware of one another and the light near them, and had eyes by which to see the light from afar. These eyes, of course, could not see the light without some light. For this reason eyes are also correctly called lights. They say that they enjoyed the sweetness of their pleasure and were determinate in the measure of their members and abodes. But unless there were some sort of beauty there, they would not love their spouses, and their bodies would not have the suitability of their parts. If this did not exist there, the things that in their madness they say happened there could not happen there. And unless there were some peace there, they would not obey their prince. Unless there were limit there, they would eat, drink, rage, or do anything else without becoming satisfied. And yet not even those who were doing this would have been determinate in their forms unless there were a limit there. But now they say that those princes did such things that they cannot deny that in all their actions they had limits suited to themselves. Unless, however, there were form there, no natural quality would exist there. Unless there were order there, some would not be masters and others would not be subjects. They would not live suitably in their elements, and, finally, they would not have members arranged in their places so that they could do all those silly things that in their myths the Manicheans say that they do.

But if they do not say that the nature of God died, what according to their nonsense does Christ raise up? If they do not say that it is ill, what does he cure? If they do not say that it forgot, what does he remind it of? If they do not say that it lacks wisdom, what does he teach it? If they do not say that it was disturbed, why does he restore it? If it was not conquered and captured, what does he set free? If it is not in need, what does he help out? If it has not lost awareness, what does he arouse? If it was not blinded, what does he enlighten? If it is not in pain, what does he relieve? If it is not sinful, what does he correct by his commandments? If it was not defiled, what does he cleanse? If it is not at war, to what does he promise peace? If it has not gone beyond the limit, on what does he impose a limit by his law? If it is not deformed, what does he restore to form? If it is not disordered, what does he correct? After all, the Manicheans say that Christ bestows all of this not on that creature which God made, which was ruined through sinning by its own choice, but on the very nature, the very substance, of God, which is identical with God.

42. What can be compared with these blasphemies? Absolutely nothing, if we consider the errors of other perverse sects. But if this error is compared with itself in another aspect, about which we have not yet spoken, it is shown to blaspheme still much worse and more detestably against the nature of God. For they say that some souls, which they want to be of the substance of God and of the very same nature, did not sin voluntarily but were defeated and overcome by the nation of darkness, which they call the nature of evil. They say that these souls came down, not of their own accord but by the command of the Father, to make war against the nation of darkness, and that these souls are detained for eternity in the horrible sphere of darkness. In that way, in accord with their sacrilegious nonsense, God set himself free from a great evil in a certain part and again condemned himself in a certain part, which he could not set free from the enemy and over which, in addition, he triumphed as if over an enemy who had been completely conquered. O the wicked and incredible audacity of believing such things, of saying such things, and of preaching such things about God! When they try to defend this, in order that they may rush into worse things with their eyes closed, they say that the mingling with the evil nature causes the good nature of God to suffer such things. For they say that his nature in itself neither could nor can suffer any of these things, as if an incorruptible nature were worthy of praise because it does not do harm to itself and not because no harm can be done to it by anything. Secondly, if the nature of darkness did harm to the nature of God and the nature of God did harm to the nature of darkness, there are consequently two evils that did harm to each other. And the nation of darkness had a better disposition because, although it did harm, it did harm unwillingly. For it did not want to harm but to enjoy the goodness of God. But God wanted to wipe it out, as Mani raves most clearly in his ruinous *Letter of the Foundation*. For he forgot that he had said a little before: "The most splendid realms of the same were founded upon the bright and blessed land so that they could never be moved or shaken by anything." And he later said:

> But the Father of the most blessed light, knowing that the great ruin and devastation which was going to arise from the darkness would threaten his holy worlds if he did not set against it some outstanding and illustrious deity powerful in might, by which he might at the same time overcome and destroy the race of darkness so that, once it was wiped out, endless peace would be prepared for the inhabitants of the light.

See, he feared the ruin and devastation threatening his worlds! They were of course founded upon the bright and blessed land so that they could never be moved or shaken by anything! See, it was out of fear that he wanted to do harm to the neighboring nation, which he tried to destroy and wipe out in order that perpetual peace might be prepared for the inhabitants of light! Why did he not add "and perpetual bondage"? Or were those souls that he confined for eternity in the sphere of darkness — of whom he clearly says, "They allowed themselves to wander from their previous bright nature" — not inhabitants of light? There, even against his will, he was forced to say that they sinned by free will, though he did not want to locate sin anywhere but in the necessity coming from the opposing nature. In every regard he is ignorant of what he is saying, and it is as if he were already confined in the sphere of darkness that he fashioned and were seeking how to get out and not finding the way.

But let him say whatever he wants to the misguided and wretched people who honor him much more than Christ in order that he may sell them such sacrilegious myths at this price. Let him say whatever he wants; let him enclose in the sphere of darkness, as if in a prison, the nation of darkness, and let him fasten on the outside the nature of the light, to which he promised perpetual peace once the enemy was defeated. See, the punishment of the light is worse than that of the darkness; the punishment of the nature of God is worse than that of the opposing nation. Even if that nation of darkness is in darkness, it belongs to its nature to dwell in darkness. But the souls, which are the same nature as God, could not be received, as he says, into those peaceful kingdoms. They are alienated from the life and freedom of the holy light and are confined in the previously mentioned horrible sphere. He says, "For this reason those same souls will cling to the things that they loved, having been abandoned in the same sphere of darkness and obtaining this for themselves by their own merits." Of course, this is not the free choice of the will! See how in his madness he does not know what he is saying and, by contradicting himself, wages a fiercer war against himself than against the god of the nation of darkness.

Next, if the souls of the light are condemned because they loved the darkness, the nation of darkness, which loved the light, is unjustly condemned. And the nation of darkness, of course, loved the light from the beginning and wanted to possess it, even if it was by violence, and not to extinguish it. But the nature of light wanted to extinguish the darkness in war. Therefore, once it was conquered, the nature of light loved the darkness. Choose which you want. Was it compelled by necessity to love the darkness or was it willingly seduced? If it was compelled by necessity, why is it condemned? If it was willing, why is the nature of God caught in such great wickedness? If the nature of God is compelled by necessity to love the darkness, it was conquered. Therefore, it does not conquer. If it was willingly seduced, why do these wretches still hesitate to attribute the will to sin to the nature that God made from nothing, for fear that they might attribute it to the light he begot?

43. What else? If we also show that before its mingling with evil — that mythical fiction in which they have believed with great insanity — there existed great evils in the nature that they call the nature of light, what will it seem possible to add to these blasphemies? After all, before the battle there was the

harsh and inevitable necessity of fighting. There you already see a great evil before the evil was mingled with the good! Let them say where this came from when no mingling had as yet been produced. But if there was no necessity, then there was will. And where did this great evil come from, so that God willed to do harm to his own nature, which could not be harmed by the enemy, when he sent it to be cruelly mingled, to be shamefully purified, and to be wickedly condemned? See the great evil of the destructive, harmful, and most cruel will before there was any mingling with evil from the opposing nation! Or did he perhaps not know that it was going to turn out that his members would love darkness and emerge as enemies to the holy light, as Mani himself says, that is, not merely to their God but also to their father, from whom they were born? Where, then, did this great evil of ignorance in God come from before there was any mingling with evil from the opposing nation? If, however, he knew that this would occur, there was in him either an everlasting cruelty if he did not grieve over the future contamination and condemnation of his own nature or an everlasting misery if he did grieve. Where did this great evil in your highest good come from before any mingling with your highest evil?

Surely, if that particle of his nature which is confined in the eternal prison of that sphere did not know that this threat hung over it, there was even in this case an everlasting ignorance in the nature of God. But if that particle did know this, there was an everlasting misery. Where did so great an evil as this come from before there was any mingling with evil from the opposing nature? Or did it perhaps rejoice with great love that through its punishment perpetual peace was being prepared for the other inhabitants of the light? Let him anathematize this who sees how wicked it is to say that the nature of God helps the nature of God in that way. But if it at least acted so that the nature of God did not become an enemy to the light, one could perhaps praise it, not like the nature of God but like a human being who chose to suffer something on behalf of his fatherland, an evil that could in fact last for some time but not for eternity. But now they say that the confinement in the sphere of darkness, not of just anything but of the nature of God, is eternal. And it would of course be a most wicked and detestable and unspeakably sacrilegious joy if the nature of God rejoiced that it was going to love the darkness and would be an enemy to the holy light. Where did this cruel and criminal evil come from before there was any mingling with evil from the opposing nation? Who would endure so perverse and so wicked a madness as to attribute to the highest evil such great goods and to attribute to the highest good, which is God, such great evils?

44. But they say that a part of the nature of God is mingled everywhere in the heavens, on the earth, and under the earth, in all bodies both dry and wet, in all kinds of flesh, in all the seeds of trees, plants, human beings, and animals. It is not present by the power of the divinity without any involvement, without any defilement and corruption, in order to govern and rule all things, as we say of

God, but it was bound, oppressed, polluted. And they say that it is released, set free, and purified not only by the course of the sun and the moon and by the power of the light but also by their Elect. It is shocking to say how this form of their most unspeakable error inclines them, even if it does not bring them, to sacrilegious and incredible shamefulness. For they say that the powers of the light are transformed into handsome males and presented to the females of the nation of darkness and that the same powers of the light are transformed into beautiful females and presented to the males of the nation of darkness so that by their beauty they may set afire the foulest passions of the princes and princesses of darkness. And in that way the vital substance, that is, the nature of God, which they say is held bound in their bodies, is released from their members (which find relief through that concupiscence), escapes, and is set free when it is taken up or purified. These unhappy people read this, say this, hear this, and believe this. This is set forth as follows in the seventh book of *The Treasury*, as they call a certain writing of Mani in which these blasphemies are written:

Then that blessed Father, who has ships of light as inns and dwellings or magnitudes, in accord with his innate mercy brings help by which his vital substance is stripped and set free from wicked snares, difficulties, and sufferings. Therefore, by an invisible nod he transforms those powers of his that are held in this very bright ship and makes them appear before the opposing powers, which are lined up in various stretches of the heavens. Because they are made up of both sexes, males and females, he commands the previously mentioned powers to appear clothed partly in the form of beardless youths for the females of the opposing nation, partly in the form of bright virgins for males of the opposing nation. For he knows that all those enemy powers are very easily captured on account of their innate, lethal, and most foul concupiscence and are trapped by the same very beautiful forms and in that way experience release. But you know that this same blessed Father of ours is the same as his powers, which for a necessary cause he transforms into the inviolate likeness of youths and virgins. But he uses them as his weapons and through them carries out his will. The ships of light are in fact full of these divine powers, which are placed, like mates, opposite the infernal kinds, and they accomplish in the same moment with speed and ease what they have in mind. And so, when the plan demands that the same holy powers appear to males, they immediately display their appearance in the guise of very beautiful virgins. Again, when they present themselves to females, they put aside their likenesses of virgins and display the form of beardless youths. But at this fair sight their passion and concupiscence grows, and in this way the restraint upon their worst thoughts is loosened, and the living soul that was held in their members finds release at this occasion, goes forth, and is mingled with his purest air where, after having been completely purified, the souls ascend to the ships of light that were readied for carrying them and transporting them to their fatherland. But that part that still bears some stains from the opposing race descends in particles by means of heat and warmth and is mingled with the trees and other plants and everything sown and is dyed various colors. And just as figures of youths and virgins from that great and very bright ship appear to the opposing powers that dwell in the heavens and have a fiery nature, and from this fair sight the part of life that is held in their members is released and pulled down into the earth through warmth, in the same way that highest power that dwells in the ship of living waters also appears through its angels in the likeness of youths and holy virgins to these powers whose nature is cold and wet and which are arranged in the heavens. And to those that are female he appears in the form of youths, to those that are male in the form of virgins. But by this change and diversity of divine and most beautiful persons the princes of the wet and cold race, whether male or female, experience release, and that which is vital in them escapes. But once that which remains is released, it is brought down into the earth through coldness and is mingled with all the elements of the earth.

Who would endure this? Who would believe this? I do not mean that it is so, but even that it could have been said. There you have people who fear to anathematize Mani when he teaches this and do not fear to believe that God does these things and endures them.

45. They say, however, that this same part and nature of God which is mingled with everything is purified by the Elect, that is, by their eating and drinking, since they say that it is held bound in all foods, and that, when for bodily refreshment they are consumed by the Elect (who are supposedly holy people) by eating and drinking, it is released, sealed, and set free by their holiness. These wretches do not consider how it is not unjustifiable to believe of them what they deny in vain, unless they anathematize those same books and cease to be Manicheans. For if, as they say, a part of God is bound in all seeds and is purified by the Elect when they eat it, who would not rightly believe that they do what they read in their *Treasury* was done between the powers of the heavens and the princes of darkness, since they do not hesitate to believe and to affirm that their own bodies come from the nation of darkness and that that vital substance, a part of God, is held bound in them? And certainly, if it is to be released and purified by being eaten, as their deadly error forces them to admit, who would not see, who would not be horrified at, the shamefulness that results and at how wicked it is?

46. For they say that certain princes of the nation of darkness created Adam, the first human being, in order that they might hold onto the light so that it would not escape. In the *Letter of the Foundation*, as they call it, Mani wrote as follows

about how the prince of darkness, whom they introduce as the father of the first man, spoke to his other companions and acted:

> With wicked designs he said to those who were present: "What do you think that this very great light that is rising is? See how it moves the pole of the world and strikes the many powers. Hence, it is right for me to ask you for the light you have in your generative powers. In that way I shall form an image of that great one who has appeared in glory, by which we may be able to reign, once we have been set free from the life of darkness." Hearing this and pondering it for a long time within themselves, they thought that it was entirely just to offer what he asked of them. For they were not confident that they would retain the same light forever; hence, they thought it better to offer it to their prince, in no way giving up the hope that they themselves would reign by that agreement. We must, therefore, consider how they offered him the same light that they had. For this light is scattered through all the scriptures of God and the heavenly mysteries. But for the wise it is not difficult to know how they gave this light. For it is immediately and clearly known by someone who is willing to investigate truthfully and faithfully. Since the group of those who assembled was a mixture, that is, of women and men, he urged them to have intercourse. In that intercourse some sowed the seed and others were impregnated. The offspring were like those who begot them, obtaining as the first offspring very much of their parents' generative powers. When he received them, their prince rejoiced as over an excellent gift. And just as we now see that the nature of evil becomes the fashioner of bodies, receiving from this source the generative powers to fashion them, so the previously mentioned prince took the offspring of his companions, which possessed its parents' senses and wisdom, and ate the light that was procreated together with them in generation. And having received much generative power from this sort of food, in which there was not only courage but even more cunning and evil thoughts from the savage mind of its parents, he summoned to himself his own spouse, who came from the same stock as he himself did. And having had intercourse with her, he, like the others, sowed the abundance of evil that he had devoured, also adding something from his own thought and power in order that his mind might be the fashioner and designer of all those whom he spilled forth. His mate received this as well-cultivated earth usually receives seed. In her were constructed and framed the images of all the heavenly and earthly powers, so that what was formed obtained the image of an entire world.

47. O the monstrous wickedness! O the accursed destruction and ruin of deceived souls! I leave out what it says of the nature of God that it is bound in this fashion. At least let these wretches, who have been deceived and poisoned by

deadly error, notice that, if a part of God is bound through the intercourse of males and females — a part they say that they release and purify by eating — the logic of this wicked error of theirs forces them to release and purify a part of God not only from bread and vegetables and fruit, which are the only things they are seen to eat in public, but also from that seed which can hold it bound if it is received in the womb of a female. It is reported in a public hearing that some individuals have confessed that they do this not only in Paphlagonia but also in Gaul, as I have heard from a certain Catholic Christian in Rome. And when they were asked for the scripture by whose authority they did this, they produced from their *Treasury* what I quoted a little before. But when this is raised as an objection to the Manicheans, they usually reply that some enemy or other from their own number, that is, from their Elect, left them, created a schism, and founded a very foul heresy of this sort. From this it is evident that, even if the Manicheans themselves engage in this practice, whoever does so does so on the basis of their books. Let them throw out those books, therefore, if they abhor the crime that they are forced to commit if they retain those books. Or if they do not commit that crime, they are trying to live more purely in opposition to those books. But what do they do when they are told, "Either purify the light from whatever seeds you can so that you do not refuse to do what you claim that you do not do, or anathematize Mani. When he says that a part of God is present in all seeds and is bound by intercourse, but that whatever light — that is, whatever part of their God — reaches the food of the Elect is purified by their eating it, you see what he is persuading you to do, and you still hesitate to condemn him"? What do they do, I ask, when this is said to them? To what means of escape do they turn when they must either anathematize so wicked a teaching or perform so shameful an action?

In comparison with this action all those intolerable evils I mentioned a little before seem tolerable, though, if they are considered by themselves, they cannot be tolerated. I had mentioned that they say of the nature of God that it is forced by necessity to wage war, that it was either carefree in everlasting ignorance or was troubled with everlasting sorrow and fear over when the corruption resulting from its being mingled with evil and the bonds of eternal condemnation would come upon it. I had mentioned next that, after having waged war, it was taken captive, overcome, and polluted, and that after a false victory it will be fastened for eternity in a horrible sphere and separated from the happiness of its origin.

48. O how great is your patience, merciful and compassionate Lord, who are longsuffering and very merciful and truthful.[8] You make your sun rise upon the

---

8. See Ps 103:8; 86:15.

good and the evil, and you send rain upon the just and the unjust.[9] You do not wish the death of a sinner as much as that he return and live.[10] You rebuke some and give them room for repentance in order that they may abandon their malice and believe in you.[11] By your patience you lead them to repentance, though in keeping with their hardness of heart and their unrepentant heart many store up for themselves wrath on the day of wrath. You repay each person according to his works.[12] You forget all their iniquities on the day on which people turn from their wickedness to your mercy and truth.[13] Give us, grant us, that, just as many have already been set free through our ministry, by which you wanted this accursed and extremely horrible error to be refuted, so others may be set free. May they merit in the sorrow of repentance to receive the forgiveness of their sins and blasphemies, by which they offended you through ignorance, either through the sacrament of holy baptism or through the sacrifice of a sorrowful spirit and a humble and contrite heart.[14] For your mercy and power and the truth of your baptism and the keys of the kingdom of heaven have such great power in your Church that we must not give up hope, even for those people, as long as they continue to live on this earth through your patience. Even though they know how evil it is to think or to say such things of you, they are detained in that evil faith because they have become used to or have attained some temporal and earthly advantage. May they at least, after they have been admonished by your rebukes, take refuge in your ineffable goodness and prefer the eternal life of heaven to all the allurements of life in the flesh.

---

9. See Mt 5:45.
10. See Ez 33:11.
11. See Wis 12:2; Jb 24:23.
12. See Rom 2:5-6.
13. See Ez 18:21-22.
14. See Ps 51:19.

Answer to Secundinus, a Manichean

(Contra Secundinum Manichaeum)

Introduction

In his *Revisions* Augustine lists the *Answer to Secundinus, a Manichean* last among his explicitly anti-Manichean writings. The *Answer* is in fact a letter written in reply to a letter from Secundinus, although it was included among his books because Augustine omitted from it the salutation that normally opened a letter. We are fortunate also to have the letter of Secundinus, who describes himself as a Roman and who, Augustine tells us, was not a member of the Manichean Elect but only a Hearer. The *Answer* was written sometime after 404, and Augustine tells us that, among his anti-Manichean writings, this was his favorite.

Though Secundinus was only a Hearer, he was obviously an intelligent and articulate Manichean who ventured to defend the teaching of Mani in the face of some of the most serious objections raised against it by Augustine,[1] for he had read a number of Augustine's writings against the Manicheans. Secundinus begins his letter by offering thanks to the Trinity for giving him the chance to greet Augustine. He goes on to pray that the Trinity will bless Augustine and rescue him from evil, not from the evil that is nothing or from the evil that human beings do, but from the evil of hell. For, as the apostle Paul taught, we have a struggle not against flesh and blood but against principalities and powers and against the spirits of wickedness (section 1). If the soul acts with the spirit of the virtues, it will attain perpetual life, but if it acts with the spirit of the vices and consents to them, it can still attain forgiveness if it repents. If it leaves this life without repentance, however, it will be cast into outer darkness and the fires of hell. Hence, Secundinus asks Augustine to return to the faith he has abandoned out of fear (section 2).

Secundinus tells Augustine that he has read some of his anti-Manichean writings and has found their author to be a highly eloquent man who would have been a great ornament to the Manichean faith if he had not turned against the truth. He pleads with Augustine not to be a lance of error by which the Lord's side is pierced, and he asks him whom he will have as an advocate when he comes to the judgment. He wishes that Augustine would have turned to the Academic skeptics or to Roman history when he left the Manicheans rather than

---

1. The Latin of the letter of Secundinus is quite difficult, at least in my judgment. I want to acknowledge the help I received from the article by Johannes van Oort, "Secundini Manichaei Epistula: Roman Manichaean Biblical Argument in the Age of Augustine," in J. van Oort, O. Wermelinger, and G. Wurst, eds., *Augustine and Manichaeism in the Latin West* (Leiden 2001) 161-173.

349

to the indecent writings of the Hebrews. He tells Augustine that he knew that Augustine always hated the immoral conduct of the patriarchs and loved loftier things. He wonders who it is that has suddenly changed Augustine (section 3). Secundinus knows that Augustine is well aware of the wickedness and malice of Satan, who tempted Peter, caused Thomas to doubt, brought Judas to the act of betrayal, and led the Jews to demand Jesus' crucifixion. The Manicheans, Secundinus says, have escaped because they have followed the spiritual savior, not someone who suffered in the flesh (section 4). Again Secundinus begs Augustine to return to the faith and to cease to enclose Christ in a womb and make the two natures one (section 5). If he has doubts concerning the initial state or about the battle between the two natures, Secundinus offers to discuss such questions in a peaceful manner and tries to explain why God fought with the evil nature (section 6). He admits that trying to explain such things to Augustine is comparable to offering water to the ocean, and he asks pardon if he has offended Augustine (section 7).

Augustine's reply to Secundinus — by way of a brief summary — begins with two introductory paragraphs in which he explains why he left the Manicheans. He then turns to a refutation of Manicheanism that is based on the contents of Secundinus' letter. He first focuses upon Secundinus' claim that Jesus Christ is the firstborn of the divine majesty and king of all the lights and shows that Secundinus can only defend such a claim by admitting that the lights of which Christ is king are creatures, not the same nature as God (sections 3 to 11). Then Augustine turns to the soul's consent to evil and develops a long argument to show that sinful consent cannot be a substance (sections 12 to 20). Next he replies to Secundinus' objections drawn from the Old Testament (sections 21 to 24). In conclusion he argues that his own conversion to the Catholic Church ought to have been impossible if Mani's teaching were true. He denounces Mani's having denied that Christ had real flesh, warns Secundinus not to be proud of the small number of Manicheans, and urges him to become a Catholic (sections 25 to 26).

The *Answer to Secundinus* starts with Augustine's acknowledgment of his correspondent's obvious good will toward him, though he warns him that he is mistaken in thinking that he had left the Manicheans out of a carnal fear of some personal loss or out of a desire for some honor that he has attained in the Catholic Church (section 1). He admits, however, that he abandoned the sect out of a fear of what the apostle Paul wrote to Timothy, when he predicted the emergence of people like the Manicheans, and out of a desire for the honor that the same apostle said was due to everyone who did good. But no one does good if he thinks that evil is found not in the mutable will but in an immutable nature. Augustine tells Secundinus that what he thinks about him is not important, but that what he thinks about the truth itself is. Hence, he cannot pass over Secundinus' error about the very light of minds, which is the truth (section 2).

Augustine tells Secundinus that he will prove the error of Manicheanism from Secundinus' own words. He points to his having called Jesus Christ the king of lights and asks what lights Christ is king of. For, if they are lights that Christ, who is equal to the Father, begot, the lights are also equal to the Father and to Christ, and Christ would in that case be king over his equals. If Christ made these lights, Augustine asks what he made them out of. If he made them out of himself, they should be equal to Christ. Or, if Christ did not make them, but they always existed, there were two natures as well as the evil nature, though Mani wanted there to be only two natures. Furthermore, by what right is Christ the king of these lights? Augustine insists that Secundinus has no alternative but to admit that Christ made these lights and rules over them as the creator over his creatures (section 3). If Secundinus asks what he made them out of, Augustine shows that he could not have made them out of himself and that he made them either out of nothing or out of something else that he had made (section 4). Secundinus had spoken of Christ as the firstborn of the ineffable and most sacred majesty. Augustine asks whether Secundinus was asserting that he was firstborn in terms of the assumption of his humanity, so that he was firstborn in relation to those whom he called to be children of God by adoption, or in terms of his divine nature, so that the lights over which he was king were his brothers. He explains that the Catholic faith distinguishes between the creator and his creatures, and he understands that Christ was the only-begotten in his divine nature but the firstborn in his human nature. Christ is the firstborn among many brothers who are the children of God not by nature but by adoption (section 5). Augustine indicates the problems that arise if one grants that Jesus Christ was the firstborn in terms of his divine substance. For example, if those lights were his brothers, by what right did he reign over them? Was it because he was the stronger or the older? Was it because more than one light was needed to battle against the darkness? Augustine warns Secundinus not to introduce time and change into the divinity (section 6). He says that the apostle would not have blamed those who worshiped a creature instead of the creator if creatures and the creator were of one and the same substance. Secundinus must cease to be a Manichean and distinguish between the creator and creatures if he wants to say that Jesus Christ is the firstborn of the divine majesty and the king of all the lights (section 7). If Augustine asks what all of creation was made out of, Secundinus will not find any answer unless he admits that all of creation was made out of nothing. For this reason creatures can tend toward nothing when they sin, and they are made subject to vanity. Augustine explains that the apostle said that all creation has been made subject to vanity because all creation is found in a human being. If Secundinus refuses to admit that all creation has been made out of nothing, he will be forced to say sacrilegious things about God. In his letter Secundinus did in fact make the soul subject to change, and his own soul proves that the soul is a mutable creature (section 8). Augustine wonders whether Secundinus meant that the soul was immutable in its own nature but mutable by reason of its mingling with the evil nature. He observes that this is like saying that the bodies of all human beings are invulnerable if they are not actually wounded. And he demonstrates that Secundinus does not want the Son of God to be born of a virgin because he believes that the Word of God can be defiled. He insists that, if he wants to avoid impiety, Secundinus must hold that God the Father and his Word are immutable and that every creature is mutable (section 9). Augustine explains that, when the apostle spoke of our struggle against the princes and powers, he did not mean that those princes and powers originated from an evil substance that God neither begot nor made. Christians hold that there is nothing contrary to God, who exists in the highest way, and that whatever else exists is good and made by God out of nothing. The princes and powers of which the apostle spoke were created good, sinned, and now try to harm others, although all power ultimately comes from God, who allows them to have power over us to test our patience and to punish our sinfulness. Even though we have been set free from our sins, we still suffer because of the mortality of our bodies, but in the resurrection our bodies will put on immortality (section 10).

To fail is to tend toward nothing, and the less anything is, the closer it is to nothing. When failures are voluntary, they are rightly blamed and called sins. Pains and difficulties, which we experience unwillingly, are just punishments for sins. Augustine tells Secundinus to read his books entitled *Free Will* if he wants a fuller explanation of these ideas (section 11). While the Manicheans say that evil is a substance, Christians say that it is not a substance but a falling away from what exists in a higher way to what exists in a lower way. Returning to his promise to prove the error of the Manicheans on the basis of Secundinus' letter, Augustine singles out the latter's statements that the soul is led to sin by its mingling with the flesh, not by its own will, and that, if it consents to evil, it sins by its own will. Augustine asks what evil the soul consents to, and he concludes that it surely must be the evil that the Manicheans say is a substance (section 12).

Augustine says that he now sees three things: the soul, the evil to which it consents, and the consent. The soul is a substance, and the evil to which it consents is, according to the Manicheans, a substance. But the consent cannot be a substance. Otherwise, there will be three substances, not two. Is the consent good or evil? If it is good, the soul does not sin by its consent. Hence, the consent must be evil, and the soul must also be evil, if they are the same substance. If Secundinus tries to escape by calling evil not the consent but that to which the soul consents, then the soul is good, but its consent and that to which it consents are evil. But if the consent does not belong to the soul, the soul does not sin. The soul, however, does consent, and the evil belongs to the soul (section 13). If this consent is a substance, then it is in the power of the soul to make an evil substance to exist or not. A substance, however, is a nature. But this nature will not be natural to the soul or to that to which the soul consents, since it depends upon the will. Secundinus, therefore, will be forced to say that this consent is a third nature that comes from the soul that consents. Augustine shows that Secundinus cannot escape from his self-imposed dilemma unless he admits that the consent, which is evil and blameworthy, is not a substance but inheres in a substance (section 14). And the substance in which the consent inheres can only be the soul. Thus, in a good substance like the soul, there can be an evil consent, which is not a substance. Augustine tells Secundinus to open his eyes and see that any substance is something good and that evil is not a substance but a failure on the part of a substance. Voluntary failures are sins, and other failures are either punishments of sins or parts of the order of temporal things that come to be and pass away (section 15). Augustine then shows that Secundinus is wrong to blame as evil that to which the soul consents. For it is possible to love wrongly something that is a good substance. Augustine uses the example of someone who wrongly loves the sun, which the Manicheans cannot deny is a good substance. Hence, that to which the soul consents is not an evil substance (section 16). Augustine then turns to the possibility that, according to Secundinus, consent is blameworthy only if the soul consents to something to which it is persuaded or forced by someone and that the evil lies in the persuasion or the forcing of that person. He insists, however, that sin consists first in preferring a good creature to the creator in one's love and only secondarily in trying to persuade or force someone to do that. The devil tries to persuade or force us to sin, but his substance is not evil insofar as it is a substance but only insofar as he abandoned the love of God for the love of himself (section 17). Augustine claims that, given Secundinus' own words that the soul sins by its will when it consents to evil, it is easy to see that evil is not an evil nature or the love of an evil nature. The Manicheans maintain two natures, one good and the other evil, but Augustine insists that a good nature becomes evil by sinning and that neither consent nor persuasion to sin is a substance (section 18).

The Manicheans ask where the evil of sin comes from if not from the nature of evil. Augustine asks in turn where evil consent comes from in the nature that the Manicheans say is good. Whatever the soul suffered, so that it consented to evil, it was able to suffer before it suffered it. Where, then, did that ability to suffer come from? Even before a good nature is changed or corrupted, there was present in it the ability to be changed or corrupted. Augustine insists that it is blasphemy to maintain that there is such mutability or corruptibility in the substance of the good, but the Manicheans, who maintain that the soul is a part of God and admit that the soul sins when it consents to evil, are forced to admit that there is mutability and corruptibility in the substance of God (section 19). The Manicheans are guilty of great blasphemies insofar as they locate in the nature of evil, which God did not make, many great goods and locate in the nature of God mutability and corruptibility, even before any mingling with evil. Augustine addresses Secundinus' explanation of why God fought with the nature of evil, namely, that God would have seemed to consent to injustice if he had not fought the invader. He insists that, according to the Manichean myth, God committed even greater injustice in handing over a part of himself to be invaded, defiled, and in part condemned for eternity. Though Daniel was able to preserve his righteousness as a captive, the Manichean God was not (section 20).

Secundinus had singled out passages of the Old Testament for attack. Augustine takes them up one by one and shows that his objections do not hold up. Secundinus, for example, was upset because in the Old Testament God had commanded Hosea to take a prostitute and have children with her. Augustine points out that the Manicheans forget that Christ said in the gospel that prostitutes and publicans would enter the kingdom of heaven before the Pharisees. He also claims that the Manicheans are more upset at the idea of Hosea's having children than they are over his fornication, since the Manichean God supposedly becomes imprisoned in the flesh when children are conceived (section 21). The Manicheans are also upset over the command that God gave to Peter in the Acts of the Apostles about killing and eating unclean animals, though Augustine suggests that they really should be in favor of butchering animals so that their Elect can set free parts of their God from the meat. Secundinus had mocked Augustine because he was saddened by the barrenness of Sarah, but Augustine accuses Secundinus of being saddened by her fertility, for the Manicheans forbid marriage and regard it as evil (section 22). Secundinus had reminded Augustine that he had always abhorred the idea of swearing by the genitals of the patriarch, Abraham, but Augustine accuses Secundinus of feigning horror at the thigh of one patriarch from which the flesh of Christ had come, while the Manichean God is bound in the flesh not only of human beings but of all animals. So Augustine also turns against Secundinus the latter's objections about all the animals and plants in the ark, about Jacob's wrestling with an angel, and about Abraham's concealing his true relationship to Sarah (section 23).

Secundinus had praised Augustine for his former way of life and said that the devil had led him to change and enter the Catholic Church. Augustine says that the fact that he changed shows that he is not what Mani had claimed. For, if his soul were a part of God, as Mani claimed, then he could not have changed. Furthermore, the devil himself does not come from the nature of evil but became evil by sinning and now begrudges human beings their place in heaven, from which he himself was cast down (section 24).

Secundinus had said that the Manicheans escaped by following the spiritual savior, that is, a Christ who did not have real flesh. Augustine points out that, if Secundinus refuses to believe in Christ, who had assumed flesh, he ought not to believe in Mani, who was born in the flesh from two parents. Secundinus had warned Augustine that he would have no patron before the judgment seat of God if he rejected Mani. Augustine replies that Secundinus is asking him to believe that Christ lied to the doubting Thomas when he showed him his wounds and that Mani is telling the truth when he says that Christ did not have real flesh. He warns Secundinus that he must flee from the lies of Mani (section 25).

Finally, Augustine tells Secundinus that he should not be misled by the small number of Manicheans, and he suggests that it is the people's horror at the impiety of the Manicheans that is responsible for their being so few in number. The number of the saints who follow the narrow path is small in comparison to the multitude of sinners, but that small number is hidden on the threshing floor of the Church. Augustine explains that the apostle Paul did not disdain the Old Testament, which foretold the coming of the true Christ, but rejected the pride of the Jews. He appeals to Secundinus to abandon Manicheanism and to be enlightened by the true light, which is something that Secundinus can only do because he is not the immutable good but a mutable creature (section 26).

Revisions II, 10 (37)

Answer to Secundinus, a Manichean, One Book

A certain Secundinus, not from among those the Manicheans call "the Elect" but from among those they call "Hearers," a man whom I did not personally know, wrote to me as a friend, reproaching me in a respectful manner because I was attacking that heresy in writing. He warned me not to do that and exhorted me rather to follow that heresy by defending it and by rejecting the Catholic faith. I replied to him, and, because I did not put at the beginning of the same work who was writing to whom, it is not included among my letters but among my books. In it his letter was also copied at the beginning. The title of this volume of mine is *Answer to Secundinus, a Manichean*. In my opinion I easily prefer it to all the books I wrote against that plague. This book begins as follows: "Your good will toward me, which is apparent in your letter."

A Letter of Secundinus, a Manichean, to Augustine

1. I am grateful and give thanks to the ineffable and most sacred Majesty and to his firstborn, Jesus Christ, the king of all lights. I am grateful and, as a suppliant, attribute it to the Holy Spirit that they gave and offered me the opportunity to greet Your Holiness, my rightly praiseworthy and uniquely venerable lord, who are salutary and most excellent. Nor is this a surprise, for they are ready enough and quite able to offer all goods and to ward off all evils, and they defend Your Goodness by their bulwarks and rescue you from that evil — not that evil which is nothing or which arises from what human beings do or have done to them but that evil which is ready to come. But woe to that man who offers himself to it as an occasion. For you are worthy to obtain such gifts from them. You are worthy to have them as the protectors of your truth, truly a light, which the right hand of the truth has set on the candlestick of your heart,[1] lest at the coming of the thief the patrimony of your treasure be plundered.[2] You are worthy that they should command that the house stand without falling, which you have not built upon the sand of error but upon the rock of knowledge,[3] and that they should repel from us the dreadful spirit that injects fear and perfidy into human beings in order to turn souls away from the narrow pathway of the savior.[4] All of his attack is poured out through those princes, whom the apostle says in the Letter to the Ephesians that he has entered into battle against. For he says that he does not have a battle *against flesh and blood, but against the princes and powers, against the spirits of wickedness that dwell in the heavens* (Eph 6:12). And who, after all, has a battle against weapons and not against someone wielding weapons who is moved to oppose him? For, as the bodies of human beings are the weapons of sin, so the salutary commandments are the weapons of justice.[5] Paul testifies to this; Mani himself testifies to this.

2. It is not, therefore, a fight against weapons but against the spirits that wield them. But they fight on account of souls. The soul, whose nature has given it the victory from the beginning, is placed in the midst of them. If it acts in accord with the spirit of the virtues, it will have endless life with him and will possess the kingdom to which our Lord invites us. But if it begins to be dragged off by the spirit of the vices and consents and then after its consent does penance, it will

---

1. See Mt 5:15.
2. See Mt 24:43.
3. See Mt 7:24-27.
4. See Mt 7:14.
5. See Rom 6:13.

357

have a source of pardon for this turpitude. For it is led by its mingling with the flesh, not by its own will. But if, after it recognizes itself, it consents to evil and does not arm itself against the enemy, it has sinned by its own will. If it is again ashamed of having gone astray, it will find the author of mercies ready to forgive. For the soul is not punished because it sinned but because it was not sorry for its sin. But if it leaves this life with the same sin without forgiveness, it will then be excluded; it will then be compared to a foolish virgin.[6] It will then be a goat on the left hand.[7] It will then, because of its dark clothing, be driven by the Lord from the wedding banquet to where there will be weeping and gnashing of teeth.[8] And it will go with the devil to the fire of his origin,[9] which in your remarkable wisdom you teach was either made out of an archangel or is nothing. Why, then, will the righteous reign? Why will the apostles and martyrs be crowned? Is all this because they conquered nothing? O how much is the power of the conqueror frustrated when the adversary is declared to be powerless! Change this idea, I beg you; set aside the perfidy of the Punic nation.[10] Turn back to the truth your withdrawal from it, for you acted out of fear; do not excuse it by these lies.

3. With the small talents, such as they are, that I have as a Roman, I have read some writings of Your Reverence, in which you are as angry with the truth as *Hortensius* was with philosophy.[11] Since, therefore, I returned again and again to them with an open mind and a quick eye, I found everywhere a consummate orator and a god of almost all eloquence. I never found a Christian, however, but a man armed against everything yet affirming nothing, though you ought to have shown yourself to be well versed in knowledge, not in speaking. But I cannot remain silent about this toward Your Holiness, who are most patient. For I thought, and it is certainly the case, that you were never a Manichean, that you could not have known the unknown mysteries of the secret of Mani, and that you are attacking Hannibal and Mithridates[12] under the name of Mani. For I admit that the marble of the house of the Anicii[13] does not gleam with as much care and industry as your writings shine with eloquence. If you wanted them to agree with the truth, it would have been a great ornament for us. Do not, I beg you, turn against your nature; do not be the lance of error by which the side of the savior is

6. See Mt 25:1-13.
7. See Mt 25:33. I have conjectured haedus in place of heres.
8. See Mt 22:2-13.
9. See Mt 25:41.
10. Since the time of Hannibal the Punic people of North Africa had been regarded as perfidious.
11. Cicero's work, *Hortensius*, which is no longer extant, spurred Augustine to a love of philosophy and eventually led to his conversion to Manicheism. Secundinus may mean that *Hortensius* was angry with the present state of philosophy and was urging its reform.
12. Hannibal (218-201 B.C.) was the great Punic general who led the armies of Carthage against Rome in the Second Punic War. Mithridates is probably Mithridates IV, king of Pontus in Anatolia (120-63 B.C.), who briefly challenged Rome's power in Asia.
13. The Anicii were one of the wealthiest families of the Roman empire.

pierced.[14] For you see that he is crucified in the whole world and in every soul, and the soul never had a nature to become angry. And so, you who come from that nature, I beg you, leave aside now your vain attacks; abandon needless controversies. When you dwelled for so long a time with your parent in the midst of darkness, you never mocked us, but now, in the face of the sun and the moon, you are found to attack us.[15] Who, then, will be your patron before the just tribunal of the judge, when you begin to be convicted by your own testimony, both by your words and by your deeds? The Persian whom you attacked will not be there. Apart from him who will console you as you weep? Who will save this Punic man? Or was there a change in the gospel, so that the wide road no longer leads to perdition?[16] Is it incorrect in Paul that individuals are going to give an account of their works?[17] O, I wish that, when you left Mani, you had sought out the Academy or had interpreted the wars of the Romans, who conquered everyone! What great, what outstanding events you would have found there, and, as a chaste man, indeed as a man of complete chastity and poverty, you would not have had recourse to the peoples of the Jews, barbarous in their way of life. You would not insert fables among the commandments and bring forth *a fornicating wife*, and, *Produce children by fornication*, and, *The land will commit fornication against the Lord* (Hos 1:2), and, "Do not wash your hands after intercourse with your wife,"[18] and, *Put your hand under my thigh* (Gn 24:2; 47:29), and, *Kill and eat* (Acts 10:13),[19] and, *Increase and multiply* (Gn 1:28). Or are you pleased with lions in a pit because there were no cages?[20] Do you grieve over the barrenness of Sarah whose modesty her husband betrayed, pretending that she was his sister?[21] Did you perhaps want Jacob to look forward to the wrestling match in the manner of the fight between Dares and Entellus?[22] Had you decided to count the multitude of the Amorites and the pancarp in the ark of Noah?[23] I know that you have always hated these things; I know that you have always loved great things that soared above the earth, that sought the

---

14. See Jn 19:34.
15. That is, before Augustine became a Manichean he never mocked its teachings, but now, after having left the sect, he attacks the God of the Manicheans.
16. See Mt 7:13.
17. See Rm 14:12.
18. Despite the way Secundinus treats it, the verse is not biblical. See Lv 15:16 as a possible source, though it says much the opposite. Van Oort suggests *nam* instead of *non* and points to possible sources in other Jewish Christian texts (see van Oort, note 16, pp. 165-166).
19. It seems odd for Secundinus to attribute this passage to the Jews, even though the Manicheans did not accept the Acts of the Apostles because they held that Mani was the Holy Spirit.
20. See Dn 6:16.
21. See Gn 12:13; 20:2.
22. See Gn 32:24-32; Virgil, *Aeneid* V, 362ff.
23. See Jos 10:5; Gn 7. Secundinus uses the term *pancarpus*, which in terms of its etymology means "all fruit." In his reply Augustine appeals to this sense.

heavens, that mortified bodies, and that vivified souls. Who, then, is it who suddenly changed you?

4. And yet it is utterly absurd to say this to Your Holiness. After all, you know quite well that he is most evil and malicious who makes war against faithful and most excellent men with such great craftiness that he forced even Peter to deny the Lord three times in one night[24] and did not permit Thomas to believe the same Lord when he rose.[25] These wounds were nonetheless healed by the medicine of forgiveness. But how boldly he acted in mixing in weeds for the Lord who sowed the best seed,[26] in taking Iscariot from that shepherd,[27] in bringing that shepherd to the ultimate punishment of the cross,[28] and in inflaming the scribes and Pharisees for his destruction, so that they shouted that Barabbas should be freed and Jesus crucified.[29] We have, therefore, escaped by following the spiritual savior. For the audacity of the devil burst forth to such a degree that, if our Lord had flesh, all our hope would have been cut away. And yet the devil could not be satisfied even by the disgrace of the cross. In fact, in his madness he forced him to be crowned with thorns[30] and given vinegar to drink,[31] to be struck by the lance of the soldiers,[32] and to suffer blasphemy from the mouth of the thief on the left.[33] But afterwards his wickedness increased so much that, when Jesus and his apostles ascended, he framed various questions — what is worse — under their name for all the superstitious, that is, in order to divide the honor of the title of "Catholic." For I pass over how he armed each of the disciples against their teachers, how he deceived Hymenaeus, how he deceived Alexander,[34] what he did at Antioch,[35] what he did at Smyrna,[36] what he did at Iconium.[37] Now I add what the present mob keeps doing; from them virtue is as distant as it is closed off to the people. For it is not virtue to which the mob attains — and a mob mostly of women. But I fear to make public their clandestine actions lest others copy the crimes they have begun. And yet it is the mark of wise men to endure both and to laugh at both and to strive only toward what wins happiness and gives birth to life.

---

24. See Mt 26:69-75; Lk 22:55-62; Jn 18:17.25-27.
25. See Jn 20:25
26. See Mt 13:24-30.
27. See Lk 22:3-4.
28. See Mt 27:35.
29. See Mt 27:21-22.
30. See Mt 27:29.
31. See Mt 27:34.
32. See Jn 19:34.
33. See Lk 23:39.
34. See 1 Tm 1:20.
35. See Acts 14:18.
36. See Rv 2:9-10.
37. See Acts 14:2.

5. And yet I beg you again and again as a suppliant. I pray, I beseech again and again, first, that you graciously pardon me if any words of mine have troubled your golden heart. For I have acted with much ardor because I do not want you to be torn from our flock, from which I myself also strayed and was almost lost, if I had not quickly removed myself from a communion of an evil sort. Secondly, I ask that you reconcile yourself to that communion which in no way wronged you. Return to her, for she will not be angry at you on account of your sin if you return. For she knows how to forgive not merely seven times;[38] in fact, she has the power of binding and loosing.[39] Do not pretend to be groping for the truth, for you have long since seen it; do not desire to learn it, for you are able to teach it. Set aside human glory if you wish to please Christ. Be a new Paul for our times. For, though he was a teacher of the Jewish law, he obtained grace from the Lord and scorned as rubbish what he had considered advantages in order to gain Christ.[40] Help your soul, which is so bright, for you do not know at what hour the thief will come.[41] Do not be an ornament of the dead, for you are an ornament of the living. Do not be a follower of the wide road, for it is looking for an Amorite. Rather, make haste to the narrow road in order that you may attain eternal life.[42] Stop, I beg you, enclosing Christ in the womb, lest you yourself again be enclosed in the womb.[43] Stop making the two natures one, for the Lord's judgment draws near. Woe to those who will receive it, that is, those who change what is sweet into bitterness!

6. If you are in doubt about the beginning, if you hesitate over the start of the fight, you can be given an explanation in a long commentary and a peaceful discussion. But I make known to Your Goodness, who are most sagacious, that there are certain things that cannot be explained in such a way as to be understood. For the divine mind exceeds the hearts of mortals. Take, for example, the question of how there are two natures or why he fought who was not able to suffer anything, as well as what the same Mani mentions concerning the new world, namely, that this world was constructed by the motions that cut into that great land. Who would admit that a fissure is produced in what is divine, however, unless, that is, you as an interpreter are creating an image for a listener? For the listener hears the words one by one, but the interpreter grasps the whole picture. And though the commentator says many things that the hearer should hold in his mind, they have not left the commentator's mind. Unless you think of that world in this way, everything that is said will seem quite foolish and

---

38. See Mt 18:21-22.
39. See Mt 18:18.
40. See Phil 3:8.
41. See Mt 24:43.
42. See Mt 7:14.
43. That is, Augustine, who believes in the incarnation of Christ in the womb of Mary, will be punished by being reincarnated.

inept. It is also the same way with the battle. For you must first suppose that God is absolute justice and that it is the ultimate crime to invade the property of another. Thus, when the contrary nature was on the verge of doing this, God could not have suffered anything. Because he had foreknowledge, he would have seemed to have consented to the crime unless he fought. And for this reason he set a great power over against the evil principle as it attacked, in order that his justice might not be defiled by any consent to sacrilege. For in that way the just one was limited by the evil nature so that he himself never sinned and never consented to the sinner. You must also presuppose that in his own kingdom God was powerful in his nature as omnipotent and as judge.

These things have been expressed not in accord with what happened to God but in accord with my inability to grasp them. They still do not do enough to dispel faithlessness. The sun does not dawn for the blind, nor is sound heard by the deaf, nor is food prepared for the dead. Places, however, cannot be assigned to the natures; this is something that our human condition calls indescribable and ineffable. But the savior, for whom everything is easy, refers to these two by "the right hand" and "the left hand," by "inside" and "outside," and by "come" and "depart."[44] You, however, do the opposite and write a verse such as: "World, life, salvation, light, law, order, and power,"[45] if you call a vowel a consonant and a long vowel short. These natures do not agree; they certainly signify two things that are also separate from each other.

7. But when I explain such matters to your admirable and lofty wisdom, it is like the Jordan offering water to the ocean, or like a lamp offering light to the sun, or like the people offering holiness to their bishop. Hence, it is necessary that you put up with whatever this letter contains. For, if I did not know your godlike patience, which readily pardons anyone, I would never have written in such a manner, although you see that I have touched upon important ideas in a summary fashion and was very careful that I not appear as a nuisance to you. Hence, may these ideas find credence with Your Holiness and show you how we may be saved. Otherwise, my lord who are rightly praiseworthy and singularly worthy of reverence, you could produce thousands of volumes on this topic. Farewell.

---

44. See Mt 25:31-46.
45. The verse begins with trochees and then breaks down unless one makes a long vowel short. In a similar way Secundinus accuses Augustine of making evil good.

Answer to Secundinus, a Manichean

1. Your good will toward me, which is apparent in your letter, is pleasing to me. But since I ought to love you in return for loving me, I am sad that you have tenaciously clung to false suspicions, in part about me, in part about the truth, which is immutable. But I readily make light of the fact that you do not hold the truth about my mind. For you hold something that one can in any event find in a human being, even if I do not recognize it in myself. Hence, even if you are mistaken about me, you are still not so mistaken that your opinion removes me from the human race. For you believe of me something that can be found in a human mind, even if it is not found in mine. Hence, there is no need for me to make a great effort to remove this suspicion from you. After all, your hope does not depend on me, nor will you be able to be a good man only if I am one. Think of Augustine what you please. May my conscience alone not accuse me in the eyes of God. For the apostle said, *It matters very little to me that I am judged by you or by any human court* (1 Cor 4:3). But I shall not repay you in turn by daring to think something of your mind to your discredit, for I cannot see it. Nor do I say that you wanted to injure me by deceit, but I only think of you insofar as you reveal yourself by your words. Hence, even if you suspected of me things that are not good, namely, that I left your heresy out of carnal fear of some disadvantage that could have befallen me because I belonged to you, or out of a desire for the honor that I have attained in the Catholic Church, I still do not in turn think bad things of you, and I believe that your suspicion is caused by good will. I think that you have written this not in order to bring accusations against me but out of a desire to correct me. But if you would show me the kindness of believing me, since you find fault with the hidden depths of my mind (which I can certainly not set before your eyes and show you), you would readily change your opinion about my mind and would no longer rashly affirm what you do not know.

2. I admit it, after all: I abandoned the Manicheans out of fear, but out of a fear of the words that were uttered by the apostle Paul, who said, *The Spirit clearly says that in the last times some will withdraw from the faith, paying attention to deceitful spirits and the teachings of demons that lie in their hypocrisy. They have their conscience seared; they forbid marriage and abstain from foods that God created for those who believe and who know the truth to receive with thanksgiving. For every creature of God is good, and nothing that is received with thanksgiving should be rejected.* (1 Tm 4:1-4) Though by these words he perhaps also described other heretics, he still briefly and clearly described the

363

Manicheans most of all. Out of this fear, then, since I still thought rather late in my life with the mind of a child, I tore myself away from that society. I admit that I also burned to depart from there out of a love for honor, but out of a love for that honor of which the same apostle says, *But glory, honor, and peace be to everyone who does good* (Rom 2:10).

Who, however, will try to do good if he thinks that evil lies not in a mutable will but in an immutable nature? For this reason the Lord himself said to those who thought that they were speaking what was good, though they were evil, *Either make the tree good and its fruit good, or make the tree bad and its fruit bad* (Mt 12:33). But the apostle said to persons who were evil and had become good, *For you were once darkness, but you are now light in the Lord* (Eph 5:8). If you do not want to believe me about my mind, think of it as you will. Only be careful what you think about the truth. Let no temptation but one that is human lay hold of you. For it is a human error to think that there occurred in my mind something that could have occurred there, even if it did not.

But when you think that the sacrilegious and not only completely false but also completely fallacious Persian myth — which is composed and made up of the foulest lies not concerning any human being but concerning the sovereign God — is the truth, this must not be passed over in the same way, nor should one make light of so great a death of the soul. This is, after all, something that I can do with you. For regarding my mind I cannot say anything more than that you should believe me, and, if you are unwilling to do that, there is nothing else for me to do. But it does not follow that, when you also think something false about the very light of minds, which rational minds gaze upon more tranquilly the purer they are, you cannot be shown, if you listen patiently, how what you hold is very far removed from the truth.

For I cannot perceive the sensation of your eye nor can you perceive that of mine, but we can only believe or not believe each other on this matter. But we can point out to each other the form that lies visible before the eyes of each of us. In the same way we should believe each other, if we want, concerning the dispositions of our minds, which we have as our own. But if we do not want to, let us not believe each other. Having set aside the fog of stubbornness, however, let us equally give our attention with peaceful minds to the nature of the truth, which is neither yours nor mine but set before both of us for our contemplation.

3. I shall offer you other proofs that reveal the error of Mani exclusively from your own letter. You write that you are "grateful and give thanks to the ineffable and most sacred majesty and to his firstborn Son, Jesus Christ, the king of all lights."[46] Tell me of which lights Jesus Christ is king. Of those that he made or of those that he begot? For we say that God the Father begot the Son as equal to himself, but created through him, that is, established or made an inferior crea-

---

46. Secundinus, Letter 1.

ture, which is certainly not the same as he who made it and as he through whom it was made. And so, because the Father made the ages through him, the apostle correctly called him *the king of the ages* (1 Tm 1:17), as someone superior over inferiors and as having the power to rule and as ruling those things that need ruling. But when you call Jesus Christ the king of lights, why are they not equal to their parent if he begot them? If, however, you say that they are equal to him, how is he their king, since a king must rule, and it is in no way possible that those that he rules should be equal to him who rules them. But if he did not beget but made these lights, I ask you what he made them from. If he propagated them from himself, why, then, are they inferior? Why have they degenerated? But if they are not from him, tell me where they came from. Or did he perhaps neither make nor beget the lights over which he reigns? They have, then, their own origin and nature, though weaker, of course, so that they either permit or desire that their more powerful neighbor may rule them.

If that is the case, do you not recognize that there are already two natures apart from the nation of darkness, that one needs the help of the other, but that neither depends upon the other as its principle? You will of course reject this opinion because it is very much opposed to Mani, who tries to convince people not of two natures that are the king of lights and the lights over which he is king, but of two natures that are the kingdom of lights and the kingdom of darkness. You will, therefore, take refuge in saying that these lights were begotten. And when I ask why they are inferior, you will perhaps try to contend that they are equal. But when I ask again what the reason is why they are ruled, you will deny that they are ruled. Here I shall reply, "Why do they have a king?" At this point I do not see what remains for a man of your talents but to regret that you put in your letter such a doorway through which you yourself cannot get out. But even when you regret this and say that Mani must not be thought to have been defeated because you put something in your letter without due caution, I shall read out for you in countless passages from the books of Mani that he called the kingdom of light — which he established to be by nature contrary to the kingdom of darkness — not a kingdom but kingdoms. For in his *Letter of the Foundation*, which is so ruinous, when he spoke of God the Father, he said, "While no one in his kingdoms is either in need or weak."[47] But where there are kingdoms, who is so blind that he does not understand that kings absolutely cannot be equal to those over whom they rule? What, therefore, is so close, if you choose to notice it, and so suited to the honesty of your heart as that you should not regret putting that in your letter?

For Jesus Christ is most truly the king of lights that are by no means his equals but his subjects, and he is ruler of the blessed. But you should instead regret that you have been a Manichean, since the truthful beginning of your letter destroys

---

47. See *Answer to the Letter of Mani Known as The Foundation* 13, 16 for the context.

all Mani's deceptive machinations by one ramming blow. After all, Christ is the king of lights and has not begotten from himself the inferiors over whom he is king, and he has not seized neighboring lights, which he neither begot nor made, in order to reign over them. Otherwise there would be two kinds of good, neither of which comes from the other or needs the other, which is an idea that is alien to the path of truth. Hence, it remains that God did not beget the lights over which he reigns, because they are inferior, nor did he steal them, because they are his, but he made and created them.

4. If you want to ask what he made them out of, and if you begin to imagine the help of some matter that he did not make, so that in this case he who is omnipotent might not seem to make what he wanted unless something that he had not made helped him, you will again suffer from inexplicable clouds of error. But the words of the prophet are added by a clearheaded stroke of intelligence in a way most fitting for the sublime and ineffable majesty: *He spoke and they were made; he gave the order and they were created* (Ps 149:5). In that way you will see how we say in the Catholic faith that from nothing God made all things very good.[48] For, if he made them of something, he of course made them either of himself or not of himself. But if it was of himself, then, he did not make them but begot them. Why, then, did he beget them as inferior to himself? After all, if they were not inferior, he could not be their king. If it was not of himself, it was certainly not of something that he himself did not make. Otherwise he made them out of something belonging to someone else, and there already was something good that he himself had not made, out of which he might establish a kingdom for himself. But if that is so, he is not the first to create good things, because there already was something good that he himself had not created. For he would not make the lights of some alien evil in order that he might reign over them. Therefore it remains that, if he made them of something, he made them of what he himself had already made.

5. And so it is that we profess that God made out of nothing the first beginnings of the things that he was going to create. Or perhaps you did not say that Jesus Christ was the firstborn of the ineffable and most sacred majesty in terms of his assumption of the man.[49] For by that assumption of the man he deigned to have, as the apostle says and as the Catholic faith believes, those who were called to adoption as his brothers, among whom he was the firstborn.[50] But you perhaps want him to be understood as firstborn rather in terms of the excellence of the divinity, so that those lights over which he reigns may be his brothers, who were not made by the Father through him but born of the Father after him. In that way they would be born later, while he would be the firstborn, though all would

---

48. See Gn 1:31.
49. See Secundinus, Letter 1.
50. See Rom 8:29.

come from the same proper substance of the Father. If you believe this, you are first of all contradicting the gospel, where he is also said to be the only-begotten. It says, *And we have seen his glory like the glory of the only-begotten of the Father* (Jn 1:14), and that would in no way be truthfully said if his everlasting power and divinity, by which he is consubstantial with the Father and exists before every creature, had brothers from the same substance. And so, since the words of God bear witness that he is the only-begotten and the firstborn — only-begotten because he has no brothers, but firstborn because he has brothers — you will not find any way to understand that both expressions pertain to him in terms of the same nature of the divinity. But the Catholic faith, which distinguishes between the creator and the creature, meets with no difficulty in understanding these two expressions. For it understands him to be the only-begotten in terms of the words of scripture: *In the beginning was the Word, and the Word was with God, and the Word was God* (Jn 1:1). But it understands him to be the firstborn of all creation in terms of the words of the apostle: *In order that he might be the firstborn among many brothers* (Col 1:18), whom the Father begot for him in order to form a society of brothers, not by an equality of substance but by the adoption of grace.

And so, read the scriptures; you will never find it said of Christ that he is the Son of God by adoption. But we read very often about ourselves: *You have received the spirit of adoption as sons, as you await the adoption, the redemption of our body* (Rom 8:15.23); *in order that we may receive adoption as sons* (Gal 4:4); *he has predestined us for adoption as sons* (Eph 1:5); *a holy nation, an adopted people* (1 Pt 2:9); *he has called you through our gospel into the adoption of the glory of our Lord Jesus Christ* (2 Thes 2:12-13); and any other such texts that occur to someone who remembers or reads them. For to be the only Son of God through the excellence of the Father is one thing; it is quite another to receive through merciful grace the power to become sons of God by believing in him. He says, *He gave them the power to become sons of God* (Jn 1:12). They were not, therefore, sons by nature, since they received the power to become sons by believing in the only Son, whom *the Father did not spare, but handed over for us all* (Rom 8:32). In that way he made him, who is by himself the only-begotten, the firstborn in relation to us. Because, then, he is the only-begotten, he was born not from the flesh, nor from blood, nor from the will of man, nor from the will of the flesh, but from God.[51] But because he became the firstborn of his brothers in the Church, *The Word was made flesh and dwelled among us* (Jn 1:14). Insofar as we were also once sons of wrath[52] — that is, sons of vengeance bound by the chain of mortality, although God creates and fashions us, who undoubtedly arranges and forms all things in measure,

---

51. See Jn 1:13.
52. See Eph 2:3.

number, and weight[53] from the highest to the lowest — we were born from flesh and blood and from the will of the flesh. But insofar as we have received the power to become children of God, we are not born from flesh and blood nor from the will of man nor from the will of the flesh but from God — not, of course, with a nature that makes us his equal, but by the grace of adoption.

6. Next, if I granted you that Jesus Christ is not the only son of the Father in accord with the same divine substance but has brothers born after him in relation to whom he is the firstborn, I ask you how he can be their king. Would you dare to say that he was born stronger because he was born earlier? Surely you would be ashamed to think that. But you do not think that. What, then, do you think? Calm your mind, and make yourself peaceful in order to consider the truth without obstinacy. For I also ask you this: How would you understand that Jesus Christ is the firstborn in that divine, perfectly good, and eternal substance? Was he born first in time so that we should understand that those in relation to whom he is the firstborn were born later in that kingdom? We could not say by how many hours, days, months, or years he who was born earlier is older, but we would nonetheless think that those births were separated by some interval of time. Or should we understand that he was the firstborn not in terms of time but in terms of the excellence of the truly sublime majesty by which he, like a son born in some princedom, merited also to be king over his brother lights?

If you reply that he is prior in time and older than his brothers, so that you contend that the kingship over his brothers was conferred on him on the basis of the fact that he preceded them in being born, and that at one point he existed when they did not yet exist, what are you saying, my brother? Will you thus cast your heart down into the pit of impiety by thinking that there is a mutability in time which is discernable in that divine and highest nature and by believing that something existed there that had not existed before? Or because the lights had to go forth against the nation of darkness, do you call those goings-forth births, which you think occurred in time in order that the battle might be fought in time? One light, then, could not suffice to carry out that whole task of war by its divine power. Or if many were needed, must we hold this in the case of spiritual realities, namely, that we should think that the gate was so narrow that they could not go forth at the same time and that, because one of the brothers emerged first, he deserved to be called the firstborn and to become the king of the others? I do not want to take up in detail the individual points for fear that I may be too much of a burden to your mind, which is capable of grasping everything from a few examples. Raise up, then, the gaze of your mind; wipe away the clouds of contention. You will immediately see that movements, goings-forth, births, deaths, or any changes in terms of places and in terms of times occur only in a mutable creature. And still, if that creature did not come from God, its artisan and creator, the

---

53. See Wis 11:21.

apostle would not have said, *And they worshiped and served a creature instead of the creator, who is blessed forever* (Rom 1:25).

7. For in this statement there are two points that are particularly important, and I ask that you look at them with me: first, that, if the creature were unrelated to God, the apostle would not call God its creator; and second, that, if the creator and the creature were of one and the same substance, he would not blame those people because *they served a creature rather than the creator*, since, whichever they served, they would not have ceased to serve the same nature and substance. For just as no one can serve the Son who does not also serve the Father, because both have one substance, neither can one serve a creature without serving the creator if both have the same substance. Hence, if you now see and understand this, you would notice that there is a very great difference between the creator and a creature, and you ought to understand that a creature is not the offspring of the creator. For, if it were, it would be not inferior but equal and of the same substance, and for this reason whoever worshiped and served it would at the same time also offer worship and service to its creator and father. But since those who worshiped and served a creature instead of the creator were blamed by the apostle and were considered contemptible, we are shown clearly enough that the two have different substances.

For, just as the Son cannot be seen, that is, understood, unless the Father is also understood in him, since he himself says, *The one who sees me sees the Father* (Jn 14:9), neither can the Son be worshiped unless the Father is also worshiped in him. And for this reason, if a creature were a son, it would not be worshiped without the creator, and those people would not be condemned who worshiped a creature rather than the creator. And so you now see, I think, that it is not appropriate for you to say that Jesus Christ is the firstborn of the most hidden and ineffable majesty and the king of all the lights unless you cease to be a Manichean and distinguish a creature from the creator. In that way Jesus Christ may be the only-begotten insofar as he is the Word of God, God with God,[54] equally immutable and equally eternal, who did not think it robbery to be equal to God,[55] and may also be the firstborn of all creation insofar as all things visible and invisible in heaven and on earth were created in him. You recognize, I think, the words of the apostle to the Colossians.[56]

8. Hence, I ask you what the universe of creatures was made out of. Although it is good in its own kind, it is still inferior to the creator and mutable, while the creator remains immutable, and you will not find anything to answer unless you admit that it was made of nothing. And for this reason it can tend toward nothing when that creature and part of creation that can sin does sin — not so that it is

---

54. See Jn 1:1.
55. See Phil 2:6.
56. See Col 1:15-16.

nothing but so that it is less vigorous and less strong. For, if you push what is less vigorous and less strong to its limit, nothing remains. That creature, therefore, willingly loves vanity when it abandons the solidity of the truth and goes after matters of opinion, that is, after mutable things. But when it pays the penalties it deserved for this, it is made subject to vanity against its will, just as creation is made subject to vanity in a human being who sins. For this reason the apostle says, *All creation has been made subject to vanity against its will* (Rom 8:20), because all creation is also present in a human being. Of course there is present in a human being something invisible in terms of the soul and something visible in terms of the body. But all creation is partly invisible and partly visible, and yet all creation is not present in an animal, in which an intellectual mind is not present. The apostle, to be sure, says that it was made subject in hope on account of the mercy of him who delivers it through the forgiveness of sins and the adoption of grace. But, if you refuse to say that creation, which is indeed good but unequal to the creator and subject to change, was made out of nothing by the Father through the Son in the goodness of the Holy Spirit, the Trinity, which remains always consubstantial, eternal, and immutable, you will certainly be forced to utter sacrileges, such as that God begot of himself something that is not equal to its parent and that can be made subject to vanity. Or, if you say that what God begot is equal to God, both will be mutable. What greater impiety is there than to believe and say these things, and to prefer to change God for the worse because of a perverse opinion than to change oneself for the better by correct reasoning?

But if you are afraid to say that God is mutable, because that is really a great and most obvious impiety, and if you say that creation is also immutable, so that you make it equal to the creator and of one and the same substance, your own letter will again reply to you. For where does that soul come from which you put in the midst of the spirits and of which you say, "It gave its own nature victory from the beginning?"[57] And you set forth for it a law and condition: "If it acts in accord with the spirit of the virtues, it will have endless life with him and will possess that kingdom to which our Lord invites us. But if it begins to be dragged off by the spirit of the vices and after its consent does penance, it will have a source of pardon for this filth."[58] You surely recognize these words from your letter, and you also recognize at the same time that you have made the nature of the soul mutable. For what else is it to consent at one point to the spirit of the vices and again to do penance but to be changed — at one time for the better, at another for the worse? And the perfectly clear truth forces you to say this. For, if you wanted to feign ignorance, your very soul would force you to notice its mutability, and, having been changed so frequently from the time when you

---

57. Secundinus, Letter 2.
58. Secundinus, Letter 2, with some variations.

were born through various desires, doctrines, moments of forgetfulness, and acts of consent, it would become a witness for itself and would not look for any proofs from elsewhere.

9. Or perhaps you think that it helps you to say that the soul is immutable, since you went on to say that the soul did not sin by its own will but under the leadership of another: "For it is led by its mingling with the flesh, not by its own will."[59] In this statement you perhaps want it to be understood that the soul is immutable in its own nature but mutable because of its mingling with the other nature, as if we were asking *why* it was so and not *whether* it was so. For in this way the bodies of Hector, Ajax, and also of all human and living beings, would be said to be invulnerable if there were no blows or mishaps that could inflict a wound upon them. But, oddly enough, it is only the body of Achilles that was said to be invulnerable, whether by poetic fiction or because of some more hidden power in things. For, even when weapons struck it, it was not pierced, and, where it could be pierced, it was not invulnerable. If the soul were immutable in that way, it would not be changed by its mingling with anything, just as a body that is invulnerable would not be wounded by contact with or an attack from anything. And so, because we say that the Word of God cannot be defiled, even after he assumed mortal and vulnerable flesh in order to teach us to regard as unimportant both death and any misfortunes of the body, we are not afraid to believe that he was born of a virgin. But because in your wicked perversity you believe that the Son of God can be defiled, you are afraid to allow him to be united with flesh. And yet, in claiming that his substance is the same as the nature of the soul, you affirm that he was mingled with flesh in such a way that you do not hesitate to think that he was even changed for the worse.

Choose, then, what you want. Do you want to say or believe that God is mutable, so that you may likewise believe that the Son was born mutable from the mutable substance of the Father? You certainly see what a great impiety this is. Or do you want to say that God is immutable but still begot a mutable Son of his own substance? Yet you see how impious and absurd it is to say this. Or do you want to confess that God is immutable, so that what he begot of his own substance may be equally unchanged and may be equally the highest and most excellent good and may, in the same manner, possess being in the highest way with an inviolable permanence, but that he made the other goods, which we call creation, not of himself but of nothing? For otherwise they would be equal to him. If you believe this, you will no longer be impious; you will forget the Persian and be one of ours.

10, 1. But the apostle says, *Our struggle is not against flesh and blood but against princes and powers* (Eph 6:12), who begrudge pious souls a return to God by turning them by their wicked will to a love of their own loftiness and

59. Secundinus, Letter 2.

dignity. But the difference between your opinion and our belief is that you think that those princes originated from some nature of their own, which God neither made nor begot but had next to him as an eternal neighbor, and that they waged war against God before the mingling of good and evil first imposed upon him the great evil of necessity. For he was forced to mingle his own substance with them to be afflicted, disturbed, changed by error, and completely submerged in forgetfulness of itself, so that it needed someone to deliver, correct, fix, and teach it. You see how foolish and fantastic it is to say this and the great crime of impiety in which it traps one. But by the Christian faith we are convinced that there is nothing contrary to God, who exists in the highest manner, save what does not exist at all, but that whatever exists in some way has it from him who exists in the highest way that it exists in any way and is good in its own kind. But some things exist to a greater degree and others to a lesser degree, and in that way all the things that God the creator made are good. And they are arranged in their various different ranks, at times by intervals and positions in place, such as all bodily things; at times by the merits of their natures, as the soul is preferred to the body; at times by the merits of rewards and punishment, as a soul is either raised up to repose or subjected to pains. And in this way those princes, against whom the apostle says we have our struggle, first suffer the punishment of their own sins before they do harm. No hateful person, after all, is not first a torment to himself before he injures someone else. But the stronger do harm to the weaker. For no one overcomes someone else save to the extent that he is more powerful. The wicked princes are nonetheless themselves weaker than if they had remained in their pristine state and righteousness.

It makes a difference, however, in what respect one is more powerful than another — whether in terms of the body, as horses are more powerful than human beings; or in terms of the nature of the soul, as a rational being is more powerful than a being without reason; or in terms of the disposition of the mind, as a just person is more powerful than someone unjust; or in terms of a degree of power, as an emperor is more powerful than a soldier or a provincial official. But we believe that power is only given by the supreme power of God, often to worse persons over better ones, that is, to unjust persons over those who either already possess justice or are striving to possess it. For it is given in order that those tested by suffering may be revealed[60] either to themselves, in order to give them hope, or to others as an example to imitate. The apostle says, *We know that tribulation produces suffering, that suffering produces tested character, and that tested character produces hope* (Rom 5:3-4).

In this sort of conflict a believer struggles against the princes and powers of the transgressor angels and against the spirits of wickedness when they receive the power to tempt him, and he is commanded to endure this. As a result, those

---

60. See 1 Cor 11:19.

spirits overcome something weaker but are overcome by something more powerful. Often they overcome the weaker body but are overcome by the stronger mind. We fight against their force by patience and against their ambushes by prudence, to be sure, in order that they may neither bend us to deadly consent by using force nor mislead us by deception. But it is truly the power and wisdom of God by which all things have been made, and when in these things that have been made the higher ones descend to lower ones, where all sin and everything that is called evil is found, violence imitates power and deceit imitates wisdom. When, however, those that have descended turn around and return, greatness of heart imitates power and learning imitates wisdom. In their impious pride sinners imitate God the Father himself; the righteous imitate him by their pious generosity. The greed of the unjust imitates the Holy Spirit; while the love of the just imitates him. From the imitation of God, from whom and through whom and in whom these natures were made, both groups start off, the former by a sinful imitation, the latter by a praiseworthy imitation. Nor is it surprising if, when those making progress and those failing enter into conflict, the imitation of those who fail is overcome by that of those making progress. For the former are hurled down by pride, but the latter rise up by humility.

10, 2. But if it bothers you that those who are stronger in mind are weaker in body, it should not surprise you that the mortality of the body tries those who have been set free by the forgiveness of sins, for they will be rewarded by its immortality. For one does not easily avoid punishment except when he who is released from the body has conquered by his merits. For this reason the apostle said, *But if Christ is in you, the body is indeed dead on account of sin, but the spirit is life on account of righteousness. If, however, the Spirit of him who raised up Jesus Christ from the dead dwells in you, he will also bring to life your mortal bodies through his Spirit who dwells in you.* (Rom 8:10-11) If the soul, then, which carries about mortal flesh as a punishment for sin, is changed for the better and does not live in accord with the mortal flesh, it will change it for the better and merit to have an immortal body. But this will come about in the end when the last enemy, death, will be destroyed, when this corruptible body will put on incorruptibility, not in that mythical sphere of yours but in that transformation of which the apostle says, *We shall all rise, but we shall not all be changed* (1 Cor 15:51). For, after he had said, *The dead will rise incorruptible, and we shall be changed* (1 Cor 15:52), he went on to add, in order to show the sort of change he was speaking about: *For this corruptible body must put on incorruptibility, and this mortal body must put on immortality* (1 Cor 15:53). He was, of course, discussing the question of the body of those who rise. He had posed the question as follows: *But someone will ask: How will the dead rise? In what sort of body will they come?* (1 Cor 15:35) Read this whole passage, then, paying attention with pious care, not disturbed by stubborn contentiousness, and, with God's help, without the need for anyone to explain it, your mind will find nothing but what I say. And then call your mind back to what we began to consider, and see now, if you can, that I am not saying that the righteous fight against nothing but against those substances that have fallen because they did not remain standing in the truth.

11. For to fail is not yet nothing, but to tend toward nothing. After all, when those things that exist to a greater degree descend to those that exist to a lesser degree, it is not those to which they come down but those that go down that fail and begin to be less than they were — not so that they become those things to which they have come down but so that they become less in accord with their own kind. For, when the soul descends toward the body, it does not become a body, but nonetheless it becomes bodily in some sense because of its defective desire. And so, when a certain angelic loftiness was more delighted by its dominion over itself, it turned its love down to what was less and it began to be less than it was, and it tended toward nothing in accord with its own level. For each thing is closer to nothing to the extent that it is less. But when these failings are voluntary, they are rightly reprehended and are called sins, but when troubles, difficulties, pains, and adversity — all of which we suffer against our wills — follow upon these voluntary failures, sins are either rightly punished by penalties or are removed by trials.

If you were willing to contemplate them with a calm mind, you would immediately cease to accuse natures and bring charges against the substances themselves. But if you want a more ample and clearer explanation of this, read our three books that are entitled *Free Will*, which you can find in Campania at Nola in the house of Paulinus, the noble servant of God. [61]

12. But I ought now to remember that I am replying to your letter with a letter, though with a much longer one. In other works, to be sure, I dealt with many points, lest I be obliged to say the same things everywhere. But I had promised to convince you, on the basis of your letter, of how false the things that you have believed are and of how true the formula of the Catholic faith is. The whole difference between us is surely that you say that evil is a kind of substance, while we say that evil is not a substance but a falling away from what exists in a higher degree to what exists in a lower degree.

Listen, then, to this as well. For you put it in your letter and say of the soul that it is led to sin by its mingling with the flesh, not by its own will, and you immediately saw there, I believe, that, if this is so, almighty God had surely to go to the help of every soul and that absolutely no soul ought to be condemned since no soul sinned by its will. And, once this has been established, the statement is destroyed that Mani utters in such a terrifying way concerning the punishment

---

61. Paulinus, bishop of Nola (d. 431), was one of Augustine's many correspondents.

of souls, even though they come from the side of the light. Hence, you added with great vigilance and said, "But if, though it knows itself, it consents to evil and does not arm itself against the enemy, it has sinned by its own will."[62] It is good, of course, that you finally admit that it is possible that the soul might sin by its own will, but to what evil does it consent when it sins by its own will? Surely to that evil which you say is a substance.

13. But now I see three things, and I think that you also see them along with me. For the soul that consents to evil and the evil to which it consents are two things, but the consent itself is a third thing. After all, you do not say that the consent is the soul but that it belongs to the soul. See, then: of these three the soul is a substance, and the evil to which the soul consents when it sins voluntarily is, according to your opinion, a substance. I ask you, then, what the consent itself is, whether you say that it is a substance or is in a substance. For, if you say that it is a substance, your opinion will hold not two substances but three. Or do you hold two because the consent of the soul, by which it consents to evil, is of the same substance as the soul? Now I ask whether this consent is evil or good. If it is good, the soul certainly does not sin when it consents to evil. Not only does the truth cry out, however, but you also write that the soul at that point sins by its will. That consent, then, is evil, and for this reason the substance of the soul is also, if the consent is the substance of the soul and the two are one substance. Do you see how you are forced to say that the soul and that evil are not the one a good substance and the other an evil substance but two evil substances?

Here you will perhaps try to ascribe the blameworthy consent not to the soul that consents to evil but to the evil to which it consents, so that in this way there can be two substances, one good and the other evil, when the soul is said to be on the side of the good, while the consent by which it consents to evil and the very evil to which it consents are situated together on the other side, and both of them are attributed by the soul to the evil substance. Who has raved more absurdly? For the soul does not consent if the consent does not belong to it. But the soul does consent; the consent, therefore, belongs to it. Now if the consent belongs to it and the consent is evil, this evil belongs to it. For, if this evil also belongs to the evil to which the soul consents, it necessarily did not have this evil before the soul consented to it. What sort of a good, then, is the soul whose coming either doubles or, to put it more mildly, increases that evil?

14. Then, if this consent, which it is agreed is evil, is a substance, we find that it lies in the power of the soul that some substance should or should not be evil, since this consent lies in the power of the soul. For, if it is not, then the soul does not consent by its own will. But you said that the soul sinned by its own will in accord with this consent. The soul, therefore, as I said, has it in its power that a particular evil substance should either exist or not exist. But what else is a substance but a

---

62. Secundinus, Letter 2.

nature? There will be some nature, therefore, that is not natural to the soul, because, if the soul does not want it, it will not exist, and that is not natural to the evil to which the soul consents. For you cannot say that it is a natural evil of the nation of darkness which is produced in it by the will of another, that is, by the will of the soul. To what nature, then, will this nature, that is, this consent, be ascribed if it is a nature that is natural neither to the soul nor to the nation of darkness, unless you argue contrary to Mani that there are not two but three natures? For, even if there were at one time two natures, yet now, after this consent has arisen, they have certainly become three. And you are certainly forced to say that this third nature, which was born from the consent of the soul and from the evil to which it consents, is like the child of the two. But since it was born of two natures, of which one is good and the other evil, I ask why it was not born as something neither good nor evil. For, just as what is born from a horse and an ass is neither a horse nor an ass, so, if what was born of the good nature and the evil nature is a nature, it ought to be neither good nor evil. But you admit that the consent is evil. For you say that the soul then sins by its own will when it consents to evil.

Or do you perhaps think that the good nature and the evil nature are male and female like the two sexes? Thus, just as from a male and a female there is not born something neither male nor female but something either male or female, so you claim that from the good and from the evil there was born not a third something that is neither good nor evil but another evil. But if that is so, where is that victorious nature of the soul? Was it overcome[63] so that another good was not born instead? And then, do you not see that you are now saying that there are different sexes, not different natures? For, if there were a difference of natures between good and evil, there would have arisen from the two only a third something that could not have been either good or evil. Or surely this union would have been infertile, and a third substance would not have been begotten from it. For, if from the union of the animals that I mentioned above nothing but a male or a female mule is born, which is neither a horse nor an ass, for how much better reason ought it to turn out this way in the case of such a great and — in fact — the very highest difference between good and evil? Or, if no new nature came to be from their union, there would not be an evil nature, even if there could not be a good one. It remains, then, that we cannot escape such incredible insanities unless we admit that the consent, which it is agreed is evil and blameworthy, is not a substance but inheres in a substance.

15. Then let us ask with the greatest diligence in what substance it inheres. Yet to whom is it not evident that, just as persuasion is only found in a nature that persuades, so consent is only found in a nature that consents? When, therefore, the soul consents to evil, the soul is a substance, but its consent is not a substance. Now you see, I think, in what substance it is found; that is, you

---

63. I have conjectured *superata* in place of *separata*.

certainly see that this consent is in the soul, and you do not doubt that this consent is a sin and is, for this reason, evil. From this you already understand that it is possible that there is some evil, which is not a substance, in a good substance like the soul, just as this consent is, and because of this evil the soul is also called evil. A sinful soul is certainly evil, but it sins when it consents to evil. One and the same thing, then, that is, the soul, is good insofar as it is a substance but evil insofar as it has some evil, which is not a substance, namely, this consent. For it has this consent as the result not of progress but of a defect.[64] Of course it is deficient when it consents to evil and begins to exist to a lesser degree and, for this reason, to be less powerful than it was when it stood firm in virtue, consenting to nothing. It is surely worse to the extent that it turns away from him who exists in the highest degree toward that which exists to a lesser degree, so that the soul itself also exists to a lesser degree. But to the extent that it exists to a lesser degree, it is closer to nothing. For what becomes less tends toward complete non-existence, and though it does not come to the point that it is nothing by completely perishing, it is still evident that any failing is a beginning to perish.

And so, open now the eyes of your heart and see, if you can, that any substance is something good and that therefore a defect of a substance is an evil, because to be a substance is good. And yet not every defect is blameworthy, but only a voluntary one by which a rational soul abandons its creator and turns its love to those things that were created beneath it. For this is what is called sin. But other defects, which are not voluntary, either are penalties, so that sins may be punished by justice, which sovereignly governs and orders everything, or they emerge from the measured stages of the lowest things by which earlier ones yield to those that follow, and in that way all temporal beauty is produced with its changes and in its own kind. After all, a speech is produced in that way as syllables die, so to speak, and are born, for they are extended over certain stretches of time and depart with the orderly succession of those that follow, once they have filled out their spaces, until the whole speech is brought to its end. And the length of time that a syllable is drawn out or hurried over, or the form by which the individual letters preserve their amounts of space, does not lie in the sounds themselves that rush on but in the control of the speaker. And yet the art itself that produces the speech is not uttered in sounds or spun out or changed in time. In that way, by the rise and fall, by the going and coming of temporal things at certain and definite periods, temporal beauty is crafted until it comes to its foreordained end. And temporal beauty is not evil because we can grasp and admire better features in spiritual creatures. Rather, it has its own splendor in its own kind and teaches those who live good lives about the supreme wisdom of God, which is its maker and governor and which is hidden on high beyond all the bounds of time.

---

64. Augustine plays on *profectus* ("progress") and *defectus* ("defect").

16. Come now, turn your attention to whether that which you called evil, by consenting to which the soul sins voluntarily, is a substance or whether here too you cannot blame a substance. For I ask what entices the consent of the soul or whether the soul rushes in without reason and is said to consent because it is moved by some delight that it finds. But if that is so, it is not logical to call something evil because it is not loved correctly. For, if I show that something is loved wrongly where it is held to be a sin not of the object loved but of the lover, you will surely admit that the beauty of anything is not necessarily vicious because the consent of the person desiring it is wrongly drawn to it. It will be evident later how much this helps me.

But to illustrate what I promised, what should I choose? For an abundance of material surrounds me. What, I repeat, should I choose rather than that which we praise as a heavenly creature but which you adore as a portion of the creator? Among all the visible beings what is more excellent than this sun? But if someone desires its light excessively, for the sake of his eyes he produces injurious conflicts. Suppose he has obtained some power by which he can accomplish what he desires and tears down the houses of his neighbors, which are set opposite his windows, so that, once the sky is less obstructed, the sun may enter his interior rooms. Is it, then, a defect of the sun because this man loved this light to the point that he dared to prefer it to the light of justice and because, in wanting to welcome in greater amounts the light of the eyes of the flesh into his body's house, he closed the door of his heart and the gaze of his mind to the light of justice? You see, then, that something good can be loved with a love that is not good. Hence, though you call that evil to which the soul consents when it sins, I call it good in its own kind — but the sort of good to which the soul should not consent insofar as the soul is better. For the soul is higher than the body and has God higher than itself, though the nature of the body is good at its own level. And yet the soul sins and by sinning becomes evil if it gives the consent of its love, which it owes to God, who is above it, to a body that is lower than it.

17. Or do you say that you do not call that consent blameworthy when a thing is loved that does not do anything to cause the consent to it but when the soul consents in a blameworthy manner,[65] when that to which the soul consents persuades it or forces it to something,[66] and that it is evil because it persuades or urges the soul to commit some evil? This is a second question and one also to be considered eventually in its proper order. But here we shall first recall what sin is, about which I think we have argued enough. It has been made clear that it is possible that something that is good in its own kind may be loved wrongly and not be blamed, though the person who loves it is blamed. What then? If a soul that is already sinful and defective because of such a love persuades someone

---

65. I have conjectured the addition of *culpabiliter*.
66. I have conjectured *illud* in place of *illum*.

else to commit the same sin, will not the soul that consents to the persuasion become evil by the same defect by which the soul it follows had become evil? The first sin, therefore, is to prefer any creature, though a good one, to the creator in one's love, but the second sin is to tempt someone else also to do that by persuasion or by force. For no one wants to lead someone else into evil unless he himself has first become evil. But they sin by will who desire to lead others to sin out of either a foolish benevolence or a malicious hatred. After all, who teaches his children — except out of a perverse love — that they should consider no gain shameful but that they should acquire more money however they can? He certainly does not hate them, and yet he persuades them harmfully. He himself has certainly already been corrupted by a love of such things, though gold and silver are not evil, just as that sun, which we discussed above, was not evil, but the disordered lover of something good is at fault. When someone wants another person to sin out of envy, however, he loves honor with an immoderate pride, and he desires to excel and to surpass the others in it. And since he sees that honor is paid more amply and more truly to virtues, he desires that others be brought down from the peak of justice to the whirlpool of wickedness for fear that he may be surpassed in honor. In this way the devil tries to persuade or to force someone to sin. But is honor itself at fault because the devil himself became impious by loving it perversely and impiously? Or is the angelic substance of the same devil, which God created, evil because it is a substance? Rather, when the devil abandoned the love of God and turned too much to a love of himself, he wanted to be thought equal to God, and for this reason he was cast down by the swelling of pride. He is evil, therefore, not insofar as he is a substance but because he was a created substance and insofar as he loved himself more than him by whom he was created. And he is evil because he exists to a lesser degree than he would have existed if he had loved that which exists in the highest degree. His defect, therefore, is evil.

Every defect, therefore, tends toward not-being from that which is, just as all progress tends toward being to a greater degree from that which is to a lesser degree. The highest honor, which the piety of devout people show him, is of course due to God. One who loves honor, therefore, imitates God. But humble souls want to be honored in God, while proud souls want to be honored in place of God. Souls humble in relation to God, however, become higher than unjust souls, while souls that rise up against God become more lowly than just souls, that is, by the distribution of rewards and punishments, because the humble souls have loved God more than themselves, while the proud souls have loved themselves more than God.

18. Now, I think, it is easy for you to understand from the words of this letter of yours, in which you said, "When it consents to evil, the soul sins by its will,"[67] that no evil is an evil nature or the love of an evil nature. But since all natures are good in their own kind, evil is a sin, which is committed by the will of the soul when it loves a creature instead of the creator, whether by its own assent when it is evil or by the persuasion of another when it consents to evil. And yet it also becomes evil by reason of the ensuing punishments, in order that the supremely good creator may arrange all things in accord with their merits in the creature that is good, but not supremely good. For God did not beget it of himself but made it from nothing.

You, however, have set up two natures, and you want one of them to be good and the other evil, or rather (since a nature also becomes evil after having been good by sinning) one of them the nature of good and the other the nature of evil. Yet you admit that the nature that you say is good acts in an evil way by consenting to evil, that is, sins by its will. I, on the other hand, maintain that both are good but that one of them acts in an evil way by persuasion, while the other acts in an evil way by consenting. But just as the consent of the one is not a nature, neither is the persuasion of the other. And just as, if this nature does not consent to evil, it will remain good, preserving the integrity of its nature, so, if that one does not persuade to evil, it will be better. But if it itself also does not commit the sin to which it does not persuade another, they will have equal integrity and praiseworthiness in their kind. For, even if that nature sins twice that commits sins and persuades another to sin, while the other sins once if it only consents to doing evil, they become evil because of their sins; they are not evil by nature. Or if that nature is evil on account of its act of persuasion, likewise this nature is evil on account of its act of consent.

But if to persuade to evil seems worse to you than to consent to it, let the one be evil and the other worse. Still, there is not such a great acceptance of persons and so unjust a partiality in judging that, though both sin, even if one sins more seriously and the other less seriously, one is said to be the nature of evil and the other the nature of good. Rather, both should be said to be good, though the one that sins less is better, or both should be said to be evil, though the one that sins more is worse.

19, 1. But what was the evil that is called sin produced from if there is no nature of evil? Tell me where that evil consent came from in the nature that you concede and teach is good. For whatever suffers so that it consents to evil, it would certainly not suffer unless it could suffer. I ask, then, where it has this ability to suffer from. After all, it would be better if it did not have it. That than which something could be better is not the nature of the highest good. Secondly, if it has it in its power to consent or not to consent, it does not therefore consent

---

67. Secundinus, Letter 2, slightly changed.

because it has been conquered. I ask, then, where it has this evil consent from, since there is no contrary nature forcing it. But if it is forced to consent so that it is not in its power to do otherwise, it does not therefore sin by its will, as you said that it does, since it does not consent with its will. But I still ask whence this ability to be deceived comes to be in it if it is deceived. For, before it was deceived, if there were not present in it the ability to be deceived so that it could suffer this, it certainly would never suffer this. And yet it consents in no other way than by the will. But if it is forced, it should be said to yield rather than to consent. But by whatever name you call it, I ask you — a sharp and clever man with your Roman mind, as you boast — whence this nature of the good has the ability to suffer what it suffers so that it consents to evil. For, before it is broken, wood has the ability to be broken, and unless the ability were present there, the wood could never be broken. Nor is wood unbreakable because no one comes along to break it. And so I ask whence this nature has the ability to be broken or to be bent before it is either broken to consent to evil or bent to it by persuasion. Or, if it already had the ability to be broken because of the proximity of the evil, as bodies are often corrupted by the vapors from a nearby swamp, it was therefore already corruptible if the pestilential infection from that vicinity could corrupt it. I ask, then, where that corruptibility came from.

19, 2. I beseech you, pay attention to what I am asking, and yield to the truth. For I am not asking where corruption comes from. After all, you will answer, "From the corrupter," and you will contend that this corrupter is some prince or other of the nation of darkness wrapped in such mythical veils that even Mani could scarcely describe and grasp him. Rather, I am asking where the corruptibility came from even before a corrupter came along. If there were no corruptibility, there either would be no corrupter or the approach of a corrupter would do no harm. Find, therefore, whence this corruptibility came to be in the good nature before it was corrupted by the contrary nature. Or, if you do not want to say that it is corrupted, at least find whence this mutability came to be in it before it was changed by that hostile opposition. For a nature is changed for the worse that becomes foolish from having been wise and that forgets itself. For you added these words when you said, "If, after it recognizes itself, it consents to evil."[68] It is changed for the worse, therefore, when it forgets itself, so that it again recognizes itself when reminded. But in no way could it have been changed unless it were changeable before it changed. When, therefore, you find whence this mutability came to be in the substance of the highest good before the mingling of good and evil was produced, you will surely stop asking me where evil comes from.

And yet, if you think of it correctly, no temporal mutability can be found in the nature of the highest good either from itself or from the approach of anything

---

68. Ibid.

else, as it can in the nature that Mani imagines and supposes is supremely good or even persuades those who believe him to think. Seek, and reply if you can, where this mutability comes from that was not discovered but revealed when the time for it came. For it could not be changed, even by an enemy, if it was not changeable. But since it could be changed, Mani showed that he had not made it unchangeable.

When you believe that this mutability exists in the substance of the highest good, that is, in the substance of God, you see, if you are not being stubborn, the great folly with which you blaspheme. But when something of the sort is said of a creature, which God has neither begotten nor brought forth of his substance but made from nothing, one is not dealing with the highest good but with a good of the sort that could only be produced by the highest good, which is God. To be sure, God, who is supremely good and immutably good, made all things not supremely or immutably good but still good, from the angels of heaven down to the least animals and plants of the earth, and he arranged all things in their proper places in accord with the dignity of each nature. But when the rational creature among these clings in the obedience of love to its creator, that is, to God, its maker and author, it preserves its own nature in God's eternity, truth, and love. But when it abandons God out of contemptuous disobedience, it implicates itself in sins through its free choice but is made unhappy because of its punishment through the just judgment of God. This is the whole of evil — partly what one does unjustly, partly what one suffers justly.

You should not ask me where it comes from, since you already answered yourself when you said, "After the soul recognizes itself, it sins by its own will if it consents to evil."[69] See where evil comes from, that is, from its own will. This is not a nature but a failing, and, for this reason, it is also contrary to the nature, which it certainly harms by depriving it of the good by which it could have been happy if it had not sinned. You think that this sinful will is not aroused in the soul except from another evil, which you believe to be a nature that God has not made, and you contend that the soul is the nature of God. And in this way, if this nature of evil, whatever it might be, produces this sinful will in the soul by persuasion, God is defeated and hurled down into sin.

20, 1. See the great impiety and the wicked and horrible blasphemies of which you refuse to strip yourself when you locate in a nature that God did not make life, sensation, speech, limit, form, order, and countless other goods, and when you locate in the very nature of God, prior to any mingling with evil, the mutability that allowed him to be taken captive and that he was forced to fear, "seeing that a great ruin and devastation would threaten his holy worlds if he did not set

---

69. Ibid., slightly changed.

against it some outstanding and illustrious deity powerful in might."[70] And why did he do all this if not in order that this nature and substance of God might subject and hold the enemy enchained in such a way that, when it sins, the nature of God would endure the enemy even while it was bound, and would not emerge wholly purified after it was defeated and, after being condemned, would still keep it enclosed within itself? But what a splendid excuse you found in your God for the necessity of war! You wanted to reply to the objection raised against you. That is, what was the nation of darkness going to do to God if God refused to fight with it? If you say that it was going to do him some harm, you admit that God is corruptible and violable. But if you say that it could not do him any harm, you will be asked: Why then did he fight? Why did he hand over to enemies his own substance to be corrupted and violated and forced into all sins? From this dilemma, then, you have never been able to escape.

20, 2. You think that you have found something important and safe to respond when you say, "It is a great injustice to desire the property of another, and God would have seemed to have consented to this injustice if he had refused to fight against the nation that had attempted this."[71] This reply would have some color of justice if the nature of your God had preserved itself whole and undefiled in this war and, after being mingled with the enemy members, had not committed any injustice either through having been forced or through having been enticed. But you say that as a captive it consents to such great crimes and outrages, and you also say that it could not be entirely purified from the very cruel impiety by which it became an enemy even of the holy light of which it was a portion. For this reason you believe that he rightly suffers the eternal punishments of that horrendous sphere. Who would not see how much better it would have been to leave the hostile foe in its injustice, while hatching its vain plans, rather than to hand over to it a part of God whose strength it would drain off and whose beauty it would corrupt and unite with its injustice?

Who is blinded by such stubbornness that he does not see and does not notice that the nation of darkness acted with much less injustice in vainly trying to invade the other nature than God acted in handing over his own nature to be invaded, to be forced into injustice, and even to be condemned to punishment in some part? Is to refuse to consent to injustice the same as to have committed so great an injustice without any necessity? Or was there some necessity — something that Mani was not ashamed to say, but that you are? Indeed, he said, "God saw that great ruin and devastation would threaten his holy worlds if he did not set against it some outstanding and illustrious deity powerful in might."[72] But you supposedly reason more cleverly. Instead of saying that God fought because

---

70. Mani, *The Letter of the Foundation.*

71. Secundinus, Letter 6, with considerable adaptation.

72. Mani, *The Letter of the Foundation.*

of that necessity, so that the nation of darkness would not harm him, you admit that God is violable and corruptible, so that it could do him some harm if he had refused to fight. Drive, therefore, and expel from your hearts and from your faith this fight, and at long last anathematize and condemn all that myth composed out of the horror of impious and impure blasphemies. For, I beg you, what does it mean that, as I said before, you are not afraid to say that that nature can be violated and God can be corrupted in such a way that, if the nature of your God could not use his strength to avoid being captured, he could not at least, as a captive, preserve justice, as Daniel did,[73] at whose lions you have dared to laugh? Because of Daniel's piety he was not compelled by any fear to consent to the injustice of those by whom he was taken captive, and he did not lose the justice and freedom of a patient and wise mind in his condition of bodily servitude.

But the nature of God was taken captive; it became unjust; it cannot be purified wholly; it is forced to be condemned in the end. If from eternity he knew that this evil would befall him, no divine honor was due to him because of what he was. You said that the places that Mani speaks of are indescribable, though the lands or territories of the kingdom of light and of the nation of darkness are next to each other in terms of proximity. These ideas are laughable for those who are wise enough to understand them. And you said that Christ called them the right hand and the left hand. We know that Christ used "the right hand" and "the left hand" not in order to refer to bodily places but in order to refer to the happiness or the unhappiness that each person merits. But your carnal thinking is tied to bodily places to such an extent that you say that this visible and hence bodily sun, which can be contained only in a bodily place, is both God and a part of God. But it is foolish to discuss this with you. Can you understand anything incorporeal, after all, if you still do not believe that God is incorruptible?

21. But like a good friend you kindly reprimand me for having left the Manicheans and for having had recourse to the books of the Jews. It is those books that strangle your error and lies. Christ is certainly foretold in them, the sort of Christ that the truth of God gave us, not the sort that the vanity of Mani made up. But, as a most urbane man, you attack the ancient scripture because it was written in the prophet: *And produce children by fornication because the land will commit fornication against the Lord* (Hos 1:2), though you hear in the gospel: *Prostitutes and tax collectors will enter the kingdom of heaven before you* (Mt 21:31). I know the reason for your indignation. For you are not as displeased at the promiscuous woman because of her fornication as you are displeased that the fornication was changed into marriage and transformed into marital chastity. For you believe that in marriage your God becomes bound in tighter chains of the flesh through the procreation of children. You think that

---

73. See Dn 6:14.

prostitutes spare your God because they try not to conceive so that they may serve a lust that is free from the duty of bearing children. In your eyes the new life in a woman is a prison and a chain for God. For this reason you are also displeased with the words, *And they will be two in one flesh* (Gn 2:24), although the apostle teaches that this is a great mystery in Christ and the holy Church.[74] For this reason you are displeased with the words, *Increase and multiply* (Gn 1:28), for fear that the prison cells of your God may be multiplied. But I confess that I learned in the Catholic Church that the soul, like the body, one of which rules while the other is subject, as well as the good of the soul and the goods of the body, come only from the highest good, from which all good things come, whether great ones or small ones, whether heavenly ones or earthly ones, whether spiritual ones or bodily ones, whether everlasting ones or temporal ones, and that the latter goods ought not to be criticized because the former are preferable.

22. But the words that you include among the passages that deserve to be blamed, *Kill and eat* (Acts 10:13), are used even in the Acts of the Apostles in a spiritual sense. Yet even in a bodily sense food is not something to blame, though overindulgence is. You above all ought to be pleased at this idea understood in a carnal sense[75] so that you might be able to butcher meat, and in that way your God would escape from his wretched imprisonment once his cell walls were broken. And if any remnants of him were left there, you would purify them in the workshop of your belly by eating them.

You insult me because I grieve over the barrenness of Sarah. I clearly do not grieve over this, because it too was prophetic. But it is appropriate for your sacrilegious myths to grieve not over Sarah's barrenness but over her fecundity, because the fecundity of every woman is a dire calamity for God. Hence, it is not surprising that what was foretold about such people — *They forbid marriage* (1 Tm 4:3) — is especially realized in you. For you do not detest intercourse as much as marriage, because in marriage intercourse for the sake of propagating children is not a vice but a duty. The continence of holy men and women is exempt from this duty not because they have avoided it as something evil but because they have chosen something better. And yet the marital duty of fathers and mothers, the sort of people Abraham and Sarah were, should be evaluated not on the basis of human society but on the basis of God's plan. For, because it was necessary that Christ come in the flesh, the marriage of Sarah served to propagate the same flesh as did the virginity of Mary.

23. For this reason Abraham said to his servant the words that you mentioned, mocking them with an amazing ignorance: *Place your hand under*

74. See Eph 5:31-32.
75. I have followed the reading in PL and omitted a *carnibus abstinere*, which the CSEL edition has.

my thigh. He said, while demanding his fidelity under an oath, *Place your hand under my thigh, and swear by the God of heaven* (Gn 24:2-3). By obeying the command the servant of course swore an oath, but by giving the command Abraham uttered a prophecy, namely, that the God of heaven was going to come into the flesh which was going to be propagated from that thigh. You scorn, detest, and despise this, you chaste and pure people. You are afraid of one womb of a virgin for the Son of God, whom no contact with the flesh could change, and you enmesh in the wombs of all females, not merely of humans but also of the other animals, the changed and polluted nature of your God. And for this reason, what thighs do you find, you people who are horrified at one thigh of a patriarch — I do not mean thighs of patriarchs but of any prostitutes where you ought not to swear by your God who has been so shamefully enchained there? Or perhaps you are not ashamed to touch chastely the member of a human body but are ashamed to swear by God, who is so shamefully chained there in such great deformity.

On account of the animals of every kind that were in it, you attack the ark of Noah[76] with the borrowed term *pancarp,* which is often eaten during the public games. By every kind of animal the ark symbolized that the Church was going to be made up of all the nations. Here I congratulate you, whether you were inattentive or ignorant, for having used that appropriate term. After all, πάγκαρπος means "all the fruits," which is true of the Church in a spiritual sense. And you do not notice that Noah and his family were much more fortunate among those wild animals, into whose midst he entered unharmed and from which he emerged unharmed, than your God was, who was torn to shreds and devoured by the fierce rage of the nation of darkness. Hence, your God clearly became not "all the fruits," but "met his match,"[77] for he was torn apart with utter ferocity.

You mock Jacob's wrestling with an angel,[78] which prophetically symbolized the future wrestling of the people of Israel with the flesh of Christ. But however you understand it, how much better would it be if your God wrestled with a human being than that he should be chained, taken captive, and torn to pieces by the nation of demons.

You falsely accuse Abraham of having sold the chastity of his wife. In that case he did not lie that she was his sister, but out of human caution he did not mention that she was his wife, while he entrusted to his God the protection of her chastity.[79] If he did not do what he could, he would have been judged not to have trusted God but to have tempted him. And yet you do not see that your God did not sell but freely gave not his wife but his own members to his enemies to be

---

76. See Gn 7.
77. Augustine plays with the words *pancarpus* and *compartus*. If *compartus* is the correct reading and not *comparcus,* which the CSEL edition has, then it means "matched as in single combat."
78. See Gn 32:24-25.
79. See Gn 12:20.

polluted, corrupted, and defiled. And you would surely hope, if it were possible, that the splendid nature of your God would return to him from his enemies as untainted as Sarah was restored untainted to her husband.

24. You praise my former way of life and aspirations and ask who suddenly changed me. Then, in approaching this point indirectly, you mention the ancient enemy of all faithful and holy men and women and of the Lord Jesus Christ. You of course want us to understand this enemy to be the devil.[80] What should I reply to you about my change other than that, if I did not believe that I became better by that change, I certainly would not have hated and condemned your error and gone over to the Catholic faith and Church? You yourself resolve for me the question of whether I did the right thing, that is, whether I was changed from evil to good, with that expression you used: "my change." For, if my soul were, as you say, the nature of God, it could never be changed either for the better, as I hope it has been, or for the worse, as you argue it has been, either by itself or by the influence of anyone else. Hence, when I left this error and chose that faith in which we piously believe that the nature of God is immutable, in order that we may come to understand it wisely, my change is only displeasing to those who are displeased at the immutability of God. But the devil is the adversary of holy men and women not because he rises up against them from an opposing principle of another nature but because he begrudges them the heavenly dignity from which he himself was cast down. For, having been changed himself, he strives to change others. After all, as you describe him in the long-windedness of that Persian myth, if the devil changes others without having been changed, he is certainly the greater and the winner. But if, as you maintain, he is not an enemy of God but a friend of the holy light and is better than those whom he deceives, who makes them enemies of the holy light of which he himself is a friend? Mani indeed says that souls will be condemned to eternal punishment in that horrible sphere because "they allowed themselves to wander from their previous bright nature and then emerged as enemies of the light."[81] For he contends that the mind of the nation of darkness, burning with a love to possess the light within itself, created the bodies of the animals. Take care to rescue yourself from these utterly empty and sacrilegious fictions so that you may be changed for the better by the help of him who is changed neither for the better nor for the worse.

25. You say, "We have escaped by following the spiritual savior. For the audacity of the devil burst forth to such a degree that, if our Lord had flesh, all our hope would have been cut away." If you say this because you do not believe that Christ had flesh, you ought not to put your faith in Mani. For you admit that he was brought to birth into the flesh from a man and a woman, like other human beings. Why, then, do you put so much hope in him? For in this letter of yours

---

80. See Letter of Secundinus 4.
81. Mani, *The Letter of the Foundation.*

you said when you were trying to terrify me, "Who, then, will be your patron before the just tribunal of the judge, when you begin to be convicted by your own testimony, both by your words and by your deeds? The Persian whom you attacked will not be there. Apart from him who will console you as you weep? Who will save this Punic man?"[82] You said that there could be no savior or consoler apart from Mani. How, then, though you were discussing the sufferings of Christ, did you say that you have escaped by following the spiritual savior, that is, one whom the enemy could not kill, as he could if he existed in the flesh? If, then, although the enemy found flesh in your Mani, he killed him in order that he might be your savior, how can you say, "Apart from him who will console you as you weep? Who will save this Punic man?" You see what is found in the heresy and in the doctrines of demons lying in their hypocrisy.[83] You want to be a true Manichean in respect to a false Christ. For, if in showing his flesh, death, resurrection, and the places of the wounds and of the nails, which he revealed to doubting disciples, he did all this as a deception and a lie, then Mani spoke the truth about Christ. But if Christ displayed real flesh and, for this reason, a real death, a real resurrection, and real scars, then Mani lied about Christ. And for this reason there is a difference on this issue between you and me: you chose to believe that Mani was truthful when you believed that Christ was a deceiver, while I believe that Mani lied about Christ, as he did about other things, rather than that Christ lied about anything. And for how much greater reason do I do so regarding that in which he located the hope of believers, that is, in his own suffering and resurrection! For someone who says, "After that supposed death of his, Christ appeared to his disciples who were doubtful, and they thought that they saw a spirit. When he said, *Touch my hands and feet, and see that a spirit does not have flesh and bones as you see that I have* (Lk 24:39), and when he said to one of them who did not believe, *Put your fingers into my side, and do not be unbelieving, but a believer* (Jn 20:27), he showed them all this not as the truth but as a lie" — someone who says this, I say, does not preach Christ but attacks him.

"But," you say, "Mani preaches Christ and says that he is his apostle." For this reason we should rather despise him and flee from him. For, if he said these things as accusations, he could at least boast of being a lover of the truth while refuting another person's lies. But now he reveals himself ignorantly and carelessly, and he demonstrates well enough to those who pay careful attention what he is doing and what he loves when he praises and preaches a liar. And so, my friend, flee from this great plague lest, by deceiving you, Mani should want to make you the sort of believer that he wants us to think that Christ made that disciple to whom he said, *Put your fingers in my side, and do not be unbelieving,*

---

82. Secundinus, Letter 3.
83. See 1 Tm 4:1-2.

but a believer (Jn 20:27). For that is impossible. After all, as the sweetest truth holds, what else did Christ say to the disciple but, "Touch the body I have; touch the body I had; touch real flesh; touch the marks of real wounds; touch the real holes made by the nails, and by believing what is real cease to be unbelieving but be a believer"? But as the sacrilegious vanity of Mani holds, what else did Christ say to the disciple but, "Touch my pretense; touch my deception"? What else did he say but, "Touch fake flesh; touch the deceptive places of fake wounds, and do not be unbelieving about my fake members, so that by believing what is false you can be a believer." Such are the believers that Mani has, believers in all the teaching of lying demons .

26, 1. Flee from these ideas, I beg you. Let not the sight of your small numbers mislead you because the Lord himself said that the few follow a narrow road.[84] You want to be among the few, but among the very worst. For it is true that few are completely innocent, but among the guilty there are fewer murderers than thieves, fewer who commit incest than adultery. Even the myths or histories of the ancients have fewer Medeas and Phaedras[85] than women who committed other crimes and outrages, fewer Orchi and Busirides[86] than men guilty of other impieties and sins. Watch out, then, that people's excessive horror of impiety is not perhaps the reason for your few numbers. Among you such things are read, said, and believed — so that one has to be surprised that any rather than only a few rush into that error and remain there. But the number of the holy, who take the narrow road, is small in comparison to the large number of sinners. This small number is hidden in the much larger amount of straw. But it is on the threshing floor of the Catholic Church where it is now to be gathered and ground, yet in the end it will be winnowed and purified.[87] You must join it if you truly desire to be a believer; otherwise, by putting your trust in what is false, you feed the winds,[88] as scripture says, that is, you become food for the unclean spirits. For the apostle Paul, whom you mention, did not regard as losses and rubbish the wise scriptures of the Old Testament and that whole prophetic dispensation of words and deeds. Rather he regarded as losses and rubbish the carnal superiority of the Jewish race, their zeal for persecuting Christians, with which he was himself ablaze — as if it were something praiseworthy — in defense of the synagogues of the people of his fathers, who were in error and

---

84. See Mt 7:14.
85. Medea was the daughter of King Aeetes of Colchis. After helping Jason to obtain the Golden Fleece, they were married. Later, when Jason deserted her, Medea killed their two children. Phaedra was the daughter of King Minos and the second wife of Theseus. Later she fell in love with Hippolytus and accused him of rape. He was put to death, and she hanged herself.
86. Ochus is probably Artaxerxes III of Persia who, to secure his hold on the kingdom, had all his relatives killed. Busiris is perhaps the mythical king of Egypt, the son of Poseidon, under whom the annual sacrifice of a foreigner was instituted to stem a plague.
87. See Mt 3:12.
88. See Prv 10:4.

recognized not Christ but the righteousness that comes from the law. For the Jews proudly boasted of the law because they did not understand the grace of God in it. How much more ought you to throw away, not as losses and rubbish but as poison, those writings full of unspeakable blasphemies in which the nature of the truth, the nature of the highest good, the nature of God, is described as so often subject to change, so often defeated, so often corrupted, so often in part inextricably defiled, and destined to be condemned by the truth in the end! And how much more ought you to put an end to your contentiousness and to cross over to the Catholic Church and faith, which has been revealed in its own time as it was foretold so long before.

26, 2. I say this to you because your mind is not the nature of evil, which does not exist at all, nor the nature of God. Otherwise, I would be speaking in vain to someone who could not change. But because your mind was changed by abandoning God and because its change is something evil, let it be changed and turned back to the immutable good by the help of this immutable good, and such a change of it will be its deliverance from evil. If you spurn this admonition, because you still believe that there are two natures, one the mutable nature of the good, which, when mingled with evil, could consent to injustice, the other the immutable nature of evil, which, even when mingled with good, could not consent to justice, you spread about that most recent and shameful myth that sows detestable and shameful blasphemies in the fornication of itching ears. And, as a result, you are in the flock of those of whom it was foretold, *There will come a time when they will not maintain sound doctrine but will gather teachers for themselves according to their desires. Their ears will itch, and turning their hearing away from the truth they will turn to myths.* (2 Tm 4:3-4)

But if you wisely accept this admonition, having turned to the immutable God, you will become by your praiseworthy change one of those of whom the apostle says, *You were once darkness, but now you are light in the Lord* (Eph 5:8). This cannot be said to the nature of God, because it was never evil and worthy of the name "darkness," nor to the nature of evil, which, if it existed, could never be changed and become light. But this was correctly and truthfully said to that nature which is not immutable but became dark in itself because it abandoned the immutable light by which it was made. Having turned to that light, it does not become light in itself but in the Lord. For it is not enlightened by itself because it is not the true light, but it is bright because it was enlightened by him of whom it was said, *He was the true light that enlightens every human being who comes into this world* (Jn 1:9). Believe this; understand this; hold onto this if you want to be good by participation in the immutable good, which you cannot be by yourself. You could neither lose this if you were immutably good, nor could you receive it if you were immutably not good.

Index of Scripture

(prepared by Michael Dolan)

The numbers after the scriptural reference refer to the section of the work

The Catholic Way of Life and the Manichean Way of Life
(pp. 17 to 103)

Revisions I, 6 (7)

Text

Galatians
1:10	I, 21, 38
5:9	I, 24, 45
5:13	II, 11, 233

Ephesians
3:14-19	I, 18, 33

Colossians
2:8a	I, 21, 38

2:8b	I, 21, 38

1 Timothy
6:10	I, 19, 35

Titus
1:15	I, 33, 71

The Two Souls
(pp. 107 to 134)

Revisions I, 15 (16)

Old Testament

Job
11:14	7

Psalms
104:26	7

New Testament

Matthew
8:11	8

Luke
19:10	8

Romans
5:12	2
7:18	2
7:20	2

Ephesians
2:3	6

Text

New Testament

Matthew
8:22	2, 2

John
1:3	7, 9
1:11	7, 9
8:47	7, 9
8:47.44	7, 9
17:3	8, 10

Romans
11:36	7, 9

1 Corinthians
8:6	7, 9
11:12	7, 9

2 Corinthians
4:18	8, 10

1 Timothy
5:6	2, 2

A Debate with Fortunatus, a Manichean
(pp. 137 to 162)

Old Testament

Genesis

3:19	22

Psalms

148:5	13

New Testament

Matthew

3:10	14
12:33	22
15:13	14

John

5:24	3
10:9	3
10:18	32
11:26	3
14:6	3
14:9	3
15:22	21

Romans

1:1-4	19

5:19	22
7:23-25	21
8:2	22
8:7	21
9:20	26

1 Corinthians

15:21	22; 25
15:50	19

Galatians

5:13	22
5:17	21
6:14	21

Ephesians

2:1-18	16
2:3	17
5:6	22

Philippians

2:5-8	7

1 Timothy

4:4	22
6:10	21

Answer to Adimantus, a Disciple of Mani
(p. 165 to 223)

Revisions I, 22 (21)

Old Testament

Proverbs

8:35 LXX	4

New Testament

Matthew

5:21.22	2
12:33	4
23:15	3

John

1:12	4
8:37	3

Romans

8:15	3

Galatians

3:7	3
4:15	3

Text

Answer to the Letter of Mani known as *The Foundation*
(pp. 227 to 267)

Answer to Felix, a Manichean
(pp. 271 to 316)

Revisions II, 8 (35)

Answer to Secundinus, a Manichean
(pp. 349 to 390)

A Letter of Secundinus,
a Manichean, to Augustine

Answer to Secundinus,
a Manichean

General Index

(prepared by Kathleen Strattan)

The Catholic Way of Life and the Manichean Way of Life
(pp. 17-103)

The first number in the Index refers to a Book
The number after the colon refers to a paragraph

Two Souls
(pp. 107-134)

The numbers in the index refer to paragraphs

justice and, *Revisions* I, 15(16):4
original, *Revisions* I, 15(16):2–3, 5, 6
and sinners, 9(7)–10(8)
and souls, condemnation of, 17(12)
and will, *Revisions* I, 15(16):2–6;
   12(9)–15(11); 21(13)
soul, souls:
  bodies, comparison to, 7(6)–8(6)
  of a fly, 4(4)
  God as source of, 1(1)–3(2)
  and God's condemnation, 17(2)
  inferior, *Revisions* I, 15(16):7; 20(13)
  intelligence of, 3(3)
  movement of (will), 16(12)
  unjust and intemperate, 5(4)–6(6)
  will and, *Revisions* I, 15(16):3, 6
souls, two, *Revisions* I, 15(16):1, 5–6;
  16(12)–24(15)
  See also evil soul; good soul
spiritual things:
  justice and, 20(13)
  love for, *Revisions* I, 15(16):8; 20(13)
stars, 6(6); 8(6)
  See also light
substance of God, Manichean belief
  regarding, 16(12); 18(12)

sun, 2(2); 6(6); 8(6)
  See also light

temperance: intemperance, 5(4)–6(6)
two souls, Manichean belief in. *See* souls, two

understanding. *See* intellect

vice, 6(6)
  See also sin
virtue, 6(6)
  lack of, vs. bodily lack, 7(6)

weakness, *Revisions* I, 15(16):2
widow: *A widow who is living in pleasure is
  dead,* 2(2)
will, free, 19(13)
  definition of, *Revisions* I, 15(16):3;
    14(10)
  as movement of the soul, *Revisions* I,
    15(16):3, 6; 16(12)
  sin and, *Revisions* I, 15(16):2–6;
    12(9)–15(11); 21(13)
  two souls and, 16(12)–24(15)

Debate with Fortunatus, a Manichean
(pp. 137-162)

The numbers in the index refer to sections

Adam, 22
adoption, 28–29
angels, *Revisions* I, 16(15):2
  wicked, 23
apostles, 22–23
  See also Paul
Augustine: as former Manichean Hearer, 1; 3;
  37

body, bodies:
  flesh, wisdom of, 21–22
  incorruptible and immortal, *Revisions* I,
    16(15):2
  vs. soul, 14; 17

Catholic faith, the, 9
  See also *specific topics*
children of wrath, 17
Christ. *See* Jesus Christ
clay pot, 26
commandments, two, *Revisions* I, 16(15):2
covetousness, 21

darkness vs. light, 14
David, 19

death:
  law of sin and death, 22
  souls as cast down to, 3–4; 6–9
  vs. life, 14
death and resurrection of Christ, 7–8
devil, 23
disciples, 22–23
Elect, Manichean, 3
Ephesians, Letter to, 16–17
evil
  See also sin; two substances, question of
  as foreign to God, 19–20
  God as not suffering, 15–16
  God as preventing, 15–16
  Manichean vs. Catholic beliefs regarding,
    19–20
  source of, *Revisions* I, 16(15):1; 21
evil substance or nature, Manichean belief in,
  21
  See also two substances
  sin and, 20
faith:
  Catholic, 9
  of Fortunatus, 3
flesh:

two substances (natures), question of, 14; 18
   See also evil substance

will. *See* free choice
wolves, 22–23

Word of God, 3
   See also Jesus Christ
wrath, children of, 17

Answer to Adimantus, a Disciple of Mani
(pp. 165-223)

The numbers in the index refer to chapters

Answer to the Letter of Mani known as *The Foundation*
(pp. 227-267)

The numbers in the index refer to sections

Answer to Felix, a Manichean
(pp. 271-316)

The first number in the index refers to a book
The number after the colon refers to a section

The Nature of the Good
(pp. 319-345)

The numbers in the index refer to paragraphs

Answer to Secundinus, a Manichean
(pp. 349-390)

The numbers in the indexes refer to sections

A Letter of Secundinus, a Manichean, to Augustine

Answer to Secundinus,
a Manichean